Play!™

Math.
Get in the Game.™

Now you and your friends can play cool video
games that help you master math.

1. Go to:
PearsonSchool.com/DimensionM

2. Download the Mission

3. Choose Your Avatar

Your Avatar Here!

4. Game On!™

DIMENSION M™

Powered By
PEARSON

Scott Foresman·Addison Wesley

enVisionMATH™

Authors

Randall I. Charles
Professor Emeritus
Department of Mathematics
San Jose State University
San Jose, California

Janet H. Caldwell
Professor of Mathematics
Rowan University
Glassboro, New Jersey

Mary Cavanagh
Mathematics Consultant
San Diego County Office of Education
San Diego, California

Dinah Chancellor
Mathematics Consultant with Carroll ISD
Southlake, Texas
Mathematics Specialist with Venus ISD
Venus, Texas

Juanita V. Copley
Professor
College of Education
University of Houston
Houston, Texas

Warren D. Crown
Associate Dean for Academic Affairs
Graduate School of Education
Rutgers University
New Brunswick, New Jersey

Francis (Skip) Fennell
Professor of Education
McDaniel College
Westminster, Maryland

Alma B. Ramirez
Sr. Research Associate
Math Pathways and Pitfalls WestEd
Oakland, California

Kay B. Sammons
Coordinator of Elementary Mathematics
Howard County Public Schools
Ellicott City, Maryland

Jane F. Schielack
Professor of Mathematics
Associate Dean for Assessment and
Pre K-12 Education, College of Science
Texas A&M University
College Station, Texas

William Tate
Edward Mallinckrodt Distinguished
University Professor in Arts & Sciences
Washington University
St. Louis, Missouri

John A. Van de Walle
Professor Emeritus, Mathematics Education
Virginia Commonwealth University
Richmond, Virginia

Consulting Mathematicians

Edward J. Barbeau
Professor of Mathematics
University of Toronto
Toronto, Canada

Sybilla Beckmann
Professor of Mathematics
Department of Mathematics
University of Georgia
Athens, Georgia

David Bressoud
DeWitt Wallace Professor of Mathematics
Macalester College
Saint Paul, Minnesota

Gary Lippman
Professor of Mathematics and Computer Science
California State University East Bay
Hayward, California

PEARSON

Glenview, Illinois • Boston, Massachusetts • Chandler, Arizona • Upper Saddle River, New Jersey

Consulting Authors

Charles R. Allan
Mathematics Education Consultant
(Retired)
Michigan Department of Education
Lansing, Michigan

Verónica Galván Carlan
Private Consultant Mathematics
Harlingen, Texas

Stuart J. Murphy
Visual Learning Specialist
Boston, Massachusetts

Grant Wiggins
Researcher and Educational Consultant
Hopewell, New Jersey

ELL Consultants/Reviewers

Jim Cummins
Professor
The University of Toronto
Toronto, Canada

Alma B. Ramirez
Sr. Research Associate
Math Pathways and Pitfalls WestEd
Oakland, California

National Math Development Team

Cindy Bumbales
Teacher
Lake in the Hills, IL

Ann Hottovy
Teacher
Hampshire, IL

Deborah Ives
Supervisor of Mathematics
Ridgewood, NJ

Lisa Jasumback
Math Curriculum Supervisor
Farmington, UT

Rebecca Johnson
Teacher
Canonsburg, PA

Jo Lynn Miller
Math Specialist
Salt Lake City, UT

Patricia Morrison
Elementary Mathematics Specialist K-5
Upper Marlboro, MD

Patricia Horrigan Rourke
Mathematics Coordinator
Holliston, MA

Elise Sabaski
Teacher
Gladstone, MO

Math Advisory Board

John F. Campbell
Teacher
Upton, MA

Enrique Franco
Coordinator Elementary Math
Los Angeles, CA

Gladys Garrison
Teacher
Minot AFB, ND

Pat Giubka
Instructional Resource Teacher
Brookfield, UT

Shari Goodman
Math Specialist
Salt Lake City, UT

Cathy Massett
Math Facilitator
Cobb County SD, GA

Mary Modene
Math Facilitator
Belleville, IL

Kimya Moyo
Math Manager
Cincinnati, OH

Denise Redington
Teacher
Chicago, IL

Arlene Rosowski
Supervisor of Mathematics
Buffalo, NY

Darlene Teague
Director of Core Data
Kansas City, MO

Debbie Thompson
Elementary Math Teaching Specialist
Wichita, KS

Michele Whiston
Supervisor
Curriculum, Instruction, and Assessment
Mobile County, AL

Scott Foresman·Addison Wesley

enVisionMATH™

ISBN-13: 978-0-328-48974-9
ISBN-10: 0-328-48974-3

4

MATH STRAND COLORS

Number and Operations

Algebra

Geometry

Measurement

Data Analysis and Probability

Problem Solving

Mathematical Processes, which include problem solving, reasoning, communication, connections, and representations, are infused throughout all lessons.

Numeration

Adding and Subtracting Whole Numbers and Decimals

Topic 2

Multiplying Whole Numbers

Dividing by 1-Digit Divisors

Topic 5 — Dividing by 2-Digit Divisors

Topic 6 — Variables and Expressions

Topic 7 — Multiplying and Dividing Decimals

Topic 8 — Shapes

Topic 9 — Fractions and Decimals

Topic 10 — Adding and Subtracting Fractions and Mixed Numbers

Topic 11 — Multiplying Fractions and Mixed Numbers

Topic 12 — Perimeter and Area

Topic 13 — Solids

Topic 14 — Measurement Units, Time, and Temperature

Topic 15 — Solving and Writing Equations and Inequalities

ix

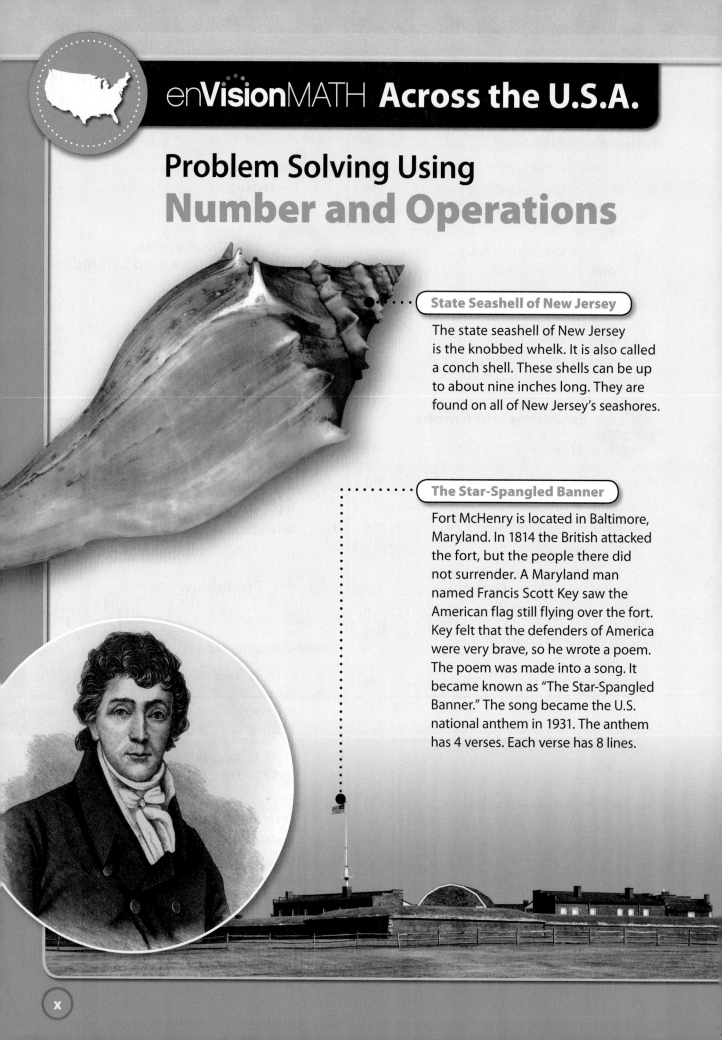

enVisionMATH Across the U.S.A.

Problem Solving Using
Number and Operations

State Seashell of New Jersey

The state seashell of New Jersey is the knobbed whelk. It is also called a conch shell. These shells can be up to about nine inches long. They are found on all of New Jersey's seashores.

The Star-Spangled Banner

Fort McHenry is located in Baltimore, Maryland. In 1814 the British attacked the fort, but the people there did not surrender. A Maryland man named Francis Scott Key saw the American flag still flying over the fort. Key felt that the defenders of America were very brave, so he wrote a poem. The poem was made into a song. It became known as "The Star-Spangled Banner." The song became the U.S. national anthem in 1931. The anthem has 4 verses. Each verse has 8 lines.

Directions: Carefully read questions 1–20. Write your answers on a separate sheet of paper.

1. What is the difference in length between a knobbed whelk shell that is $8\frac{1}{2}$ inches long and one that is $5\frac{1}{2}$ inches long?

A 4 inches   **C** 2 inches

B 3 inches   **D** 1 inch

2. How many total lines are in "The Star-Spangled Banner"?

A 8   **C** 24

B 16   **D** 32

3. What fraction of the "The Star-Spangled Banner" is two verses?

A $\frac{1}{4}$ **C** $\frac{2}{3}$

B $\frac{1}{2}$ **D** $\frac{2}{5}$

4. The length between the two main towers of the Mackinac Bridge is 3,800 feet. Between which two numbers is 3,800?

A 1,000 and 3,000   **C** 3,000 and 3,900

B 3,000 and 3,700   **D** 3,900 and 4,000

5. About 0.33 of the total length of the Mackinac Bridge is a suspension bridge. Which is equivalent to 0.33?

A $30 + 3$ **C** $0.3 + 0.3$

B $0.3 + 0.03$ **D** $0.30 + 0.3$

6. James walked across the Mackinac Bridge in 1.8 hours. Gene walked the same distance in 2.3 hours. How much longer did it take Gene to walk across the bridge than James?

A 0.5 hour   **C** 3.5 hours

B 1.9 hours   **D** 4.1 hours

Mackinac Bridge, Michigan

The Mackinac Bridge connects the upper and lower peninsulas of Michigan. The bridge is about 5 miles long. The middle part of the bridge is a suspension bridge—one of the world's longest. A suspension bridge has large cables that hang from towers. These cables hold up the roadway. On one day each year, some lanes of the Mackinac Bridge are closed to traffic. On that day people can walk the full length of the bridge.

enVisionMATH Across the U.S.A.

Problem Solving Using
Geometry

• • • **Arizona State Flag**

The top half of the state flag of Arizona has thirteen red and yellow rays. The rays stand for the thirteen original colonies of the United States. The bottom half of the flag is blue. It is the same shade of blue as in the U.S. flag. The star in the center of the flag is copper-colored. Copper mining is important to Arizona's economy.

Peach Water Tower in South Carolina • • •

Peach farming is important in South Carolina. The South Carolina Peach Festival is held in the city of Gaffney every July. The city has a water tower shaped like a peach. Its base is circular. The tower has more than 20 colors of paint on it. The peach has a large metal leaf and a circular stem.

7. Look at the star in the center of the Arizona state flag. Which describes the type of angle that makes up each point of the star?

A Acute angle
B Obtuse angle
C Right angle
D Straight angle

8. Which term names the measure of the distance around the circular base of the peach water tower?

A Radius
B Diameter
C Chord
D Circumference

9. The "stem" on the peach water tower has a diameter of 18 inches. How long is its radius?

A 6 inches
B 9 inches
C 27 inches
D 36 inches

Problem Solving Using
Measurement

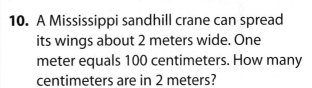

Mississippi Sandhill Cranes

The only place in the world where Mississippi sandhill cranes live is in Mississippi. The cranes live in a place where animals are protected. Sandhill cranes are large, tall birds with long legs and necks. They eat roots, nuts, and berries, as well as other parts of plants. They also eat insects and other small animals.

10. A Mississippi sandhill crane can spread its wings about 2 meters wide. One meter equals 100 centimeters. How many centimeters are in 2 meters?

A 0.2
B 20
C 200
D 2,000

11. A group of birdwatchers saw a Mississippi sandhill crane at 2:43 P.M. The group saw another crane 38 minutes later. At what time did the group see the second crane?

A 1:59 P.M.
B 2:05 P.M.
C 3:21 P.M.
D 4:01 P.M.

12. What is the height (in inches) of a Mississippi sandhill crane that is 4 feet tall? One foot equals 12 inches.

A 24 inches
B 36 inches
C 48 inches
D 60 inches

Problem Solving Using
Data Analysis and Probability

Copper in Arizona ·····················

Arizona produces more copper than any other state in the United States. Copper is a metal. It has many uses, including wires for electronic products. Mines in Arizona also produce large amounts of coal, sand, and gravel.

13. Look at the table of the amount of copper produced in Arizona. What is the greatest amount listed?

   A 885,000 metric tons
   B 767,000 metric tons
   C 723,000 metric tons
   D 691,000 metric tons

14. Which is the best estimate for the difference in the amount of copper produced in 2002 and in 2003 in Arizona?

   A 30,000 metric tons
   B 20,000 metric tons
   C 10,000 metric tons
   D 3,000 metric tons

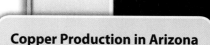

Copper Production in Arizona

Year	Amount (metric tons)
2001	885,000
2002	767,000
2003	741,000
2004	723,000
2005	691,000

15. Look at the table that shows statehood dates and release dates of state quarters. Find the difference between the year Georgia became a state and the year the Georgia state quarter was released.

   A 209 years   **C** 211 years
   B 210 years   **D** 212 years

The U.S. Mint has made state quarters. The Massachusetts quarter shows a drawing of a statue. The statue is called *The Minuteman*. Minutemen were soldiers in the Revolutionary War. They fought on the side of the American colonies and helped defeat the British. The U.S. Mint has released state quarters in the order of statehood. The date of statehood is the date on which a state joined the United States. The table shows the release dates for the first six state quarters.

Statehood Dates and Release Dates of State Quarters

State	Date of Statehood	Release Date of Quarter
Delaware	December 7, 1787	January 4, 1999
Pennsylvania	December 12, 1787	March 8, 1999
New Jersey	December 18, 1787	May 17, 1999
Georgia	January 2, 1788	July 19, 1999
Connecticut	January 9, 1788	October 12, 1999
Massachusetts	February 6, 1788	January 3, 2000

State Fossil of Missouri

Long ago an ocean covered the land that is now Missouri. Creatures called crinoids lived in that ocean. Some people think that crinoids look like plants. However, crinoids are animals. Today Missouri is far from the ocean. Fossils of crinoids are found in Missouri's rocks. In 1989 the crinoid became the state fossil of Missouri. Some types of crinoids live in today's ocean.

16. Look at the table that shows statehood dates and release dates of state quarters. When did Pennsylvania become a state?

 A December 12, 1787
 B January 2, 1788
 C February 6, 1788
 D March 8, 1999

17. A bag contains 10 quarters. Four are Massachusetts quarters. What is the probability that a person will choose a Massachusetts quarter from the bag?

 A $\frac{1}{10}$ **C** $\frac{3}{10}$
 B $\frac{2}{10}$ **D** $\frac{4}{10}$

18. How likely is it that a person would find a crinoid living in the wild in Missouri today?

 A Certain
 B Likely
 C Unlikely
 D Impossible

Problem Solving Using
Algebra

State Insect of Pennsylvania

The state insect of Pennsylvania is the firefly. Fireflies make flashes of light. The pattern of flashes depends in part on the type of firefly. The insects use their lights to send signals to other fireflies. Some fireflies use their lights to attract other types of fireflies and then eat them.

19. Suppose a firefly flashes once every 5 seconds for 35 seconds. Which equation shows the total number of flashes?

   A $5 \times 35 = x$
   B $35 \div 5 = x$
   C $\frac{5}{35} = x$
   D $35 - 5 = x$

20. Look at the table of firefly flashes. How many times would you expect five fireflies to flash in one minute?

   A 36
   B 48
   C 60
   D 72

Example of the Number of Firefly Flashes in One Minute

Number of Fireflies	Number of Flashes
1	12
2	24
3	36
4	48
5	n

Problem-Solving Handbook

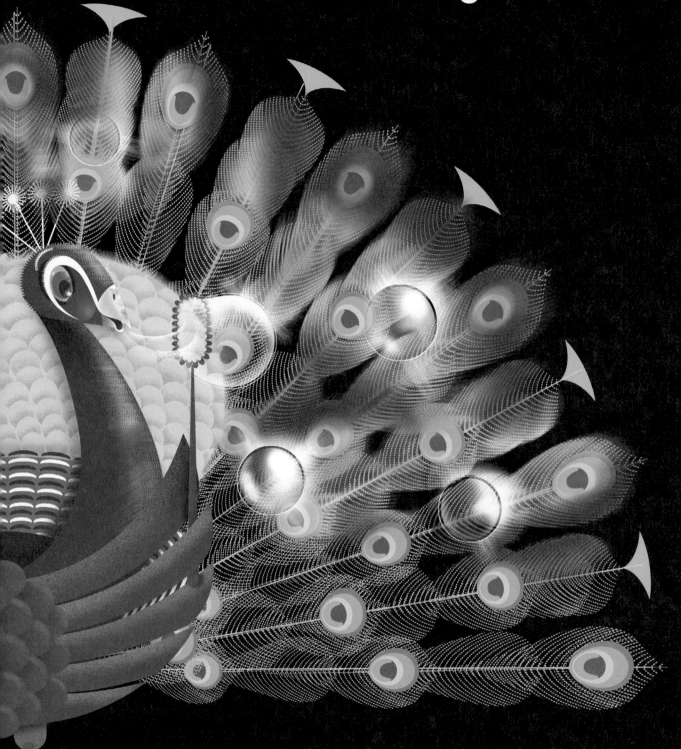

Scott Foresman·Addison Wesley

enVisionMATH™

Problem-Solving Handbook

Use this Problem-Solving Handbook throughout
the year to help you solve problems.

Everybody can
be a good
problem solver!

Don't
give up!

There's almost always
more than one way to
solve a problem!

Don't trust
key words.

Pictures help me
understand!

Explaining helps me
understand!

Problem-Solving Process

Read and Understand

❓ What am I trying to find?
- Tell what the question is asking.

❓ What do I know?
- Tell the problem in my own words.
- Identify key facts and details.

Plan and Solve

❓ What strategy or strategies should I try?

❓ Can I show the problem?
- Try drawing a picture.
- Try making a list, table, or graph.
- Try acting it out or using objects.

❓ How will I solve the problem?

❓ What is the answer?
- Tell the answer in a complete sentence.

Strategies
- Show What You Know
  - Draw a Picture
  - Make an Organized List
  - Make a Table
  - Make a Graph
  - Act It Out/ Use Objects
- Look for a Pattern
- Try, Check, Revise
- Write an Equation
- Use Reasoning
- Work Backward
- Solve a Simpler Problem

Look Back and Check

❓ Did I check my work?
- Compare my work to the information in the problem.
- Be sure all calculations are correct.

❓ Is my answer reasonable?
- Estimate to see if my answer makes sense.
- Make sure the question was answered.

Using Bar Diagrams

Use a bar diagram to show how what you know and what you want to find are related. Then choose an operation to solve the problem.

Problem 1

Carrie helps at the family flower store in the summer. She keeps a record of how many customers come into the store. How many customers came into the store on Monday and Wednesday?

Customers

Days	Customers
Monday	124
Tuesday	163
Wednesday	151
Thursday	206
Friday	259

Bar Diagram

TOTAL: Total number of customers → ?

124	151

PART: Customers on Monday   PART: Customers on Wednesday

124 + 151 = ▢

 Think I can add to find the total.

Problem 2

Kim is saving to buy a sweatshirt from the college her brother attends. She has $18. How much more money does she need to buy the sweatshirt?

Bar Diagram

TOTAL: Cost of the sweatshirt → 32

18	?

PART: Amount she has   PART: Amount she needs

32 − 18 = ▢

 Think I can subtract to find the missing part.

Pictures help me
understand!

Don't trust
key words!

Problem 3

Season tickets to the community
theater cost only $105 each no matter
what age you are. What is the cost of
tickets for four people?

Bar Diagram

TOTAL: Total cost
of the tickets →

?

| 105 | 105 | 105 | 105 |

↑
PART:
Cost of
each ticket

4 × 105 = ▢

 Think I can multiply because the
parts are equal.

Problem 4

Thirty students traveled in 3 vans to
the zoo. The same number of students
were in each van. How many students
were in each van?

Bar Diagram

TOTAL: Total number of
students →

30

| ? | ? | ? |

↑
PART:
Number in
each van

30 ÷ 3 = ▢

 Think I can divide to find how many
are in each part.

Problem-Solving Strategies

Strategy	Example	When I Use It
Draw a Picture	The race was 5 kilometers. Markers were at the starting line and the finish line. Markers showed each kilometer of the race. Find the number of markers used.	Try drawing a picture when it helps you visualize the problem or when the relationships such as joining or separating are involved.
Make a Table	Phil and Marcy spent all day Saturday at the fair. Phil rode 3 rides each half hour and Marcy rode 2 rides each half hour. How many rides had Marcy ridden when Phil rode 24 rides?	Try making a table when: • there are 2 or more quantities, • amounts change using a pattern.
Look for a Pattern	The house numbers on Forest Road change in a planned way. Describe the pattern. Tell what the next two house numbers should be.	Look for a pattern when something repeats in a predictable way.

Draw a Picture diagram:

Start Line ————————————— Finish Line

Start Line — 1 km — 2 km — 3 km — 4 km — Finish Line

Make a Table:

Rides for Phil	3	6	9	12	15	18	21	24
Rides for Marcy	2	4	6	8	10	12	14	16

Look for a Pattern houses: 3, 6, 10, 15, ?, ?

Strategy	Example	When I Use It
Make an Organized List	How many ways can you make change for a quarter using dimes and nickels?	Make an organized list when asked to find combinations of two or more items.

1 quarter =

1 dime + 1 dime + 1 nickel

1 dime + 1 nickel + 1 nickel + 1 nickel

1 nickel + 1 nickel + 1 nickel + 1 nickel + 1 nickel

Strategy	Example	When I Use It
Try, Check, Revise	Suzanne spent $27, not including tax, on dog supplies. She bought two of one item and one of another item. What did she buy? $8 + $8 + $15 = $31 $7 + $7 + $12 = $26 $6 + $6 + $15 = $27	Use Try, Check, Revise when quantities are being combined to find a total, but you don't know which quantities.

Dog Supplies Sale!
Leash $8
Collar $6
Bowls $7
Medium Beds $15
Toys $12

Strategy	Example	When I Use It
Write an Equation	Maria's new CD player can hold 6 discs at a time. If she has 204 CDs, how many times can the player be filled without repeating a CD? Find $204 \div 6 = n$.	Write an equation when the story describes a situation that uses an operation or operations.

Even More Strategies

Strategy	Example	When I Use It
Act It Out	How many ways can 3 students shake each other's hand?	Think about acting out a problem when the numbers are small and there is action in the problem you can do.
Use Reasoning	Beth collected some shells, rocks, and beach glass. **Beth's Collection** 2 rocks 3 times as many shells as rocks 12 objects in all How many of each object are in the collection?	Use reasoning when you can use known information to reason out unknown information.
Work Backward	Tracy has band practice at 10:15 A.M. It takes her 20 minutes to get from home to practice and 5 minutes to warm up. What time should she leave home to get to practice on time?	Try working backward when: • you know the end result of a series of steps, • you want to know what happened at the beginning.

I can think about
when to use
each strategy.

Strategy	Example	When I Use It

Solve a Simpler Problem 	Each side of each triangle in the figure at the left is one centimeter. If there are 12 triangles in a row, what is the perimeter of the figure?
	
	 I can look at 1 triangle, then 2 triangles, then 3 triangles.
	
	  perimeter = 3 cm
	
	  perimeter = 4 cm
	
	  perimeter = 5 cm
		Try solving a simpler problem when you can create a simpler case that is easier to solve.

Make a Graph	Mary was in a jump rope contest. How did her number of jumps change over the five days of the contest? 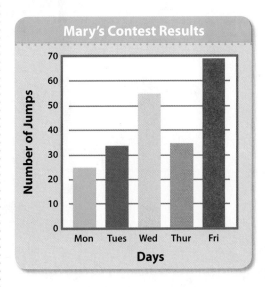	Make a graph when: • data for an event are given, • the question can be answered by reading the graph.

Writing to Explain

Here is a good math explanation.

Writing to Explain What happens to the area of the rectangle if the lengths of its sides are doubled?

■ = $\frac{1}{4}$ of the whole rectangle

The area of the new rectangle is 4 times the area of the original rectangle.

Tips for Writing Good Math Explanations....

A good explanation should be:
- correct
- simple
- complete
- easy to understand

Math explanations can use:
- words
- pictures
- numbers
- symbols

Explaining helps me understand!

This is another good math explanation.

Writing to Explain Use blocks to show 13 × 24.
Draw a picture of what you did with the blocks.

First we made a row of 24 using
2 tens and 4 ones. Then we made
more rows until we had 13 rows.
Then we said 13 rows of 2 tens is
13 × 2 tens = 26 tens or 260.
Then we said 13 rows of 4 ones is
13 × 4 = 52. Then we added the parts
260 + 52 = 312   So, 13 × 24 = 312.

Problem-Solving Recording Sheet

Name __Jane__

Problem-Solving Recording Sheet

Problem:
On June 14, 1777, the Continental Congress approved the design of a national flag. The 1777 flag had 13 stars, one for each colony. Today's flag has 50 stars, one for each state. How many stars were added to the flag since 1777?

Find?

Number of stars added to the flag

Know?

Original flag
13 stars

Today's flag
50 stars

Strategies?

Show the Problem
- ☑ Draw a Picture
- ☐ Make an Organized List
- ☐ Make a Table
- ☐ Make a Graph
- ☐ Act It Out/Use Objects

- ☐ Look for a Pattern
- ☐ Try, Check, Revise
- ☑ Write an Equation
- ☐ Use Reasoning
- ☐ Work Backwards
- ☐ Solve a Simpler Problem

Show the Problem?

50

13	?

Solution?

I am comparing the two quantities.
I could add up from 13 to 50. I can also subtract 13 from 50. I'll subtract.

$$\begin{array}{r} 50 \\ -\ 13 \\ \hline 37 \end{array}$$

Answer?

There were 37 stars added to the flag from 1777 to today.

Check? Reasonable?

37 + 13 = 50 so I subtracted correctly.

50 − 13 is about 50 − 10 = 40
40 is close to 37. 37 is reasonable.

Name __Benton__

Teaching Tool
1

Problem-Solving Recording Sheet

Problem:

Suppose your teacher told you to open your math book to the facing pages whose page numbers add to 85. To which two pages would you open your book?

Find?

Two facing page numbers

Know?

Two pages.
Facing each other.
Sum is 85.

Strategies?

Show the Problem
☑ Draw a Picture
☐ Make an Organized List
☐ Make a Table
☐ Make a Graph
☐ Act It Out/Use Objects

☐ Look for a Pattern
☑ Try, Check, Revise
☑ Write an Equation
☐ Use Reasoning
☐ Work Backwards
☐ Solve a Simpler Problem

Show the Problem?

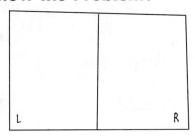

$L + R = 85$
L is 1 less than R

Solution?

I'll try some numbers in the middle.
$40 + 41 = 81$, too low
How about 46 and 47?
$46 + 47 = 93$, too high
Ok, now try 42 and 43.
$42 + 43 = 85$.

Answer?

The page numbers are 42 and 43.

Check? Reasonable?

I added correctly.
$42 + 43$ is about $40 + 40 = 80$
80 is close to 85.
42 and 43 is reasonable.

Numeration

1 How many driver ants can live in one colony? You will find out in Lesson 1-1.

2 Can you guess the size of a grain of sand? You will find out if you are right in Lesson 1-4.

Review What You Know!

Vocabulary

Choose the best term from the box.

- digits
- place value
- period
- whole numbers

1. __?__ are the symbols used to show numbers.

2. A group of 3 digits in a number is a __?__.

3. __?__ is the position of a digit in a number that is used to determine the value of the digit.

Adding Whole Numbers

Find each sum.

4. $800 + 90 + 2$

5. $3,000 + 400 + 50$

6. $10,000 + 2,000 + 60 + 1$

7. $37 + 85$

8. $124 + 376$

Comparing

Compare. Use $<$, $>$, or $=$ for each $\bigcirc$.

9. $869 \bigcirc 912$　　10. $9,033 \bigcirc 9,133$

11. $1,338 \bigcirc 1,388$　　12. $7,325 \bigcirc 7,321$

Place Value

13. **Writing to Explain** In the number 767, does the first 7 have the same value as the final 7? Why or why not?

3

How would you compare the surface area of the Earth to the surface area of the Moon? You will find out in Lesson 1-2.

4

The longest stick insect in the world lives in Borneo. How long is the Borneo stick insect? You will find out in Lesson 1-3.

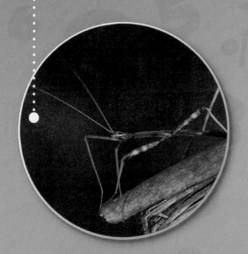

Place Value

How can you read and write large numbers?

A place-value chart is helpful in reading and writing a number such as 1,600,000,000. The digits 0, 1, 2, 3, 4, 5, 6, 7, 8, and 9 are used to write numbers. The place of a digit in a number tells you its value.

It would take about 1,600,000,000 quarters laid end-to-end to circle the world at the equator one time.

Guided Practice*

Do you know HOW?

In **1** through **3**, write each number in standard form.

1. forty billion, forty-eight million

2. 90,000,000,000 + 5,000,000 + 300

3. six billion, two hundred million, twelve thousand, six

Do you UNDERSTAND?

4. Look at the number in the example at the top. In what place is the digit 6? What is its value?

5. In which period does the 1 occur on the place-value chart? How does the period name help you read a large number?

Independent Practice

Write each number in word form.

6. 7,123   **7.** 18,345   **8.** 10,010,468   **9.** 300,014,000,056

Write each number in standard form.

10. 8,000,000 + 300 + 9   **11.** 60,000,000 + 10,000 + 20 + 3

12. 114,000,000,000 + 70,000 + 8,000 + 7   **13.** 50,000,000,000 + 200,000 + 30,000

Write each number in expanded form.

14. 670,200,640   **15.** 1,000,102,200   **16.** 85,000,011,000

What is the value of the underlined digit in each number?

17. 6<u>7</u>,100   **18.** 6,800,000

DIGITAL   Animated Glossary
www.pearsonsuccessnet.com

*For another example, see Set A on page 20.

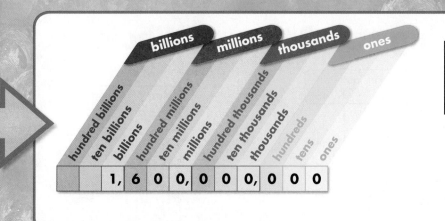

1 is in the billions place.
Its value is 1,000,000,000

Standard form:
1,600,000,000

Expanded form:
1,000,000,000 + 600,000,000

Word form:
one billion, six hundred million

| | | 1, | 6 | 0 | 0, | 0 | 0 | 0, | 0 | 0 | 0 |

Problem Solving

19. The Milky Way Galaxy has at least two hundred billion stars. Write this number in standard form.

20. Neptune is 4,498,252,900 km from the Sun. Write this number in expanded form.

21. Janet purchased 3 T-shirts and 2 blouses. Each T-shirt cost $12 and each blouse cost $23. What was the total cost of Janet's purchase?

22. Number Sense Write three different 10-digit numbers that have a 7 in the millions place.

23. In a recent U.S. Census, the population of Illinois was 12,419,293. What is this population after

a an increase of 100,000.

b an increase of 1,000,000.

c a decrease of 10,000.

24. Writing to Explain For the standard form of two billion, three hundred fifty thousand, four, Danielle wrote 2,350,400,000. What error did she make? What is the correct standard form of the number?

25. There can be up to 22,000,000 individuals in a colony of driver ants. Write this number in word form and expanded form.

26. What is the value of the underlined digit in 90,80<u>5</u>,001,021?

A 5,000   **C** 500,000

B 50,000   **D** 5,000,000

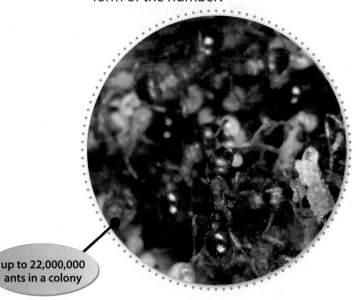

up to 22,000,000 ants in a colony

Comparing and Ordering Whole Numbers

Portland, OR
pop 529,121

Nashville, TN
pop 545,524

Charlotte, NC
pop 540,828

How can you compare and order whole numbers?

Which city has the greater population, Charlotte or Nashville?

Another Example How do you order numbers?

Order the cities by their populations from greatest to least.

To order whole numbers, line up the digits by place value. Start from the left and compare digits until they are different.

Step 1 Write the numbers. Line up the places. Begin at the left, at the greatest place-value position. Compare.

545,524 ← greatest number
540,828
529,121

Step 2 Look at the two remaining numbers. Compare.

540,828 ← greater number
529,121

Step 3 Write the numbers from greatest to least.

545,524   540,828   529,121

In order of their populations from greatest to least, the cities are Nashville, Charlotte, and Portland.

Explain It

1. Explain why 89,010,000 is greater than 89,000,101.

2. How can you order three whole numbers, each with a different number of digits, without comparing digits?

Line up the places.   545,524

540,828

Begin at the left.

Compare.

Use > for greater than.
Use < for less than.

Find the first place   545,524
where the digits
are different.   540,828

Compare   5 > 0

Think 5 thousands > 0 thousands

So, 545,524 > 540,828. Nashville has a greater population than Charlotte.

Guided Practice*

Do you know HOW?

Copy and complete. Write <, > or = for each ○.

1. 9,445,000 ○ 10,000,000

2. 496,256,001 ○ 496,155,001

3. 20,003,888,065 ○ 20,003,868,001

Do you UNDERSTAND?

4. Writing to Explain Why do you compare numbers beginning from the left after you line them up by place value?

5. In a recent U.S. Census, Long Beach had a population of 491,564 and Fresno had a population of 464,727. Which city has a greater population?

Independent Practice

Copy and complete. Write <, > or = for each ○.

6. 3,456 ○ 3,543

7. 9,999 ○ 10,000

8. 98,325 ○ 98,325

9. 789,124 ○ 789,300

10. 4,701,045,756 ○ 4,701,045

11. 3,000,010 ○ 3,000,000,010

12. 29,374,087,210 ○ 28,124,087,210

13. 13,059 ○ 9,898

14. 6,012,907,000 ○ 6,012,907,000

15. 8,937,051 ○ 8,937,501

16. 1,790,023,901 ○ 1,090,023,901

17. 45,034,521 ○ 45,034,251

18. 990,148,632,109 ○ 990,149,632,109

*For another example, see Set B on page 20.

Order each set of numbers from greatest to least.

19. 65,081,127 7,000,128 9,910,001

20. 90,459,012,045 91,459,012,045 90,459,010,045

21. 15,100,000,022 1,510,000,022 10,010,899,002

22. 186,347,987 100,389,120 18,121,817 1,500,987

Problem Solving

23. Number Sense Write three numbers that are greater than 154,000 but less than 155,000.

24. The U.S. Postal Service delivers about 212,000,000,000 pieces of mail every year. Which digit is in the ten billions place?

25. Writing to Explain Here is how Marek ordered three numbers from least to greatest:
870,990; 4,970,070; 1,426,940

What mistake did Marek make? Explain how to correct his mistake.

26. Four brothers each bought a $9 movie ticket and a $4 bag of popcorn. Bottled water cost $2. Together the brothers had $60. How much was left?

27. Algebra Find all the digits that can replace the missing digit to make this comparison true.
    496,▮56,200 > 496,745,310

28. Which of the numbers below is the greatest?
9,781   9,178   9,817
9,187   8,971

  A 9,178   **C** 9,781

  B 9,817   **D** 8,971

29. Glory Bicycle Company made $589,029 in sales. Right Bicycles made $590,011. Coastal Bikes made more than Glory Bicycle Company, but less than Right Bicycles. How much did Coastal Bikes make?

  A $589,020   **C** $590,101

  B $589,300   **D** $590,100

30. The surface area of the moon is 37,900,000 km². Which has a larger surface area?

The surface area of Earth is 510,066,000 km².

31. Reasoning If a number is greater than 800,000,000,000 but less than 801,000,000,000, what digit will be in the billions place?

Mixed Problem Solving

Use the table at the right to answer **1** and **2**.

1. Which city will have the least population in 2015? The greatest?

2. Arrange the cities in order from the least projected population to the greatest projected population.

City	Projected Populations in 2015
Tokyo, Japan	26,400,000
Mumbai, India	26,100,000
Sao Paulo, Brazil	20,400,000
Lagos, Nigeria	23,200,000
Mexico City, Mexico	19,000,000

Use the table at the right to answer **3** and **4**.

3. The Indian Ocean has an area of about 73,556,000 km². Is the area of Indian Ocean greater than or less than the area of the Atlantic Ocean?

4. Order the areas of bodies of water from greatest to least.

Body of Water	Area (sq km)
Atlantic Ocean	82,400,000
Bay of Bengal	2,172,000
Hudson Bay	1,232,300
Pacific Ocean	166,241,000

Use the table at the right to answer **5** through **7**.

5. The United Kingdom had 37,800,000 Internet users in 2006. Which countries had a greater number of Internet users than the United Kingdom?

6. The number of Internet users in India in 2005 was 50,600,000. Between which two countries in the table should India be placed?

7. **Strategy Focus** Using the strategy, Make an Organized List, find how many outfits Eileen can make with 5 different blouses and 5 different skirts.

Country	Population	Internet Users
United States	299,093,237	203,824,428
China	1,306,724,067	111,000,000
Japan	128,389,000	86,300,000
Germany	82,515,988	48,722,055

Decimal Place Value

How can you represent decimals?

Orchid seeds are extremely small. A single orchid seed can weigh only 0.000035 ounce.

What are some different ways you can represent 0.000035?

A single seed of certain orchids can weigh 0.000035 ounce.

Another Example **What are equivalent decimals?**

Equivalent decimals name the same amount.

Name two other decimals equivalent to 1.4.

One and four tenths is the same as one and forty hundredths.
So, 1.4 = 1.40.

One and four tenths is the same as one and four hundred thousandths.
So, 1.4 = 1.400.

So, 1.4 = 1.40 = 1.400.

 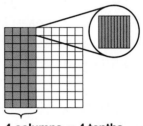

1 whole

4 columns = 4 tenths
40 small squares = 40 hundredths
= 400 thousandths

Guided Practice*

Do you know HOW?

Write the word form for each number and give the value of the underlined digit.

1. 4.7<u>3</u>7

2. 9.806<u>4</u>15

Write each number in standard form.

3. $6 + 0.6 + 0.03 + 0.007 + 0.0001$

4. four and sixty-eight hundredths

Write two decimals that are equivalent to the given decimal.

5. 3.700

6. 5.60

Do you UNDERSTAND?

7. Writing to Explain The number 3.453 has two 3s. Why does each 3 have a different value?

8. How do you read the decimal point in word form?

9. José finished a race in 2.6 hours and Pavel finished the same race in 2.60 hours. Which runner finished the race first?

DIGITAL   Animated Glossary, eTools
www.pearsonsuccessnet.com

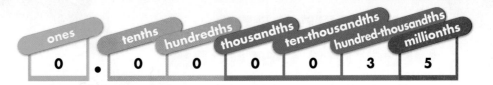

Standard Form: 0.000035

⌐ The 5 is in the millionths place. Its value is 0.000005.

Expanded Form: 0.00003 + 0.000005

Word Form: thirty-five millionths

Independent Practice

Write the word form for each number and give the value of the underlined digit.

10. 2.3̲00

11. 9.000̲27

12. 1.98̲2

13. 6.00017̲8

Write each number in standard form.

14. two and six hundred thousandths

15. five and one hundred four millionths

16. 3 + 0.3 + 0.009 + 0.0005

17. 7 + 0.6 + 0.05 + 0.007 + 0.0001 + 0.00003

Write two decimals that are equivalent to the given decimal.

18. 2.200

19. 8.1

20. 9.50

21. 4.2000

Problem Solving

22. Writing to Explain Kay is buying juice at the market. She has $9 and each bottle of juice costs $2. Does she have enough money to buy 5 bottles of juice? Explain.

23. Which point on the number line below best represents 0.368?

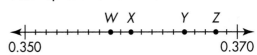

A W **B** X **C** Y **D** Z

24. The Borneo stick insect has a total length, including legs, of 21.5 inches. Write 21.5 in word form.

25. Worker leafcutter ants can measure 0.5 inches. Name two decimals that are equivalent to 0.5.

26. Writing to Explain Why are 7.630 and 7.63000 equivalent?

Comparing and Ordering Decimals

How can you compare and order decimals?

Scientists collected and measured the lengths of different cockroach species. Which cockroach had the greater length, the American or the Oriental cockroach? Use these three steps to find out.

Oriental
3.432 centimeters

American
3.576 centimeters

Australian
3.582 centimeters

Another Example How can you order decimals?

Order the cockroaches from least to greatest length. Use the three steps below to help you.

Step 1

Write the numbers, lining up the decimal points. Start at the left. Compare digits of the same place-value.

3.576
3.432
3.582

3.432 is the least.

Step 2

Write the remaining numbers, lining up the decimal points. Start at the left. Compare.

3.576
3.582

3.582 is the greater.

Step 3

Write the numbers from least to greatest.

3.432, 3.576, 3.582

In order of their lengths from least to greatest, the cockroaches are the Oriental, the American, and the Australian.

Guided Practice*

Do you know HOW?

Compare the two numbers. Write >, <, or = for each ◯.

1. 3.692 ◯ 3.697   **2.** 7.216 ◯ 7.203

Order these numbers from least to greatest.

3. 5.540, 5.631, 5.625, 5.739

4. 0.675, 1.529, 1.35, 0.693

Do you UNDERSTAND?

5. Write a number that is greater than 4.508 but less than 4.512.

6. Scientists measured a Madeira cockroach and found it to be 3.438 cm long. If they were ordering the lengths of the cockroaches from least to greatest, between which two cockroaches would the Madeira cockroach belong?

Step 1	Step 2	Step 3

Step 1

Line up the decimal points.

Start at the left.

Compare digits of the same place-value.

3.576

3.432

Step 2

Find the first place where the digits are different.

3.576

3.432

Step 3

Compare.

5 > 4

Think 0.5 > 0.4

So, 3.576 > 3.432.

The American cockroach is longer than the Oriental cockroach.

Independent Practice

Copy and complete. Write >, <, or = for each ◯.

7. 0.890 ◯ 0.89

8. 5.733 ◯ 5.693

9. 9.707 ◯ 9.717

10. 4.953 ◯ 4.951

11. 1.403 ◯ 1.4

12. 3.074 ◯ 3.740

Order from least to greatest.

13. 2.912, 2.909, 2.830, 2.841

14. 8.541, 8.314, 8.598, 8.8

Order from greatest to least.

15. 5.132, 5.123, 5.312, 5.231

16. 62.905, 62.833, 62.950, 62.383

Problem Solving

17. Writing to Explain Why do you need to line up the decimal points before comparing and ordering numbers with decimals?

18. Judith wants to buy her mother flowers. Judith earns $4 a week doing chores. If each flower costs $2, how many flowers can Judith buy her mother if she saves for three weeks?

19. There are five types of grains of sand: coarse, very coarse, medium, fine, and very fine. A grain of fine sand can have a diameter of 0.125 millimeters.

Which number is less than 0.125?

A 0.5

C 0.13

B 0.2

D 0.12

Problem Solving

Look for a Pattern

There are patterns in decimal number charts. Continue the pattern to label the other squares.

0.01	0.02	0.03					0.08		0.1
				0.15	0.16			0.19	
								0.29	
	0.32		0.34			0.37			

Another Example

In this decimal number chart, what are the patterns in the diagonals?

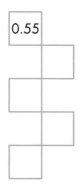

Using the same system as above, you could fill in the diagonals of a decimal number chart.

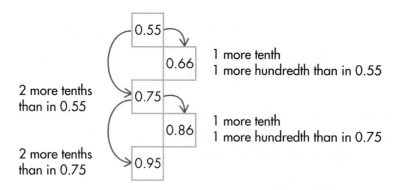

0.55

0.66 — 1 more tenth
1 more hundredth than in 0.55

2 more tenths than in 0.55 → 0.75

0.86 — 1 more tenth
1 more hundredth than in 0.75

2 more tenths than in 0.75 → 0.95

Explain It

1. If the grid in Another Example above were extended by 2 cells in the same design, what decimals would be used to complete the grid?

What are the missing decimals?

0.01

As you work with vertical columns, you will see the tenths increase by 1 and the hundredths stay the same as you move down.

0.01
0.11
0.21
0.31

What are the missing decimals?

		0.29	

Moving from left to right, tenths are the same in each row except for the last number; the hundredths increase by 1.

0.26	0.27	0.28	0.29	0.30

Guided Practice*

Do you know HOW?

In **1** and **2**, determine the patterns, and then complete the grids.

1.

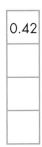

2.

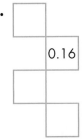

Do you UNDERSTAND?

3. In a completed decimal chart, look at the first row, which begins with 0.01, 0.02.... If Rene were to create a thousandths chart, what two numbers would immediately follow 0.001?

4. Write a real-world problem that you could solve by looking for a pattern.

Independent Practice

In **5** and **6**, determine the patterns, and then complete the grids.

5.

6.

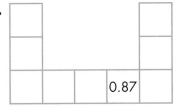

Stuck? Try this....

- What do I know?
- What am I asked to find?
- What diagram can I use to help understand the problem?
- Can I use addition, subtraction, multiplication, or division?
- Is all of my work correct?
- Did I answer the right question?
- Is my answer reasonable?

7. Describe the patterns you should use to complete the following grid, then complete it.

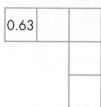

8. Determine the patterns, and then complete the grid.

9. Determine the patterns, and then complete the grid.

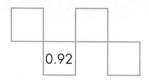

10. What is the missing number in the grid?

	0.27	0.28	0.29

11. Drake drew a grid of five cells in a row. The number 0.75 was in the middle cell. What did Drake's grid look like?

12. Determine a pattern, and then complete the grid.

0.004	0.005	

13. Juan and his family went to a movie. They bought 2 adult tickets for $8 apiece and 3 student tickets for $5 apiece. They paid with two $20 bills. How much change did they get?

14. The greatest distance of Mercury from Earth is 136,000,000 miles. Write this number in expanded form.

Think About the Process

15. You buy three items that cost $0.37, $0.35, and $0.19, and give the clerk $1.00. Which expression shows how to find the amount of change you would get from $1.00?

  A $0.37 + $0.35 + $0.19 + $1.00

  B $1.00 − $0.37

  C $1.00 − ($0.37 + $0.35 + $0.19)

  D $1.00 + $0.37 + $0.35 − $0.19

16. If 100 people are waiting in line to buy tickets and only 53 tickets are available, which expression would you use to find how many people won't be able to buy tickets?

  A 100 + 53

  B 100 − 53

  C 100 × 53

  D 53 + 53

Decimal Place Value

To subtract 0.008 from 3.695, you can subtract 0.01, and then add 0.002.
Do this subtraction on the calculator.
Next, tell how to change 3.695 to 3.685, and then 3.685 to 3.687 on a calculator.

Step 1   Turn the calculator on, enter 3.695.
Subtract 0.01 and add 0.002.

Press: 3.695 [−] 0.01 [+] 0.002 [ENTER =]

Display: *3.687*

Step 2   When 3.695 changes to 3.685, the digit in the hundredths place decreases from 9 to 8, so subtract one hundredth, or 0.01.

Press: 3.695 [−] 0.01 [ENTER =]

Display: *3.685*

Step 3   When 3.685 changes to 3.687, the digit in the thousandths place increases from 5 to 7, so add two thousandths, or 0.002.

Press: [+] 0.002 [ENTER =]

Display: *3.687*

Press (Clear) before starting a new problem.

Practice

Make each change on a calculator and tell how you made it.

1. 2.659 to 2.658

2. 8.356 to 8.456

3. 7.348 to 7.328

4. 5.148 to 5.178

5. 4.251 to 4.253

6. 9.462 to 9.062

7. 3.272 to 3.27

8. 1.605 to 1.635

9. 6.537 to 6.534

10. 0.659 to 0.658

11. 7.492 to 7.495

12. 5.219 to 5.209

13. 8.674 to 8.676

14. 3.21 to 3.23

15. 7.41 to 7.45

16. 3.673 to 3.671

17. 5.483 to 5.479

18. 3.618 to 3.612

1. About 885,000,000 people speak Mandarin Chinese. How is 885,000,000 written in words? (1-1)

   A eight hundred million, eighty-five thousand

   B eight hundred eighty-five million

   C eight billion, eighty-five million

   D eight hundred eighty-five billion

2. A National Park in Alaska has eighty thousand, nine-hundred twenty-three and eighty-six hundredths acres of nonfederal land. Which shows this number in standard form? (1-3)

   A 80,923.68

   B 80,923.86

   C 80,923.086

   D 80,923.806

3. About 1,300,000,000 people ride the New York Subway System each year. What is the value of the 3 in 1,300,000,000? (1-1)

   A Three hundred thousand

   B Three million

   C Three hundred million

   D Three billion

4. The circumference of a bowling ball is less than 27.002 inches. Which of the following numbers is less than 27.002? (1-4)

   A 27.02

   B 27.2

   C 27.004

   D 27

5. In the year 2000, the population of New York City was about 14,700,000. Which of the following is another way to write this number? (1-1)

   A 10,000,000 + 4,000,000 + 70,000

   B 10,000,000 + 4,000 + 700

   C 10,000,000 + 4,000,000 + 700

   D 10,000,000 + 4,000,000 + 700,000

6. The average daily temperatures in July of some cities in Texas are shown in the table. Which of the following lists the cities from greatest temperature to least temperature? (1-4)

City	Average Daily Temperature
Austin	84.5°F
Dallas	85.9°F
San Antonio	85°F
Fort Worth	85.3°F

   A Dallas, Fort Worth, San Antonio, Austin

   B Austin, Fort Worth, San Antonio, Dallas

   C Dallas, Austin, Fort Worth, San Antonio

   D San Antonio, Fort Worth, Dallas, Austin

7. Lead melts at 327.46°C. What is the value of the 6 in 327.46? (1-3)

   A 6 hundreds

   B 6 tenths

   C 6 hundredths

   D 6 thousandths

8. Which of the following shows the numbers in order from least to greatest? (1-2)

A 201,008 201,080 201,800

B 201,080 201,800 201,008

C 201,080 201,008 201,800

D 201,008 201,800 201,080

9. A certain machine part must be between 2.73 and 3.55 inches. Which number is greater than 2.73 and less than 3.55? (1-4)

A 3.73

B 3.6

C 2.55

D 2.75

10. As of 2006, which country listed had the greatest number of cell phones? (1-2)

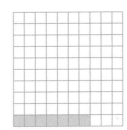

Country	Cell Phones
Mexico	38,451,100
South Korea	36,586,100
Spain	38,646,800
Turkey	34,707,500

A Mexico

B South Korea

C Spain

D Turkey

11. Which statement is true? (1-2)

A 157,324,113 > 157,323,113

B 157,324,113 < 157,323,113

C 157,323,113 > 157,332,113

D 157,332,113 < 157,324,113

12. Which decimal is one and twenty-one millionths in standard form? (1-3)

A 1.00021

B 1.000021

C 1.021

D 1.21

13. Which of the following is less than 2.08? (1-4)

A 2.7

B 2.1

C 2.080

D 2.07

14. What part of the figure is shaded? (1-3)

A 0.7

B 0.70

C 0.07

D 0.007

15. Where will the shaded square be located in the next figure of the pattern? (1-5)

A lower right corner

B lower left corner

C upper right corner

D upper left corner

Set A, pages 4–5

Write the word form and tell the value of the underlined digit for 930,365.

Nine hundred thirty thousand, three hundred sixty-five.

Since the 0 is in the thousands place, its value is 0 thousands or 0.

Write the word form and tell the value of the underlined digit for 65,467,386,941.

Sixty-five billion, four hundred sixty-seven million, three hundred eighty-six thousand, nine hundred forty-one

Since the 6 is in the ten billions place, its value is 60,000,000,000.

Remember that, starting from the right, each group of three digits forms a period. Periods are separated by commas.

Write the word form and tell the value of the underlined digit.

1. 9,000,009
2. 300,000,000,000
3. 25,678
4. 17,874,000,000
5. 4,000,345,000
6. 105,389
7. 876,400,000,000
8. 600,309,470
9. 135,000
10. 2,647,000
11. 4,104,327,894

Set B, pages 6–8

Compare. Write $<$, $>$, or $=$.

2,876,547 ◯ 2,826,547.

Line up the numbers above one another.

2,876,547   Begin at the left and compare.
             Notice that the ten thousands
2,826,547   are different.

7 ten thousands $>$ 2 ten thousands

So, 2,876,547 $>$ 2,826,547

Remember that lining up place values helps you compare numbers.

Compare. Write $>$, $<$, or $=$.

1. 9,990 ◯ 9,099
2. 89,128 ◯ 90,000
3. 1,000,000 ◯ 999,999
4. 300,300 ◯ 303,000
5. 6,752,100 ◯ 6,752,000
6. 9,314 ◯ 9,314
7. 17,320 ◯ 17,212
8. 45,006 ◯ 45,060
9. 22,009 ◯ 22,090
10. 8,374 ◯ 8,374

Set C, pages 10–11

Write the word form and tell the value of the underlined digit for the number 8.0000<u>2</u>6.

Write the numbers on a place value chart.

ones		tenths	hundredths	thousandths	ten-thousandths	hundred-thousandths	millionths
8	•	0	0	0	0	2	6

Eight and twenty-six millionths

The 2 is in the hundred-thousandths place. Its value is 0.00002.

Remember to write the word *and* for the decimal point.

Write the word form and tell the value of each underlined digit.

1. 8.<u>5</u>9

2. 2.2<u>5</u>1

3. 7.00<u>3</u>

4. 3.002<u>4</u>

5. 6.<u>8</u>37

6. 0.00063<u>6</u>

Set D, pages 12–13

Compare. Write <, >, or =.

8.45 ◯ 8.47.

Line up the numbers above each other by the decimals.

8.4<u>5</u>

8.4<u>7</u>

5 hundredths < 7 hundredths

So, 8.45 < 8.47.

Remember that equivalent decimals, such as 0.45 and 0.450, can help you compare numbers.

Compare. Write >, <, or =.

1. 0.584 ◯ 0.58

2. 9.327 ◯ 9.236

3. 5.2 ◯ 5.20

4. 5.643 ◯ 5.675

5. 0.07 ◯ 0.08

Set E, pages 14–16

The table below shows the number of new members each month for a club. If the pattern continues, how many new members will there be in June?

Jan.	Feb.	Mar.	Apr.	May	June
15	30	60	120		

Pattern: The number doubles each month.

May: 120 × 2 = 240   June: 240 × 2 = 480

In June, there will be 480 new members.

Remember to look for a pattern.

1. On the board, Andrea's teacher wrote the pattern below. Find the next three numbers in the pattern.

2, 4, 8, 14, 22, ▨ , ▨ , ▨

2. Sean bought a rare stamp for $15. He was told that it would increase in value by $11 each year. What will the stamp's value be after 4 years?

Topic 2

Adding and Subtracting Whole Numbers and Decimals

1 Golden Gate Park is a very large urban park in San Francisco. About how many more acres does this park cover than the number of acres Central Park in New York City covers? You will find out in Lesson 2-3.

2 What is the total number of hours that astronauts in the Space Shuttle program have spent in space? You will find out in Lesson 2-5.

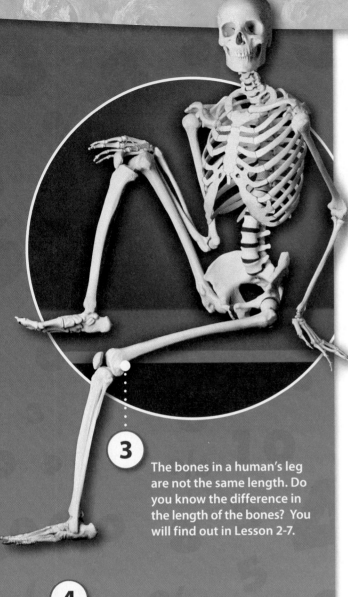

Review What You Know!

Vocabulary

Choose the best term from the box.

- Associative Property of Addition
- Commutative Property of Addition
- difference
- sum

1. Using the __?__ you can add two numbers in any order.

2. The __?__ is the answer to a subtraction problem.

3. When you can change the grouping of numbers when adding you are using the __?__.

4. The answer in an addition problem is called the __?__.

Rounding

Round each number to the nearest hundred.

5. 748　　　6. 293　　　7. 139

Round each number to the nearest thousand.

8. 3,857　　9. 2,587　　10. 2,345

Round each number to the underlined digit.

11. 84.59　　12. 2.948　　13. 3.0125

Estimating

Writing to Explain Write an answer for the question.

14. Explain how to use rounding when estimating.

3 The bones in a human's leg are not the same length. Do you know the difference in the length of the bones? You will find out in Lesson 2-7.

4 The world's largest aloha shirt measures more than 4 meters around the chest. What is the actual measure of this part of the shirt? You will find out in Lesson 2-2.

Mental Math

How can you use mental math to add and subtract?

Jon bought 3 items. Properties of addition can help him find the sum of the cost.

Commutative Property:	Associative Property:
You can add two numbers in any order.	You can change the grouping of addends.
$17 + 9 = 9 + 17$	$17 + (9 + 3) = (17 + 9) + 3$

$9

$17

$3

Another Example How can you use compensation to add or subtract?

Sometimes you can change an addition or subtraction problem to make it simpler. With compensation you adjust one number to make computation easier and compensate by changing the other number.

Using compensation to add

Find $39 + 17$ mentally.

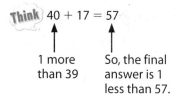

Think $40 + 17 = 57$

1 more than 39   So, the final answer is 1 less than 57.

$39 + 17 = 56$

Using compensation to subtract

Find $86 - 19$ mentally.

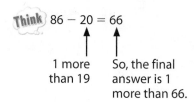

Think $86 - 20 = 66$

1 more than 19   So, the final answer is 1 more than 66.

$86 - 19 = 67$

Explain It

1. In the first example above, why is the answer 1 less than 57? In the second example above, why is the answer 1 more than 66?

2. The equation $0 + 7 = 7$ is an example of the Identity Property of Addition. What is the sum when you add zero to any number?

What You Think

The Commutative and Associative Properties make it easy to add 17 + 9 + 3.

17 and 3 are compatible numbers. These are numbers that are easy to compute mentally.

17 + 3 = 20

20 + 9 = 29

So, 17 + 9 + 3 = 29.

The total cost is $29.

Why It Works

Commutative Property: change the order

17 + (9 + 3) = 17 + (3 + 9)

Associative Property: change the grouping

17 + (3 + 9) = (17 + 3) + 9

Guided Practice*

Do you know HOW?

In **1** through **6**, use mental math to add or subtract.

1. 21 + 9 + 12

2. 35 + 46 + 4

3. 19 + 34

4. 38 + 15

5. 47 − 19

6. 86 − 49

Do you UNDERSTAND?

7. Writing to Explain Which numbers are easier to subtract, 141 − 99 or 142 − 100? Explain.

8. Jim earns $22, $14, and $8 on three different days. How much did he earn in all? Use mental math to find the sum.

Independent Practice

In **9** through **26**, use mental math to add or subtract.

 Tip *When you add 3 or more numbers, look for compatible numbers.*

9. 66 + 18 + 2

10. 97 + 3 + 64

11. 22 + 46 + 4

12. 237 + 195 + 5

13. 39 + 23 + 1

14. 57 + 42 + 3

15. 96 + 73 + 4

16. 299 + 34 + 1 + 6

17. 306 + 199

18. 453 − 98

19. 49 + 87

20. 68 − 29

21. 1,003 + 58

22. 468 − 190

23. 379 + 621

24. 230 + 215 + 70

25. 201 − 99

26. 101 + 17 + 99

DIGITAL — Animated Glossary
www.pearsonsuccessnet.com

27. **Writing to Explain** Use the Equal Additions Property shown at the right to find each difference mentally. Explain how you found each difference.

    a 67 − 29   b 456 − 198

Equal Additions Property:

Subtract 369 − 199 mentally.

369 − 199.   *If the same number*
                      is added to each, the
+1   +1   *difference is the same.*
↓   ↓
370 − 200 = 170

28. Use mental math to find how many points the football team had scored after the first three quarters.

Quarter	Points
1	14
2	9
3	6
4	10

29. On three different days at her job, Sue earned $27, $33, and $49. She needs to earn $100 to buy a desk for her computer. The cost of the desk includes tax. If she buys the desk, how much money will she have left over?

30. A CD shelf can hold 50 CDs. Jill has 27 CDs. She plans to buy 5 new ones. Each CD costs $9. After she buys the new ones, how many more CDs will the shelf hold?

31. Three different gymnasts had scores of 8.903, 8.827, and 8.844. Order the scores from greatest to least.

    A 8.827, 8.844, 8.903

    B 8.844, 8.903, 8.827

    C 8.903, 8.844, 8.827

    D 8.827, 8.903, 8.844

32. Which shows the Associative Property of Addition?

    A 3 + 10 = 10 + 3

    B 10 + 0 = 10

    C (3 + 10) + 7 = 3 + (10 + 7)

    D (3 + 10) + 7 = (10 + 3) + 7

33. André buys 12 apples at $1 each. He uses a coupon for $1.50 off the total purchase. How much did André spend on apples?

    A $10.50

    B $11.00

    C $11.50

    D $12.00

34. Which number, when rounded to the nearest ten thousand, is 70,000?

    A 6,499

    B 7,499

    C 64,985

    D 74,999

1. How many more species of fish are there than mammals?

fish	19,000	
mammals	4,000	?

2. What is total number of species of fish, birds, and mammals?

Some Facts About Animal Species

Animal	Species
Arthropods	1,100,000
Fish	19,000
Birds	9,000
Mammals	4,000
Reptiles	6,000
Amphibians	4,000

3. Is the number of arthropods greater or less than a million? By how much?

4. What is the total number of species of birds, mammals, reptiles, and amphibians? Is the total greater or less than the number of species of fish? By how much?

5. What is the total number of reptiles and amphibians? Is the total greater or less than the number of species of birds? By how much?

6. Arthropods have the most species. Find the total number of species of fish, birds, mammals, reptiles, and amphibians. How many more arthropod species are there than that total?

7. A zoo has 1,123 mammals, 745 birds, 1,078 fish and 134 amphibians. They want to increase the number of amphibians to 200. How many more amphibians do they need?

8. The diagram below shows about how much of the Earth's surface is covered by water. About how much of the Earth's surface is not covered by water?

9. A single drip of water doesn't seem like much, but many drips of water from one faucet can quickly add up to several gallons per day. If the number of drips from a faucet is 30 per minute, how many drips is this for 10 minutes? Use repeated addition.

Rounding Whole Numbers and Decimals

How can you round whole numbers?

Rounding replaces one number with another number that tells about how many or how much.
Round 634 to the nearest hundred.

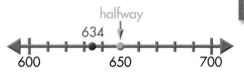

Think Is 634 closer to 600 or 700?

Another Example ## How do you round decimals?

How do you round 2.36 to the nearest tenth?

Think Is 2.36 closer to 2.3 or 2.4?

Step 1

Find the rounding place. Look at the digit to the right of the rounding place.

2.3̲6

Step 2

If the digit is 5 or greater, add 1 to the rounding digit. If the digit is less than 5, leave the rounding digit alone.

Since 6 > 5, add 1 to the 3.

Step 3

Drop the digits to the right of the rounding digit.

2.36 rounds to 2.4

Guided Practice*

Do you know HOW?

In **1** through **6**, round each number to the place of the underlined digit.

1. 1̲6

2. 5̲6.1

3. 1.3̲2

4. 4̲27,841

5. 1̲,652

6. 5̲82,062

Do you UNDERSTAND?

7. To round 7,458 to the nearest hundred, which digit do you look at? What is 7,458 rounded to the nearest hundred?

8. A runner is running on a track with markers every 10 meters. If the runner has run 368 meters, is she closer to the 360-meter marker or the 370-meter marker?

Animated Glossary
www.pearsonsuccessnet.com

For another example, see Set B on page 52.

Step 1	Step 2	Step 3

Step 1

Find the digit in the rounding place. Underline this digit.

6<u>3</u>4

Step 2

Look at the digit to the right of the rounding place. If this digit is 5 or greater, add 1 to the rounding digit. If the digit is less than 5, leave the rounding digit alone.

6<u>3</u>4 $3 < 5$

Leave 6 the same.

Step 3

Change all the digits to the right of the rounding digit to zeros.

634 rounds to 600.

Independent Practice

In **9** through **16**, round each whole number to the place of the underlined digit.

9. 6<u>7</u>7

10. 4,5<u>2</u>6

11. 12,0<u>6</u>4

12. 5<u>7</u>3

13. 34,<u>7</u>39

14. 5<u>9</u>,304

15. 930,<u>9</u>98

16. 7<u>4</u>8,397

In **17** through **24**, round each number to the place of the underlined digit.

17. 7<u>5</u>.8

18. 0.7<u>5</u>8

19. 64<u>3</u>.82

20. 0.<u>4</u>72

21. 84.<u>7</u>32

22. 738.2<u>9</u>

23. 5.0<u>2</u>8

24. 23.00<u>9</u>

Problem Solving

25. The world's largest aloha shirt measures 4.26 meters around the chest. Round 4.26 to the nearest ones place and to the nearest tenths place.

26. In the first 3 quarters of a basketball game, a team scored 17, 25, and 13 points. Their final score was 75. How many points did the team score in the fourth quarter?

27. An African Watusi steer's horn measures 95.25 cm around. What is 95.25 when rounded to the nearest tenth? Nearest whole number? Nearest ten?

28. In a recent year, the population of Illinois was 12,653,544. What is that population when rounded to the nearest million?

    A 10,000,000   **B** 12,000,000   **C** 12,600,000   **D** 13,000,000

29. The world land speed record set on October 15, 1997, was 763.03 miles per hour. What is this speed rounded to the nearest one?

Estimating Sums and Differences

How can you estimate sums?

Students are collecting cans of dog food to give to an animal shelter. Estimate the sum of the cans collected in Weeks 3 and 4.

Week	Cans of dog food
1	172
2	298
3	237
4	345
5	338

Another Example How can you estimate differences?

Estimate 22.8 − 13.9.

One-Way

Round each addend to the nearest whole number.

$$
\begin{array}{r}
22.8 \longrightarrow 23 \\
-\ 13.9 \longrightarrow -\ 14 \\
\hline
9
\end{array}
$$

22.8 − 13.9 is about 9.

Another Way

Substitute compatible numbers.

$$
\begin{array}{r}
22.8 \longrightarrow 25 \\
-\ 13.9 \longrightarrow -\ 15 \\
\hline
10
\end{array}
$$

22.8 − 13.9 is about 10.

Explain It

1. Which estimate is closer to the actual difference? How can you tell without subtracting?

2. When is it appropriate to estimate an answer?

Guided Practice*

Do you know HOW?

In **1** through **6**, estimate the sums and differences.

1. 49 + 22

2. 86 − 18

3. 179 + 277

4. 232 − 97

5. 23.8 − 4.7

6. 87.2 + 3.9

Do you UNDERSTAND?

7. Give an example of when estimating is useful.

8. In the example at the top, the students collected more cans of dog food in week 4 than in week 3. Estimate about how many more cans.

*For another example, see Set C on page 53.

Round each addend to the nearest hundred.

$$237 \longrightarrow 200$$
$$+\ 345 \longrightarrow +\ 300$$
$$500$$

237 + 345 is about 500. The students collected about 500 cans of dog food in Weeks 3 and 4.

Substitute compatible numbers. Compatible numbers are easy to add.

$$237 \longrightarrow 250$$
$$+\ 345 \longrightarrow +\ 350$$
$$600$$

237 + 345 is about 600. The students collected about 600 cans of dog food in Weeks 3 and 4.

Independent Practice

Estimate each sum or difference.

9.
$$79$$
$$+\ 32$$

10.
$$788$$
$$-\ 572$$

11.
$$103$$
$$+\ 798$$

12.
$$2,488$$
$$-\ 1,320$$

13.
$$64$$
$$+\ 48$$

14.
$$837$$
$$+\ 488$$

15.
$$51$$
$$-\ 18$$

16.
$$7,889$$
$$+\ 6,455$$

17.
$$184$$
$$-\ 58$$

18.
$$847$$
$$-\ 379$$

19.
$$3,856$$
$$-\ 2,357$$

20.
$$7,647$$
$$-\ 369$$

21. 3,205 − 2,812   **22.** 93 − 46   **23.** 1,052 + 963   **24.** 149 − 51

Estimate each sum or difference.

25.
$$2.9$$
$$+\ 3.9$$

26.
$$7.28$$
$$-\ 1.32$$

27.
$$\$11.33$$
$$+\ 32.43$$

28.
$$\$12.99$$
$$-\ 3.95$$

29.
$$8.1$$
$$3.7$$
$$+\ 7.9$$

30.
$$3.8$$
$$4.1$$
$$+\ 3.3$$

31.
$$67.9$$
$$+\ 81.34$$

32.
$$78.11$$
$$+\ 46.03$$

33. 77.11 − 8.18   **34.** 35.4 − 7.8   **35.** 89.66 − 27.9   **36.** 99.9 − 27.9

37. 22.8 + 49.2 + 1.7   **38.** 67.5 − 13.7   **39.** $9.10 + $48.50 + $5.99

40. Writing to Explain The cost of one CD is $16.98 and the cost of another CD is $9.29. Brittany estimated the cost of these two CDs to be about $27. Did she overestimate or underestimate? Explain.

41. Martha cycled 14 miles each day on Saturday and Monday and 13 miles each day on Tuesday and Thursday. How many miles did she cycle in all?

42. One fifth-grade class has 11 boys and 11 girls. A second fifth-grade class has 10 boys and 12 girls. There are 6 math teachers. To find the total number of fifth-grade students, what information is not needed?

  A The number of girls in the first class.

  B The number of boys in the first class.

  C The number of math teachers.

  D The number of boys in the second class.

43. On vacation, Steven spent $13 each day on Monday and Tuesday. He spent $9 each day on Wednesday and Thursday. If Steven brought $56 to spend, how much did he have left to spend?

44. Estimate 74.05 + 9.72 + 45.49 by rounding to the nearest whole number. What numbers did you add?

  A 75, 10, and 46   **C** 74, 10, and 45

  B 74.1, 9.7, and 45.5   **D** 75, 10, and 50

45. Golden Gate Park is located in San Francisco, California. The park covers 1,017 acres and has been compared to the size and shape of Central Park in New York City. Central Park covers 843 acres. About how many more acres does Golden Gate Park cover than Central Park?

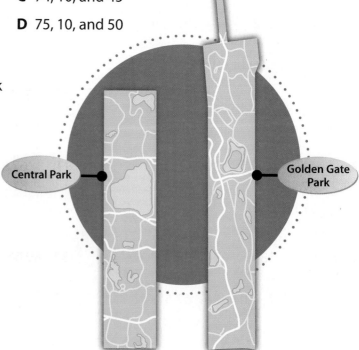

Algebra Connections

Number Patterns

The following numbers form a pattern.

3, 7, 11, 15, 19, …

In this case the pattern is a simple one. The pattern is add 4.

Some patterns are more complicated. Look at the following pattern.

20, 24, 30, 34, 40, 44, 50, …

In this case, the pattern is add 4, add 6.

> **Example**:
>
> What are the next two numbers in the pattern?
>
> 24, 29, 28, 33, 32, 37, 36, …
>
> **Think** The first number is increased by 5. The next number is decreased by 1. I see that the pattern continues.
>
> 24, 29, 28, 33, 32, 37, 36, …
>   +5   −1   +5   −1   +5   −1
>
> To find the next two numbers, add 5, and then subtract 1. The next two numbers are 41 and 40.

Look for a pattern. Find the next two numbers.

1. 9, 18, 27, 36, 45, …

2. 90, 80, 70, 60, 50, …

3. 2, 102, 202, 302, …

4. 26, 46, 66 , 86, …

5. 20, 31, 42, 53, 64, …

6. 100, 92, 84, 76, 68, …

7. 1, 3, 9, 27, …

8. 800, 400, 200, 100, …

9. 20, 21, 19, 20, 18, 19, 17, …

10. 10, 11, 21, 22, 32, 33, …

11. 25, 32, 28, 35, 31, 38

12. 5, 15, 10, 20, 15, 25, 20

13. The following numbers are called Fibonacci numbers.

1, 1, 2, 3, 5, 8, 13, 21, 34, 55 …

Explain how you could find the next two numbers.

14. **Write a Problem** Make up a number pattern that involves two operations.

Problem Solving

Draw a Picture and Write an Equation

Three friends have music collections. How many more CDs does Susan have than Larry?

Data

Music Collections	
	Number of CDs
Susan	42
Chad	17
Larry	26

Another Example

Rori had some balloons and then gave 35 of them away. She now has 21 left. How many balloons did Rori have to begin with?

x

35	21

One Way

 The total is unknown.

35 were given away and 21 are left.

Write an Equation

$x - 35 = 21$

$21 + 35 = 56$, so 56 is the total.

$x = 56$

Another Way

 35 were given away. Rori has 21 left.

The total is unknown.

Write an Equation

$35 + 21 = x$

$35 + 21 = 56$, so 56 is the total.

$x = 56$

Rori had 56 balloons to begin with.

Explain It

1. Why do both ways use addition to solve for x?

2. How can you check if 56 is a reasonable answer?

What do I know?

Susan has 42 CDs
and Larry has 26 CDs.

What am I asked to find?

The difference between
the number of CDs from
these two collections.

Draw a Picture

Susan	42 CDs

Larry	n	26

Write an Equation

Let n = the number of
additional CDs Susan has.

$42 - 26 = n$

$$\begin{array}{r} \overset{3}{\not{4}}\,\overset{1}{2} \\ -\ 2\ 6 \\ \hline 1\ 6 \end{array}$$

Susan has 16 more CDs in her collection than Larry.

Guided Practice*

Do you know HOW?

Draw a picture and write an equation. Solve.

1. Alec prints digital photos at a camera store. The first order was for 24 prints. The second order was for 85 prints, and the third for 60 prints. How many fewer prints were in the first order than the third order?

Do you UNDERSTAND?

2. What phrase from the above example gives you a clue that you will use subtraction in your drawing to solve the problem?

3. **Write a Problem** Write a real-world problem that uses subtraction and can be solved by drawing a picture and writing an equation.

Independent Practice

In **4**, copy and complete the picture. Then write an equation and solve.

4. Rose needs 22 tacos for a party. She has made 12 tacos so far. How many more tacos does Rose need to make?

	12

In **5**, draw a picture, write an equation in two different ways, then solve.

5. Aryanna is planning to spend a certain number of days on a trip to Florida. If she plans to spend 5 of the days in Orlando, she'll have 16 more days for the rest of her vacation. How many days does Aryanna plan to spend in Florida?

Stuck? Try this....

- What do I know?
- What am I asked to find?
- What diagram can I use to help understand the problem?
- Can I use addition, subtraction, multiplication, or division?
- Is all of my work correct?
- Did I answer the right question?
- Is my answer reasonable?

Independent Practice

For **6**, use the bar graph at the right.

6. Foster Middle School raised money to help care for some endangered animals. The bar graph shows the number of animals they will help with the money raised.

   a How many sea turtles and snow leopards can they help?

   b What is the difference between the greatest number of animals to be helped and the least number to be helped?

   c Show how you can use mental math to find the total number of animals helped.

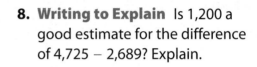

Endangered Animals to Help

Number of Animals — Animal: Sea Turtles, Elephants, Snow Leopards, Bison

7. **Writing to Explain** Don is adding 407 and 512. How do you know his sum will be less than 1,000?

8. **Writing to Explain** Is 1,200 a good estimate for the difference of 4,725 − 2,689? Explain.

9. A planetarium is 39 miles from Marco's school. The class leaves for the field trip at 8:00 A.M. After driving for 17 minutes and traveling 15 miles, the driver of the bus got caught in traffic. How many more miles are left to travel to the planetarium? Write an equation to solve.

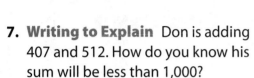

39 miles

| n | 15 |

10. Marlee is taking a class to improve her reading. She began reading a book on Monday and completed 3 pages. Tuesday she read 6 pages, Wednesday, 12 pages. If this pattern continues, how many pages will Marlee read on Friday?

Think About the Process

11. Three fifth-grade classes took a survey and found that 35 students take the bus to school, 25 come by car, 15 walk, and 5 ride their bikes. Which shows how to find how many more students take the bus than walk?

   A Subtract 35 from 5

   B Subtract 15 from 35

   C Add 15 and 35

   D Add 35 and 5

12. Darcy brought home 43 seashells from his vacation. Rich brought home x shells. Together they brought home 116 seashells. Which equation can you solve to find the number of shells Rich brought home?

   A $43 + x = 116$

   B $116 + x = 43$

   C $116 + 43 = x$

   D $x - 43 = 116$

Reasonableness of Differences

Estimate 4.72 − 2.85. Use a calculator to subtract. Then explain whether or not the sum you found is reasonable.

Step 1 Estimate 4.72 − 2.85.

$$5 - 3 = 2$$

Step 2 Use a calculator to subtract.

Press: 4.72 [−] 2.85 [ENTER =]

Display: `1.87`

Step 3 Explain whether or not the difference is reasonable.

Since 1.87 is close to the estimate of 2, the difference is reasonable.

Press (Clear) before starting a new problem.

Estimate 7.51 − 6.49 and use a calculator to subtract. Explain the difference between the estimation and the calculator result.

The estimated difference is 2, and the calculator result is 1.02. The two answers have a difference of about 1, because the first number rounded up and the second number rounded down.

Practice

Estimate each difference. Find the difference on a calculator. Then explain whether or not the difference is reasonable.

1. 28.34 − 7.85

2. 6.86 − 2.18

3. 5.2 − 0.74

4. 1.73 − 0.8

5. 14.97 − 12.39

6. 9.05 − 5.92

7. 2.4 − 0.56

8. 65.47 − 38.19

9. 16.15 − 3.9

10. 3.7 − 1.2

11. 2.82 − 1.21

12. 5.76 − 3.21

13. 8.47 − 7.08

14. 6.59 − 6.03

15. 8.88 − 3.84

Understand It!
Place value can be used to add and subtract whole numbers.

Adding and Subtracting

How can you add and subtract whole numbers?

What was the total number of motor vehicles made in the United States and Japan in one year?

Choose an Operation

Add to join groups.

Find $11,989,387 + 10,511,518$.

Estimate:

$12,000,000 + 11,000,000 = 23,000,000$

Country	Number of motor vehicles produced in one year
United States	11,989,387
Japan	10,511,518
Germany	5,569,954

Another Example **How can you subtract across zeros?**

Find $5,002 - 2,684$. Since addition and subtraction have an inverse relationship, check your subtraction by adding.

Step 1

Subtract the ones. Think of 5,000 as 500 tens. Regroup.

```
  4 9 9 12
  5, 0 0 2
- 2, 6 8 4
          8
```

Step 2

Subtract the tens, hundreds, and thousands.

```
  4 9 9 12
  5, 0 0 2
- 2, 6 8 4
  2, 3 1 8
```

Check

Add the difference to the number you subtracted. The answer checks.

```
    2, 3 1 8
  + 2, 6 8 4
    5, 0 0 2
```

Explain It

1. Explain the regrouping in Step 1 of the subtraction example above.

2. Why can you check a subtraction problem by adding?

Line up numbers by place value.
Add the ones, tens, and hundreds.

$$
\begin{array}{r}
\overset{1\ 1}{11{,}989{,}387} \\
+\ \ 10{,}511{,}518 \\
\hline
905
\end{array}
$$

Continue adding. Regroup if needed.
Insert commas in the sum to separate
periods.

$$
\begin{array}{r}
\overset{1\ 11\ \ \ 11}{11{,}989{,}387} \\
+\ \ 10{,}511{,}518 \\
\hline
22{,}500{,}905
\end{array}
$$

The sum is reasonable since the estimate was
23,000,000.

In one year a total of 22,500,905 vehicles
were made.

Guided Practice*

Do you know HOW?

Add.

1. $5{,}741 + 31{,}018$

2. $7{,}110 + 499$

Subtract.

3. $9{,}234 - 2{,}387$

4. $110{,}652 - 8{,}600$

Do you UNDERSTAND?

5. Writing to Explain In Step 2 of the
example above, explain how you
regrouped the tens place.

6. In the example above, how many cars
did the United States and Germany
make altogether?

Independent Practice

In **7** through **12**, add.

7. $7{,}469 + 8{,}374$

8. $19{,}335 + 24{,}281$

9. $40{,}742 + 22{,}597$

10. $102{,}369 + 60{,}320$

11. $18{,}269 + 109{,}347$

12. $75{,}977 + 24{,}683$

In **13** through **18**, subtract. Check your answer by adding.

13. $4{,}002 - 3{,}765$

14. $58{,}005 - 1{,}098$

15. $113{,}300 - 1{,}774$

16. $454{,}900 - 33{,}870$

17. $31{,}483 - 29{,}785$

18. $103{,}558 - 64{,}671$

19. Reasoning Why should you estimate before you find the sum or difference of large numbers?

20. About 66,150,000 households in the U.S. have cats and about 58,200,000 households have dogs. About how many more households have cats than dogs?

21. Write a Problem Use 1,400 and 986 to write a real-world addition problem.

22. Humans are born with 350 bones. Some of these bones fuse together as humans grow. Adults only have 206 bones. How many more bones does a baby have than an adult?

350 bones

?	206

23. Find each sum and difference. Write >, <, or = for each ◯.

a 1,233 + 486 ◯ 2,200 − 481

c 544 + 4,732 ◯ 2,512 + 1,930

b 193 + 233 ◯ 309 + 118

d 9,491 − 6,230 ◯ 7,020 − 3,759

The table at the right shows the amount of time (rounded to the nearest hour) that astronauts have spent in space for several space programs.

24. For the five space programs listed, what is the total number of hours astronauts spent in space?

A 14,608 hours

C 19,988 hours

B 17,621 hours

D 20,038 hours

Data

Program	Years	Total Hours
Mercury	1961–1963	54
Gemini	1965–1966	970
Apollo	1968–1972	2,502
Skylab	1973–1974	4,105
Space Shuttle	1981–1995	12,407

25. How much longer did astronauts in the Space Shuttle program spend in space than all of the other programs combined?

A 631 hours

C 4,776 hours

B 2,194 hours

D 12,407 hours

26. Lisa has a basket of 17 tomatoes. She makes sauce with 9 tomatoes. If Lisa wants to split up the rest between 3 friends and herself, how many tomatoes does each person get?

27. There are about 44,000 farms in Florida and about 38,000 farms in New York. Are the total number of estimated farms in Florida and New York greater or less than 100,000?

Mixed Problem Solving

Newbery Medal Winners for Children's Literature

Author	Title of Book	Year	Pages
Jerry Spinelli (1941–Present)	*Maniac Magee*	1991	184
Beverly Cleary (1916–Present)	*Dear Mr. Henshaw*	1984	160
Nancy Willard (1936–Present)	*A Visit to William Blake's Inn*	1982	48
E.L. Konigsburg (1930–Present)	*From the Mixed-Up Files of Mrs. Basil E. Frankweiler*	1968	176

For **1** through **6**, use the table above.

1. Which writer has lived the longest?

2. The first Newbery Medal was awarded in 1923. How many years after this first award did Jerry Spinelli receive his award?

3. How old was E.L. Konigsburg when she published *From the Mixed-Up Files of Mrs. Basil E. Frankweiler*?

4. What is the difference in the number of pages between the shortest and longest books in the table?

5. How much older is the author of *Dear Mr. Henshaw* than the author of *A Visit to William Blake's Inn*?

6. Strategy Focus Solve using the strategy Draw a Picture and Write an Equation.

In the first quarter of the year, Paul has to write two book reports. He chose to read *Maniac Magee* and *Dear Mr. Henshaw*. What is the total number of pages Paul will need to read? Use the diagram at the right to write and solve an equation. Let p = the number of pages Paul has to read.

p pages in all	
184	160

Adding Decimals

How can you add decimals?

What was the combined time for the first two legs of the relay race?

Choose an Operation Add to join groups.

Find 21.49 + 21.59.

Estimate: 21 + 22 = 43

Swimmers	Times in Seconds
Caleb	21.49
Bradley	21.59
Vick	20.35
Matthew	19.03

Data

Guided Practice*

Do you know HOW?

In **1** through **6**, find each sum.

1. 0.82 + 4.21　　**2.** 9.1 + 7.21

3. 9.7 + 0.24　　**4.** 3.28 + 6.09

5. 0.26 + 8.3　　**6.** 4.98 + 3.02

Do you UNDERSTAND?

7. Reasonableness How do you know the total time for the first two legs of the race is reasonable?

8. Writing to Explain How is finding $4.25 + $3.50 like finding 4.25 + 3.5? How is it different?

Independent Practice

In **9** through **26**, find each sum.

9.　　1.03
　　+ 0.36

10.　　6.9
　　+ 2.8

11.　　45.09
　　+ 2.005

12.　　2.02
　　+ 0.78

13.　　13.094
　　+ 4.903

14.　　356.2
　　+ 12.45

15.　　4.298
　　+ 0.65

16.　　9.001
　　+ 1.999

17.　　$8.23
　　+ $64.10

18.　　$44.00
　　+ $91.46

19.　　17.49
　　+ 9

20.　　42.89
　　+ 8.2

21. $271.90 + $34.22

22. 658.2 + 0

23. 0.922 + 6.4

24. 8.02 + 9.07

25. 13.9 + 0.16

26. 0.868 + 15.973

*For another example, see Set F on page 54.

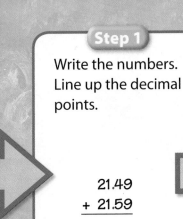

Step 1

Write the numbers. Line up the decimal points.

$$\begin{array}{r} 21.49 \\ + \ 21.59 \\ \hline \end{array}$$

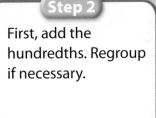

Step 2

First, add the hundredths. Regroup if necessary.

$$\begin{array}{r} \overset{1}{2}1.49 \\ + \ 21.59 \\ \hline 8 \end{array}$$

Step 3

Add the tenths, ones, and tens. The decimal point in the sum is aligned with the decimal point in the addends. Check the sum with your estimate.

$$\begin{array}{r} \overset{1}{}\overset{1}{2}1.49 \\ + \ 21.59 \\ \hline 43.08 \end{array}$$

The total time for the first two legs of the race was 43.08 seconds.

Problem Solving

27. A balloon mural of the Chicago skyline measures 17.6 m on two sides and 26.21 m on the other two sides. What is the perimeter of the mural?

A 38.81 m **B** 48.21 m **C** 55.74 m **D** 87.62 m

28. Writing to Explain Juan adds $3.8 + 4.6$ and gets a sum of 84. Is his answer correct? Tell how you know.

29. **Think** **About the Process** Jamie earned $27 taking care of a neighbor's dog for one week. She spent $19.95 on a new DVD. Later, she earned $15 for raking leaves. Which expression shows how to find the money Jamie has left?

A $27 + $19.95 + $15
C $27 − $19.95 + $15
B $19.95 − $15 + $27
D $27 − $19.95 − $15

30. At a flower shop, Teri sees that roses are $3 each, carnations are $4 for 3 flowers, and tulips are $4 for 4 flowers. She buys 3 roses and 3 carnations. She has $20. How much change does Teri get back?

31. Which two cities had the greatest combined rainfall for the period given?

  A Caribou and Boise

  B Springfield and Macon

  C Macon and Boise

  D Caribou and Springfield

Location	Rainfall amount in a typical year (in inches)
Macon, GA	45
Boise, ID	12.19
Caribou, ME	37.44
Springfield, MO	44.97

32. What is the typical yearly rainfall for all four cities?

33. Which location had less than 45 inches of rain but more than 40 inches of rain?

Subtracting Decimals

How can you subtract decimals?

What is the difference in the wingspans of the two butterflies?

Understand It!
Place value can be used to subtract decimals.

Choose an Operation
Subtract to find the difference.

Find 5.92 − 4.37.
Estimate: 6 − 4 = 2

4.37 cm

5.92 cm

Other Examples

Using 0 as a placeholder

Find 49.59 − 7.9.

$$
\begin{array}{r}
\overset{8\ \ 15}{4\ \cancel{9}.\ \cancel{5}\ 9} \\
-\ \ 7.\ 9\ 0 \\
\hline
4\ 1.\ 6\ 9
\end{array}
$$

Annex a 0 as a placeholder to show hundredths.

Using 0 as a placeholder

Find 24.6 − 8.27.

$$
\begin{array}{r}
\overset{1\ \ 14\ \ 5\ \ 10}{\cancel{2}\ \cancel{4}.\ \cancel{6}\ \cancel{0}} \\
-\ \ 8.\ 2\ 7 \\
\hline
1\ 6.\ 3\ 3
\end{array}
$$

← Annex a 0 as a placeholder to show hundredths.

Subtracting Money

Find $26.32 − $5.75.

$$
\begin{array}{r}
\overset{\ \ \ \ \ \ \ \ 12}{\overset{5\ \ \cancel{2}\ \ 12}{\$2\ \cancel{6}.\ \cancel{3}\ \cancel{2}}} \\
-\ \ \ \ 5.\ 7\ 5 \\
\hline
\$2\ 0.\ 5\ 7
\end{array}
$$

Guided Practice*

Do you know HOW?

In **1** through **8**, find each difference.

1.
$$
\begin{array}{r}
16.82 \\
-\ \ 5.21 \\
\hline
\end{array}
$$

2.
$$
\begin{array}{r}
7.21 \\
-\ \ 6.1 \\
\hline
\end{array}
$$

3.
$$
\begin{array}{r}
23.06 \\
-\ \ 8.24 \\
\hline
\end{array}
$$

4.
$$
\begin{array}{r}
\$4.08 \\
-\ \ 2.12 \\
\hline
\end{array}
$$

5. 56.8 − 2.765

6. $43.80 − $16.00

7. 22.4 − 10.7

8. $36.40 − $21.16

Do you UNDERSTAND?

9. Reasonableness Explain why 1.55 cm is a reasonable answer for the difference in the wingspans of the two butterflies.

10. In the other examples above, is the value of 7.9 changed when you annex a zero after 7.9? Why or why not?

11. Writing to Explain How is finding 9.12 − 4.8 similar to finding $9.12 − $4.80? How is it different?

Step 1

Write the numbers, lining up the decimal points.

$$
\begin{array}{r}
5.\,9\,2 \\
-\ 4.\,3\,7 \\
\hline
\end{array}
$$

Step 2

Subtract the hundredths. Regroup if needed.

$$
\begin{array}{r}
5.\,\overset{8}{\cancel{9}}\,\overset{12}{\cancel{2}} \\
-\ 4.\,3\,7 \\
\hline
5
\end{array}
$$

Step 3

Subtract the tenths and ones. Bring down the decimal point.

$$
\begin{array}{r}
5.\,\overset{8}{\cancel{9}}\,\overset{12}{\cancel{2}} \\
-\ 4.\,3\,7 \\
\hline
1.\,5\,5
\end{array}
$$

The difference is reasonable since the estimate was 2.

The difference in the wingspans is 1.55 cm.

Independent Practice

In **12** through **23**, find each difference.

12.
$$
\begin{array}{r}
7.8 \\
-\ 4.9 \\
\hline
\end{array}
$$

13.
$$
\begin{array}{r}
\$20.60 \\
-\ \$14.35 \\
\hline
\end{array}
$$

14.
$$
\begin{array}{r}
43.905 \\
-\ 7.526 \\
\hline
\end{array}
$$

15.
$$
\begin{array}{r}
65.29 \\
-\ 28.038 \\
\hline
\end{array}
$$

16. $15.03 - 4.121$

17. $13.9 - 3.8$

18. $65.18 - 12.005$

19. $\$52.02 - \$0.83$

20. $7.094 - 3.657$

21. $34.49 - 12.619$

22. $85.22 - 43.548$

23. $\$10.05 - \$4.50$

Problem Solving

24. Writing to Explain Why is it necessary to line up decimal points when subtracting decimals?

25. Reasonableness Sue subtracted 2.9 from 20.9 and got 1.8. Explain why this is not reasonable.

26. The pyramid of Khafre measured 143.5 meters high. The pyramid of Menkaure measured 65.5 meters high. What is the difference in the heights of these two pyramids?

A 68.8 meters

B 69.3 meters

C 78 meters

D 212.3 meters

27. An average person's upper leg bone measures 19.88 in. and the lower leg bone measures 16.94 in. How much longer is the upper leg bone than the lower leg bone?

upper leg bone	19.88 in.	
lower leg bone	?	16.94 in.

Khafre
143.5 meters

Menkaure
65.5 meters

Understand It!
Identifying and answering hidden questions can help when solving multiple-step problems.

Problem Solving

Multiple-Step Problems

Monica wants to buy all of the fruit shown on this sign. She has coupons for $0.45 off the cost of one pint of blueberries, and $0.35 off one watermelon. What will Monica's total cost be after the discounts?

FRESH FRUIT TODAY

(3 lb) $1.29

(1 pt) $3.29

(2 lb) $0.92

(each) $5.65

Another Example

A children's news and talk show is broadcast for 2 hours each weekday. On Saturday and Sunday, the show is an hour longer than during the week. How many hours is this show broadcast each week?

What is one hidden question?

How many hours of the show are broadcast during weekdays?

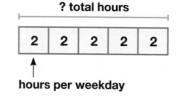

? total hours

| 2 | 2 | 2 | 2 | 2 |

↑ hours per weekday

$5 \times 2 = 10$

The show is on for 10 hours during weekdays.

What is another hidden question?

How many hours of the show are broadcast during the weekend?

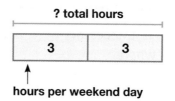

? total hours

| 3 | 3 |

↑ hours per weekend day

$2 \times 3 = 6$

The show is on for 6 hours during the weekend.

Add the number of weekday and weekend hours.

10 weekday hours + 6 weekend hours = 16 hours
The show is on for 16 hours each week.

Check for reasonableness: I can estimate 2 hrs $\times$ 7 days = 14 hrs. This is close to 16 hours.

Explain It

1. Why do you find and answer the hidden questions before solving the problem?

What do I know?

Monica wants to buy the fruit with prices shown on a store sign. She has coupons for $0.45 and $0.35 off the price of one pint of blueberries and one watermelon.

What am I asked to find?

The cost of all the fruit after the discount

Find and answer the hidden question or questions.

1. How much does the fruit cost?

? total cost			
$1.29	$3.29	$0.92	$5.65

$1.29 + $3.29 + $0.92 + $5.65 = $11.15

2. How much are the coupons worth?

? total saved	
$0.45	$0.35

$$\begin{array}{r} \$0.45 \\ + \$0.35 \\ \hline \$0.80 \end{array}$$

Subtract the total saved from the cost of the fruit.
$11.15 − $0.80 = $10.35

Monica will pay $10.35 for the fruit after the discount.

Guided Practice*

Do you know HOW?

Solve.

1. Nate has a $5 bill and a $10 bill. He spends $2.50 for a smoothie and $2 for a muffin. How much money does he have left?

Do you UNDERSTAND?

2. What are the hidden questions and answers for Problem 1?

3. Write a Problem Write a real-world multiple-step problem that can be solved using addition and subtraction.

Independent Practice

In **4** through **6**, write and answer the hidden question or questions. Then solve.

4. Elias saved $30 in July, $21 in August, and $50 in September. He spent $18 on movies and $26 on gas. How much money does Elias have left?

5. Paige takes riding lessons 5 days per week for 2 hours each day. Maggie takes guitar lessons twice a week for $2\frac{1}{2}$ hours each day, and piano lessons three days per week for 1 hour each day. Which girl spends more hours on lessons? How many more hours?

6. Lonny planted 15 roses, 12 geraniums, and 6 daisies. His dog digs up 4 roses and 2 daisies. How many flowers are left planted?

Stuck? Try this....

- What do I know?
- What am I asked to find?
- What diagram can I use to help understand the problem?
- Can I use addition, subtraction, multiplication, or division?
- Is all of my work correct?
- Did I answer the right question?
- Is my answer reasonable?

For another example, see Set H on page 55.

For **7** and **8**, write and answer the hidden question or questions. Then solve.

7. At the right is a driving log that Mr. Smith kept for the last three days of his trip. How many more miles did he drive for business than for personal use?

Driving Log		
	Business	**Personal Use**
Monday	48 mi	11 mi
Tuesday	59 mi	8 mi
Wednesday	78 mi	28 mi

8. The table at the right shows the amount of salad a deli had on Monday morning. During the morning, the deli sold 5 lb of macaroni salad, 16 lb of pasta salad, and 14 lb of potato salad. How many total pounds of salad did the deli have left Monday afternoon?

Salad Inventory	
Macaroni Salad	11 lb
Pasta Salad	22 lb
Potato Salad	15 lb

9. At the craft festival, Tuan spent $12 for food, $19.50 for a small painting, and $6 for a straw hat. Tuan had $4 left. How much did Tuan spend on the small painting and the hat together? Draw a picture and write an equation to solve.

10. Look for a pattern, and then describe it. What are the next three missing numbers?

0.39, 0.45, 0.51, ▨ , ▨ , ▨

11. **Writing to Explain** Pull-over shirts cost $24.95 each. Describe how to estimate the cost of 4 shirts. What is the estimate?

Think About the Process

12. A men's store has 63 blue oxford shirts and 44 tan oxford shirts. The same store has 39 red rugby shirts. Which hidden question needs to be answered to find the difference between the number of oxford shirts and rugby shirts?

    A How many oxford shirts does the store have?

    B How many blue and red shirts does the store have?

    C How many total shirts does the store have?

    D Why does the store sell oxford shirts?

13. Rita budgeted $250 to refurnish her home. She spent $156 on two rugs and $205 on a new lamp. Rita wants to know how much more money she'll need. Which expression can be evaluated to answer this hidden question: How much has Rita spent on the rugs and the lamp?

    A $156 + $205

    B $250 − $156

    C $156 + $250

    D $250 + $205

Adding Decimals

Use ⚙ **tools**

Place-Value Blocks

Use the Place-Value Blocks eTool to add 1.46 + 0.285.

Step 1 Go to the Place-Value Blocks eTool. Use the pull-down menu at the top of the page to select Large as the unit block. Select the two-part workspace icon. Click on the large cube, which represents one whole, and then click in the top part of the workspace. In the same way as above, show 4 flat place-value blocks and 6 long place-value blocks. The odometer should read 1.460.

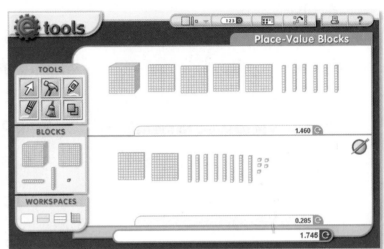

Step 2 Show 0.285 in the bottom part of the workspace, using the small cube for thousandths. The odometer for the bottom workspace should read 0.285.

Step 3 Use the arrow tool to select the 5 thousandths in the bottom part of the workspace and move them to the top. Move the 8 hundredths so they are next to the 4 hundredths in the top. Click on the glue icon, and then click on a long block. This will change 10 hundredths to 1 tenth. Move the remaining 2 tenths to the top space and look at the blocks to find the sum. 1.46 + 0.285 = 1.745.

Practice

Use the Place-Value Blocks eTool to find each sum.

1. 1.728 + 0.154   **2.** 0.375 + 0.29   **3.** 0.569 + 0.253   **4.** 0.86 + 0.649

5. 1.649 + 0.123   **6.** 1.223 + 0.789   **7.** 0.123 + 1.223   **8.** 0.789 + 1.649

9. 1.518 + 0.456   **10.** 1.527 + 0.912   **11.** 0.456 + 1.527   **12.** 0.912 + 1.518

13. 1.312 + 0.708   **14.** 1.630 + 0.815   **15.** 1.847 + 0.217   **16.** 1.309 + 0.219

1. The Chen family's home has 1,515 square feet downstairs and 625 square feet upstairs. Which of the following is the best estimate of the total square footage in the home? (2-3)

   A 2,100

   B 2,200

   C 2,300

   D 2,500

2. What is 2.934 rounded to the nearest hundredth? (2-2)

   A 2.90

   B 2.93

   C 2.94

   D 3.00

3. Eduardo is training for a marathon. He ran his first mile in 12.567 minutes and his second mile in 12.977 minutes. What is his combined time for the first two miles? (2-6)

   A 24.434 minutes

   B 24.544 minutes

   C 25.444 minutes

   D 25.544 minutes

4. To add 18 + 25 using mental math, Braxton did the following. What is the missing number that makes the statement true? (2-1)

   18 + 25 = 18 + (2 + 23) = (18 + ▢) + 23

   A 43

   B 25

   C 20

   D 2

5. Which two trails combined are less than 4 miles? Use estimation to decide. (2-3)

Trails	Red	Blue	Yellow	Green
Miles	2.75	3.5	2.95	1.2

   A Red and Yellow

   B Blue and Green

   C Red and Green

   D Blue and Yellow

6. The Thomas Jefferson Memorial is on 18.36 acres of land and the Franklin Delano Roosevelt Memorial is on 7.5 acres of land. How many more acres of land is the Jefferson Memorial on than the Roosevelt Memorial? (2-7)

   A 9.86

   B 10.86

   C 11.31

   D 17.61

7. The table shows the areas of two islands. How many more square miles is the area of Greenland than the area of New Guinea? (2-5)

Island	Area (square miles)
Greenland	839,999
New Guinea	316,615

   A 1,156,614

   B 1,145,504

   C 587,716

   D 523,384

8. In 2005, there were 2,100,990 farms in the United States. Which of the following is 2,100,990 rounded to the nearest thousand? (2-2)

 A 2,101,100

 B 2,101,000

 C 2,100,900

 D 2,100,000

9. Which picture represents the problem? Parson's Sporting Goods ordered 56 T-shirts in sizes small, medium and large. If 23 T-shirts are medium and 12 T-shirts are large, how many are small? (2-4)

A 56 shirts in all

23	12	?

B ? shirts in all

23	12	56

C 56

23	?

D 56 + ?

23	12

10. A lecture hall has 479 desk chairs and 216 folding chairs. How many seats are there in all? Use mental math to solve. (2-1)

 A 615

 B 685

 C 695

 D 785

11. Parker had a batting average of 0.287 and Keenan had an average of 0.301. How much higher was Keenan's batting average than Parker's? (2-7)

 A 0.256

 B 0.14

 C 0.023

 D 0.014

12. Monica bought a skirt for $15 and a hat for $12. Which is a way to find how much change she would get from $40? (2-8)

 A Add 40 to the difference of 15 and 12

 B Add 12 to the difference of 40 and 15

 C Subtract the sum of 15 and 12 from 40

 D Subtract 15 from the sum of 12 and 40

13. What is 87.25 + 7.69? (2-6)

 A 79.56

 B 94.2569

 C 94.94

 D 95.94

14. In the 2004 Presidential Election, 62,040,610 people voted for George W. Bush and 59,028,439 people voted for John F. Kerry. What was the total number of votes for the two men? (2-5)

 A 121,069,049

 B 121,068,049

 C 111,069,049

 D 121,169,049

Set A, pages 24–26

Add 53 + 11 + 7 using mental math.

Use compatible numbers.

 Compatible numbers are easy to add.

53 and 7 are compatible numbers.

The Commutative Property of Addition allows us to add in any order.

$$53 + 11 + 7 = 53 + 7 + 11$$
$$= \quad 60 + 11$$
$$= \quad 71$$

So, 53 + 11 + 7 = 71

Remember that you can use compatible numbers or compensation to find sums and differences.

Use mental math to add.

1. 67 + 28

2. 130 + 470

3. 35 + 14 + 6

4. 96 + 234 + 4

5. 276 − 99

6. 127 + 99

7. 241 + 2 + 98

8. 86 − 49

Set B, pages 28–29

Round 12.0<u>8</u>7 to the place of the underlined digit.

12.0<u>8</u>7   Look at the digit following the underlined digit. Look at 7.

         Round to the next greater digit of hundredths because 7 > 5.

12.087 is about 12.09.

Round <u>9</u>.073 to the place of the underlined digit.

<u>9</u>.073   Look at the digit following the underlined digit. Look at 0.

         Since 0 < 5 the digit in the ones place remains the same.

9.073 is about 9.

Remember that rounding a number means replacing it with another number that tells about how much or how many.

Round each number to the place of the underlined digit.

1. 10.2<u>4</u>5   **2.** 7<u>3</u>.4

3. 9.14<u>5</u>   **4.** 3.9<u>9</u>9

5. 67,<u>9</u>01   **6.** 13.0<u>2</u>3

7. <u>9</u>9,102   **8.** 45.3<u>9</u>8

9. 0.1<u>5</u>3   **10.** 0.62<u>5</u>

11. <u>8</u>.978   **12.** 5.7<u>3</u>9

13. 9,99<u>9</u>   **14.** 79.<u>5</u>

15. 3.0<u>9</u>1   **16.** 2.4<u>3</u>2

Set C, pages 30–32

Estimate 19.9 + 17.03.

$$
\begin{array}{r}
19.9 \longrightarrow \quad 20 \\
+\ 17.03 \longrightarrow \quad +\ 17 \\
\hline
37
\end{array}
$$

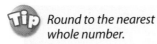 *Round to the nearest whole number.*

19.9 + 17.03 is about 37.

Estimate 22.4 − 16.2.

$$
\begin{array}{r}
22.4 \longrightarrow \quad 20 \\
-\ 16.2 \longrightarrow \quad -\ 15 \\
\hline
5
\end{array}
$$

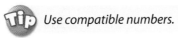 *Use compatible numbers.*

22.4 − 16.2 is about 5.

Remember using compatible numbers to estimate is easier than rounding.

Estimate each sum or difference.

1. 76 + 23

2. 15.01 − 4.4

3. 8,001 + 2,890

4. 25,003 − 12,900

5. 9.5 + 9 + 8.6

6. 34 + 37 + 30

Set D, pages 34–36

Draw a picture and write an equation. Solve.

Over the summer, Martin exercises 190 minutes more each week than during the school year. If Martin exercises 910 minutes per week in the summer, how many minutes per week does he exercise during the school year?

910 minutes	
m	190 min.

Let *m* = minutes per week of exercise during the school year

$$910 - 190 = m$$
$$m = 720$$

$$
\begin{array}{r}
\overset{\scriptstyle 8\ 1}{9\!\!\!/10} \\
-\ 190 \\
\hline
720
\end{array}
$$

Martin exercises 720 minutes per week during the school year.

Remember that drawing a picture can help you before writing an equation to solve a problem.

Draw a picture and write an equation. Solve.

1. Jay's parents celebrated their 25th wedding anniversary in 2005. In what year were they married?

2. One football stadium, built in 1982, has 64,035 seats. Another stadium, built in 1987, has 74,916 seats. How many more seats does the newer stadium have?

3. In Helen's class, there are 13 girls and 17 boys. Megan's class has the same number of students, but there are 20 girls in her class. How many boys are in Megan's class?

Set E, pages 38–40

Find 6,259 − 2,488.

Estimate: 6,000 − 2,000 = 4,000

Step 1 Subtract each place, starting from the right. Regroup as necessary. Check your work.

$$
\begin{array}{r}
\overset{\scriptstyle 11}{} \\
\overset{5}{\cancel{6}},\,\overset{\cancel{X}}{2}\,\overset{\cancel{15}}{5}\,9 \\
-\ 2,\ 4\ 8\ 8 \\
\hline
3,\ 7\ 7\ 1
\end{array}
$$

Step 2 Check.

$$
\begin{array}{r}
\overset{1}{}\ \ \overset{1}{} \\
3,\ 7\ 7\ 1 \\
+\ 2,\ 4\ 8\ 8 \\
\hline
6,\ 2\ 5\ 9
\end{array}
$$

The difference 3,771 is reasonable because it is close to the estimate, 4,000.

Remember to estimate first and then check that your answer is reasonable.

Find each sum or difference.

1.	9,371 + 6,059	**2.**	14,506 − 8,759
3.	41,974 + 32,821	**4.**	178,312 − 140,987
5.	12,364 + 87,112	**6.**	83,096 + 55,112

7. 72,555 + 38,055

8. 222,078 − 93,359

9. 51,716 + 8,422

10. 322,671 − 109,999

Set F, pages 42–43

Find 9.326 + 2.95.

Estimate: 9 + 3 = 12

Step 1 Write the numbers. Line up the decimal points. Annex zeros to show place value and to act as placeholders.

$$
\begin{array}{r}
9.\ 3\ 2\ 6 \\
+\ 2.\ 9\ 5\ 0 \\
\hline
\end{array}
$$

Step 2 Add as you would whole numbers. Bring the decimal point down into the answer.

$$
\begin{array}{r}
\overset{1}{} \\
9.\ 3\ 2\ 6 \\
+\ \ 2.\ 9\ 5\ 0 \\
\hline
1\,2.\ 2\ 7\ 6
\end{array}
$$

The sum 12.276 is reasonable because it is close to the estimate, 12.

Remember to line up the decimal points before you add.

Find each sum.

1. 3.77 + 4.66

2. 12.68 + 31.919

3. 6.142 + 1.322

4. 67.8 + 14.755

5. 7.029 + 48.7

6. 10.93 + 0.967

7. 1.47 + 1.80

8. 125.9 + 6.777

Set G, pages 44–45

Find 7.83 − 3.147.

Estimate: 8 − 3 = 5.

Step 1 Write the numbers. Line up the decimal points. Annex zeros to show place value and act as placeholders.

$$\begin{array}{r} 7.830 \\ -\ 3.147 \\ \hline \end{array}$$

Step 2 Subtract as you would whole numbers. Bring the decimal point down into the answer.

$$\begin{array}{r} {\scriptstyle 7\ \ 12\ 10} \\ 7.\cancel{8}\cancel{3}\cancel{0} \\ -\ 3.1\ 4\ 7 \\ \hline 4.6\ 8\ 3 \end{array}$$

Step 3 Check your answer by adding. The answer checks.

$$\begin{array}{r} {\scriptstyle 1\ \ 1} \\ 4.6\ 8\ 3 \\ +\ 3.1\ 4\ 7 \\ \hline 7.8\ 3\ 0 \end{array}$$

The difference 4.683 is reasonable because it is close to the estimate, 5.

Remember that you can check your answer by adding.

Find each difference.

1. 9.21 − 1.72

2. 15.51 − 11.302

3. 5.7 − 0.623

4. 16.209 − 14.5

5. 17.099 − 9.7

6. 81.12 − 37.202

7. 61.1 − 0.008

8. 19.006 − 7.5

Set H, pages 46–48

Gene wants to buy a catcher's mitt for $52.00 and baseball shoes for $95.75. He has a coupon for $8.50 off the price of the catcher's mitt. How much money will Gene owe for his total purchase?

What is the hidden question or questions?

How much will Gene have to pay for the catcher's mitt after he uses the coupon?

$52.00

$8.50	? cost after coupon

$52.00 − $8.50 = $43.50

Solve the problem.

Add the discounted price of the mitt to the price of the shoes to find the total amount Gene owes.
$43.50 + $95.75 = $139.25

Gene will pay $139.25 for his purchase.

Remember to look for the hidden question or questions first to solve the problem.

Write and answer the hidden question or questions. Then solve.

1. Pedro earned money doing different jobs for neighbors. He kept a table of what he earned. If Pedro bought a magazine subscription for $16.95 from his earnings, how much money did he have left?

Job	Earnings
Mowing lawn	$13.50
Raking leaves	$11.00
Walking dogs	$14.75

Multiplying Whole Numbers

1 This Black-chinned Hummingbird is eating nectar from a redbud. How can you make food for a hummingbird? You will find out in Lesson 3-4.

2 Kilauea is the most active volcano in the world. About how many cubic meters of lava does it discharge every minute? You will find out in Lesson 3-3.

Review What You Know!

3 Technology companies design and build digital products. How many images can a 32 MB memory stick for a digital camera hold? You will find out in Lesson 3-4.

4 One man balanced 75 drinking glasses on his chin. What was the capacity of the drinking glasses he balanced? You will find out in Lesson 3-5.

Vocabulary

Choose the best term from the box.

- equation
- product
- factors
- round

1. A(n) _?_ is another word for a number sentence.

2. One way to estimate a number is to _?_ the number.

3. A(n) _?_ is the answer to a multiplication problem.

4. In the equation $9 \times 5 = 45$, 9 and 5 are both _?_.

Multiplication Facts

Find each product.

5. 3×9 **6.** 5×6 **7.** 4×8

8. 6×9 **9.** 7×4 **10.** 9×8

Rounding

Round each number to the nearest hundred.

11. 864   **12.** 651   **13.** 348

14. 985   **15.** 451   **16.** 749

Multiplying Three Factors

Writing to Explain Write an answer to the question.

17. Gina wants to multiply $9 \times 2 \times 5$. How can Gina group the factors to make it easier to multiply?

Multiplication Properties

What are the properties of multiplication?

Do 2 groups of 5 beach balls equal 5 groups of 2 beach balls?

Commutative Property of Multiplication

The order of factors can be changed, but the product stays the same.

$2 \times 5 = 5 \times 2$

Guided Practice*

Do you know HOW?

In **1** through **5**, write the multiplication property used in each equation.

1. $65 \times 1 = 65$

2. $45 \times 6 = 6 \times 45$

3. $33 \times 0 = 0$

4. $11 \times 9 = 9 \times 11$

5. $(6 \times 20) \times 5 = 6 \times (20 \times 5)$

Do you UNDERSTAND?

6. Using equations, give an example for each property of multiplication.

7. In the following equations, what number should replace each ▨? Which property of multiplication is used?

a $40 \times 8 = \boxed{} \times 40$

b $1{,}037 \times \boxed{} = 1{,}037$

Independent Practice

In **8** through **19**, write the multiplication property used in each equation.

8. $537 \times 1 = 537$

9. $24 \times 32 = 32 \times 24$

10. $400 \times 0 = 0$

11. $73 \times 14 = 14 \times 73$

12. $5 \times (40 \times 9) = (5 \times 40) \times 9$

13. $1 \times 111 = 111$

14. $0 \times 1{,}247 = 0$

15. $8 \times (4 \times 3) = (8 \times 4) \times 3$

16. $(9 \times 3) \times 5 = 9 \times (3 \times 5)$

17. $1 \times 90 = 90 \times 1$

18. $76 \times 1 = 76$

19. $0 \times 563 = 0$

For another example, see Set A on page 80.

Associative Property of Multiplication	Identity Property of Multiplication	Zero Property of Multiplication
You can change the grouping of the factors. The product stays the same.	When you multiply any number by 1, the product is that number.	When you multiply any number by 0, the product is 0.
$(2 \times 5) \times 3 = 2 \times (5 \times 3)$	$5 \times 1 = 5$	$5 \times 0 = 0$

Reasoning In **20** through **25**, use the multiplication properties to determine the number that belongs in each box.

20. $1{,}037 \times \boxed{} = 1{,}037$

21. $5 \times (20 \times 9) = (5 \times 20) \times \boxed{}$

22. $(635 \times 47) \times \boxed{} = 0$

23. $8 \times (\boxed{} \times 4) = (8 \times 5) \times 4$

24. $75 \times \boxed{} = 42 \times 75$

25. $(9 \times 6) \times 4 = 9 \times (\boxed{} \times 4)$

Problem Solving

26. Writing to Explain Haley said that she would always know her 0 and 1 multiplication facts. Explain why Haley would say this.

27. Writing to Explain How can one of the multiplication properties help you evaluate $(77 \times 25) \times 4$?

28. Last month 48,097 people visited the zoo. The number 48,097 is how many more than 25,000?

    A 2,079   **C** 23,097

    B 12,097   **D** 320,079

29. Think About the Process Naomi ordered 2 bottles of water for $1.00 each and 1 turkey sandwich for $3.00. Which expression would you use to find how much Naomi paid?

    A $(2 \times \$1) \times \$3$

    B $2 \times (1 \times \$3)$

    C $(2 + \$1) + \$2$

    D $(2 \times \$1) + (1 \times \$3)$

30. Compare. Write $>$, $<$, or $=$ for each $\bigcirc$.

    a 34,304 $\bigcirc$ 43,403

    b 5.70 $\bigcirc$ 5.7

    c 21,978 $\bigcirc$ 21,789

31. Three hundred fifty 10-year-olds registered for a city-wide bowling tournament. If 205 participants are boys, how many are girls?

32. Critical Thinking Think of two numbers that will round to 14,000.

Understand It!
Using basic facts, patterns, and properties can be helpful when multiplying mentally.

Using Mental Math to Multiply

How can you use mental math to multiply by multiples of 10, 100, or 1,000?

Factors are <u>numbers that are multiplied to get a product.</u>

A multiple of a number is <u>a product of a given whole number and another whole number.</u>

factors   product

$$3 \times 10 = 30$$

30 is a multiple of 10.
30 is a multiple of 3.

Another Example **How can multiplication properties help you use mental math?**

Use the properties of multiplication and mental math to find $25 \times 17 \times 4$.

What You Think

25 and 4 are compatible numbers. They are easy to multiply in my head.

$25 \times 4 = 100$ and $100 \times 17 = 1,700$.

So, $25 \times 17 \times 4 = 1,700$

What You Write

Step 1 Using the Commutative Property,
$25 \times (17 \times 4) = 25 \times (4 \times 17)$.

Step 2 Using the Associative Property,
$25 \times (4 \times 17) = (25 \times 4) \times 17$

Guided Practice*

Do you know HOW?

In **1** through **8**, use patterns and properties to compute mentally.

1. $3 \times 7 =$ ▢
$30 \times 7 =$ ▢
$300 \times 7 =$ ▢

2. $4 \times 8 =$ ▢
$40 \times 8 =$ ▢
$400 \times 8 =$ ▢

3. $20 \times 50 \times 7$

4. $50 \times 32 \times 2$

5. 600×90

6. $4 \times 33 \times 25$

7. 80×500

8. $10 \times 783 \times 10$

Do you UNDERSTAND?

9. Writing to Explain Why are there two zeros in the product of 5×40?

10. When you find $50 \times 32 \times 2$, which two numbers are easy to multiply? Which multiplication property allows you to think of $50 \times 32 \times 2$ as $50 \times 2 \times 32$?

DIGITAL
Animated Glossary
www.pearsonsuccessnet.com

*For another example, see Set B on page 80.

300 is a multiple of 3 and 100, since $3 \times 100 = 300$.

It is easy to multiply by multiples of 10, 100, and 1,000.

Notice the pattern.

$5 \times 7 = 35$
$50 \times 7 = 350$
$500 \times 7 = 3,500$

$5 \times 70 = 350$
$50 \times 70 = 3,500$
$500 \times 70 = 35,000$

Step 1 Find the product of the non-zero digits.

Step 2 Count the total number of zeros in both factors.

Step 3 Place the total number of zeros after the product of the non-zero digits.

Independent Practice

In **11** through **22**, use patterns and properties to compute mentally.

11. 120×30

12. $600 \times 40 \times 0$

13. $110 \times 2,000$

14. $800 \times 40 \times 3$

15. $3,000 \times 700$

16. $60 \times 90 \times 1$

17. 500×500

18. $1,000 \times 100$

19. 50×60

20. 70×80

21. 400×800

22. $1 \times 6 \times 250$

Problem Solving

23. A box of printer paper has 10 packages, with 500 sheets in each package. If a principal orders 10 boxes, how many sheets of paper does he order?

24. Draw a Picture A post will be put on every corner and every 6 feet of a fence that is 42 feet long and 36 feet wide. How many posts are needed?

25. Writing to Explain Write a rule that tells how to use mental math to find the product of $30,000 \times 50,000$.

26. Algebra $a \times b = 3,500$. If a and b are two-digit multiples of 10, what numbers could a and b represent?

27. Which is a possible solution for

$$\boxed{} \times \boxed{} \times \boxed{} = 1,500?$$

A $50 \times 30 \times 0$

C $5 \times 30 \times 10$

B $3 \times 5 \times 10$

D $10 \times 5 \times 10$

28. Geometry Name the solid figure shown below.

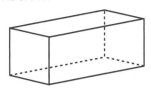

29. It takes Isaac 10 minutes to ride his bike down the hill to school and 20 minutes to ride up the hill from school. He attends school Monday through Friday. How many minutes does he spend biking to and from school in two weeks?

Estimating Products

How can you estimate products?

Understand It!
There is more than one way to estimate products of whole numbers.

A store needs to take in at least $15,000 in sales per month to make a profit. If the store is open every day in March and takes in an average of $525 per day, will the store make a profit in March?

store makes $15,000?

Another Example How can you use compatible numbers to estimate products?

Estimate 24 × 39.

You can also use compatible numbers to estimate products.

It is easy to find 25 × 40, since 25 and 40 are compatible numbers. Remember that 25 × 4 = 100. So, 25 × 40 = 1,000, and 1,000 is a good estimate for 24 × 39.

Both numbers used to estimate were greater than the actual numbers. So, 1,000 is an overestimate.

Guided Practice*

Do you know HOW?

In **1** and **2**, estimate by using rounding. Tell if your estimate is an overestimate or underestimate.

1. 58 × 6   **2.** 733 × 21

In **3** and **4**, estimate by using compatible numbers. Tell if your estimate is an overestimate or underestimate.

3. 43 × 27 × 4   **4.** 38 × 69

Do you UNDERSTAND?

5. Writing to Explain Susan used rounding to estimate 243 × 4 and found 200 × 4. Jeremy used compatible numbers and found 250 × 4. The actual product is 972. Whose method gives an estimate closer to the actual product?

6. Reasonableness In the example above, why is it better to adjust $525 to 500 rather than leave the number at 525?

DIGITAL   Animated Glossary
www.pearsonsuccessnet.com

You can use rounding to estimate.

$525 rounds to $500.

31 rounds to 30.

Find 30 × 500.   **Think** I know that
3 × 5 = 15.
30 × 500 = 15,000

Both numbers used to estimate were less than the actual numbers, so 15,000 is an underestimate. The store will actually take in more than $15,000.

So, the store will make a profit in March.

Independent Practice

In **7** through **18**, estimate each product.

7. 75 × 28

8. 3 × 118

9. 39 × 58

10. 97 × 15

11. 513 × 19

12. 64 × 55

13. 286 × 9

14. 11 × 83

15. 10 × 66

16. 26 × 29 × 41

17. 18 × 586

18. 26 × 3 × 101

Problem Solving

19. Reasoning Estimate 53 × 375. Is the estimated product closer to 15,000 or 20,000?

20. Kilauea has been active since 1983. About how many cubic meters of lava is discharged in one minute?

21. Writing to Explain Samuel needs to estimate the product of 95 × 23 × 4. Explain two different methods Samuel could use to estimate.

22. Give two factors whose estimated product is about 800.

23. Jacque uses 11 sheets of notebook paper each day at school. If he has a package of 150 sheets, will that be enough paper for him to use for 3 weeks at school? Use an estimate to find out.

Lava is discharged from the volcano at about 7 cubic meters per second.

Understand It!
To find products, use place value to break apart factors.

Multiplying by 1-Digit Numbers

How do you multiply by 1-digit numbers?

How many beads are in 7 containers?

Choose an Operation
Multiply to join equal groups.

36 Beads

Another Example How do you multiply a 1-digit number by a 3-digit number?

A theater has 5 sections with 347 seats in each section. What is the total number of seats in the theater?

A 1,505 seats   **C** 1,705 seats

B 1,535 seats   **D** 1,735 seats

? seats in theater

| 347 | 347 | 347 | 347 | 347 |

└ seats in each section

Choose an Operation Multiply to join equal groups.

Step 1

Multiply the ones, and regroup if necessary.

$$\begin{array}{r} 3 \\ 347 \\ \times\ 5 \\ \hline 5 \end{array}$$

5 × 7 ones = 35 ones
Regroup 35 ones as
3 tens 5 ones.

Step 2

Multiply the tens.
Add any extra tens.
Regroup if necessary.

$$\begin{array}{r} 23 \\ 347 \\ \times\ 5 \\ \hline 35 \end{array}$$

5 × 4 tens = 20 tens
20 tens + 3 tens = 23 tens
Regroup as 2 hundreds
3 tens.

Step 3

Multiply the hundreds.
Add any extra hundreds.
Regroup if necessary.

$$\begin{array}{r} 23 \\ 347 \\ \times\ 5 \\ \hline 1{,}735 \end{array}$$

5 × 3 hundreds = 15 hundreds
15 hundreds + 2 hundreds =
17 hundreds
Regroup as 1 thousand 7 hundreds.

The theater has 1,735 seats, so the correct choice is **D**.

Explain It

1. In Step 1, how do you know that 35 ones is 3 tens and 5 ones?

2. In Step 3, why are 2 hundreds added to the 15 hundreds?

Remember how to multiply using partial products.

$$36$$
$$\times \ \ 7$$
$$42 \longleftarrow 7 \times 6$$
$$+ \ 210 \longleftarrow 7 \times 30$$
$$252$$

The partial products are 42 and 210. You add them to find the product.

Step 1 Multiply the ones. Regroup if necessary.

$$\overset{4}{36}$$
$$\times \ \ 7$$
$$2$$

7×6 ones = 42 ones
Regroup 42 ones as 4 tens 2 ones.

Step 2 Multiply the tens. Add any extra tens. Regroup if necessary.

$$\overset{4}{36}$$
$$\times \ \ 7$$
$$252$$

7×3 tens = 21 tens
21 tens + 4 tens = 25 tens
Regroup 25 tens as 2 hundreds 5 tens.

There are 252 beads in 7 containers.

Guided Practice*

Do you know HOW?

In **1** and **2**, find each product. Estimate to check that your answer is reasonable.

1.
$$63$$
$$\times \ \ 8$$

2.
$$274$$
$$\times \ \ \ 3$$

Do you UNDERSTAND?

3. **Writing to Explain** In Step 2 of Another Example, why is it necessary to regroup the 23 tens?

4. In the example above, how many beads would be in 9 containers?

Independent Practice

In **5** through **29**, find each product. Estimate to check that your answer is reasonable.

5.
$$111$$
$$\times \ \ \ 7$$

6.
$$873$$
$$\times \ \ \ 6$$

7.
$$795$$
$$\times \ \ \ 5$$

8.
$$227$$
$$\times \ \ \ 3$$

9.
$$459$$
$$\times \ \ \ 4$$

10.
$$25$$
$$\times \ \ 9$$

11.
$$633$$
$$\times \ \ \ 9$$

12.
$$41$$
$$\times \ \ 8$$

13.
$$552$$
$$\times \ \ \ 6$$

14.
$$69$$
$$\times \ \ 7$$

15. 62×7

16. 124×2

17. 921×8

18. 55×4

19. 438×3

20. 29×6

21. 73×9

22. 264×4

23. 18×5

24. 38×8

25. 705×9

26. 351×2

27. 826×3

28. 79×8

29. 26×6

30. How do you know if the actual product of 26 × 44 is between 800 and 1,500?

31. Algebra Find the value of x.

$$x + 100 = 100,000,000$$

32. Estimation Estimate the product of 76 and 8. Do you have an underestimate or overestimate?

33. Geometry What is the perimeter of a rectangle measuring 5 cm by 9 cm?

34. A memory stick can be used to store images from a digital camera. The first memory stick was available in 1998. A 32 MB memory stick can hold up to 491 images. How many images can 7 memory sticks hold?

35. Writing to Explain Paul needs to estimate the product of 87 × 23 × 4. Explain two different estimation strategies he can use.

36. Use partial products to find 89 × 6.

37. When multiplying 37 × 4, how would you regroup the 14 tens?

38. **Think About the Process** A popular Mexican restaurant has 48 tables. On each table are 3 different types of salsa. In one day, all of the tables are used for 9 different sets of customers. Which expression can be used to estimate how many containers of salsa are needed for all the tables in one day?

A 50 × 9

C 50 × 3 × 10

B 47 × 3 × 9

D 40 × 5 × 5

39. A group of 24 students and 2 teachers went to a school fair. Each student and teacher spent $8 on tickets and $3 on snacks. What information is NOT needed to find out how much the 24 students and 2 teachers spent on tickets?

A The number of teachers

B The amount spent on snacks

C The amount spent on tickets

D The number of students

40. A man set a world record by holding nine eggs in one hand. Each egg weighed about 57 grams. What was the total weight of all of the eggs?

A 513 grams

B 456 grams

C 540 grams

D 570 grams

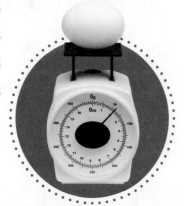

41. One type of food that hummingbirds like to eat is a simple syrup made from sugar and water. To make simple syrup you need 4 parts sugar and 1 part water. If you have 12 cups of water, how many cups of sugar do you need?

? cups of sugar

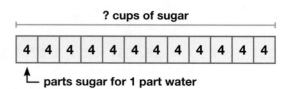

parts sugar for 1 part water

Algebra Connections

Simplifying Numerical Expressions

In order to simplify numerical expressions, you must follow the order of operations.

- Complete the operations inside the parentheses.

- Multiply and/or divide in order from left to right.

- Add and/or subtract in order from left to right.

Example:

Simplify $50 - (9 \times 3)$.

Start with the operation inside the parentheses. What is 9×3?

$9 \times 3 = 27$

Then subtract.

$50 - 27 = 23$

So, $50 - (9 \times 3) = 23$.

Simplify. Follow the order of operations.

1. $4 + 2 \times 9$

2. $16 + 8 \div 2$

3. $25 + (3 \times 6) - 5$

4. $8 \times 6 + 9$

5. $10 + 27 \div 3$

6. $(6 + 3) \times 5$

7. $(5 \times 2) + (10 \div 2)$

8. $5 \times 7 \times (6 - 3)$

9. $(12 - 3) \times (3 + 4)$

10. $35 + 5 \div 5 - 2$

11. $20 \times 2 + 3 \times (8 + 2)$

12. $(10 + 7) \times 3 - 4 \times (2 + 5)$

13. $3 \times 3 \div 3 + 6 - 3$

14. $(5 + 63) - 4 \times (12 \div 4)$

. . . .

Insert parentheses to make each statement true.

15. $11 - 6 - 1 = 6$

16. $10 + 2 \times 4 + 1 = 60$

17. $30 - 4 \times 2 + 5 = 2$

18. $64 \div 2 \times 4 \div 2 = 4$

19. **Write a Problem** Write a real-world problem that you could solve by simplifying the expression $50 - (2 \times 9)$.

Understand It!
To find products, use place value to break apart factors.

Multiplying 2-Digit by 2-Digit Numbers

How do you multiply by 2-digit numbers?

Sammy's Car Wash had 38 full-service car washes in one day. How much money did Sammy's Car Wash make in one day from full-service car washes?

Choose an Operation
Multiply to join equal groups.

CAR WASH	
SERVICE	COST
EXTERIOR ONLY	$8.00
FULL SERVICE	$12.00
VACUUM	$5.00

Guided Practice*

Do you know HOW?

In **1** through **4**, find each product. Estimate to check that your answer is reasonable.

1.   72
       × 16

2.   84
       × 21

3. 25 × 13

4. 34 × 22

Do you UNDERSTAND?

5. Writing to Explain How can you use estimation to decide if the $456 that Sammy's Car Wash made is reasonable?

6. In the example at the top, what would the car wash make if it charged $15 for each full-service wash?

Independent Practice

Leveled Practice In **7** through **23**, find each product. Estimate to check that your answer is reasonable.

7.   44
       × 23
          2
        8 0
        1

8.   89
       × 11
         8
        0
       9

9.   67
       × 57
         69
        350
       3 1

10.   98
        × 45
          9
        3 20
        4 0

11.   17
        × 12
          3
        1 0
         4

12.   35
        × 71
           5
        2 5
        2 8

13.   26
        × 18

14.   35
        × 29

15.   72
        × 51

16.   19
        × 15

17.   83
        × 47

18.   45
        × 16

19. 52 × 36

20. 77 × 18

21. 24 × 21

22. 64 × 32

23. 96 × 33

*For another example, see Set D on page 81.

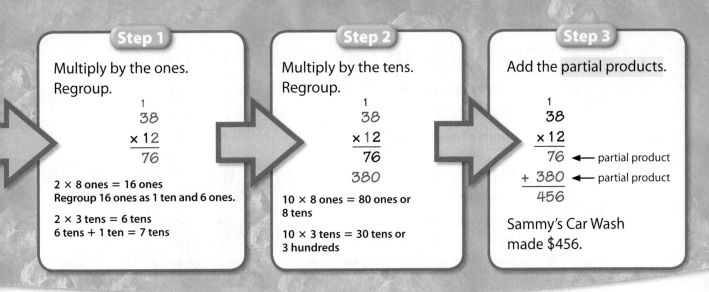

Step 1

Multiply by the ones. Regroup.

$$
\begin{array}{r}
1 \\
38 \\
\times 12 \\
\hline
76
\end{array}
$$

2 × 8 ones = 16 ones
Regroup 16 ones as 1 ten and 6 ones.

2 × 3 tens = 6 tens
6 tens + 1 ten = 7 tens

Step 2

Multiply by the tens. Regroup.

$$
\begin{array}{r}
1 \\
38 \\
\times 12 \\
\hline
76 \\
380
\end{array}
$$

10 × 8 ones = 80 ones or 8 tens

10 × 3 tens = 30 tens or 3 hundreds

Step 3

Add the partial products.

$$
\begin{array}{r}
1 \\
38 \\
\times 12 \\
\hline
76 \\
+ 380 \\
\hline
456
\end{array}
$$

76 ← partial product
380 ← partial product

Sammy's Car Wash made $456.

Problem Solving

24. The 2001 record for balancing drinking glasses was 75 glasses. If the capacity of each glass was 20 fluid ounces, how many total fluid ounces could all of the glasses contain?

25. The principal of a school is buying 3 computers at $900 each. She can pay $98 per month instead of paying for them at once. Will she have paid for the computers by the end of 12 months?

26. Writing to Explain How can finding the product of 5 × 700 help you check the product of 5 × 789?

27. The label on a jigsaw puzzle states that it has more than 1,000 pieces. After Bonnie put the puzzle together, she counted 44 pieces across the top and 28 pieces down the side. Estimate to determine if the label was correct.

28. There are 21 classrooms at Pine School. There are between 27 and 33 students per room. Which is the best estimate of the total number of students in the school?

   A 300   **B** 400   **C** 500   **D** 600

For **29** and **30**, use the table at the right.

29. The Explorer Hiking Club has 64 members. How much will it cost for all members to buy new Terrain backpacks?

30. The club also needs to buy 16 dome tents and 16 propane stoves. Will they spend more or less on these items than on the backpacks? How much more or less?

Camping Gear Prices	
Gear	**Price**
Dome Tent	$99
Propane Stove	$28
Terrain Backpack	$87

Multiplying Greater Numbers

How do you multiply 3-digit numbers by 2-digit numbers?

Understand It!
To find products, use place value to break apart factors.

Last month a bakery sold 389 trays of bagels. How many bagels did the store sell last month?

Choose an Operation
Multiply to join equal groups.

12 bagels
per tray

Guided Practice*

Do you know HOW?

In **1** through **4**, find each product. Estimate to check that your answer is reasonable.

1. $\begin{array}{r} 236 \\ \times\ \ 46 \\ \hline \end{array}$

2. $\begin{array}{r} 425 \\ \times\ \ 61 \\ \hline \end{array}$

3. 827×23

4. 745×13

Do you UNDERSTAND?

5. In Step 2 of the example at the top, do you multiply 1×9 or 10×9?

6. **Writing to Explain** Is 300×10 a good estimate for the number of bagels sold at the bakery?

Independent Practice

In **7** through **31**, find each product. Estimate to check that your answer is reasonable.

7. $\begin{array}{r} 451 \\ \times\ \ 10 \\ \hline \end{array}$

8. $\begin{array}{r} 892 \\ \times\ \ 18 \\ \hline \end{array}$

9. $\begin{array}{r} 655 \\ \times\ \ 98 \\ \hline \end{array}$

10. $\begin{array}{r} 132 \\ \times\ \ 47 \\ \hline \end{array}$

11. $\begin{array}{r} 381 \\ \times\ \ 27 \\ \hline \end{array}$

12. $\begin{array}{r} 901 \\ \times\ \ 62 \\ \hline \end{array}$

13. $\begin{array}{r} 185 \\ \times\ \ 55 \\ \hline \end{array}$

14. $\begin{array}{r} 227 \\ \times\ \ 87 \\ \hline \end{array}$

15. $\begin{array}{r} 946 \\ \times\ \ 33 \\ \hline \end{array}$

16. $\begin{array}{r} 735 \\ \times\ \ 41 \\ \hline \end{array}$

17. 25×100

18. 529×47

19. 19×763

20. 498×42

21. 106×72

22. 289×26

23. 390×59

24. 35×515

25. 81×11

26. 785×58

27. 25×314

28. 602×14

29. 40×719

30. 500×62

31. 199×99

Step 1

Multiply by the ones, and regroup if necessary.

$$\begin{array}{r} \overset{1\ 1}{389} \\ \times\ 12 \\ \hline 778 \end{array}$$

2 × 9 ones = 18 ones or 1 ten and 8 ones

2 × 8 tens = 16 tens
16 tens + 1 ten = 17 tens
17 tens = 1 hundred 7 tens

2 × 3 hundreds = 6 hundreds
6 hundreds + 1 hundred = 7 hundreds

Step 2

Multiply by the tens, and regroup if necessary.

$$\begin{array}{r} 389 \\ \times\ 12 \\ \hline 778 \\ +\ 3890 \end{array}$$

10 × 9 ones = 90 ones
10 × 8 tens = 80 tens or
8 hundreds
10 × 3 hundreds = 30 hundreds
or 3 thousand

Step 3

Add the partial products.

$$\begin{array}{r} 389 \\ \times\ 12 \\ \hline 778 \\ +\ 3890 \\ \hline 4,668 \end{array}$$

The store sold 4,668 bagels last month.

Problem Solving

For **32** through **34**, use the data chart.

32. How many times does a dog's heart beat in 15 minutes?

33. In 20 minutes, how many more times does a gerbil's heart beat than a rabbit's?

Animal	Heart Rate (beats per minute)
Dog	100
Gerbil	360
Rabbit	212

34. **Think About the Process** Which expression shows how to find the total number of heartbeats in 1 hour for a dog and a rabbit?

A $(100 \times 1) + (212 \times 1)$

B $60 \times 100 \times 212$

C $(60 \times 100) + (60 \times 212)$

D $(212 \times 100) + 60$

35. The length of the Nile River in Africa is about 14 times the length of Lake Michigan. About how many miles long is the Nile River?

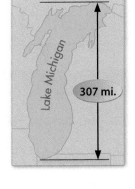

Lake Michigan — 307 mi.

36. The fifth-grade class at Monticello Middle School sold more bags of popcorn than any other class. They ordered 17 cases of popcorn. Each case had 242 bags. How many bags of popcorn did the class sell?

37. A nursery sells plants in flats. There are 6 plants in each tray. Each flat has 6 trays. The nursery sold 18 flats on Saturday and 21 flats on Sunday. How many plants did the nursery sell in all?

38. **Writing to Explain** Is 3,198 a reasonable product for 727 × 44? Why or why not?

39. A theater in Darling Harbour, Australia, can seat 540 people at one time. How many tickets can be sold if the theater sells out every seat for one 30-day month?

Understand It!
Exponents are used to show the number of times a factor is repeated.

Exponents

How can you use exponents to write large numbers?

A box of cubes has 5 layers. Each layer has 5 rows, with 5 cubes in each row.

There are $5 \times 5 \times 5$ cubes in the box.

You can use exponential notation to represent repeated multiplication of the *same* number such as $5 \times 5 \times 5$.

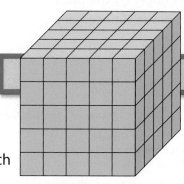

Other Examples

Exponential notation
Write $4 \times 4 \times 4$ in exponential notation.

$4 \times 4 \times 4 = 4^3$

Expanded form
Write 10^4 in expanded form.

$10^4 = 10 \times 10 \times 10 \times 10$

Standard form
Write 2^5 in standard form.

$2^5 = 2 \times 2 \times 2 \times 2 \times 2$
$\qquad = 32$

An exponent is also called a power. You can read 4^6 as "4 to the sixth power". The second and third powers have special names. Read 3^2 as "3 to the second power," or 3 squared. Read 6^3 as "6 to the third power," or 6 cubed.

Guided Practice*

Do you know HOW?

1. Write 3^5 in expanded form.

2. Write 2^4 in standard form.

3. Write $7 \times 7 \times 7 \times 7 \times 7$ using exponential notation.

4. Write 5^4 in expanded form and standard form.

Do you UNDERSTAND?

5. In 3^5, what is the base? The exponent?

6. In the example at the top, how is 125 written in expanded form?

7. What is the standard form of 3 squared? For 6 cubed?

DIGITAL

Animated Glossary
www.pearsonsuccessnet.com

For another example, see Set E on page 81.

The base is the number to be multiplied.

The exponent is the number that tells how many times the base is used as a factor.

factors   exponent

$5 \times 5 \times 5 = 5^3$

base

Numbers involving exponents can be written in three different forms.

Exponential notation	5^3
Expanded form	$5 \times 5 \times 5$
Standard form	125

Independent Practice

In **8** through **14**, write in exponential notation.

8. $10 \times 10 \times 10 \times 10 \times 10$ **9.** $9 \times 9 \times 9$ **10.** 81×81 **11.** $5 \times 5 \times 5 \times 5$

12. $7 \times 7 \times 7$ **13.** $13 \times 13 \times 13 \times 13 \times 13 \times 13$ **14.** $6 \times 6 \times 6 \times 6$

In **15** through **22**, write in expanded form.

15. 17^5 **16.** 35 squared   **17.** 4^3 **18.** 7^6

19. 55^4 **20.** 11^6 **21.** 8 cubed   **22.** 1^9

In **23** through **30** write in standard form.

23. 5^4 **24.** 10^3 **25.** $4 \times 4 \times 4$ **26.** 12 squared

27. 1^{10} **28.** 2^6 **29.** 3 cubed   **30.** 9^4

Problem Solving

31. Writing to Explain Why is the standard form of 8^2 NOT equal to 16?

32. Number Sense Find the number that equals 81 when it is squared.

33. Darnell earned $10 each week for 10 weeks walking a neighbor's dog.

 a How much did he earn?

 b Write the amount Darnell earned using exponential notation.

34. Which of the following, when written in standard form, is equal to the standard form of 2^6?

 A 6^2 **C** 8^2

 B 3^4 **D** 4^4

Problem Solving

Draw a Picture and Write an Equation

In 1990, a painting was bought for $575. In 2006 the same painting sold for 5 times as much. What was the price of the painting in 2006?

Another Example

Each artist at a large art show is assigned to a team of 3 judges. There are 9 teams of judges at the show. If each team reviews the work of 27 artists, how many artists attend the show?

Think There are 9 teams of judges. Each team reviews 27 artists. The total number of artists at the show is unknown.

Draw a Picture

a **number of artists**

| 27 | 27 | 27 | 27 | 27 | 27 | 27 | 27 | 27 |

number of artists for each team of judges

Write an Equation

Let *a* = the number of artists at the show.

$9 \times 27 = a$

$a = 243$

$$\begin{array}{r} \overset{6}{27} \\ \times\quad 9 \\ \hline 243 \end{array}$$

There are 243 artists at the show.

Explain It

1. Which of the 2 diagrams shown in the 2 examples models "times as many"?

2. What does the variable *a* represent in the example?

3. How can you check if 243 is a reasonable product?

What do I know?

The 1990 price of the painting was $575. In 2006 the same painting sold for 5 times as much as the 1990 price.

What am I asked to find?

The price of the painting in 2006.

Draw a Picture

p price in 2006

| 2006 | $575 | $575 | $575 | $575 | $575 | 5 times as much |

| 1990 | $575 |

Write an Equation

Let p = the price of the painting in 2006.

$575 \times 5 = p$ So, $p = \$2,875$

In 2006, the painting sold for $2,875.

$$\begin{array}{r} {\scriptstyle 3\,2} \\ 575 \\ \times\quad 5 \\ \hline 2,875 \end{array}$$

Guided Practice*

Do you know HOW?

Copy and complete the picture and write an equation. Solve.

1. Sharon's Stationery Store has 219 boxes of cards. May's Market has 3 times as many boxes of cards. How many boxes of cards does May's Market have?

   b boxes of cards

   | | | |

   | |

Do you UNDERSTAND?

2. What phrase from the top example gives you a clue that you will use multiplication in your drawing to solve the problem?

3. **Write a Problem** Write a real-world problem that uses multiplication and can be solved by drawing a picture and writing an equation.

Independent Practice

For **4** through **8**, draw a picture and write an equation. Solve.

4. Brad lives 10 times as far away from Dallas as Jennie. If Jennie lives 44 miles from Dallas, how many miles from Dallas does Brad live?

5. Gamal helped his dad clean the garage and attic over the weekend. They took eight 15-minute breaks. How many minutes did they spend on breaks?

Stuck? Try this....

- What do I know?
- What am I asked to find?
- What diagram can I use to help understand the problem?
- Can I use addition, subtraction, multiplication, or division?
- Is all of my work correct?
- Did I answer the right question?
- Is my answer reasonable?

For another example, see Set F on page 81.

6. Jupiter is about 5 times the distance Earth is from the Sun. How far is Jupiter from the Sun?

93,000,000 miles

7. Ralph's Roadhouse serves breakfast, lunch and dinner. The menu at Ralph's Roadhouse has 39 different items. Ruby's Café has 3 times the menu items as Ralph's. How many menu items does Ruby's Café have?

8. Harry earned $35 mowing grass this summer. Howard earned 6 times as much money as Harry. How much money has Howard earned?

9. Jake searches online and finds a pair of in-line skates. He asks his mom to order them since they are less expensive than in the store. The price of the skates is $56.95. The shipping charge is $10.65. What is the total price for the in-line skates?

10. Elsie practiced playing the clarinet from 3:10 to 4:15 on Monday afternoon. Tuesday night she practiced from 6:45 to 7:20. How many minutes in all did she practice?

11. Suzanne worked 1 hour on Monday, $2\frac{1}{2}$ hours on Tuesday, and 4 hours on Wednesday. If this pattern continues, how long will she work on Friday?

Think About the Process

12. Frieda decorates her friends' jackets with antique buttons. She uses 6 buttons for men's jackets and twice as many buttons for women's jackets. Which equation shows how to find the number of buttons Frieda will need for a women's jacket?

A $6 \div 2 = b$

B $2 + 6 = b$

C $2 \times 6 = b$

D $6 - 2 = b$

13. Emilio has to sell more than $200 worth of tickets to the fundraising dinner to win a prize. He makes 16 sales, and each sale is worth $12. How can Emilio find out if he has sold enough to win a prize?

A He can subtract $16 - 12$ and compare the difference to 200.

B He can multiply 12×16 and compare the product to 200.

C He can multiply 12×200 and add the product to 16.

D He can add $16 + 12$ and subtract the sum from 200.

Multiplication Patterns

Use  tools
Spreadsheet/Data/Grapher

Use a pattern to find $400 \times 6,000$. Describe the pattern that relates the number of zeros in 400 and 6,000 to the number of zeros in the product.

Step 1 ⬈ Select the Spreadsheet/Data/Grapher eTool. Use the arrow tool to select rows 1 to 10 and columns A to C. Use the .00 pull-down menu at the top of the workspace to select 0 decimal places. Type in the numbers shown below.

B9	6000					
	A	B	C	D	E	F
1	4	60				
2	4	600				
3	4	6000				
4	40	60				
5	40	600				
6	40	6000				
7	400	60				
8	400	600				
9	400	6000				
10						

Step 2 Cell C1 is in column C and row 1. In cell C1, type $= A1*B1$ and press enter. This will multiply the 4 in cell A1 by the 60 in cell B1. In cell C2, type $= A2*B2$ and press enter. Do the same for cells C3 to C9. Notice the pattern. To find $400 \times 6,000$, first find $4 \times 6 = 24$. Then annex the total number of zeros in both numbers. So $400 \times 6,000 = 2,400,000$.

Practice

Use the Spreadsheet/Data/Grapher to find the product for each.
Hint: Do not delete the formulas.

1. $300 \times 7,000$

2. $600 \times 5,000$

3. $500 \times 8,000$

4. $200 \times 6,000$

5. $500 \times 2,000$

6. $100 \times 5,000$

7. $400 \times 1,000$

8. $300 \times 4,000$

9. $600 \times 3,000$

1. Dr. Peterson works about 11 hours each day. Which of the following can be used to find the best estimate of the number of hours he works in 48 days? (3-3)

   A 10×40

   B 9×50

   C 10×50

   D 15×45

2. A banana contains 105 calories. Last week, Brendan and Lea ate a total of 14 bananas. How many calories does this represent? (3-6)

   A 525

   B 1,450

   C 1,470

   D 4,305

3. Four bags with 7 apples in each bag is the same amount as 7 bags with 4 apples in each bag. Which property of multiplication does this represent? (3-1)

   A Associative

   B Commutative

   C Identity

   D Zero

4. A cube with sides 2 inches long has a volume of 2^3 cubic inches. Which of the following is equal to 2^3? (3-7)

   A 6

   B 8

   C 9

   D 36

5. The latest mystery novel costs $24. The table shows the sales of this novel by a bookstore. What is the the total amount of sales on Saturday? (3-6)

Day	Books Sold
Thursday	98
Friday	103
Saturday	157
Sunday	116

   A $3,768

   B $3,748

   C $2,784

   D $942

6. Mr. Leim spends $24 on parking each week. He works 48 weeks a year. How much does he spend on parking in a year? (3-5)

   A $1,152

   B $1,122

   C $1,022

   D $288

7. Jasmin's parents allow her to use the family computer 90 minutes each day. How many minutes is she allowed to use the computer during a month that is 30 days in length? (3-2)

   A 120

   B 270

   C 1,200

   D 2,700

8. The average rainfall at Mt. Waialeale in Hawaii is 460 inches per year. How much rain would this location expect to receive in 5 years? (3-4)

   A 2,000

   B 2,030

   C 2,300

   D 2,305

9. A small town newspaper prints 9,000 copies each day. How many copies will the newspaper print in 40 days? (3-2)

   A 13,000

   B 36,000

   C 360,000

   D 3,600,000

10. Tyrone scored 24 touchdowns this year. Each touchdown scored was 6 points. How many points did Tyrone score this year? (3-4)

    A 30

    B 124

    C 144

    D 164

11. Which of the following is the best estimate of $4 \times 26 \times 7$ using compatible numbers? (3-3)

    A 800

    B 700

    C 650

    D 400

12. Which of the following is equal to 4^5? (3-7)

    A 4×5

    B $5 \times 5 \times 5 \times 5$

    C $4 \times 4 \times 4 \times 4$

    D $4 \times 4 \times 4 \times 4 \times 4$

13. Four buses are available for a field trip. If each bus can hold 48 people, which of the following can be used to find the number of people that can ride the buses? (3-8)

p people on buses			
48	48	48	48

    A $4 \times 48 = p$

    B $48 \div 4 = p$

    C $4 + 48 = p$

    D $48 - 4 = p$

14. What number makes the number sentence true? (3-1)

    $(4 \times 8) \times 7 = 4 \times (8 \times \quad)$

    A 3

    B 7

    C 28

    D 56

Set A, pages 58–59

Property of Multiplication	Example
Commutative	$4 \times 8 = 8 \times 4$ $32 = 32$
Associative	$(4 \times 5) \times 6 = 4 \times (5 \times 6)$ $120 = 120$
Zero	$12 \times 0 = 0$
Identity	$9 \times 1 = 9$

Remember to use the multiplication properties to determine what number must be in the box.

1. $256 \times \boxed{} = 256$

2. $157,678 \times 0 = \boxed{}$

3. $7,000 \times \boxed{} = 20 \times 7,000$

4. $(12 \times 3) \times 4 = 12 \times (\boxed{} \times 4)$

5. $\boxed{} \times 1 = 1,234,005$

6. $40 \times 60 = 60 \times \boxed{}$

Set B, pages 60–61

Find $3,000 \times 500$.

Step 1	Find the product of the non-zero digits.	$3 \times 5 = 15$
Step 2	Count the total number of zeros in both factors.	5 zeros
Step 3	Place the total number of zeros after the product of the non zero digits.	1,500,000

Remember to count the total number of zeros in both factors.

Find each product.

1. 12×30 **2.** 600×40

3. $10 \times 9,000$ **4.** $5,000 \times 80$

5. $9 \times 10 \times 800$

6. $7,000 \times 400 \times 3$

7. $8 \times 5 \times 22,000$

Set C, pages 62–63

Estimate 37×88.

| **Step 1** | Round both factors. | 37 is about 40 and 88 is about 90. |
| **Step 2** | Use mental math and multiply the rounded factors. | $40 \times 90 = 3,600$ |

Remember to either round the factors or use compatible numbers.

Estimate each product.

1. 7×396 **2.** 17×63

3. 91×51 **4.** 70×523

5. 32×400 **6.** 116×787

7. $4 \times 24 \times 91$ **8.** $29 \times 51 \times 67$

Set D, pages 64–66; 68–69; 70–71

Find 425 × 38.

Step 1	Step 2	Step 3
Multiply the ones.	Multiply the tens.	Add the partial products.

$$
\begin{array}{r}
{\scriptstyle 2\,4} \\
425 \\
\times\ \ 38 \\
\hline
3400
\end{array}
$$

$$
\begin{array}{r}
{\scriptstyle 1} \\
425 \\
\times\ \ 38 \\
\hline
3400 \\
12750
\end{array}
$$

$$
\begin{array}{r}
425 \\
\times\ \ 38 \\
\hline
3400 \\
+\ 12750 \\
\hline
16{,}150
\end{array}
$$

Remember to regroup if necessary. Estimate to check that your answer is reasonable.

Find each product.

1. 54 × 9   **2.** 92 × 6

3. 189 × 3   **4.** 708 × 5

5. 67 × 48   **6.** 81 × 19

7. 51 × 605   **8.** 32 × 871

Set E, pages 72–73

Write 7^3 in expanded form and standard form.

 The base is 7.
The exponent is 3.

Exponential notation: 7^3
Expanded form: 7 × 7 × 7
Standard form: 343

Remember that the exponent tells how many times the base is used as a factor.

Write each in expanded form and standard form.

1. 17^2 **2.** 10^5 **3.** 2^6 **4.** 5^4

Set F, pages 74–76

Draw a picture and write an equation. Solve.

The length of James's pool is 16 ft. The length of the pool at Wing Park is 4 times as long. How long is the pool at Wing Park?

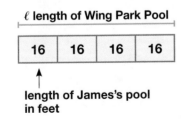

ℓ length of Wing Park Pool

| 16 | 16 | 16 | 16 |

length of James's pool in feet

Let ℓ = the length of Wing Park pool.

16 × 4 = ℓ
ℓ = 64 ft

$$
\begin{array}{r}
{\scriptstyle 2} \\
16 \\
\times\ \ 4 \\
\hline
64
\end{array}
$$

The length of Wing Park pool is 64 ft.

Remember that a picture can help you visualize an equation.

Solve.

1. Mia has a collection of 34 dolls. A toy store's warehouse has 15 times as many dolls. How many dolls are in the warehouse?

2. Lea has given 23 surveys at school. She needs to give twice this amount before the end of the week. How many more surveys does Lea need to give?

Dividing by 1-Digit Divisors

1 Radar measures over 19 hands. How many feet tall is Radar? You will find out in Lesson 4-2.

2 Scientists have been tagging turtles at Turtle Island for years in order to study their behavior. How many turtles have the scientists tagged? You will find out in Lesson 4-5.

Review What You Know!

3 The roadrunner prefers to run than fly. What is the prime factorization of the number that represents the top speed of a roadrunner? You will find out in Lesson 4-8.

Vocabulary

Choose the best term from the box.

> • compatible numbers   • multiple
> • inverse   • quotient

1. The number 800 is a(n) __?__ of 100.

2. One way to estimate is to use __?__.

3. In the equation $12 \div 4 = 3$, the number 3 is the __?__.

4. Multiplication and division have a(n) __?__ relationship.

Place Value

Copy and complete with the word tens, hundreds, or thousands.

5. 6,200 is the same as 6 __?__ and 2 __?__.

6. 150 is the same as 15 __?__.

7. 2,300 is the same as 23 __?__.

8. 750 is the same as 75 __?__.

Rounding

Round each number to the place value of the underlined digit.

9. 4<u>5</u>6   10. <u>3</u>8   11. <u>1</u>,600

12. <u>9</u>20   13. <u>6</u>1   14. 3,<u>2</u>05

Writing to Explain Write an answer to the question.

15. Explain how to round 768 to the hundreds place.

Understand It!
Dividing multiples of 10 and 100 is easy to do mentally.

Dividing Multiples of 10 and 100

How can you divide mentally?

Five friends want to share these comic books equally. Can you use mental math to find how many comic books each friend will get?

Choose an Operation Divide to find how many are in each group.

1,000 comic books

Guided Practice*

Do you know HOW?

In **1** through **6**, use mental math to find each quotient.

1. $540 \div 9$
2. $490 \div 7$
3. $28,000 \div 4$
4. $48,000 \div 6$
5. $360 \div 6$
6. $81,000 \div 9$

Do you UNDERSTAND?

7. **Writing to Explain** How can you use the division fact $54 \div 9$ to find $5,400 \div 9$?

8. In the example at the top, how many comic books would each friend get if there were 300 comic books?

9. How could you use multiplication to check your answer of 200 comic books per person?

Independent Practice

In **10** through **29**, use mental math to find each quotient.

10. $22 \div 2$
11. $220 \div 2$
12. $2,200 \div 2$
13. $22,000 \div 2$

14. $63 \div 9$
15. $630 \div 9$
16. $6,300 \div 9$
17. $63,000 \div 9$

18. $72 \div 8$
19. $720 \div 8$
20. $7,200 \div 8$
21. $72,000 \div 8$

22. $36 \div 3$
23. $360 \div 3$
24. $3,600 \div 3$
25. $36,000 \div 3$

26. $42 \div 6$
27. $420 \div 6$
28. $4,200 \div 6$
29. $42,000 \div 6$

DIGITAL

Animated Glossary
www.pearsonsuccessnet.com

*For another example, see Set A on page 116.

Notice the pattern.

$10 \div 5 = 2$

$100 \div 5 = 10 \text{ tens} \div 5 = 2 \text{ tens} = 20$

$1,000 \div 5 = 10 \text{ hundreds} \div 5 = 2 \text{ hundreds} = 200$

$10,000 \div 5 = 10 \text{ thousands} \div 5 = 2 \text{ thousands} = 2,000$

Use the division fact $10 \div 5 = 2$.

Count the additional zeros in the dividend (the number you are dividing). The number you are dividing by, in this case 5, is the divisor.

There are two more zeros in 1,000 than in 10. Annex the additional zeros to the quotient (the number that is the result of dividing).

So, $1,000 \div 5 = 200$.

Each friend will get 200 comic books.

Problem Solving

30. The Paloma family has 1,000 minutes per month on their cell phone plan. Mr. and Mrs. Paloma each use the number of minutes shown, and their children divide the remaining minutes equally. How many minutes do the children use per month?

Name	Minutes
Mr. Paloma	400 minutes
Mrs. Paloma	440 minutes
Maria	minutes
Luz	minutes

31. Writing to Explain How can you find the quotient of $56,000 \div 7$ mentally? Find the quotient.

32. Estimation Estimate the product of 88×7. Do you have an underestimate or an overestimate?

33. Algebra If $18,000 \div n = 300$, then what is the value of n?

34. Writing to Explain Why does $3,600 \div 6$ have the same quotient as $1,800 \div 3$?

35. If a cyclist rides 200 miles in 5 days and rides the same distance each day, how many miles does the cyclist ride each day?

36. DVDs at the mall are on sale 3 for $25. If 400 DVDs are put on 5 shelves with an equal number on each shelf, how many DVDs are on each shelf?

A 8

B 80

C 800

D 8,000

37. Saturn's average distance from the Sun is 886,000,000 miles. Jupiter's average distance from the Sun is 484,000,000 miles. Which planet's distance from the Sun is greater?

38. Number Sense For each pair, determine if the quotient is the same or different. Explain.

a $72,000 \div 9$ and $40,000 \div 5$

b $3,600 \div 12$ and $1,800 \div 6$

Estimating Quotients

How can you estimate quotients?

Jorge is putting shells into 6 boxes. He wants to put about the same number in each box. About how many shells could Jorge put in each box?

Choose an Operation Divide to separate an amount into equal groups.

Understand It!
There is more than one way to estimate quotients.

258 total shells

Guided Practice*

Do you know HOW?

In **1** through **8**, estimate each quotient.

1. 520 ÷ 4   **2.** 444 ÷ 8

3. 640 ÷ 6   **4.** 310 ÷ 5

5. 683 ÷ 2   **6.** 297 ÷ 3

7. 700 ÷ 9   **8.** 507 ÷ 7

Do you UNDERSTAND?

9. Reasonableness In the rounding example above, how do you know the actual quotient should be less than 50?

10. In the example above, about how many shells could Jorge put into each box if he had 8 boxes?

Independent Practice

In **11** through **22**, use rounding to estimate each quotient.

11. 312 ÷ 5   **12.** 792 ÷ 4   **13.** 834 ÷ 2   **14.** 518 ÷ 4

15. 586 ÷ 5   **16.** 419 ÷ 7   **17.** 635 ÷ 8   **18.** 287 ÷ 2

19. 975 ÷ 5   **20.** 359 ÷ 6   **21.** 695 ÷ 7   **22.** 187 ÷ 4

In **23** through **34**, use compatible numbers to estimate each quotient.

23. 263 ÷ 3   **24.** 317 ÷ 7   **25.** 477 ÷ 6   **26.** 378 ÷ 9

27. 641 ÷ 6   **28.** 433 ÷ 4   **29.** 256 ÷ 3   **30.** 182 ÷ 7

31. 545 ÷ 8   **32.** 239 ÷ 5   **33.** 772 ÷ 7   **34.** 324 ÷ 8

*For another example, see Set B on page 116.

Use rounding to estimate 258 ÷ 6.

Remember that you can round to the nearest tens or hundreds.

Round 258 to 300.

$300 \div 6 = 50$

50 shells is an overestimate, since 258 was rounded up to 300.

Another Way

Use compatible numbers.

Replace 258 with 240.

240 and 6 are compatible, since $24 \div 6 = 4$. You can use mental math to find $240 \div 6 = 40$.

40 shells is an underestimate, since 258 was rounded down to 240.

Jorge should put between 40 and 50 shells in each box.

Problem Solving

35. While shopping, Tina's mom bought 7 tacos for the family for lunch. Each taco cost $2.25, including tax. How much change did Tina's mom get from a $20 bill?

36. Writing to Explain If you want to use compatible numbers to estimate $262 \div 7$, is it better to use $210 \div 7$ or $280 \div 7$? Explain.

37. Seven friends collected coats for a clothing drive. The students gathered 61 coats. Each person collected about the same number. About how many coats did each student collect?

38. The town of Kingswood just completed building a new auditorium. There are 7 sections in the auditorium. The auditorium seats 560 people. How many seats are in each section?

560 people

?					

↑
seats in each section

39. Toby earned $596 in 3 months for mowing lawns. If he was paid the same amount each month, about how much did he earn per month?

40. **Think About the Process** A digital camera costs $499. A laser printer for the camera costs $277. If you have $100 to spend, which expression can you use to find how much more money you need to save to buy the digital camera?

A $499 - 100$

B $277 + 100 + 499$

C $499 + 100$

D $277 - 100$

41. Horses are measured in hands. Three hands equal 1 foot. Radar, the world's tallest horse, is about 19 hands high. About how many feet tall is Radar?

A 5 feet

B 6 feet

C 7 feet

D 8 feet

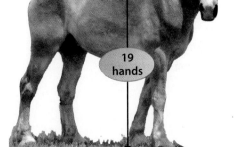

19 hands

Understand It!
Always look back and check for reasonableness when solving problems.

Problem Solving

Reasonableness

There are 60 students attending a field trip. One chaperone is needed for every 8 students. How many chaperones are needed?

Answer: 60 ÷ 8 = 7 R4
So, 7 chaperones are needed.

After you solve a problem, check to see if your answer is reasonable.

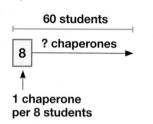

60 students

8 | ? chaperones →

↑
1 chaperone
per 8 students

Guided Practice*

Do you know HOW?

Look back and check. Tell if the answer is reasonable. Explain why or why not.

1. Myrna has 26 daisies. She can plant 3 daisies in each pot. How many pots can she completely fill?

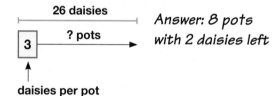

26 daisies

3 | ? pots →

↑
daisies per pot

Answer: 8 pots
with 2 daisies left

Do you UNDERSTAND?

2. In the problem above, why did the remainder need to be interpreted before the final answer was given?

3. **Write a Problem** Write a real-world problem that you can solve by dividing. Give an answer to be checked for reasonableness.

Independent Practice

In **4** through **6**, look back and check. Tell if the answer is reasonable. Explain why or why not.

4. In the school cafeteria, each table holds 10 students. There are 48 students who will eat lunch. How many tables are needed to seat all of the students?

   Answer: Four tables with 8 students left

Stuck? Try this....

- What do I know?
- What am I asked to find?
- What diagram can I use to help understand the problem?
- Can I use addition, subtraction, multiplication, or division?
- Is all of my work correct?
- Did I answer the right question?
- Is my answer reasonable?

*For another example, see Set C on page 116.

Is my calculation reasonable?

 I can check by using multiplication.

I know that $7 \times 8 = 56$. I can add the remainder to the product. $56 + 4 = 60$.

So, 7 R4 is reasonable.

Did I answer the right question?

 The question asks for the number of chaperones needed for ALL students. Seven chaperones is not reasonable because 4 students will be without a chaperone.

 When there is remainder in a division problem, you must always interpret the remainder.

So, the correct answer should be that 8 chaperones are needed for the field trip.

For **5** and **6**, the table at the right shows how many students can use each supply per case.

5. Mrs. Goia has 49 students in her art classes. She is ordering art supplies.

   a How many cases of pastels does she need to order?

     Answer: 17 cases

   b How many cases of charcoals does she need to order?

     Answer: 8 cases with 1 student left

Art Supplies	
Item	**Number of Students**
Case of pastels	3
Case of paints	4
Case of charcoals	6

6. Lionel is buying ice chests to hold 144 bottles of lemonade for a picnic. Each ice chest holds 20 bottles. How many ice chests should he buy?

   Answer: 8 chests

7. Estimation Bridget sold 62 tickets to a school concert at $3.95 each. About how much money did she collect for all 62 tickets?

8. How many 6-bottle packages of bottled water must Rashmi's mom buy if she plans to serve 1 bottle to each of the 28 people who will attend the school fair?

9. Marcia has 27 red beads and 42 blue beads. How many beads does she have in all? Write an equation and solve.

b	
27	42

10. Pia needs 100 red beads to make a necklace. She already has 38 red beads. How many more red beads does she need? Write an equation and solve.

100	
38	r

11. A wood carver has made 179 carved animals. The animals will be shipped in boxes that hold only 8 animals each. How many boxes will be completely filled? How many animals will be left over?

Hands-On
play money

Connecting Models and Symbols

How can you model division?

Abbott Middle School raised $148 selling spaghetti at the school's fund-raiser dinner. How can the principal divide the money equally among 4 school projects?

Choose an Operation Divide since you are sharing.

Another Example How can you record division?

Suppose 4 people needed to share $148.

What You Think

The $100 bill needs to be shared. Exchange the $100 bill for ten $10 bills. There are now 14 $10 bills.

Each person gets three $10 bills. (4 × 3 = 12).

Two $10 bills are left to share. Exchange the $10 bills for 20 $1 bills.

That gives 28 $1 bills to be divided into four groups.

Each person gets seven $1 bills (4 × 7 = 28).

After each person gets seven $1 bills, there is no money left to share.

What You Write

$$\begin{array}{r} 3 \\ 4\overline{)148} \\ -12 \\ \hline 2 \end{array}$$

$$\begin{array}{r} 37 \\ 4\overline{)148} \\ -12 \\ \hline 28 \\ -28 \\ \hline 0 \end{array}$$

Each person gets $37.

Explain It

1. Explain how you can exchange bills to divide four $10 bills equally among 5 people.

2. Suppose Abbott Middle School raised $76 more. In all, how much would each of the four projects receive?

Exchange the $100 bill for ten $10 bills. There are now 14 $10 bills. Share the $10 bills. Each project gets three $10 bills. Two $10 bills are left.

Exchange the two remaining $10 bills for 20 $1 bills. This gives 28 $1 bills.

Each project gets a total of $37.

Guided Practice*

Do you know HOW?

In **1** through **4**, use models to help you divide.

1. $3\overline{)69}$ **2.** $7\overline{)490}$

3. $9\overline{)225}$ **4.** $3\overline{)186}$

Do you UNDERSTAND?

5. Writing to Explain In the example above, why do you have to exchange the two remaining $10 bills?

6. If 4 people divide $244 equally, how much will each person get?

Independent Practice

Leveled Practice In **7**, use play money or draw diagrams of the bills shown at the right to symbolize division. Copy and complete the calculation as you answer the questions below.

7. Six people need to share $576 equally.

  a All $100 bills are replaced with $10 bills. How many $10 bills are there altogether?

  b How many $10 bills will each person get?

  c How many $10 bills are left?

  d Replace the remaining $10 bills with $1 bills. How many $1 bills are left in all to divide among 6 people?

  e What is the total amount each person gets?

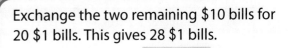

five $100 bills

seven $10 bills

six $1 bills

$$6\overline{)576}$$
$$-$$
$$6$$
$$-$$

eTools
www.pearsonsuccessnet.com

For another example, see Set D on page 117.

In **8** through **17**, copy and complete. You may use play money to help you divide.

8. $5\overline{)355}$ **9.** $7\overline{)693}$ **10.** $4\overline{)364}$ **11.** $6\overline{)492}$

12. 484 divided by 4 **13.** 672 divided by 6

14. 312 divided by 2 **15.** 765 divided by 5

16. 385 divided by 7 **17.** 759 divided by 3

Problem Solving

18. Twenty bags of dog food were donated to the animal shelter. The total cost of the dog food, including $5.95 tax, was $145.95. How much did one bag of dog food cost before taxes?

19. Paulo helped his grandmother with her garden for five days after school. He worked for two hours each day. Paulo's grandmother gave him $75. How much money did Paulo earn each day?

20. **Number Sense** Nick and 3 friends unloaded 224 folding chairs for the community theater. Each person unloaded the same number of chairs. How many chairs did Nick unload?

21. **Writing to Explain** Explain how division facts and patterns can help you find 20,000 ÷ 5.

22. The Stanton Ferry transports a maximum of 756 people to Green Island in 4 trips. How many people can the ferry transport in 1 trip?

    A 151   **C** 189

    B 164   **D** 199

23. The Napoleon Bonaparte Broward Bridge is 10,646 feet long. The Sunshine Sky Bridge is 29,040 feet long. Which bridge is shorter and by how much?

24. **Writing to Explain** Why is 3.892 greater than 3.289?

25. **Think About the Process** The art museum sold 1,770 tickets to the modern art exhibit on Sunday. Each ticket cost $12. The ticket holders were divided into five groups to organize the viewing for that day. Which expression tells how to find the number of people in each group?

    A 1,770 ÷ $12 + 5

    B 1,770 ÷ 5 + $12

    C 1,770 ÷ $12

    D 1,770 ÷ 5

26. Kirstin is starting a swimming club. She is the only member the first month. She plans to have each member find 2 new members each month. How many members will the club have at the end of 4 months?

27. Find the next three numbers in the pattern shown below.

    10, 15, 12, 17, 14, . . .

Algebra Connections

Completing Number Sentences

Remember that a number sentence has two numbers or expressions that are connected by the symbols >, <, or =.

Estimation can be used to see if the left or right side is greater.

Copy and complete the comparisons using estimation. Check your answers.

Remember:
> means "is greater than."
< means "is less than."
= means "is equal to."

Example: 6 × 80 ◯ 6 × 77

 Is 6 groups of 80 more than 6 groups of 77?

Since 80 is more than 77, 6 groups of 80 is more than 6 groups of 77. Complete the comparison with ">."

$$6 \times 80 > 6 \times 77$$

This means 6 groups of 80 is greater than 6 groups of 77.

Copy and complete. Write <, >, or = in the circle.

1. 6 × 50 ◯ 51 × 6

2. 40 × 5 ◯ 45 × 5

3. 56 + 56 ◯ 55 × 2

4. 7 × 67 ◯ 67 × 7

5. 320 ◯ 8 × 43

6. 8 × 72 ◯ 560

7. 20 × 20 ◯ 17 × 18

8. 5 × 20 ◯ 100

9. 3 + 48 ◯ 3 × 48

10. 3 × 19 ◯ 60

11. 5 × 20 ◯ 19 × 4

12. 6 + 18 ◯ 6 × 18

For **13** through **14**, write a number sentence to help solve each problem.

13. Marina bought a lavender backpack for herself and a green backpack for her brother. Charley bought an orange backpack. Who spent more money?

14. Mr. Wozniak purchased a green backpack. Ms. Chivas purchased 4 lavender backpacks. Who paid more?

15. Write a Problem Write a word problem using the price of the backpacks.

$9

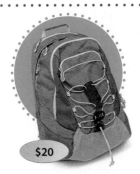
$20

$40

$50

Dividing by 1-Digit Divisors

Why use division?

Students are selling candles to raise money. A shipment arrived yesterday. The candles will be sold in boxes of 6 each. How many boxes can be filled? A diagram can help you decide what operation to use.

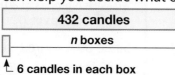

432 candles

432 candles

_n_ boxes →

⌐ 6 candles in each box

6 candles per box

Another Example **How do you find a quotient with a remainder?**

2-digit quotient with remainder

Find 380 ÷ 6.

$$\begin{array}{r} 6 \\ 6\overline{)380} \\ -36 \\ \hline 2 \end{array}$$

$$\begin{array}{r} 63\ R2 \\ 6\overline{)380} \\ -36\downarrow \\ \hline 20 \\ -18 \\ \hline 2 \end{array}$$

 Tip *380 is the dividend, 6 is the divisor, 63 is the quotient, and 2 is the remainder.*

3-digit quotient with remainder

Find 547 ÷ 4.

$$\begin{array}{r} 1 \\ 4\overline{)547} \\ -4 \\ \hline 1 \end{array}$$

$$\begin{array}{r} 13 \\ 4\overline{)547} \\ -4\downarrow \\ \hline 14 \\ -12 \\ \hline 2 \end{array}$$

$$\begin{array}{r} 136\ R3 \\ 4\overline{)547} \\ -4\downarrow \\ \hline 14 \\ -12\downarrow \\ \hline 27 \\ -24 \\ \hline 3 \end{array}$$

Explain It

1. Name the quotient, divisor, remainder, and dividend in these two examples.

2. Why did the second example have a 3-digit quotient?

Find 432 ÷ 6.

Estimate. Decide where to place the first digit in the quotient.

Use compatible numbers.
420 ÷ 6 = 70
The first digit is in the tens place.

Divide the tens.
Multiply and subtract.

$$\begin{array}{r} 7 \\ 6\overline{)432} \\ -\ 42 \\ \hline 1 \end{array}$$

Divide. 43 ÷ 6 ≈ 7
Multiply. 7 × 6 = 42
Subtract. 43 − 42 = 1
Compare. 1 < 6

Bring down the ones. Divide the ones. Multiply and subtract.

$$\begin{array}{r} 72 \\ 6\overline{)432} \\ -\ 42\downarrow \\ \hline 12 \\ -\ 12 \\ \hline 0 \end{array}$$

Divide. 12 ÷ 6 = 2
Multiply. 2 × 6 = 12
Subtract. 12 − 12 = 0
Compare. 0 < 6

There can be 72 boxes filled with candles.

Guided Practice*

Do you know HOW?

In **1** through **6**, find each quotient.

1. 9)270

2. 6)684

3. 3)65

4. 5)339

5. 5)564

6. 4)724

Do you UNDERSTAND?

7. Writing to Explain How can estimating with compatible numbers help you find the quotient?

8. In the first example, find the quotient if the total number of candles is 561.

Independent Practice

In **9** through **16**, use compatible numbers to estimate each quotient. Then decide where to place the first digit of the quotient.

9. 5)762

10. 3)289

11. 8)607

12. 3)567

13. 6)960

14. 7)973

15. 5)373

16. 9)462

In **17** through **28**, copy and complete the calculation.

17. 8)616

18. 6)486

19. 4)448

20. 9)828

21. 2)131

22. 9)836

23. 5)413

24. 5)469

25. 7)644

26. 2)995

27. 4)139

28. 5)625

29. Writing to Explain How can you tell, before you divide 387 by 4, that the first digit of the quotient is in the tens place?

30. Writing to Explain Why is the following incorrect? 296 ÷ 6 = 48 R8. Write your answer before you complete the calculation.

31. Think About the Process A team of 10 people in the Netherlands rolled a 140-lb barrel a distance of 164 miles in 24 hours. Each person rolled the same distance. Which of the following shows how to determine how many miles each person rolled the barrel?

A 164 ÷ 24   **C** 140 ÷ 24

B 164 ÷ 10   **D** 140 ÷ 10

32. Ray walked for 9 hours to raise money for his favorite charity. He raised $225. How much money did he raise for each hour he walked?

33. Over 9 years, scientists tagged 450 turtles at Turtle Island. How many turtles did they tag each year if each year they tagged the same number of turtles?

450 turtles								
?	?	?	?	?	?	?	?	?

34. The High Sierra Trail at Mt. Whitney is 49 miles long each way. Park rangers report that to walk the trail one way takes hikers 6 days. About how many miles must the hikers walk each day to finish all 49 miles in 6 days?

A 6 miles   **C** 10 miles

B 8 miles   **D** 12 miles

35. Algebra What is the value of c in the equation c × 3 = 324?

A 18   **C** 180

B 108   **D** 1,080

36. Algebra Find the value of n.

3 × 7 = n × 3

37. Geometry What is the perimeter of the rectangle in inches? (Hint: 1 ft = 12 in.)

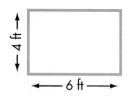

38. Suppose there were 8 cowboys that herded 104 cattle. If each cowboy herded the same number of cattle, how many animals was each cowboy responsible for?

39. Draw It Sears Tower in Chicago is 1,450 feet tall. First Interstate Plaza in Houston is 973 feet tall. How many feet taller is the Sears Tower than the First Interstate Plaza building? Finish drawing the picture. Write an equation, then solve. Let h = the difference in height.

	h

Find the product. Estimate to check if the answer is reasonable.

| 1. | 58 $\times$ 4 | 2. | 355 $\times$ 7 | 3. | 6,044 $\times$ 6 | 4. | 5,137 $\times$ 3 |

| 5. | 236 $\times$ 17 | 6. | 23 $\times$ 25 | 7. | 117 $\times$ 33 | 8. | 65 $\times$ 29 |

9. 45×12 **10.** $1,001 \times 25$ **11.** $8 \times 3,030$ **12.** $6 \times 3,373$

Find the sum. Estimate to check if the answer is reasonable.

| 13. | 76,095 $+$ 3,950 | 14. | 9,713 $+$ 9,328 | 15. | 888 $+$ 726 | 16. | 7,566 $+$ 8,092 | 17. | 27,444 $+$ 9,507 |

Error Search Find each answer that is not correct.
Write it correctly and explain the error.

| 18. | 703 $\times$ 88 — 11,248 | 19. | 348 $\times$ 17 — 5,916 | 20. | 202 $\times$ 15 — 1,010 | 21. | 19 $\times$ 18 — 344 | 22. | 2,456 $\times$ 73 — 179,288 |

Number Sense

Estimating and Reasoning Write whether each statement is
true or false. Explain your reasoning.

23. The product of 7 and 6,943 is closer to 42,000 than 49,000.

24. The difference of 15.9 and 4.2 is closer to 11 than 12.

25. The sum of 33,345 and 60,172 is less than 93,000.

26. The product of 43 and 5,116 is greater than 200,000.

27. The sum of $3.98 + 4.62$ is 0.02 less than 8.62.

28. The product of 9 and 48 is 18 less than 450.

Understand It!
There are times when it is necessary to place a zero in the quotient.

Zeros in the Quotient

When do you write a zero in the quotient?

On vacation the McQueen family drove a total of 830 miles in four days. What is the average number of miles they drove each day?

Choose an Operation Divide to find how many miles per day.

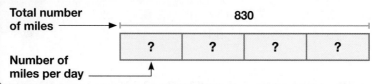

Total number of miles ——→ 830

| ? | ? | ? | ? |

Number of miles per day ——→

Another Example **When do you write a zero in the ones place in the quotient?**

Find 520 ÷ 4

Step 1   Estimate. Decide where to place the first digit in the quotient. Use compatible numbers. 400 ÷ 4 = 100

$$\begin{array}{r} 1 \\ 4\overline{)520} \\ -\ 4 \\ \hline 1 \end{array}$$ 5 ÷ 4 ≈ 1
1 × 4 = 4
5 − 4 = 1
1 < 4

The first digit in the quotient is in the hundreds place.

Divide the hundreds. Multiply, subtract, and compare.

Step 2   Bring down the tens.
Divide the tens.
Multiply, subtract, and compare.

$$\begin{array}{r} 13 \\ 4\overline{)520} \\ -\ 4\downarrow \\ \hline 12 \\ -\ 12 \\ \hline 0 \end{array}$$ 12 ÷ 4 = 3
3 × 4 = 12
12 − 12 = 0
0 < 4

Step 3   Bring down the ones.
There are 0 ones.
Write 0 in the ones place in the quotient.

$$\begin{array}{r} 130 \\ 4\overline{)520} \\ -\ 4 \\ \hline 12 \\ -\ 12 \\ \hline 00 \end{array}$$ There are 0 ones. Write 0 in the ones place in the quotient.

Explain It

1. In the example at the top, why is the zero in the tens place of the quotient, but in the ones place in Another Example?

2. Explain how to check your answers in both examples.

Find 830 ÷ 4.

Estimate first. Use compatible numbers. 800 ÷ 4 = 200
So, the first digit in the quotient is in the hundreds place. Divide the hundreds.

$$4\overline{)830}$$ gives 2
$$- 8$$
$$\overline{0}$$

Divide. $8 ÷ 4 = 2$
Multiply. $2 × 4 = 8$
Subtract. $8 − 8 = 0$
Compare. $0 < 4$

$$\begin{array}{r} 20 \\ 4\overline{)830} \\ -8\downarrow \\ \hline 03 \end{array}$$

You cannot divide the tens. Write 0 in the tens place.

$$\begin{array}{r} 207 \text{ R2} \\ 4\overline{)830} \\ -8\downarrow \\ \hline 030 \\ -28 \\ \hline 2 \end{array}$$

$30 ÷ 4 ≈ 7$
$7 × 4 = 28$
$30 − 28 = 2$
$2 < 4$

The McQueens drove about 207 miles each day.

Guided Practice*

Do you know HOW?

In **1** through **4**, find each quotient. Check your answers.

1. $9\overline{)972}$ **2.** $7\overline{)714}$

3. $5\overline{)453}$ **4.** $2\overline{)941}$

Do you UNDERSTAND?

5. Writing to Explain In the example at the top, what would happen if you do not bring down the zero in the ones place?

6. Suppose the McQueens only drove 424 miles in 4 days. If they drove an equal number of miles each day, how many miles did they drive in 1 day?

Independent Practice

In **7** through **24**, find each quotient. Check your answers.

7. $2\overline{)880}$ **8.** $5\overline{)540}$ **9.** $6\overline{)840}$

10. $3\overline{)323}$ **11.** $7\overline{)563}$ **12.** $3\overline{)624}$

13. $2\overline{)801}$ **14.** $5\overline{)180}$ **15.** $8\overline{)816}$

16. $3\overline{)912}$ **17.** $5\overline{)547}$ **18.** $7\overline{)284}$

19. $9\overline{)455}$ **20.** $2\overline{)420}$ **21.** $6\overline{)648}$

22. $4\overline{)816}$ **23.** $3\overline{)512}$ **24.** $7\overline{)776}$

25. Elena spent $25 on a ring. She paid using $10, $5, and $1 bills. If Elena gave the clerk 8 bills, how many of each bill did she give the clerk?

26. Raul bought a collection of 856 baseball cards for $40. If only 8 cards can fit on one page of an album, how many pages will Raul have to buy?

27. The grandstand at the stadium has 648 seats. There are 6 equal sections. How many seats are in each section?

28. Ali ran 120 kilometers over a four week period. On average, how many kilometers did he run each week?

29. **Number Sense** Harry filled one box with 9 pints of blueberries. He picked 97 pints of blueberries. If Harry filled 10 boxes, how many pints were left for the last box?

30. A school raised $306 washing cars. The money will be used to buy new recycling containers for the school. If each container costs $8, how many containers can the school buy?

31. **Writing to Explain** Clare's teacher has a box of 180 stickers for a group of students to share equally. Does each student get more stickers if there are 6 students or if there are 9 students?

32. Each car of the roller coaster can hold 6 people. If 63 people are waiting in line to ride the roller coaster, how many cars will be needed?

33. Dora has 24 pairs of earrings. She keeps them in 6 boxes. Each box has the same number of earrings. Each pair of earrings costs between $10 and $20. How many pairs of earrings are in each box?

A 4

B 8

C 10

D 12

34. **Think About the Process** A home and garden show ran for two days. Tickets cost $2 each. On the first day, ticket sales totaled $322. On the second day, ticket sales were $294. Which of the following shows how to determine the number of tickets sold?

A $(322 + 294) \div 2$

B $322 \times 294 \div 2$

C $(322 + 294) \times 2$

D $322 \div 2 + 294$

35. The world's longest cartoon strip has 242 panels. It was drawn by 35 artists in about 8 hours. About how many panels were drawn in one hour?

A 15   **B** 20   **C** 30   **D** 45

Choose a Computation Method

In many airports, people ride minibuses between terminals. The minibuses leave only when they are full. If a minibus carried 297 passengers in a day, and it holds 11 passengers at a time, how many times did it fill up?

Step 1 Draw a picture and choose an operation.

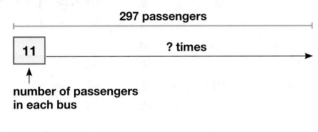

Divide 297 ÷ 11.

Step 2 Choose the best computation method. Decide whether to use mental math, paper and pencil, or a calculator.

Since 11 has two-digits, use a calculator.

Step 3 Solve.

Press: 297 ÷ 11 ENTER =   Display: 27

The minibus filled up 27 times.

Practice

For each problem, draw a picture and choose an operation. Then choose the best computation method and solve.

1. If each of the 297 passengers paid $2, how could the driver find the amount of money he collected? How much did he collect?

2. Four drivers had 293, 147, 307, and 284 passengers. How many passengers did the four drivers have in all?

3. One of the drivers had 150 passengers on Monday and 250 passengers on Tuesday. How many passengers does he need on Wednesday to have 500 passengers for the week?

4. A special pass for frequent travelers cost $50 a year. If 200 travelers bought the special pass, how much was the bus company paid?

Understand It!
There are rules that make it easy to tell if a number is divisible by 2, 3, 4, 5, 6, 9, or 10.

Understanding Factors

How can you find all the factors of a number?

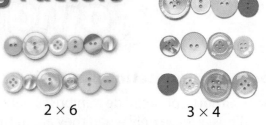

Three possible arrays of 12 buttons are shown. The arrays can help find all the factors of 12. The factors of 12 are 1, 2, 3, 4, 6, and 12.

2 × 6

3 × 4

1 × 12

Another Example How can you use divisibility rules to find factors?

A factor pair is a pair of whole numbers whose product equals a given whole number. A factor pair for 12 is 3 and 4.

Find all the factor pairs of 32. Then list all the factors of 32.

Try	Is It a Factor?	Factor Pair
1	Yes, 1 is a factor of every whole number.	1 and 32
2	Yes, because 32 is even.	2 and 16
3	No. Since 3 + 2 = 5, it is not divisible by 3.	
4	Yes; 32 is divisible by 4.	4 and 8
5	No, because 32 does not end in 0 or 5.	
6	No, because 32 is not divisible by both 2 and 3.	
7	No.	
8	Yes; 32 is divisible by 8.	4 and 8

Numbers greater than 8 do not need to be tested because after 8 the factor pairs repeat. The factors of 32 are 1, 2, 4, 8, 16, and 32.

Explain It

1. Why is it helpful to know the divisibility rules?

2. If 15 and 14 are factors of a number, what other numbers will be factors of the same number? Explain.

Arrays can help you find all the factors of a number. However, an easier way is to use divisibility rules.

A whole number is <u>divisible</u> by another when the quotient is a whole number and the remainder is 0.

Divisibility Rules

A number is divisible by

2 → If the number is even.

3 → If the sum of the digits of the number is divisible by 3.

4 → If the last two digits are divisible by 4.

5 → If the last digit is 0 or 5.

6 → If the number is divisible by BOTH 2 and 3.

9 → If the sum of the digits is divisible by 9.

10 → If the last digit is 0.

Guided Practice*

Do you know HOW?

In **1** through **4**, list all the factors of each number.

1. 25   **2.** 42

3. 36   **4.** 18

Do you UNDERSTAND?

5. What factor pair does every number have?

6. List the possible arrays you can arrange 18 buttons in.

Independent Practice

In **7** through **12**, name two different factor pairs of the given number.

7. 30   **8.** 32   **9.** 36

10. 40   **11.** 42   **12.** 39

In **13** through **24**, list all the factors of each number.

13. 45   **14.** 48   **15.** 50

16. 54   **17.** 60   **18.** 70

19. 84   **20.** 98   **21.** 108

22. 114   **23.** 8   **24.** 55

Animated Glossary
www.pearsonsuccessnet.com

For another example, see Set G on page 118.

Lesson 4-7   **103**

25. A restaurant wall was divided into 4 equal parts as shown. What fraction of the wall is the

a mirror?

b paneling?

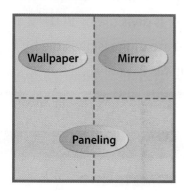

26. A museum has 80 African baskets. Which list shows all the different possible arrangements so that all the rows have the same number? Assume that an arrangement such as 4 × 20 is the same as 20 × 4.

A 1 × 80; 4 × 20; 8 × 10

B 1 × 80; 2 × 40; 4 × 20; 5 × 16; 8 × 10

C 2 × 40; 5 × 16; 8 × 10

D 2 × 40; 4 × 20; 5 × 16; 8 × 10

27. The list shows all the factors for which number?

4, 8, 14, 7, 2, 1, 56, 28

A 9

B 28

C 56

D 14

28. Name a fraction and a decimal for the shaded part of the figure below.

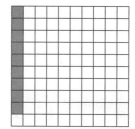

29. Which number is NOT a factor of 36?

A 1   **C** 20

B 18   **D** 36

30. Name the fraction and decimal at *F*.

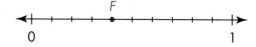

31. (Think) About the Process The town meeting hall was set up in 18 rows with 15 chairs in each row. There were also 10 chairs at the speakers' table. Which expression shows how many chairs were in the meeting hall?

A (18 + 15) + 10   **C** (18 × 15) + 10

B (15 × 10) + 18   **D** (10 × 15) × 18

32. List the factors of 24. Then list the factors of 16. What factors do they share in common? Which of those common factors is the greatest number?

Algebra Connections

Find a Rule

Remember that tables can be used to show relationships between pairs of numbers.

Number of Feet	1	2	3	4
Number of Inches	12	24	36	48

If you know a length in feet, you can multiply by 12 to find the length in inches. When you know a length in inches, you can divide by 12 to find the length in feet.

Example:
What rule connects the number of hours to the number of days? Find the missing numbers.

Number of Days	1	2	3	4	■	■
Number of Hours	24	48	72	96	120	240

Rule:
Divide the number of hours by 24 to find the number of days.

$120 \div 24 = 5$. So, 120 hours = 5 days.
$240 \div 24 = 10$. So, 240 hours = 10 days.

For **1** through **7**, find a rule. Then find the missing numbers in the chart.

1.

Quarters	4	8	12	16	20	60
Dollars	1	2	3	4	■	■

2.

Apples	30	35	40	45	50	75
Baskets	6	7	8	9	■	■

3.

Loaves	1	2	3	4	5	9
Slices	20	40	60	80	■	■

4.

Cups	3	4	5	6	7	10
Fluid Ounces	24	32	40	48	■	■

5.

Marbles	Bags
50	1
100	2
150	3
200	■
450	■

6.

Tomatoes	Containers
30	2
45	3
60	4
75	5
120	■

7.

Yards	Inches
1	36
2	72
3	108
4	144
10	■

Prime and Composite Numbers

What are prime and composite numbers?

Every whole number greater than 1 is either a prime number or a composite number. A prime number has exactly two factors, 1 and itself. A composite number has more than two factors.

●●●
$1 \times 3 = 3$

●●●●●●●●
$1 \times 8 = 8$

●●●●
●●●●
$2 \times 4 = 8$

Another Example How can you write a composite number as a product of prime factors?

Write 24 as a product of prime factors.

A product of prime factors is called the prime factorization of a number. A factor tree is a diagram that shows the prime factorization of a composite number.

One Way

Step 1 Find a factor pair for 24.

$$24$$
$$4 \times 6$$

Step 2 Write each factor that is not prime as a product of prime numbers.

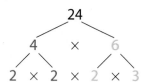

Last "branch" of the tree contains all prime numbers.

So, $24 = 2 \times 2 \times 2 \times 3$.

Another Way

You can use a different factor pair for 24.

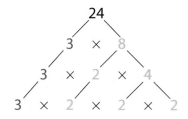

Tip Continue until all "branches" end in prime numbers.

Explain It

1. What are the first 10 prime numbers? How do you know?

2. When you write the prime factorization of a composite number, why do you not include 1 and the number itself?

Prime or Composite?

Is 27 a prime number or a composite number?

You can use divisibility rules to help you decide.

Since 27 is an odd number it is not divisible by 2.

Since the sum of the digits is $2 + 7 = 9$, then 27 is divisible by 3. So, 27 also has factors of 3 and 9.

So, 27 is composite.

Is 11 prime or composite?

Since 11 is an odd number, it is NOT divisible by 2.

It is also NOT divisible by 3, 4, 5, 6, 7, 8, 9, or 10.

So, 11 is prime.

Guided Practice*

Do you know HOW?

For **1** through **6**, write whether the number is prime or composite.

1. 41   **2.** 72

3. 22   **4.** 37

5. 106   **6.** 287

Do you UNDERSTAND?

7. The prime factorization of a number is $2 \times 3 \times 3 \times 5 \times 7$. What is the number?

8. When beginning a factor tree for a composite number, does it matter which factor pair you start with? Explain.

Independent Practice

In **9** through **20**, use a factor tree to find the prime factorization of each number.

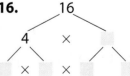
Think of the basic multiplication facts to use for the factor pairs.

Leveled Practice

9.

10.

11.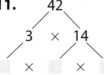

12.

13.

14.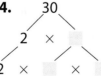

15.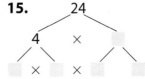

16.

17. 23   **18.** 40   **19.** 60   **20.** 45

Animated Glossary
www.pearsonsuccessnet.com

21. Two composite numbers have 2, 3, and 5 in their prime factorizations. One of the numbers is twice as large as the other. What could the two composite numbers be?

23. Which numbers between 40 and 49 have both 2 and 3 in their prime factorizations?

24. The prime factorization of 25 is 5 × 5. Using mental math, what is the prime factorization of 75?

26. Roadrunners live year-round throughout the southwestern part of the U.S., and can get to a top speed of 15 miles per hour. What is the prime factorization of 15?

A 3 × 15   **C** 1 × 2 × 3 × 5

B 2 × 3 × 5   **D** 3 × 5

22. **Think About the Process** Every Sunday Jay walks 6 blocks one way to his grandmother's house for lunch. After lunch, he walks 2 blocks farther to the park. He then walks home on the same exact route. Which shows how to find the number of blocks Jay walks in 4 weeks?

A (6 + 2) × (4 + 6)   **C** 6 × 2 × 2

B 6 × (2 × 4)   **D** (6 + 2) × 2 × 4

25. **Reasonableness** Shirley multiplied 379 × 8 and got 3,032. Use estimation to check the reasonableness of her answer.

27. Which pair of compatible numbers would be best to estimate the sum of 249 and 752?

A 200 and 700   **C** 300 and 800

B 250 and 750   **D** 400 and 700

28. Eratosthenes was born in Cyrene (now Libya) about 230 B.C. He developed a method for deciding if a number is prime. It is called the Sieve of Eratosthenes because it "strains out" prime numbers from other numbers. Use a hundred chart to find all the prime numbers between 1 and 100.

a Cross out 1. It is neither prime nor composite.

b Circle 2, the least prime number. Cross out every second number after 2.

c Circle 3, the next prime number. Cross out every third number after 3 (even if it has already been crossed out.)

d Circle 5, and repeat the process.

e Circle 7, and repeat the process.

f Circle all the remaining numbers that have not been crossed out. The numbers that are circled are the prime numbers less than 100. There should be 25.

Going Digital

Divisibility Rules

Use 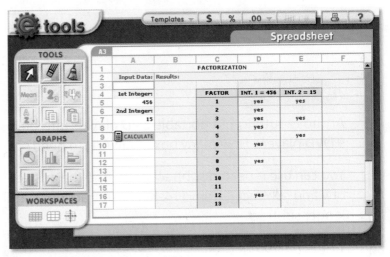 **tools**

Spreadsheet/Data/Grapher

If the sum of the digits of a number is divisible by 3, is the number divisible by 3? If the sum of the digits of a number is divisible by 9, is the number divisible by 9?

Step 1 Go to the Spreadsheet/Data/Grapher eTool. Choose *Factorization* from the Templates pull-down menu at the top of the page. To test a number, enter 456 under *1st Integer* and press Enter. Add the digits in 456 mentally. The sum is $4 + 5 + 6 = 15$. Enter 15 under *2nd Integer* and press Enter. Click Calculate. The *yes* next to 3 in the Integer 1 column means that 456 is divisible by 3. The *yes* next to 3 in the Integer 2 column means that 15 is divisible by 3. So, both 456 and 15 are divisible by 3. The blanks next to 9 mean that neither 456 nor 15 is divisible by 9.

Step 2 Enter 837 under *1st Integer*. The sum of the digits in 837 is $8 + 3 + 7 = 18$. Enter 18 under *2nd Integer*. The results show that both 837 and 18 are divisible by 3 and by 9.

Practice

Copy and complete the table.

Number	Sum of Digits	Sum Divisible by 3?	Sum Divisible by 9?	Number Divisible by 3?	Number Divisible by 9?
984	21	yes	no	yes	no
371	11				
585					
714					

Understand It!
Drawing a picture can help when writing and solving an equation.

Draw a Picture and Write an Equation

There are 112 campers going boating. The size of the boat and number of people it can hold is shown at the right. How many boats will be needed to hold all the campers?

Another Example

Arturo is putting 114 portable DVD players into boxes. Each box holds 9 DVD players. How many boxes will Arturo need?

You can use repeated subtraction to find the answer. Take one group of 9 and subtract it from 114. Keep subtracting 9 until you can no longer subtract.

$114 - 9 = 105$
$105 - 9 = 96$
$96 - 9 = 87$
$87 - 9 = 78$
$78 - 9 = 69$
$69 - 9 = 60$
$60 - 9 = 51$
$51 - 9 = 42$
$42 - 9 = 33$
$33 - 9 = 24$
$24 - 9 = 15$
$15 - 9 = 6$ You cannot subtract 9 from 6, so 6 players are left over.

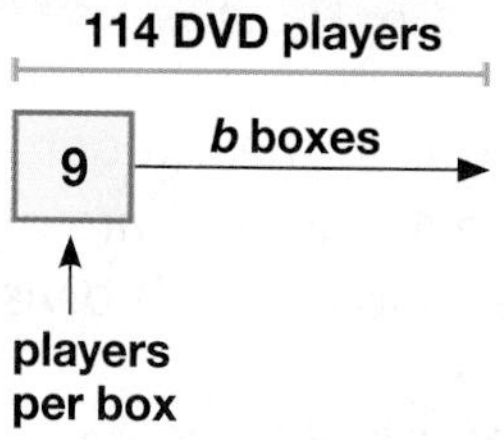

114 DVD players

| 9 | _b_ boxes → |

↑
players
per box

Tip You can also draw a picture and write an equation to solve.

Let _b_ = the number of boxes needed.

$114 \div 9 = b$
$b = 12 \text{ R}6$

Since you can subtract 9 *twelve times* and have 6 *left over*,
$114 \div 9 = 12 \text{ R}6$.

Since there are 6 players left without a box, Arturo needs 13 boxes to pack all 114 DVD players.

Explain It

1. Why does Arturo need 13 boxes and not 12?

Read and Understand

What do I know?	There are 112 campers. Six people can fit in a boat.
What am I asked to find?	The number of boats needed to hold all the campers.

Plan

Draw a picture.

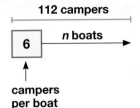

112 campers

6   *n* boats →

campers per boat

Write an equation.

Let *n* = the number of boats needed.

$$112 \div 6 = n$$

$$n = 18 \text{ R}4$$

For all campers to go boating, 19 boats will be needed.

```
      18 R4
6)112
    - 6
     52
    - 48
      4
```

Guided Practice*

Do you know HOW?

Solve. Copy and complete the picture. Then, write an equation.

1. If each van holds 9 people, how many vans will be needed to take 137 people to a concert?

9 →

Do you UNDERSTAND?

2. How do you know your answer for Exercise 1 is reasonable?

3. **Write a Problem** Write a real-world problem that you can solve by using repeated subtraction.

Independent Practice

In **4** through **8**, draw a picture, write an equation, then solve.

4. Steven has 140 photos. A page from a photo album contains 8 photos. How many pages does Steven have?

5. If you buy a digital music player for $246, including tax, and are allowed to pay for it in 6 equal payments, how much will each payment be?

6. There are 7 players on each academic team. If there are 175 total players at the tournament, how many teams are there?

Stuck? Try this....

- What do I know?
- What am I asked to find?
- What diagram can I use to help understand the problem?
- Can I use addition, subtraction, multiplication, or division?
- Is all of my work correct?
- Did I answer the right question?
- Is my answer reasonable?

7. The theater in the wilderness exhibit seats only 9 students at a time. If there are 106 students attending the field trip, how many times will the movie be shown so that all students can view it?

8. Joanna's family is driving to their summer cottage that is 441 miles away. It takes them 7 hours to drive there. What is the average number of miles the family travels each hour?

9. Brenda says a good estimate for 50×31 is 800. Is she correct? Explain.

10. Wanda needs to buy at least 50 stickers. Will this 1 sheet of stickers be enough? How do you know?

11. Jin's friends collected 149 bottles of water for riders going on a bike trip. If each rider needs 4 bottles, how many riders can they supply with water?

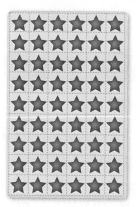

12. Brown bats sleep 20 hours each day. How many hours per week are they awake? How many hours per year are they awake?

13. Writing to Explain Tell how you can check to see if 54 R2 is the quotient for $164 \div 3$.

14. If you divide 152 flowers into 7 arrangements, how many flowers should there be in each arrangement?

15. Greg spends $10.95 on a basketball uniform and $3.50 on socks. How much money does Greg spend in all?

16. In 1916, the first international women's ice hockey tournament was held in Cleveland, Ohio. In 1998, women's ice hockey was represented for the first time in the Winter Olympics. Give the number of years between these two events.

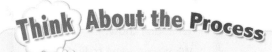

17. A ticket to Los Angeles costs $390, and a ticket to New York costs $425. Which equation can you solve to show how much less the ticket to Los Angeles cost?

  A $390 + $425 = c

  B $425 − $390 = c

  C $425 × $390 = c

  D (2 × $390) + (2 × $425) = c

18. Each shelf holds 24 books. There are 8 shelves. Which equation would you solve to find how many books there are in all?

  A 24 + 8 = b

  B 24 − 8 = b

  C 24 × 8 = b

  D 24 ÷ 8 = b

Finding Remainders

Tell how to find 573 ÷ 7, including the remainder, on a calculator.

Step 1   Divide 573 by 7.

Press: 573 [÷] 7 [ENTER =]

Display: 81.857143

Step 2   Interpret the result and find the remainder.

The result means 573 ÷ 7 is 81 with a remainder.
To find the remainder, multiply 7 by 81 and
subtract the result from 573.

Press: 7 [×] 81 [ENTER =]

Display: 567

Press: 573 [−] 567 [ENTER =]

Display: 6

573 ÷ 7 = 81 R6

Press (Clear) before starting a new problem.

Step 3   Another way to solve this problem on a calculator is to
change the calculator mode to numerator and denominator.

Press (Mode). Use the arrow keys to select _n/d_ .

Press [ENTER =] (Mode) again. Enter the problem as above.

Display: $81\frac{6}{7}$

The numerator in the fraction is the remainder.

Practice

Find each quotient and remainder.

1. 312 ÷ 5

2. 295 ÷ 4

3. 529 ÷ 9

4. 158 ÷ 8

5. 254 ÷ 3

6. 191 ÷ 2

1. If the money shown is to be divided among 4 people, what should be the first step? (4-4)

A Exchange the $100 bill for eight $10 bills and twenty $1 bills.

B Exchange the four $10 bills for forty $1 bills.

C Exchange the $100 dollar bill for a hundred $1 bills.

D Exchange the $100 dollar bill for ten $10 bills.

2. If $2,400 is divided evenly by 3 charities, how many dollars does each charity get? (4-1)

A 60

B 80

C 800

D 8,000

3. If 283 is divided by 4, where should the first digit of the quotient be placed? (4-5)

A Because 4 is greater than 2, it should be in the tens place.

B Because 4 is less than 2, it should be in the tens place.

C Because 4 is greater than 2, it should be in the hundreds place.

D Because 4 is less than 2, it should be in the hundreds place.

4. Which of the following is the best estimate of 913 ÷ 4? (4-2)

A 200

B 225

C 250

D 300

5. The table shows the amount raised by teams for the children's hospital. Raquel's team raised 4 times the amount that Jeremy's team raised. How much did Jeremy's team raise? (4-6)

Team Leader	Amount Raised
Raquel	$836
Jeremy	
Charles	$448

A $209

B $204

C $112

D $29

6. Which of the following shows the best way to estimate 712 ÷ 8 using compatible numbers? (4-2)

A 700 ÷ 8

B 720 ÷ 8

C 730 ÷ 8

D 800 ÷ 8

7. Which of the following is a prime number? (4-8)

A 21

B 14

C 12

D 11

8. The student council has 186 members divided as evenly as possible into 8 committees. How many members are on each committee? (4-5)

A There are 194 members in the student council.

B There are 23 members on each committee with 2 members left.

C There are 22 members on each committee.

D There are 22 members on each committee with 2 members left.

9. A marathon race has 522 runners divided into 6 groups. What is a reasonable number of runners in each group? (4-3)

A 112, because 522 ÷ 6 is about 550 ÷ 5 = 110

B 98, because 522 ÷ 6 is about 500 ÷ 5 = 100

C 87, because 522 ÷ 6 is about 540 ÷ 6 = 90

D 82, because 522 ÷ 6 is about 480 ÷ 6 = 80

10. Which of the following has factors of 1, 2, 4, 8, and 16? (4-7)

A 20

B 16

C 8

D 2

11. A florist is making flower arrangements. She has 108 roses to place in 9 arrangements. Which of the following equations can be used to find *r*, the number of roses in each arrangement? (4-9)

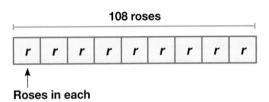

108 roses

Roses in each arrangement

A $108 + 9 = r$

B $108 - 9 = r$

C $108 \times 9 = r$

D $108 \div 9 = r$

12. A high school has $1,016 available for scholarships and $2,592 available for grants. If 8 students are awarded equal parts of the money for scholarships, how much does each student receive? (4-5)

A $102

B $120

C $127

D $217

13. Which of the following is the prime factorization of 84? (4-8)

A $2 \times 2 \times 3 \times 7$

B $4 \times 3 \times 7$

C $2 \times 2 \times 21$

D $2 \times 2 \times 2 \times 7$

Set A, pages 84–85

Find 48,000 ÷ 6.

Identify a basic fact.   48 ÷ 6 = 8

Look for a pattern.   480 ÷ 6 = 80
4,800 ÷ 6 = 800
48,000 ÷ 6 = 8,000

Remember to use basic facts and patterns to divide mentally.

1. 810 ÷ 9   **2.** 360 ÷ 6

3. 2,400 ÷ 6   **4.** 4,500 ÷ 9

5. 64,000 ÷ 8   **6.** 42,000 ÷ 7

Set B, pages 86–87

Estimate 330 ÷ 8.

Think of a number close to 33 that is a multiple of 8, so a basic fact can be used. Then divide.

32 ÷ 8 = 4
320 ÷ 8 = 40

So, 330 ÷ 8 is about 40.

Remember to use rounding or compatible numbers when estimating quotients.

Estimate.

1. 410 ÷ 6   **2.** 653 ÷ 8

3. 8,243 ÷ 9   **4.** 14,368 ÷ 5

5. 26,952 ÷ 7   **6.** 22,487 ÷ 3

Set C, pages 88–89

A company ships 4 basketballs in a box. How many boxes will be needed to ship 30 balls?

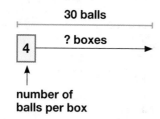

Calculate the division.

$$\begin{array}{r} 7\ R2 \\ 4\overline{)30} \\ -\ 28 \\ \hline 2 \end{array}$$

Seven boxes will be completely filled, but another box is needed to hold the remainder of 2 balls.

It is reasonable to say that 8 boxes are needed to ship 30 balls.

Remember you need to check the reasonableness of a solution by interpreting a remainder of a division problem.

Solve.

1. Sarah's DVD collection is stored in a cabinet that holds 6 DVDs on each shelf. How many shelves will she need to hold her collection of 89 DVDs?

2. There are 135 fifth-grade students in a certain school. Each table in the lunchroom seats six students. How many tables are needed to seat all fifth graders?

3. A large group of people are going to the baseball game. If 97 people are going, and each bus holds 32 people, how many buses will need to be ordered?

Set D, pages 90–92

Tell how much each person will get if 4 people share $212 equally.

What You Think

Exchange the two $100 bills for twenty $10 bills. Each person gets five $10 bills. Exchange the one $10 bill and two $1 bills for twelve $1 bills. Divide the twelve $1 bills by 4. $12 ÷ 4 = $3.

What You Write

$$
\begin{array}{r}
\$53 \\
4\overline{)212} \\
-20 \\
\hline
12 \\
-12 \\
\hline
0
\end{array}
$$

Each person will get $53.

Remember to regroup when necessary.

Use play money to divide. Tell how much each person will get.

1. 6 people share $240 equally
2. 5 people share $510 equally
3. 3 people share $252 equally
4. 6 people share $336 equally
5. 8 people share $1,136 equally
6. 9 people share $783 equally
7. 7 people share $672 equally
8. 5 people share $995 equally

Set E, pages 94–96

Find 549 ÷ 6.

Estimate first. 540 ÷ 6 = 90.

$$
\begin{array}{r}
91 \text{ R}3 \\
6\overline{)549} \\
-54 \\
\hline
09 \\
-6 \\
\hline
3
\end{array}
$$

Check:

$$
\begin{array}{r}
91 \\
\times 6 \\
\hline
546 \\
+3 \\
\hline
549
\end{array}
$$

The quotient 91 R3 is close to the estimate, 90.

Remember that you can check your answer by multiplying the quotient and the divisor, and then add the remainder.

Divide.

1. 74 ÷ 5
2. 89 ÷ 9
3. 232 ÷ 4
4. 488 ÷ 8
5. 682 ÷ 7
6. 735 ÷ 6
7. 856 ÷ 4
8. 492 ÷ 6

Set F, pages 98–100

Find 839 ÷ 4.

Estimate first. 800 ÷ 4 = 200.

```
      209 R3
  4)839
   - 8
     03
    - 0
      39
    - 36
       3
```

Check:
```
      209
    ×   4
      836
    +   3
      839
```

The quotient 209 R3 is close to the estimate, 200. The answer is reasonable.

Remember that you sometimes need to write a zero in the quotient when you divide.

Divide. Estimate to check that your answer is reasonable.

1. 720 ÷ 6

2. 661 ÷ 3

3. 424 ÷ 4

4. 914 ÷ 3

5. 6)185

6. 9)1,872

7. 7)2,940

8. 5)1,532

Set G, pages 102–104

Determine all the factor pairs for 12.

Factors are numbers you multiply to give a particular product. Two factors form a factor pair.

Shown below are factor pairs for 12.

1 × 12 = 12,
2 × 6 = 12,
3 × 4 = 12

1 and 12, 2 and 6, 3 and 4 form factor pairs.

Each of these factor pairs gives the product 12.

Remember that you can use divisibility rules to help find factors of a number.

Determine all the factor pairs for each number.

1. 15

2. 20

3. 24

4. 36

5. 70

6. 80

7. 85

8. 98

Set H, pages 106–108

Is 6 a prime or composite number?

A prime number is a whole number with no other factors besides 1 and itself.

A composite number is a number that is not prime; it has factors other than 1 and itself.

Factors of 6: 1 and 6, and 2 and 3

The number 6 is composite.

Is 47 a prime or composite number?

Since the only factors of 47 are 1 and 47, it is a prime number.

Remember that a prime number is a whole number that is greater than 1 and has exactly two factors, 1 and itself.

Classify each as prime or composite.

1. 11
2. 15
3. 18
4. 19
5. 27
6. 33
7. 200
8. 555

Set I, pages 110–112

Eight friends want to share 131 postcards. How many postcards will each person get if each person gets the same number of cards? Draw a picture and write an equation to solve.

131 postcards

8 people
p

number of postcards per person

$131 \div 8 = p$

$$\begin{array}{r} 16 \text{ R3} \\ 8)\overline{131} \\ \underline{8} \\ 51 \\ \underline{48} \\ 3 \end{array}$$

$p = 16$ R3

Since there is a remainder of 3 postcards, there are not enough for each person to get 17 cards.

Each friend will receive 16 postcards.

Remember that you may need to interpret the remainder before solving each problem.

Draw a picture and write an equation. Solve.

1. A total of 60 students are being separated into 5 equal teams. How many students are on each team?

2. Nancy has 35 bottles of water that she wants to put into portable coolers. Each cooler can hold 6 bottles. How many coolers will Nancy need?

3. A restaurant made 142 pancakes. Each serving had 3 pancakes on a plate. How many servings were there?

Dividing by 2-Digit Divisors

1 How fast can the Thorny Devil Lizard eat ants, which is one of its favorite foods? You will find out in Lesson 5-6.

2 About how many arches per mile would you see while driving through Arches National Park in Utah? You will find out in Lesson 5-7.

3

Some comets can be seen from Earth fairly often. About how many of these comets are seen each year? You will find out in Lesson 5-2.

Review What You Know!

Vocabulary

Choose the best term from the box.

- dividend
- divisor
- quotient
- remainder

1. In the equation $180 \div 45 = 4$, the number 180 is the __?__ and the number 4 is the __?__.

2. The number used to divide another number is the __?__.

3. $15 \div 6 = 2$ with a __?__ of 3.

Place Value

Copy and complete.

4. 7,896 is the same as 7 __?__ + 8 __?__ + 9 __?__ + 6 __?__.

5. 36,000 is the same as 36 __?__.

6. 75,800 is the same as 75 __?__ + 8 __?__.

Rounding

Round each number to the place of the underlined digit.

7. 6<u>7</u>9

8. <u>3</u>,769

9. 90,<u>3</u>24

10. <u>8</u>77

11. <u>6</u>,542

12. 42,3<u>7</u>6

Writing to Explain Write an answer to the question.

13. Explain one way to estimate $738 \div 84$.

Using Patterns to Divide

How can patterns help you divide large multiples of 10?

A jet carries 18,000 passengers in 90 trips. The plane is full for each trip. How many passengers does the plane hold?

Choose an Operation Divide to find how many people were on each trip.

18,000 passengers in 90 trips

Understand It!
Basic facts and place value patterns can help when finding quotients such as 6,300 ÷ 90.

Guided Practice*

Do you know HOW?

In **1** through **4**, find each quotient. Use mental math.

1. 210 ÷ 30 = 21 tens ÷ 3 tens = ▢

2. 480 ÷ 60 = 48 tens ÷ 6 tens = ▢

3. 8,100 ÷ 90 = ▢

4. 2,800 ÷ 70 = ▢

Do you UNDERSTAND?

5. In Exercise 1, why is 210 ÷ 30 the same as 21 tens ÷ 3 tens?

6. In the example at the top, if the jet carried 10,000 people in 40 trips, how many people did it carry for each trip?

Independent Practice

In **7** through **22**, use mental math to find the missing numbers.

7. 560 ÷ 70 = 56 tens ÷ 7 tens = ▢

8. 360 ÷ 60 = 36 tens ÷ 6 tens = ▢

9. 6,000 ÷ 50 = 600 tens ÷ 5 tens = ▢

10. 24,000 ÷ 60 = 2,400 tens ÷ 6 tens = ▢

11. 2,000 ÷ 20 = ▢

12. 6,300 ÷ 90 = ▢

13. 240 ÷ 10 = ▢

14. 21,000 ÷ ▢ = 700

15. 8,100 ÷ 90 = ▢

16. 72,000 ÷ ▢ = 200

17. 30,000 ÷ ▢ = 600

18. 7,200 ÷ ▢ = 80

19. 56,000 ÷ ▢ = 800

20. 10,000 ÷ 100 = ▢

21. 25,000 ÷ 50 = ▢

22. 45,000 ÷ 90 = ▢

*For another example, see Set A on page 142.

Think of a basic fact to help you solve.

$18 \div 9 = 2$

Think about multiples of 10:

$180 \div 90 = 18$ tens $\div 9$ tens $= 2$

$1{,}800 \div 90 = 180$ tens $\div 9$ tens $= 20$

$18{,}000 \div 90 = 1{,}800$ tens $\div 9$ tens $= 200$

The pattern shows us that $18{,}000 \div 90 = 200$.

So, the jet can hold 200 people during each trip.

You can multiply to check your answer.

$200 \times 90 = 18{,}000$

Problem Solving

For **23** and **24**, use the information at the right.

23. If all the flights were full and all planes carried the same number of passengers, how many people were on each flight?

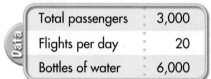

Data		
Total passengers	:	3,000
Flights per day	:	20
Bottles of water	:	6,000

24. If each flight was stocked with the same number of bottles of water, how many bottles were on each flight?

25. There are 12 school campuses in the community. Each campus has a 14-member volleyball team. How many students play volleyball?

26. Helen bowled 5 games. Her scores were 97, 108, 114, 99, and 100. What was the total of her scores?

27. **Think About the Process** Dividing 480 by 60 is the same as

  A dividing 48 ones by 6 ones.

  B dividing 48 tens by 6 ones.

  C dividing 48 tens by 6 tens.

  D dividing 48 hundreds by 6 tens.

28. Suppose there are 1,500 pencils in 20 bins. You want to put the same number of pencils in each bin. Which expression shows how to find the number of pencils in each bin?

  A $1{,}500 + 20$ **C** $1{,}500 \times 20$

  B $1{,}500 - 20$ **D** $1{,}500 \div 20$

29. One dozen eggs is 12 eggs. A farmer harvested 1,260 eggs from the hen-house. Which expression shows how to find how many dozen eggs the farmer harvested?

  A $1260 + 12$ **C** $1260 \div 12$

  B $1260 - 12$ **D** 1260×12

30. It takes 18,000 kg of sand to fill 600 school sandboxes. How much sand will a construction company need to put in each of the 600 sandboxes to get ready for the new school year?

Understand It!
There are different ways to adjust whole numbers to estimate quotients.

Estimating Quotients with 2-Digit Divisors

How can you use compatible numbers to estimate quotients?

$159 for 75 bracelets

Betty made $159 by selling 75 bracelets. Each bracelet costs the same. About how much did each bracelet cost?

Choose an Operation We know the total amount made and the number of bracelets. Divide to find the price.

Guided Practice*

Do you know HOW?

In **1** through **6**, estimate using compatible numbers.

1. 287 ÷ 42

2. 320 ÷ 11

3. 208 ÷ 72

4. 554 ÷ 62

5. 1,220 ÷ 59

6. 3,390 ÷ 42

Do you UNDERSTAND?

7. Writing to Explain If you use rounding to estimate in the example above, can you divide easily? Explain.

8. Reasonableness Betty has 425 more bracelets to sell. She wants to store these in plastic bags that hold 20 bracelets each. She estimates she will need about 25 bags. Is she right? Why or why not?

Independent Practice

In **9** through **26**, estimate using compatible numbers.

9. 412 ÷ 84

10. 288 ÷ 37

11. 2,964 ÷ 73

12. 228 ÷ 19

13. 1,784 ÷ 64

14. 7,620 ÷ 53

15. 2,280 ÷ 12

16. 485 ÷ 92

17. 540 ÷ 61

18. 1,710 ÷ 32

19. 2,740 ÷ 67

20. 4,322 ÷ 81

21. 5,700 ÷ 58

22. 7,810 ÷ 44

23. 6,395 ÷ 88

24. 4,877 ÷ 74

25. 2,495 ÷ 48

26. 6,284 ÷ 93

*For another example, see Set B on page 142.

The question asks, "About how much?" So, an estimate is enough.

Use compatible numbers to estimate 159 ÷ 75.

Find compatible numbers for 159 and 75.

 16 can be divided evenly by 8.

160 and 80 are close to 159 and 75.

So, 160 and 80 are compatible numbers.

Divide.

$160 ÷ 80 = 2$.

So, Betty charged *about* $2 for each bracelet.

Check for reasonableness:

$2 × 80 = 160$

Problem Solving

27. A high school volleyball team has made it to the state tournament. There are 586 students that want to go, and 32 students can fit on each bus. About how many buses are needed?

28. Each player contributed $3 for a gift for the head coach. The two assistant coaches each donated $10. If there were 22 players on the team, how much money did the team raise in all?

29. There are 135 comets that are visible from Earth every 20 years or less. What is an estimate of how many of these comets are seen each year?

30. Leon bought 8 CDs on sale for $88. The regular price for 8 CDs is $112. How much did Leon save per CD by buying them on sale?

31. Estimate the product for the following expression.

$805 × 62$

A 4,800

B 48,000

C 54,000

D 64,000

32. Which property does the following equation illustrate?

$2 + (11 + 19) = (2 + 11) + 19$

A Commutative Property of Addition

B Associative Property of Addition

C Identity Property of Addition

D Commutative Property of Multiplication

33. Donald bought a clock radio. The radio weighs 18 ounces. Donald paid $12 less than the normal sales price. If the normal sales price was $38, how much did Donald spend on the radio?

34. **Writing to Explain** Autumn needs to estimate the quotient $817 ÷ 91$. Explain how she can use compatible numbers to make a reasonable estimate.

Lesson
5-3

Understand It!
Identifying hidden
questions is helpful
when solving
multiple-step
problems.

Multiple-Step Problems

For three months, a fifth-grade class held a fun fair to raise money for charities. The funds raised are shown in the table. If the class divides the money equally among 30 different organizations, how much will each organization receive?

Funds Raised	
September	$435
October	$460
November	$605

Data

Guided Practice*

Do you know HOW?

1. A keyboardist has a digital camera that holds 156 photos. Of these photos, 114 were taken on a vacation, and the rest at a concert. The keyboardist wants to print and mount the photos of the concert on 7 pages of an album with the same number of photos on each page. How many photos will be on each page?

Do you UNDERSTAND?

2. What is the hidden question and answer in Problem 1?

3. **Writing to Explain** Were you able to use mental math in Problem 1?

4. **Write a Problem** Write a real-world multiple-step problem that can be solved by using division.

Independent Practice

In **5** through **9**, write and answer the hidden question or questions. Then solve.

5. Ralph's Nursery sold 62 cherry trees, 36 orange trees, and 42 fig trees during 14 days. If the nursery sold the same number of trees each day, how many trees were sold each day?

6. A high-rise apartment building in New York has 15 floors with 26 apartments on each floor. There are 3 kinds of apartments in the building: one-, two-, and three-bedroom. If each floor has the same number of these kinds of apartments, how many of each kind are in the building?

Stuck? Try this....

- What do I know?
- What am I asked to find?
- What diagram can I use to help understand the problem?
- Can I use addition, subtraction, multiplication, or division?
- Is all of my work correct?
- Did I answer the right question?
- Is my answer reasonable?

*For another example, see Set C on page 142.

What do I know?

A class raised $435, $460, and $605. Thirty charities will receive the same amount of money from the total amount raised.

What am I asked to find?

The amount of money each charity will receive.

Find the hidden question or questions.

How much money was raised altogether?

? total amount raised		
$435	$460	$605

$435 + $460 + $605 = $1,500

Solve. Use mental math.

$1,500 ÷ 30 = ☐

Think 150 tens ÷ 3 tens = 50

Each charity will receive $50.

---

7. The table at the right shows the typical number of calories for certain kinds and amounts of food. Which combination of food items contains more calories: 1 apple and 1 cooked fish stick or 1 slice of Italian bread and 1 ounce of cheddar cheese? How many more calories?

Calories in Food	
Food Description	**Calories**
1 apple	125
1 slice Italian bread	85
1 cooked fish stick	70
1 oz cheddar cheese	115

Data

8. Nina has enrolled in a modern dance class. The class meets the same number of hours each day, Monday through Friday, for 6 weeks. If the total number of hours is 90, how many hours does Nina spend in class each weekday?

9. Franco changes the oil in his car every 3,000 miles. If Franco uses 4 quarts of oil for each oil change, how many quarts of oil has he already used if his car has 24,000 miles?

10. During school spirit week, Lynn sold 85 green and gold spirit ribbons. How many ribbons did Lynn sell each day if she sold the same number of ribbons each day? Draw a picture, write an equation, then solve.

11. In 2006, Preston wrote a 5-page paper on Martin Luther King Jr.'s life. One of the events Preston wrote about was Rev. King's famous I Have a Dream speech. The speech was given in 1963. How many years after this speech was Preston's paper written?

12. Melanie took a bag containing 700 quarters to the bank and exchanged them for dollar bills. How much money did she receive?

13. Tony bought *n* football cards. He gave half of them to Karen. Then he gave 2 cards to Jeff and had 6 cards left. How many cards did Tony buy?

Dividing by Multiples of 10

What are the steps in dividing by a multiple of ten?

This year, a group of 249 students are taking a field trip. One bus is needed for every 20 students. How many buses are needed?

Choose an Operation Divide to find the number of buses.

20 students per bus

Guided Practice*

Do you know HOW?

In **1** through **6**, divide.

1. $30\overline{)345}$ **2.** $20\overline{)282}$

3. $50\overline{)467}$ **4.** $60\overline{)841}$

5. $40\overline{)413}$ **6.** $80\overline{)766}$

Do you UNDERSTAND?

7. In the example above, if only 137 students were going on the trip, how many buses would be needed?

8. **Reasonableness** In the example above, why is 12 buses a reasonable estimate?

Independent Practice

Leveled Practice Copy and complete.

9.
$$\begin{array}{r} 5\,R1 \\ 20\overline{)318} \\ 2 \\ \hline 1 \\ 1 \\ \hline 1 \end{array}$$

10.
$$\begin{array}{r} 1R\,2 \\ 60\overline{)712} \\ 6 \\ \hline 1 \\ 6 \\ \hline 2 \end{array}$$

11.
$$\begin{array}{r} 1R \\ 30\overline{)328} \\ \\ \hline \\ 0 \\ \hline 2 \end{array}$$

12. $40\overline{)348}$ **13.** $70\overline{)618}$ **14.** $80\overline{)939}$

15. $697 \div 90$ **16.** $114 \div 30$ **17.** $766 \div 50$

18. $724 \div 60$ **19.** $841 \div 20$ **20.** $222 \div 30$

21. $936 \div 40$ **22.** $295 \div 20$ **23.** $479 \div 60$

Step 1

Find 249 ÷ 20.

Estimate: 240 ÷ 20 = 12

Divide the tens.

$$\begin{array}{r} 1 \\ 20\overline{)249} \\ -\,20 \\ \hline 4 \end{array}$$

Divide   24 ÷ 20 = 1
Multiply   1 × 20 = 20
Subtract   24 − 20 = 4
Compare   4 < 20

Step 2

Bring down the ones. Divide the ones.

$$\begin{array}{r} 12\ R9 \\ 20\overline{)249} \\ -\,20\downarrow \\ \hline 49 \\ -\,40 \\ \hline 9 \end{array}$$

Divide   49 ÷ 20 = 2
Multiply   2 × 20 = 40
Subtract   49 − 40 = 9
Compare   9 < 20

Since the remainder is 9, one more bus is needed. A total of 13 buses are needed.

The answer is reasonable since 13 is close to the estimate, 12.

Problem Solving

Use the chart to answer **24** through **26**.

24. Rita's family is moving from Grand Junction to Dallas. The van that is moving them averages 60 miles an hour. About how many hours does it take the family to reach their new home in Dallas?

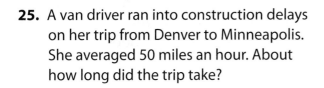

Data		
Dallas, TX, to Grand Junction, CO	980 miles
Nashville, TN, to Norfolk, VA	670 miles
Charleston, SC, to Atlanta, GA	290 miles
Denver, CO, to Minneapolis, MN	920 miles
Little Rock, AR, to Chicago, IL	660 miles

25. A van driver ran into construction delays on her trip from Denver to Minneapolis. She averaged 50 miles an hour. About how long did the trip take?

26. Charlie has to pay a toll of $2 for every 30 miles on his trip from Charleston to Atlanta. How much money does Charlie pay in tolls?

27. Manchaca school district has 32,020 students, while the Saddle River school district has 56,212 students. How many more students are there in the Saddle River than in the Manchaca school district?

28. The Port Lavaca fishing pier is 3,200 feet long. If there is one person fishing every ten feet, then how many people could fish from the pier at once?

29. Each person on a boat ride pays $26 for a ticket. There are 63 passengers. How much money is collected from all the passengers?

  A $89

  B $504

  C $1,538

  D $1,638

30. **Think About the Process** What is the first step in finding 383 ÷ 30?

  A Regroup 8 tens as 80 ones

  B See how many are in the remainder

  C Regroup 3 hundreds as 30 tens

  D Multiply 3 by 38

1-Digit Quotients

What are the steps for dividing by 2-digit numbers?

A theater sold 428 tickets for a show. A section in this theater has 64 seats. How many sections must there be to seat all the ticket holders?

Choose an Operation Divide to find the total number of sections.

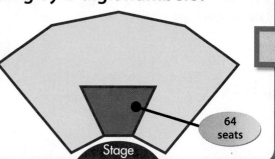

64 seats

Stage

Another Example **How do you revise an estimate when dividing?**

Find $330 \div 42$.

Step 1

Estimate first.

$330 \div 42$ is about $320 \div 40$, or 8.

Tip *Think of 32 tens $\div 4$ tens $= 8$.*

Step 2

Divide the ones. Multiply and subtract.

8 groups of 42 or $8 \times 42 = 336$.

Since $336 > 330$, my estimate is too high.

$$\begin{array}{r} 8 \\ 42\overline{)330} \\ -\ 336 \\ \hline \text{Oops!} \end{array}$$

Step 3

Revise your estimate. Since 8 was too high, try 7 and divide.

7 groups of 42 or $7 \times 42 = 294$

$330 - 294 = 36$

$36 < 42$, so I do not have to divide again.

$$\begin{array}{r} 7 \\ 42\overline{)330} \\ -\ 294 \\ \hline 36 \end{array}$$

Answer: 7 R36

Step 4

Check your work.

Multiply the divisor by the quotient. Add the remainder.

$$\begin{array}{r} 42 \\ \times\ \ \ 7 \\ \hline 294 \\ +\ \ 36 \\ \hline 330 \end{array}$$

Explain It

1. In Step 1, how did the estimate tell you to start dividing ones?

2. In Step 2, how did you know that your first estimate of 8 was too high?

Step 1	Step 2	Step 3

Step 1

Estimate to help decide where to place the first digit in the quotient.

428 ÷ 64 is about 420 ÷ 70, or 6.

Start dividing ones.

Step 2

Divide the ones. Multiply and subtract.

```
      6 R44
64)428
  − 384
     44
```

428 ÷ 64 = 6 R44

Step 3

Check:

```
      64
   ×   6
     384
  +   44
     428
```

So, the theater must have 7 sections.

Guided Practice*

Do you know HOW?

Copy and complete.

1. 12)115

2. 31)243

Do you UNDERSTAND?

3. Can the remainder in either example be greater than the divisor? Why or why not?

4. In the example above, if the theater had sold 612 tickets, how many sections must it have?

Independent Practice

Leveled Practice Copy and complete.

5.
```
       R2
38)325
 − 3
    2
```

6.
```
      7 R 9
52)403
 −   4
     9
```

7.
```
      R 7
74)693
 − 66
    7
```

8.
```
       R
33)301
 −
```

In **9** through **24** divide.

9. 57)550 **10.** 29)254 **11.** 46)260 **12.** 56)528

13. 51)293 **14.** 19)119 **15.** 91)628 **16.** 40)180

17. 396 ÷ 42 **18.** 275 ÷ 38 **19.** 179 ÷ 22 **20.** 345 ÷ 85

21. 214 ÷ 28 **22.** 748 ÷ 81 **23.** 671 ÷ 79 **24.** 476 ÷ 68

For another example, see Set E on page 143.

25. Use the table at the right to answer the following questions.

a What is the total capacity for all four exhibits at the History Museum?

b How many class groups of 24 could view the showing at the Interactive Exhibit at the same time?

History Museum Capacity	
Governor Exhibit	68
Landmark Exhibit	95
Early 1900s Exhibit	85
Interactive Exhibit	260

26. Chen's band put on a concert at school. There were 702 people in the audience. Each ticket cost $8. The audience was seated in 13 sections. If each section had the same number of people, how many people were in each section?

27. Mrs. Dugan collects antiques. She bought 7 antique chairs for which she paid a total of $1050. Each chair was made with a different type of wood. If each chair cost the same amount, how much did each chair cost?

28. Mr. Nolan changes the oil in his car every 4,000 miles. He uses 3 quarts of oil each time. How many quarts of oil will he have used after 12,000 miles?

29. If you estimate 125×22 by rounding to the nearest ten, will you get an overestimate or an underestimate?

30. Twenty members of the photography club took 559 pictures. If they use memory cards that hold 85 pictures per card, how many cards will they use?

31. The annual music festival featured different posters for sale. The sale of jazz band posters brought in $1,312. If each poster was $16, how many were sold?

32. **Writing to Explain** Explain how you know the answer to the problem shown below has an error.

$$\begin{array}{r} 8 \text{ R24} \\ 16\overline{)152} \\ -128 \\ \hline 24 \end{array}$$

33. Rachel wanted to get 8 hours of sleep before a test. She went to bed at 9:00 P.M. and woke up at 6:00 A.M. How many more hours of sleep did Rachel get than the 8 hours she wanted?

A 3 more hours   **C** 1 more hour

B 9 more hours   **D** No more hours

34. **Writing to Explain** Explain why 0.2 and 0.02 are NOT equivalent.

35. In a large restaurant, there are 9 times as many chairs as tables. The restaurant is famous for its very spicy chili. If the restaurant has 342 chairs, how many tables are in the restaurant?

Algebra Connections

Completing Tables

Remember that multiplication and division have an inverse relationship.

Since $9 \times 7 = 63$, you also know:

$$63 \div 9 = 7$$
$$63 \div 7 = 9$$

You can use inverse relationships to help complete tables.

Example:

There are 4 quarts in a gallon. Complete the table.

gallons	1	3	8	
quarts	4	12		40

You can multiply the number of gallons by 4 to find the number of quarts.

$8 \times 4 = 32$. So, 8 gallons = 32 quarts.

You can divide the number of quarts by 4 to find the number of gallons.

$40 \div 4 = 10$. So, 40 quarts = 10 gallons.

Copy and complete each table below.

1. Each box holds 5 pencils.

Pencils	15	30	35	40	45
Boxes	3				9

2. Each shelf has 10 books.

Shelves	2	3	4		
Books	20			50	90

3. A frame holds 4 photos.

Frames	2	3		5	
Photos			16		36

4. Each package has 8 markers.

Packages	2	4	5		
Markers				72	80

5. Mallory swims 2 miles per day.

Days	1	3		10	
Miles			16		60

6. Each week has 7 days.

Weeks	2	4			12
Days			35	63	

2-Digit Quotients

How can you divide larger numbers?

So far, 467 tortillas have been made. These tortillas will be placed in packages of 15. How many complete packages will be filled?

Choose an Operation Divide to find the number of packages of tortillas.

15 tortillas per package

Understand It!
Estimation, multiplication, subtraction, and comparing are used to find quotients.

Guided Practice*

Do you know HOW?

Copy and complete.

1. 47)985
   R
   –

2. 33)678
   R
   –

For **3** and **4**, divide.

3. 16)298

4. 23)292

Do you UNDERSTAND?

5. **Writing to Explain** In the problem above, why will 31 packages be filled instead of 32?

6. How many packages will 627 tortillas fill?

7. How do you decide where to place the first digit in the quotient for Exercises 1–4?

Independent Practice

Leveled Practice Copy and complete.

8. 36)584
   R
   –
   – 1
      8

9. 45)981
   R
   – 0
      1
   –

10. 56)674
    R
    –
    –

In **11** through **22**, divide.

11. 76)864

12. 23)279

13. 63)710

14. 18)638

15. 48)582

16. 26)784

17. 13)989

18. 72)2,532

19. 4,328 ÷ 93

20. 678 ÷ 27

21. 980 ÷ 45

22. 717 ÷ 31

*For another example, see Set E on page 143.

Step 1

Estimate to help decide where to place the first digit in the quotient.

Use compatible numbers.

$450 \div 15 = 30$

Start dividing tens.

Step 2

Divide the tens. Multiply and subtract. Continue the process.

$$\begin{array}{r} 31 \text{ R2} \\ 15\overline{)467} \\ -\ 45 \\ \hline 17 \\ -\ 15 \\ \hline 2 \end{array}$$

Step 3

Check:

$$\begin{array}{r} 31 \\ \times\ 15 \\ \hline 155 \\ +\ 310 \\ \hline 465 \end{array}$$

$465 + 2 = 467$

So far, 31 packages of tortillas will be filled.

Problem Solving

23. Writing to Explain If you are asked to find $621 \div 59$, how do you know the quotient will be greater than 10 before you actually divide?

24. Julita bought a sandwich for $3.50 and a glass of juice for $1.75. The tax was $0.42. She paid with a $10 bill. How much change did she get?

25. An outdoor concert company is putting on 12 concerts this summer. Each concert is sold out. The company sold a total of 972 seats. How many people will attend each performance?

  A 8   **C** 80

  B 79   **D** 81

26. Julio spends about $\frac{1}{2}$ hour reading every night. He owns 8 science fiction books, 12 mystery books, and 7 history books. He wants to add enough books to his collection to have 40 books. How many more books does he need?

27. There are 120 minutes in 2 hours. How many minutes are there in 15 hours?

28. What compatible numbers can you use to estimate $803 \div 86$?

29. One of the Thorny Devil lizard's favorite foods is ants. It can eat up to 45 ants per minute. How long would it take it to eat 540 ants?

  A 9 minutes

  B 10 minutes

  C 12 minutes

  D 15 minutes

30. Number Sense Decide if each statement is true or false. Explain.

  a $710 \div 20$ is greater than 30.

  b $821 \div 40$ is less than 20.

  c $300 \div 15$ is exactly 20.

31. Braedy had $5.00 when she left the county fair. She spent $11.00 on her ticket, and she bought lunch for $6.00. After lunch, she spent $17.00 on games and rides. How much money did Braedy bring to the county fair?

Understand It!
A calculator can be used when dividing greater numbers.

Estimating and Dividing with Greater Numbers

How do you solve problems involving division of greater numbers?

In one season, all the teams in a basketball league scored 7,832 points. If the season lasted 14 weeks, on average, how many points were scored each week?

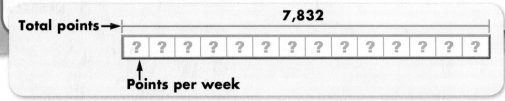

Total points → 7,832

? ? ? ? ? ? ? ? ? ? ? ? ? ?

↑
Points per week

Guided Practice*

Do you know HOW?

For **1** through **8**, estimate first. Then use a calculator to find the quotient. Round to the nearest hundredth if necessary.

1. $12\overline{)1,455}$

2. $23\overline{)3,189}$

3. $27\overline{)2,264}$

4. $59\overline{)6,214}$

5. $19\overline{)4,657}$

6. $44\overline{)7,894}$

7. $68\overline{)5,201}$

8. $81\overline{)9,222}$

Do you UNDERSTAND?

9. In the example above, calculate the average points per week if the season had 11 weeks instead of 14.

10. **Writing to Explain** For Exercises 1 and 2, how do you know the first digit of the quotient is in the hundreds?

11. **Writing to Explain** Why was the quotient rounded to the nearest hundredth?

Independent Practice

For **12** through **31**, estimate first. Then use a calculator to find the quotient. Round to the nearest hundredth if necessary.

12. $4,457 \div 31$

13. $5,232 \div 47$

14. $9,137 \div 84$

15. $3,201 \div 68$

16. $5,792 \div 51$

17. $7,274 \div 68$

18. $8,728 \div 83$

19. $8,415 \div 81$

20. $3,972 \div 32$

21. $6,281 \div 24$

22. $8,264 \div 35$

23. $5,423 \div 71$

24. $4,896 \div 71$

25. $2,482 \div 25$

26. $5,016 \div 50$

27. $2,915 \div 52$

28. $6,321 \div 84$

29. $9,852 \div 11$

30. $3,233 \div 77$

31. $8,932 \div 92$

Estimate

7,832 ÷ 14 is close to 7,500 ÷ 15, or 500.

The quotient should be close to 500.

Use a Calculator

Dividing on a calculator gives 559.428 … , or 559 R6.

7,832 ÷ 14 = 559.428 … .

Round 559.428 to the nearest hundredth—559.43.

Since 559.43 is close to the estimate—500, it is reasonable.

About 559 points were scored during each week of the basketball season.

Problem Solving

32. The city of Linton is holding a chess tournament. Use the data at the right to answer the problems.

a The total student entry fees paid were $3,105. How many students participated?

b There are about ten times as many students as adults registered for the tournament. About how many adults are registered?

Chess Tournament	
Student entry fee	$15
Adult entry fee	$18
Reserve a chess board	$12

33. Number Sense Give three factors whose product is about 10,000.

34. There are 12 inches in 1 foot. How many inches are there in 120 feet?

35. There are 1,185 possible words that can be used for the spelling bee. This number is 15 times more than will be used in the contest. How many words will be used in the contest?

A 7.9 words   **C** 709 words

B 79 words   **D** 790 words

36. The Arches National Park in Utah covers more than 73,000 acres and has 2,000 stone arches. A 40-mile road in the park takes visitors past most of the arches. If a visitor drove the entire paved road, about how many arches would he or she see per mile?

A 20   **B** 26   **C** 50   **D** 75

37. Tabitha's class is making flash cards to study the 1,185 words for the spelling bee. There are 5 teams in her class. How many flash cards will each team need to make?

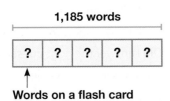

1,185 words

? ? ? ? ?

Words on a flash card

38. Darci wants to buy a computer that costs $1,236. She works at the grocery store where she earns $11 an hour. How many hours will she have to work to earn enough money to purchase the computer?

Problem Solving

Missing or Extra Information

A 1920 antique bicycle that had once belonged to 2 owners recently sold for $850. A 2008 lightweight mountain bike recently sold for 3 times as much. What was the cost of the 2008 bike?

$?

Guided Practice*

Do you know HOW?

For **1** and **2**, decide if each problem has extra or missing information. Solve if possible.

1. An adult male gorilla eats about 40 pounds of food each day. An adult female gorilla eats about half as much. How many pounds of food does an adult male gorilla eat in one week?

2. Lacey is buying dried fruit to feed her pet bird. How much will it cost to feed the bird for one month?

Do you UNDERSTAND?

3. Draw a diagram to show what you know and want to find in Problem 1.

4. **Writing to Explain** Why is it important to find the extra or missing information before solving a problem?

5. **Write a Problem** Write a real-world problem that does not include all of the information to solve it. Under the problem, write the missing information.

Independent Practice

For **6** and **7**, decide if each problem has extra or missing information. Solve if possible.

6. Eli has played 5 baseball games so far this season. How many runs did he score if he scored 2 runs each game for the first 4 games?

7. Sonja posted 45 band concert flyers in 2 days. Over the next 2 days, Elsie posted 60 flyers, and Frank posted 30 flyers. How many flyers did the 3 students post altogether?

Stuck? Try this....

- What do I know?
- What am I asked to find?
- What diagram can I use to help understand the problem?
- Can I use addition, subtraction, multiplication, or division?
- Is all of my work correct?
- Did I answer the right question?
- Is my answer reasonable?

Read and Understand

Draw a diagram to show what you know and want to find.

? cost of 2008 bicycle

| 2008 mountain bike | $850 | $850 | $850 | 3 times as much |
| 1920 bicycle | $850 | | | |

Plan

Is there extra information not needed to solve the problem?

Yes. The years, 1920 and 2008, are not needed. Also, it does not matter that the antique bike once had 2 owners.

Is there missing information needed to solve the problem?

No. All the information I need is given in the problem.

Since 3 × $850 = $2,550, the cost of the 2008 bike was $2,550.

8. Mrs. Torance has invited 16 people to a party. What information is missing if she wants to serve enough submarine sandwiches at her party?

Each sub feeds 3 children or 2 adults

9. Kara and her 4 friends went camping. Each day they hiked 2 miles before lunch and 3 miles after lunch. How many total miles did all the girls hike on their camping trip? Provide possible information needed to solve the problem, then solve it.

10. Fox Meadow Farm boards show horses. Fifteen of their horses are in the arena. The other 21 horses are in the barn. How many horses board at the farm? Draw a picture and write an equation to solve.

11. Jun and his sister visited Texas State Aquarium in Corpus Christi. While there, they learned that 1 catfish produces 40 eggs. How many eggs will 60 catfish produce?

12. Sylvia had $20 to spend at the circus. She spent $5.00 on admission. During lunch, Sylvia bought a hot dog and drink for $6.50. How much money did Sylvia have left to spend after lunch?

13. Greg bought a sandwich and a drink at Dunstan's Deli. He paid $4.50. Which sandwich and drink did he buy?

Dunstan's Deli	
Chicken	$4.25
Roast Beef	$3.75
Tuna	$3.50
Milk	$0.60
Juice	$0.75

14. Roses are on sale at the market 2 for $1.00. Mindy has $20.00. If she buys 16 roses, how much will they cost?

15. **Writing to Explain** There are 24 hours in one day. How can you use addition to find the number of hours in one week? How can you use multiplication?

16. **Reasoning** One decade equals 10 years and one century equals 100 years. Are there more years in 11 decades or 1 century?

1. The city of Seattle has 1,242 law enforcement officers in the police department. If the officers are divided into groups of 18, about how many officers will be in each group? (5-7)

   A 30

   B 60

   C 130

   D 700

2. Which of the following is the best way to estimate 487 ÷ 67 with compatible numbers? (5-2)

   A 480 divided by 70

   B 485 divided by 60

   C 490 divided by 60

   D 490 divided by 70

3. There are 40 windows on each floor of a 20 story building. If a window washer can wash 50 windows in one day, which of the following can be used to find how long it will take to wash all the windows in the building? (5-3)

   A $20 \times 40 \div 50 = 16$ days

   B $20 + 40 \div 50 = 21$ days

   C $20 \times 50 \div 40 = 25$ days

   D $40 \times 50 \div 20 = 100$ days

4. The carnival committee has purchased 985 small prizes. If the prizes are to be divided among the 20 game booths, how many prizes will each booth have and how many prizes will be left over? (5-4)

   A 44 per booth with 5 left over

   B 49 per booth with none left over

   C 49 per booth with 5 left over

   D 490 per booth with 5 left over

5. Which of the following is another way to think of 27,000 ÷ 30? (5-1)

   A 27 tens ÷ 30 tens

   B 27 tens ÷ 3 tens

   C 270 tens ÷ 3 tens

   D 2,700 tens ÷ 3 tens

6. The table shows the number of people who have signed up to attend a company picnic. Cases of water bottles with 24 bottles in each case are to be purchased for the event. How can the organizer find the number of cases needed if each person receives one bottle? (5-3)

Group	Number signed up to attend
Accounting	137
Marketing	146
Central Office	84

   A Subtract 84 from the sum of 137 and 146, and divide the result by 24.

   B Add 137, 146, and 84, and multiply the sum by 24.

   C Add 137, 146, and 84, and divide the sum by 24.

   D Add 137, 146, and 84, and subtract 24 from the result.

7. Shady Rivers summer camp has 188 campers this week. If there are 22 campers to each cabin, what is the least number of cabins needed? (5-5)

   A 7

   B 8

   C 9

   D 10

8. Mrs. Delgato needs to buy 160 begonias for her flowerbed. According to the prices shown, how much would she save if she bought them by the flat instead of buying them separately? (5-3)

A $8

B $10

C $40

D $80

Begonia Prices	
One Plant	$2
One Flat (20 plants per flat)	$30

9. Alberto is saving for an item that costs $384. If he saves $30 each week, how long will it take him to buy the item? (5-4)

A 11 weeks

B 12 weeks

C 13 weeks

D 20 weeks

10. The lengths of two canals are given in the table. About how many times longer is the Erie Canal than the Chesapeake and Delaware Canal? (5-2)

Ship Canal	Length (in miles)
Chesapeake and Delaware Canal	14
Erie Canal	363

A 25

B 30

C 36

D 180

11. About 300,000 Mexican Free-tailed Bats occupy the caves at Carlsbad Caverns during the summer months. Each bat can eat about 800 insects in one hour. What other information is needed to find the number of insects a bat can eat each day? (5-8)

A The number of hours a bat sleeps

B The number of hours a bat spends eating each day

C The weight of each bat

D The average weight of each insect

12. A company ordered 384 note pads. If there are 48 note pads in each box, how many boxes were ordered? (5-5)

A 7

B 8

C 9

D 12

13. Morning Star Farm purchased 2,400 apple trees. If 80 trees can be planted on each acre of land, how many acres will be needed to plant all the trees? (5-1)

A 3,000

B 300

C 30

D 3

14. The cost to rent a lodge for a reunion is $975. If 65 people attend, and pay the same price each, how much will each person pay? (5-6)

A $150

B $35

C $25

D $15

Set A, pages 122–123

Find 32,000 ÷ 80 using mental math.

Use basic facts and patterns to help.

32 ÷ 8 = 4

320 ÷ 80 = 4

3,200 ÷ 80 = 40

32,000 ÷ 80 = 400

Think 32,000 ÷ 80 is the same as 3,200 tens ÷ 8 tens.

Remember that if the basic fact has a zero in the dividend, it should NOT be used to find the number in the quotient.

1. 360 ÷ 40 = 　　　 **2.** 270 ÷ 90 = 　　
3. 180 ÷ 20 = 　　　 **4.** 750 ÷ 50 = 　　
5. 2,100 ÷ 30 = 　　 **6.** 4,800 ÷ 80 = 　　
7. 5,400 ÷ 60 = 　　 **8.** 6,300 ÷ 90 = 　　
9. 30,000 ÷ 50 = 　　 **10.** 21,000 ÷ 30 = 　　
11. 72,000 ÷ 80 = 　　 **12.** 81,000 ÷ 90 = 　　

Set B, pages 124–125

Estimate 364 ÷ 57.

Use compatible numbers and patterns to divide.

364 ÷ 57
↓　　↓
360 ÷ 60 = 6

So, 364 ÷ 57 is about 6.

Remember that compatible numbers are numbers that are easy to compute in your head.

1. 168 ÷ 45 　　　 **2.** 525 ÷ 96
3. 379 ÷ 63 　　　 **4.** 234 ÷ 72
5. $613 ÷ 93 　　 **6.** $748 ÷ 92

Set C, pages 126–127

The football coach spent a total of $890.40 including $50.40 tax for 35 shirts for the team. The price of each shirt was the same. How much did one shirt cost before tax was added?

Identify the hidden question or questions.

How much did all the shirts cost without tax?

$890.40 − $50.40 = $840.00

Solve the problem.

$840 ÷ 35 = $24　Each shirt cost $24.00.

Remember that you need to identify the hidden question or questions and answer them before solving the problem.

Write and answer the hidden question or questions. Then solve.

1. At the city triathlon, athletes bike 110 miles, run a 23.5-mile marathon, and swim. If the total distance of this triathlon is 135.7 miles, how far do the athletes swim?

2. A gymnast practices 6 days per week. If the same gymnast practices a total of 120 hours in a 4-week period, how many hours per day does the gymnast practice?

Set D, pages 128–129

Find 461 ÷ 30.

Estimate to decide where to put the first digit in the quotient.

Use compatible numbers.   450 ÷ 50 = 9

Start dividing the ones. Multiply and subtract. Compare the remainder to the divisor.

$$\begin{array}{r} 9 \text{ R11} \\ 50\overline{)461} \\ -\ 450 \\ \hline 11 \end{array}$$ To check, compare the quotient to your estimate.

Remember that if the product of your first quotient and the divisor is larger than the dividend, your estimate is too high. Try dividing again with the next lower number.

1. $20\overline{)428}$ **2.** $30\overline{)547}$

3. $40\overline{)387}$ **4.** $50\overline{)653}$

5. $60\overline{)589}$ **6.** $70\overline{)912}$

7. $80\overline{)698}$ **8.** $90\overline{)849}$

Set E, pages 130–132, 134–137

Find 789 ÷ 19.

Estimate first.

800 ÷ 20 = 40.

Divide the tens. Multiply, subtract, and compare.

Bring down the ones. Divide the ones. Multiply, subtract, and compare. Check the quotient with your estimate.

$$\begin{array}{r} 41 \text{ R10} \\ 19\overline{)789} \\ -\ 76 \\ \hline 29 \\ -\ 19 \\ \hline 10 \end{array}$$

Remember that you can check your answer by multiplying the quotient by the divisor, and then adding the remainder to that product. The sum should be your dividend.

1. $74\overline{)389}$ **2.** $28\overline{)119}$

3. $36\overline{)234}$ **4.** $38\overline{)792}$

5. $42\overline{)523}$ **6.** $47\overline{)5,190}$

7. $58\overline{)7,211}$ **8.** $12\overline{)3,549}$

Set F, pages 138–139

Decide if the problem has missing or extra information. Solve if possible.

Kay has 3 folders. Each folder has 6 pockets for subjects. How many sheets of paper are in each folder?

What you know: 3 folders, 6 pockets per folder.

What you want to find: How many sheets of paper in each folder.

Can you solve? No, it does not mention paper being in folders or pockets.

Remember that some problems have too much information, but can be solved.

1. Mario has $40.20. He went to the store and bought apples, cereal, and bread. How much change did he get back?

2. Alanna bought 6 books. Each book costs $13 and each bookmark cost $2. How much did she spend on books?

Variables and Expressions

1

Passengers on a cruise ship can go ashore when the ship stops at ports of call. How can order of operations be used to find the number of passengers left on the ship when other passengers get off the ship? You will find out in Lesson 6-5.

2

How can an algebraic expression be used to show the number of minutes you spend exercising each day? You will find out in Lesson 6-3.

Review What You Know!

Vocabulary

Choose the best term from the box.

- difference • quotient
- product • sum

1. The answer to a division problem is the __?__.

2. The __?__ of 5 and 7 is 12.

3. To find the __?__ between 16 and 4 you subtract.

4. Multiplying is the same as finding the __?__.

Mixed Practice

Find each answer.

5. $32 \div 4$

6. 35×100

7. $47 + 92$

8. $\frac{1}{4} + \frac{2}{4}$

9. $3.4 - 2.7$

10. $1.9 + 7$

11. $3 + \frac{1}{2}$

12. $75 \div 5$

13. $\$3.75 + \$2.49$

14. $8\frac{5}{8} - 1\frac{2}{8}$

Patterns

Writing to Explain Write an answer for the question.

15. What equation comes next in the pattern below? Explain how you know.

$$7 \times 10 = 70$$
$$7 \times 100 = 700$$
$$7 \times 1,000 = 7,000$$

3

If a hermit crab grows 1 inch per year, how long will it be in 5 years? 10 years? x years? You will find out in Lesson 6-2.

4

What is the height of a sculpture made entirely of jeans? You will find out in Lesson 6-1.

Variables and Expressions

4 oz

How can you translate words into expressions?

What expression shows the weight of the mixed nuts after the weight of the jar is subtracted?

A **variable** is a letter or symbol that represents an unknown amount that can vary, or change.

> **Understand It!**
> Variables can be used to write algebraic expressions that describe real-world situations.

Guided Practice*

Do you know HOW?

In **1** through **4**, use a variable to write an algebraic expression that represents the word phrase.

1. twice the number of people

2. $7 less than the current price

3. 8 more gumballs than Javier has

4. a number of students divided into 2 teams

Do you UNDERSTAND?

5. What would the expression for the weight of the mixed nuts be if the weight of the jar was 8 oz?

6. **Writing to Explain** Why is a variable used in the example at the top?

7. Write two word phrases that could be translated as $25 \times p$.

Independent Practice

For **8** through **11**, translate each algebraic expression into words.

8. $n + 9$ 9. $x \div 12$ 10. $y - 4$ 11. $8m$

For **12** through **20**, write each word phrase as an algebraic expression.

12. subtract a number from 10

13. the product of 9 and a number

14. add 6 to a number

15. 6 divided by a number

16. a number decreased by 12

17. 9 plus a number

18. a number added to 19

19. the quotient of a number and 8

20. 4 less a number

Animated Glossary
www.pearsonsuccessnet.com

For another example, see Set A on page 166.

An algebraic expression is a mathematical phrase involving variables, numbers, and operations.

Operation	Word Phrase	Algebraic Expression
Addition	a number *plus* 4 a number *added* to 4	$w + 4$
Subtraction	a number *minus* 4 a number *less* 4	$w - 4$
Multiplication	4 *times* a number	$4 \times w$ or $4w$
Division	a number *divided* by 4	$w \div 4$ or $\frac{w}{4}$

Since the weight of the mixed nuts varies, let w represent the total weight of the jar and the mixed nuts.

So, $w - 4$ is the weight of the mixed nuts after the weight of the jar is subtracted.

Problem Solving

21. You and three of your friends are going to share a package of granola bars equally. Write an algebraic expression to show this situation.

22. In January, Winifred had $1,369.57 in her savings account. In December, she had $2,513.34 in her account. How much more money did she have in December than in January?

23. Jeff added $\frac{4}{5}$ cup of water to $\frac{2}{3}$ cup of lemonade concentrate. Is there more water or concentrate?

24. Writing to Explain How are the expressions $7 - g$ and $g - 7$ different?

25. **Think About the Process** Nao has 6 fewer CDs than Emily. If c represents the number of CDs Emily has, which expression tells how many CDs Nao has?

  A $c + 6$ **C** $6 - c$

  B $c - 6$ **D** $6 + c$

26. A person has to be at least 48 inches tall to ride a roller coaster. Jill, who is 12 years old, is taller than 48 inches. Which expression shows Jill's height?

  A $(12 + t) - 48$ **C** $(48 - 12) + t$

  B $48t$ **D** $48 + t$

27. This drawing of the sculpture of a ball of jeans shows a stand beneath it. If the stand and sculpture measure 18 feet, which equation shows how to find the height of the sculpture?

  A $18 + x = 2$ **C** $x - 18 = 2$

  B $x + 2 = 18$ **D** $2 - 18 = x$

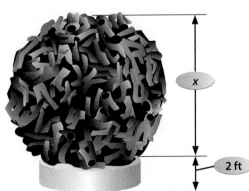

28. Juan is planning to buy a new computer monitor. He has already saved $250. Let n equal the amount Juan still needs to save. Write an algebraic expression that represents the cost of the monitor.

Patterns and Expressions

How can you use patterns to show relationships?

Shawna wanted to buy tickets to the concert for herself and some friends. What is the total cost of all of the tickets?

Let t = the number of tickets purchased.

Other Examples

How can you evaluate an algebraic expression?

You replace the variable with a number, and then perform the computation.

Evaluating an Addition Expression

Evaluate $x + 7$ for $x = 6$.
Replace x with 6 in the expression.
$x + 7$
↓
$6 + 7 = 13$

Evaluating a Division Expression

Evaluate $z \div 3$ for $z = 9$.
Replace z with 9 in the expression.
$z \div 3$
↓
$9 \div 3 = 3$

Writing and Evaluating an Expression

After 5 weeks, Sean's plant was h inches tall and Fred's plant was 3 inches taller.

Write an algebraic expression to represent the height of Fred's plant.

$h + 3$

Evaluate the expression for $h = 3$ and $h = 5$

h	3	5
$h + 3$	$3 + 3 = 6$	$5 + 3 = 8$

Explain It

1. Explain how you could figure out the height of Fred's plant if you knew the height of Sean's plant.

2. What is the shortest possible height of Fred's plant after 5 weeks? Explain.

Shawna made a table.

Number of Tickets	Total Cost (in dollars)
2	8
3	12
4	16
5	20
t	$4 \times t$

+4
+4
+4

Shawna saw a pattern: For each ticket, the total cost increased by $4.

She wrote an algebraic expression to show the relationship between the number of tickets and the total cost.

The total cost of tickets for any number of friends can be represented by the algebraic expression $4 \times t$.

Guided Practice*

Do you know HOW?

1. Megan and Travis have the same birthday, but Travis is 6 years older. In the table, m is Megan's age and $m + 6$ is Travis's age. Complete the table.

m	3	5	
$m + 6$			14

Do you UNDERSTAND?

2. When Megan was 5 years old, how old was Travis?

3. What was Megan's age when Travis was 14?

4. **Writing to Explain** If you know Travis's age, how can you find Megan's age?

Independent Practice

In **5** through **19**, evaluate each expression for $n = 5$ and $n = 2$.

5. $\frac{40}{n}$

6. $4.5 + n$

7. $n \times 16$

8. $50 - n$

9. $12n$

10. $\frac{30}{n}$

11. $8.6 + n$

12. $9n$

13. $36 - n$

14. $8 \times n$

15. $\frac{10}{n}$

16. $3n$

17. $n + 5$

18. $7 - n$

19. $\frac{70}{n}$

In **20** through **31**, evaluate each expression for $n = 10$ and $n = 12$.

20. $\frac{n}{2}$

21. $n + 4.9$

22. $18n$

23. $44.7 - n$

24. $n - 5$

25. $n + 6.2$

26. $10n$

27. $33.6 - n$

28. $\frac{60}{n}$

29. $3n$

30. $n - 8$

31. $n + 3.17$

32. Strategy Focus Use the strategy Make a Table to solve the following problem. There are 3 classrooms in the second grade. There are 24 students in Mrs. Smithfield's room, 27 students in Mr. Rodger's room, and 21 students in Miss Jones's room. Each student gets 2 tangerines for a snack. How many tangerines does each teacher need?

33. Henry has 7 quarters, 4 dimes, 17 nickels, and 26 pennies in his bank. If he doesn't count the pennies, what is the value of his other coins?

A $2.15

B $2.60

C $3.00

D $3.26

34. A plane can travel 400 miles for each hour it flies. How long will it take you to travel approximately 1,600 miles from Oakland, California, to Beaumont, Texas?

35. Joseph is 50 inches tall. Paul is y inches taller than Joseph, and 3 inches taller than Dan. Write an expression for how much taller Paul is than Joseph.

36. Which number is less than 0.09?

A 0.9   **C** 0.11

B 0.1   **D** 0.01

37. Write an algebraic expression to represent the cost of a CD for m dollars with a $2 off coupon.

38. What is another way to write the expression $\frac{56}{n}$?

39. Writing to Explain Why can a variable be used to represent a number?

40. For a science experiment, you need to mix 4 grams of baking soda for every 25 milliliters of vinegar. How many grams of baking soda do you need to do an experiment with 75 milliliters of vinegar? How did you find the answer?

41. Think About the Process A century is a period of time that is 100 years long. Which expression can be used to find the number of years in x centuries?

A $100 + x$ **C** $\frac{100}{x}$

B $100 - x$ **D** $100x$

42. Writing to Explain The size of the hermit crab's shell depends on the size of the crab. If a 2-inch hermit crab grows 1 inch per year, use words to describe a rule that will show how long a 2-inch crab will grow in x years. Study the table below. Write an expression to find how large this crab will grow in x years.

Length	2	3	4	5	6	7	8	9	10	11	12	
Number of Years	0	1	2	3	4	5	6	7	8	9	10	x

Expressions and Tables

Use  **tools**
Spreadsheet/Data/Grapher eTool

Copy and complete the table. Then, create more tables with other operations.

Pizza slices (s)	24	48	60	84
Number of pizzas (s ÷ 12)	2	▪	5	▪

Step 1 ↗ Go to the Spreadsheet/Data/Grapher eTool. Use the arrow tool to select at least 2 rows and 5 columns. Set the number of decimal places at zero using the .00 pull-down menu. In the first row, enter the word "slices" in column A and the numbers 24, 48, 60, and 84 in the subsequent columns. Use the tab or arrow keys to move between cells. Enter the word "pizzas" in column A of row 2. Note: If you use a capital P, the page will print.

Step 2 Cell B2 is in column B, row 2. In cell B2, type = B1/12. This will divide the 24 in cell B1 by 12. In cell C2, type = C1/12. Do the same for cells D2 and E2. This will give you the numbers needed to complete the table.

				Spreadsheet	
E2	=E1/12				
	A	B	C	D	E	F
1	slices	24	48	60	84	
2	pizzas	2	4	5	7	
3						
4						

Step 3 Use + for addition, − for subtraction, and * for multiplication. Create other tables using these operations.

Practice

Copy and complete each table.

1.

n	500	692	714	905
n − 347	153	▪	▪	▪
n + 263	763	▪	▪	▪

2.

n	5	20	25	50
18 × n	90	▪	▪	▪
500 ÷ n	100	▪	▪	▪

More Patterns and Expressions

How can you write and evaluate expressions with variables?

Write an expression for finding the total cost of a service call from Matteo's Electrical Repair. Evaluate the expression for service calls that last 2 hours, 4 hours, and 5 hours.

MATTEO'S ELECTRICAL REPAIR

SERVICE CALL CHARGES

$55 Fee Plus $65 Per Hour

Another Example How can you write a word phrase as an algebraic expression?

Let *n* represent the number.

Word Phrase	Algebraic Expression
Five times a number, plus two	$5n + 2$
Two less than five times a number	$5n - 2$
Two more than five times a number	$5n + 2$
Two minus five times a number	$2 - 5n$

Sometimes a word phrase can be interpreted in different ways. The word phrase below can be interpreted in two different ways. Parentheses are used to make the algebraic expressions clear.

Word Phrase: Five times a number plus 2

Algebraic Expressions: $(5 \times n) + 2$, or $5 \times (n + 2)$

  Remember that operations inside parentheses are completed first.

Explain It

1. Why is the comma in the first word phrase above important?

2. How do the parentheses make the expressions $(5 \times n) + 2$ and $5 \times (n + 2)$ different?

The total cost is the fee plus the charge per hour times the number of hours.

Write an expression for the total cost. Let h represent the number of hours.

The expression for the total cost in dollars is $55 + 65h$.

Evaluate the expression for various numbers of hours. Substitute each value for h in the expression $55 + 65h$.

For 2 hours: $55 + (65 \times 2) = 55 + 130 = 185$

For 4 hours: $55 + (65 \times 4) = 55 + 260 = 315$

For 5 hours: $55 + (65 \times 5) = 55 + 325 = 380$

The total cost for a 2-hour service call is $185, for a 4-hour service call is $315, and for a 5-hour service call is $380.

Guided Practice*

Do you know HOW?

Write an algebraic expression for each word phrase. Let x represent the number.

1. Three times a number, plus 10

2. Four less than a number times 2

3. Eight plus a number times 5

4. Forty minus two times a number

Do you UNDERSTAND?

5. How much does Matteo Electrical Repair charge for 3 hours of work?

6. Evaluate $3n + 18$ for $n = 2$.

7. Evaluate $3n + 18$ for $n = 3$.

8. Does $3n + 18$ have the same meaning as $3 \times n + 18$? Explain.

Independent Practice

For **9** through **12**, write an algebraic expression for each phrase. Let n represent the number.

9. Nine times a number, minus six

10. Seven less than a number times three

11. Four more than a number, times twelve

12. Eight plus a number times sixteen

For **13** through **16**, evaluate the expressions for $p = 21$ and $k = 64$.

13. $3p + 52$

14. $10k - 249$

15. $432 - 2p$

16. $3p + 4k$

For **17** through **20**, evaluate the expressions for $r = 13$ and $h = 52$

17. $(8 + r) \times 3$

18. $352 - 4h$

19. $5r + 97$

20. $9r - 2h$

You walk for 30 minutes each day on a treadmill. You also do a number of weight-lifting exercises. You do each weight-lifting exercise for 5 minutes.

21. Write an algebraic expression for the number of minutes you spend exercising each day. Let *e* represent the number of weight-lifting exercises.

22. How many minutes do you exercise on a day when you do 3 weight-lifting exercises? 6 weight-lifting exercises?

Sasha works in a clothing store. He earns $20 per day, plus a $2 commission for each sale.

23. Write an algebraic expression for the amount of money Sasha earns each day. Let *s* represent the number of sales he makes.

24. How much does Sasha earn per day if he has 12 sales? 19 sales? 32 sales?

For **25** through **27**, use the table at the right.

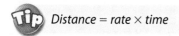 *Distance = rate × time*

25. A plane travels at a rate of 425 miles per hour. Write an expression to show the distance it travels, if *t* represents hours.

Travel Times	
From Los Angeles, CA	**Time**
To Dallas, TX	3 hrs
To Tampa, FL	5 hrs

26. How far is it from Los Angeles to Tampa?

27. How far is it from Los Angeles to Dallas?

28. A plane traveled 200 miles before arriving in Cleveland. It then departed Cleveland and traveled at a speed of 395 miles per hour. Write an algebraic expression for the total distance it will have traveled when it reaches the next stop.

29. Josephine fixes cars at the rate of $50 an hour. She also charges a cleanup fee of $30. Write an expression for her total charges.

30. A human infant can weigh about 8 pounds. A baby humpback whale can weigh over 500 times as much. About how much can a baby humpback whale weigh?

31. All DVDs at the See These video store cost $12. You have a coupon for $2 off the total purchase. Which expression represents the total cost of *d* videos?

A $2 - 12d$ **B** $12d - 2d$ **C** $12d - 2$ **D** $12 - 2d$

Find the product. Estimate to check if the answer is reasonable.

1.	692 × 414	2.	365 × 212	3.	405 × 326	4.	444 × 222

5.	732 × 551	6.	605 × 706	7.	117 × 515	8.	275 × 625

Find the quotient.

9. 720 ÷ 9   **10.** 3,200 ÷ 8   **11.** 30,000 ÷ 50   **12.** 48,000 ÷ 6

13. 54,000 ÷ 90   **14.** 21,000 ÷ 70   **15.** 30,000 ÷ 5   **16.** 2,700 ÷ 30

Error Search Find each answer that is not correct.
Write it correctly and explain the error.

17. 42,000 ÷ 70 = 6,000   **18.**   398   **19.** 180 ÷ 6 = 20   **20.**   883
                                              × 602   × 445
                                             ──────   ──────
                                             24,676   392,935

Number Sense

Estimating and Reasoning Write whether each statement is true or false. Explain your reasoning.

21. The quotient of 388 ÷ 8 is closer to 50 than 40.

22. The sum of 4.95 + 3.68 is 0.05 more than 8.68.

23. The product of 5 and 3,003 is 15 more than 15,000.

24. The product of 28 and 485 is greater than 15,000.

25. The quotient of 4,479 ÷ 61 is closer to 80 than 70.

26. The product of 7 and 409 is greater than the product of 4 and 709.

27. The quotient of 42,000 ÷ 6 is greater than 700 and less than 70,000.

Understand It!
The distributive property breaks numbers apart so they are easier to multiply.

Distributive Property

How can you use the distributive property to write expressions and solve equations?

What expressions can you write to represent the number of square units inside the rectangle?

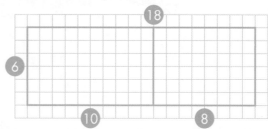

Guided Practice*

Do you know HOW?

1. Use the distributive property to complete the equation.

   $12 \times 308 = 12 \times (\boxed{} + 8)$

   $= (12 \times \boxed{}) + (\boxed{} \times 8)$

   $= \boxed{} + \boxed{}$

   $= \boxed{}$

2. Show how you can use the distributive property to find the product of 4×105.

3. Show how you can use the distributive property to find the product of 20×32.

Do you UNDERSTAND?

4. Do these expressions name the same number of square units in the shaded area?

   $4 \times (13 - 5)$ and $(4 \times 13) - (4 \times 5)$

   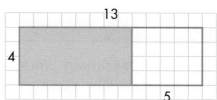

5. Write the distributive property to state that multiplication distributes over subtraction.

6. **Writing to Explain** Is $20 - (4 \times 2) = (20 - 4) \times (20 - 2)$? Explain your answer.

Independent Practice

Use the distributive property to complete each equation.

7. $509 \times 11 = (500 + 9) \times 11$

   $= (500 \times \boxed{}) + (9 \times \boxed{})$

   $= \boxed{} + 99$

   $= \boxed{}$

8. $12 \times 47 = 12 \times (50 - \boxed{})$

   $= (12 \times \boxed{}) - (12 \times 3)$

   $= 600 - \boxed{}$

   $= \boxed{}$

Animated Glossary
www.pearsonsuccessnet.com

For another example, see Set D on page 167.

Three ways to find the number of square units:

1) Think of 6 rows with 18 in each row. **6 × 18**

2) Think of 18 as 10 + 8. **6 × (10 + 8)**

3) Think of the figure in two parts.
The orange part has 6 × 10 square units.
The green part has 6 × 8 square units.

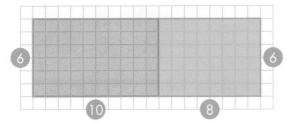

The total is the sum of the two parts.
(6 × 10) + (6 × 8)

Since the expressions name the same number of square units, you can write an equation.

6 × (10 + 8) = (6 × 10) + (6 × 8)

The <u>distributive property</u> states: <u>Multiplying a sum (or difference) by a number is the same as multiplying each number in the sum (or difference) by that number and adding (or subtracting) the products.</u>

For **9** through **16**, rewrite each expression using the distributive property. Then find each product.

9. 7 × 86

10. 7 × 420

11. 220 × 8

12. 45 × 60

13. 80 × 64

14. 16 × 102

15. 101 × 23

16. 390 × 40

Problem Solving

For **17** through **19**, use the table at the right and the following information.

Wendy brought the lemonade and iced tea for the school picnic. Since more people like lemonade than iced tea, she brought 2 gallons of lemonade for every 10 people. She also brought 5 gallons of iced tea for people who don't like lemonade.

Number of People	Gallons of Lemonade	Total Gallons
10	2	
20		
30		
40		

17. Write an algebraic expression to show the total number of gallons Wendy would need to bring. Let *n* represent the number of groups of ten people.

18. How many gallons does Wendy need for 10 people?

19. Complete the rest of the table.

20. Use the distributive property to find another expression for 3(2x + 7).

A 6x + 7

B 3(14x)

C (9x) × 3

D 6x + 21

21. Estimation The highest point in Colorado is Mount Elbert, at 14,433 feet. About how many miles is that?

 1 mile = 5,280 feet

Order of Operations

How can you evaluate a numerical expression with more than one operation?

Two students evaluated the same expression but got different answers.

To avoid getting more than one answer, use the order of operations. Rebecca used the correct order.

Find the value of $12 \div 4 + (9 - 2) \times (3 + 5)$.

Rebecca's Way	Juan's Way
$36 + 9 \div 3 \times 5$	$36 + 9 \div 3 \times 5$
$36 + 3 \times 5$	$45 \div 3 \times 5$
$36 + 15$	15×5
51	75

Another Example **How can you evaluate an algebraic expression with more than one operation?**

You can use order of operations when evaluating algebraic expressions.

What is the value of $4v + 2w - 3$, if $v = 5$ and $w = 3$?

Step 1 Replace all of the variables with given values. Remember that $4v$ means $4 \times v$.

Step 2 Using the order of operations, multiply or divide in order from left to right.

Step 3 Add or subtract in order from left to right.

The value of the expression is 23.

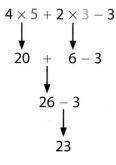

Explain It

1. How could the value of a numerical expression such as $4 \times 5 + 2 \times 3 - 3$ be changed?

Guided Practice*

Do you know HOW?

For **1** through **4**, name the operation you should do first.

1. $6 + 27 \div 3$

2. $5 \times 2 + 12 \div 6$

3. $17 - (4 + 3)$

4. $(14 - 7) + (3 + 5)$

Do you UNDERSTAND?

5. In the first example, why was Juan's answer incorrect?

6. Insert parentheses to make the following statement true.
$3 + 5 \times 2 - 10 = 6$

Step 1

In using order of operations, do the operations inside parentheses first.

$$12 \div 4 + (9 - 2) \times (3 + 5)$$
$$\downarrow \quad \downarrow \qquad \downarrow \qquad \downarrow$$
$$12 \div 4 + \quad 7 \quad \times \quad 8$$

Remember to rewrite the operations not yet performed.

Step 2

Then, multiply and divide in order from left to right.

$$12 \div 4 + 7 \times 8$$
$$\downarrow \qquad \downarrow$$
$$3 \quad + \quad 56$$

Step 3

Finally, add and subtract in order from left to right.

$$3 + 56$$
$$\downarrow$$
$$59$$

Independent Practice

For **7** through **18**, find the value of each expression using order of operations.

7. $3 + 7 \times 6 \div 3 - 4$

8. $(29 - 18) + 14 \div 2 + 6$

9. $64 \div 8 \times 2$

10. $(19 - 5) \times 3 + 4$

11. $3(6 + 2) - 12 \times 2$

12. $36 - 5(16 - 11)$

13. $8 \times (3 + 2) - 6$

14. $3 \div (9 - 6) + 4 \times 2$

15. $(3 + 4) \times (3 + 5)$

16. $25 + 18 \div 6 - 1$

17. $4 \times (3 - 2) + 18$

18. $8 \times 6 - 4 \times 3$

For **19** through **24**, insert parentheses to make each statement true.

19. $30 - 4 \times 2 + 5 = 2$

20. $17 - 8 - 5 = 14$

21. $10 \div 2 - 3 + 1 = 3$

22. $30 - 4 \times 2 + 5 = 57$

23. $17 - 8 - 5 = 4$

24. $10 \div 2 - 3 + 1 = 1$

25. Writing to Explain Would the value of the expression in Exercise 21 be different if no parentheses were used?

For **26** through **34**, evaluate each expression for $x = 16$ and $y = 4$.

26. $3x - 3y$

27. $x \div (2y - 4)$

28. $5y + x \div 8$

29. $4x - 2y$

30. $y \div (x \div y)$

31. $3y + 2x - 7$

32. $5x - 4y$

33. $x \div y$

34. $2x + 4y - 10$

Animated Glossary
www.pearsonsuccessnet.com

DIGITAL

*For another example, see Set E on page 167.

35. Draw the next figure in the following pattern.

For **36** through **38**, use the table at the right.

36. The girls' gym teacher needs to purchase 15 softballs, 5 packages of tennis balls, and 2 soccer balls. She plans to collect $1 from each of her 15 students to help pay for the balls. Write and evaluate an expression to show how much more the teacher will have to pay.

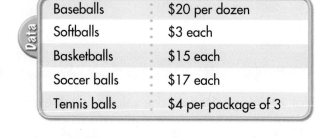

Data		
Baseballs		$20 per dozen
Softballs		$3 each
Basketballs		$15 each
Soccer balls		$17 each
Tennis balls		$4 per package of 3

37. The boys' gym teacher needs to buy 2 dozen baseballs, 4 basketballs, and 24 tennis balls. Write and evaluate an expression to show how much the balls will cost.

38. **Writing to Explain** Did you use parentheses in the expression you wrote for Exercise 36? Why or why not?

39. A small cruise ship has 220 passengers. At the Port of San Juan, 2 groups of 12 passengers go ashore to shop and 5 groups of 6 passengers go sightseeing. Evaluate $220 - (2 \times 12) - (5 \times 6)$ to find the number of passengers that are left on the ship.

40. **Geometry** The state of Montana is about 630 miles long and about 280 miles wide. The area of Montana could fit 3 states the size of Pennsylvania. What is the approximate area of Montana?

 Area = length × width.

41. At a ski lift, 41 people are waiting to board cars that hold 6 people each. How many cars will be completely filled? How many people are left to board the last car?

  A 6; 6   **C** 5; 6

  B 6; 5   **D** 5; 5

43. **Number Sense** True or false? Explain.
$4(3 + 5) - 10 = 4 \times 3 + 5 - 10$

42. Mark bought 3 boxes of pencils that contained 20 pencils each and 4 boxes of pens that contained 10 pens each. Which expression represents the total number of pencils and pens Mark bought?

  A $(3 \times 10) + (4 \times 20)$

  B $(3 \times 4) + (10 \times 20)$

  C $(3 \times 20) + (4 \times 10)$

  D $(3 + 20) + (4 + 10)$

Mixed Problem Solving

A state song is an official symbol of the state it represents. Each of the 50 states, with the exception of New Jersey, has at least one state song. Some of the states chose songs that are famous on their own, while other states chose a song that is known only as a state song. Here are a few examples of some of the state songs:

Data

United States State Songs			
State	**Song Title**	**Year Written**	**Year Adopted**
California	"I Love You, California"	1913	1988
Kentucky	"My Old Kentucky Home"	1853	1928
Oklahoma	"Oklahoma"	1943	1953
Maryland	"Maryland, My Maryland"	1861	1939

For **1** through **5**, use the table above.

1. How many years passed between the time Kentucky's state song was written before it was adopted?

2. About how many decades passed between the writing of *"I Love You, California"* and its adoption?

3. How many years earlier was *"Maryland, My Maryland"* written than *"Oklahoma"*?

4. Put the years each song was adopted in order from least to greatest.

5. **Writing to Explain** A lustrum is a period of 5 years. Richard said that 15 lustrums occurred between California's state song being written and then adopted by the state. Is he correct? Explain.

6. **Strategy Focus** Solve using the strategy Draw a Picture and Write an Equation.

   Tricia ran 5 times as far as Ali. Ali ran 375 meters. How far did Tricia run?

Problem Solving

Act It Out and Use Reasoning

A children's zoo displays birds in 3 different cages. The zoo has three kinds of birds. There are 36 birds in all. How many of each type of bird are in the zoo?

Use objects to show the birds and then use reasoning to solve the problem.

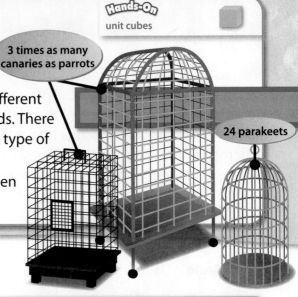

Hands-On
unit cubes

3 times as many canaries as parrots

24 parakeets

Guided Practice*

Do you know HOW?

Solve. You can use cubes to act out the problem.

1. The Rodriquez family is donating 25 baseball caps to a charity auction. There are 11 blue caps. There are 2 more white caps than green caps. How many of each color caps are they donating?

Do you UNDERSTAND?

2. If you use 25 cubes to represent all the caps and 11 are used to show the blue caps, how many cubes are left for the white and the green caps?

3. **Write a Problem** Write a real-world problem that can be solved by acting it out and using reasoning.

Independent Practice

Solve. Use cubes to act out the problems.

4. Mr. Niles has a box of accessories for clarinets. He has a total of 42 objects. He has 12 mouthpieces. He has four times as many reeds as neck straps. How many of each object does he have?

5. Sylvia has a jewelry collection of bracelets, necklaces, and earrings. She has 16 bracelets. The number of earrings is 2 times the number of necklaces. She has 43 pieces of jewelry in all. How many of each piece of jewelry does she have?

Stuck? Try this....

- What do I know?
- What am I asked to find?
- What diagram can I use to help understand the problem?
- Can I use addition, subtraction, multiplication, or division?
- Is all of my work correct?
- Did I answer the right question?
- Is my answer reasonable?

Use objects and show what you know.
Let 36 cubes represent all the birds.
Use reasoning to make conclusions.

24 parakeets

12 canaries and parrots

There are 24 parakeets and 36 birds in all. That leaves a total of 12 canaries and parrots.

Use 12 cubes. There are 3 times as many canaries as parrots.

There are 24 parakeets, 9 canaries, and 3 parrots.
$24 + 9 + 3 = 36$, so the answer is correct.

For **6** through **8**, use and complete the table at the right.

6. Brady joined the band. In Group 1, there are a total of 44 students. There are 8 students who play the oboe. There are $\frac{1}{2}$ as many students playing the clarinet as the flute. How many students from Group 1 play each instrument?

7. There are 41 students in Group 2. Twice as many students play the trumpet as play the trombone, but 8 students play the saxophone. How many students in Group 2 play each instrument?

Instrument	Number of Students
Group 1	44
Oboe	8
Clarinet	
Flute	
Group 2	41
Saxophone	8
Trumpet	
Trombone	

8. Later, 7 students joined Group 2 and 1 student left to join Group 1. Some students decided to play a different instrument. Now 20 students play trombone and 7 more students play trumpet as play saxophone. How many students play each instrument?

9. Jane worked 1.5 hours on Monday, 3 hours on Tuesday, and 4.5 hours on Wednesday. If the pattern continues, how many hours will she work on Friday?

10. Reggie earned $360 in the summer. If he earned $40 per week, how many weeks did he work?

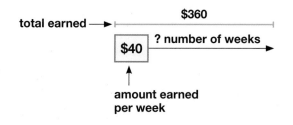

total earned → $360
$40 | ? number of weeks
amount earned per week

11. The Garden Theater presented a play. A total of 179 people attended in 3 days. The first day, 58 people attended. On the second day, 47 people attended. How many attended on the third day?

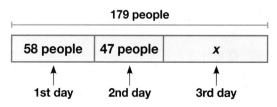

179 people

| 58 people | 47 people | x |

1st day   2nd day   3rd day

1. Which expression can be used to represent the phrase "three times the amount of money"? (6-1)

   A $3 + m$

   B $3 - m$

   C $3 \times m$

   D $3 \div m$

2. If Lisa travels an average of 65 miles per hour for 8 hours, she will travel 8×65 miles. Which of the following is equal to 8×65? (6-4)

   A $(8 + 60) \times (8 + 5)$

   B $(8 + 60) - (8 + 5)$

   C $(8 \times 60) + (8 \times 5)$

   D $(8 \times 60) - (8 \times 5)$

3. Ryan had 18 more shots on goal during the soccer season than Peyton, who had 36. Evaluate the expression $x + 18$ for $x = 36$. (6-2)

   A 2

   B 18

   C 52

   D 54

4. Jerry has a coupon for \$3 off the price of an item. If p represents the original price of a shirt, which expression tells Jerry's cost, before tax, when he uses the coupon? (6-1)

   A $p \div 3$

   B $3 - p$

   C $p - 3$

   D $p + 3$

5. The expression $f - 3$ represents the number of years Mark has taken piano lessons when Fatima has taken lessons for f years. How many years of lessons will Mark have when Fatima has 9 years? (6-2)

   A 27

   B 12

   C 6

   D 3

6. What is the first step in evaluating the expression shown below? (6-5)

   $8 - 7 + 12 \div (3 + 1)$

   A Add 3 and 1.

   B Divide 12 by 3.

   C Add 7 and 12.

   D Subtract 7 from 8.

7. What value of n makes the equation true? (6-4)

   $15 \times 110 = (15 \times 100) + (15 \times n)$

   A 10

   B 15

   C 90

   D 110

8. The cost for n students to attend a workshop is $7n + 12$ dollars. What is the cost for 6 students to attend? (6-3)

   A \$25

   B \$54

   C \$126

   D \$156

9. Tennessee, New Mexico, and Michigan have a total of 27 representatives in the U.S. House of Representatives. Michigan has 15 representatives and Tennessee has 3 times as many as New Mexico. How many representatives does the state of Tennessee have? (6-6)

A 12

B 9

C 6

D 3

10. The expression $n \div 6$ can represent which of the following phrases? (6-1)

A n students divided into groups of 6

B 6 times n students

C 6 students divided into n groups

D 6 less than n students

11. What is the value of the expression $6 + (13 - 1) \div 4 + 2$? (6-5)

A 20

B 11

C 8

D 3

12. Which expression can be used to represent the phrase "3 more than 7 times the number of pages, p"? (6-3)

A $7p + 3$

B $p + 3 \times 7$

C $3p + 7$

D $7p - 3$

13. The expression $8 - 2x$ can be used to represent which phrase? (6-3)

A Eight less than two times a number

B Two less than eight times a number

C Eight more than two times a number

D Eight minus two times a number

14. What is the value of $7 + 3m - 2$ when $m = 4$? (6-5)

A 11

B 17

C 20

D 38

15. Which of the following expressions has a value equal to 3? (6-5)

A $8 + (4 \div 2) - 1 \times 3$

B $8 + 4 \div (2 - 1) \times 3$

C $(8 + 4 \div 2) - 1 \times 3$

D $(8 + 4) \div 2 - 1 \times 3$

16. The table shows the cost to board Lucy's dog at a kennel. Which expression shows the cost to board the dog for d days? (6-2)

Number of Days	Total Cost
3	$36
4	$48
5	$60

A $d + 36$

B $d + 12$

C $36d$

D $12d$

Set A, pages 146–147

Translate a word phrase into an algebraic expression.

Five more cards than Steve owns

Step 1

Decide what the variable will represent.

Let s = cards Steve owns

Step 2

What operation should be used? The word *more* is a clue.

Addition

Step 3

Write an algebraic expression.

$s + 5$

Remember to look for words that give you clues as to what operation to use.

Write an algebraic expression for each.

1. A puzzle costs p less than a magazine. The magazine costs $1.99. How much is the puzzle?

2. The evergreen is twice as tall as a hosta. The hosta is h inches tall. How tall is the evergreen?

Set B, pages 148–150

When you evaluate an algebraic expression, you replace the variable with a given number value.

Evaluating a Division Expression

Evaluate $\frac{t}{6}$ for $t = 18$.

Replace t with 18 in the expression.

$\frac{18}{6}$

Divide.

$\frac{18}{6} = 3$

Remember to replace the variable with the given values and perform the operation.

Evaluate each expression for $d = 2$ and $d = 3$.

1. $\frac{30}{d}$

2. $3.6 + d$

3. $d \times 20$

4. $57 - d$

5. $11d$

Set C, pages 152–154

Write an algebraic expression for the following word phrase. Let n represent the number.

Word Phrase
five less than three times a number

Algebraic Expression
$3n - 5$

Remember that placing a number next to a variable means to multiply.

Write an algebraic expression for each. Let n represent the number.

1. Four times a number, plus 8

2. Six less than three times a number

3. Ten more than four times a number

4. Fifty minus the quotient of five and a number.

Set D, pages 156–157

The Distributive Property states that multiplying a sum by a number is the same as multiplying each number in the sum by the number, and then adding the products.

Use the Distributive Property to find 5×23.

Think of 23 as $20 + 3$.

$$
\begin{aligned}
5 \times 23 &= 5 \times (20 + 3) \\
&= (5 \times 20) + (5 \times 3) \\
&= 100 + 15 \\
&= 115
\end{aligned}
$$

Remember that you write one of the numbers as a sum, multiply each of those numbers by the other number, and then add the products.

Use the Distributive Property to find each product.

1. 7×45 **2.** 29×9

3. 72×6 **4.** 3×46

5. 5×78 **6.** 29×5

Set E, pages 158–160

When evaluating an expression, you need to use the order of operations. Otherwise, more than one answer is possible.

Evaluate $(8 + 2) \times (3 + 7) + 50$.

Step 1

Perform the operations inside the parentheses.

$(8 + 2) \times (3 + 7) + 50$
$= 10 \times 10 + 50$

Step 2

Multiply and divide in order from left to right.

$10 \times 10 + 50$
$= 100 + 50$

Step 3

Add and subtract in order from left to right.

$100 + 50$
$= 150$

Remember that there is an order of operations that you must use when you evaluate an expression with more than one operation. Otherwise, more than one answer is sometimes possible.

Find the value of each expression using the order of operations.

1. $4 + 8 \times 6 \div 2 + 3$

2. $(18 - 3) \div 5 + 4$

3. $8 \times 5 + 7 \times 3 - (10 - 5)$

4. $10 \times 10 + 5 \times 2 - 3 \times 5$

Set F, pages 162–163

Use objects to show what you know and then use reasoning to solve the problem.

A pet shop has a total of 19 dogs, cats, and ferrets. There are 4 ferrets, and twice as many cats as dogs. How many of each kind of pet are in the shop?

Use 19 cubes and let 4 of them represent the ferrets. That leaves 15 cubes to represent the cats and dogs. There must be 10 cats and 5 dogs.

Remember that objects can help you reason through a problem.

1. Kerry has 12 paperweights in her collection. She has twice as many glass paperweights as metal, and 3 are wood. How many of each type of paperweight does she have?

Topic 7

Multiplying and Dividing Decimals

1 How many hours does it take to drive from Cheyenne, Wyoming, to the Devil's Tower National Monument in Wyoming? You will find out in Lesson 7-7.

2 How many times as fast does a quarter horse run than a garden snail moves per hour? You will find out in Lesson 7-8.

Review What You Know!

The fastest growing flowering plant is the *Hesperoyucca Whipplei*. How many centimeters did one of these plants grow in 7 days? You will find out in Lesson 7-2.

Vocabulary

Choose the best term from the box.

- equivalent fractions • mixed numbers
- factors • product

1. In the equation 5 × 5 = 25, the number 25 is the __?__ and the digits 5 and 5 are __?__.

2. __?__ have a whole number and a fraction.

3. Fractions that name the same part of a whole are __?__.

Number Theory

Write whether each number is prime or composite.

4. 32   **5.** 7   **6.** 45

List all the factors for each number.

7. 10   **8.** 18   **9.** 50

Fractions

Write each quotient as a fraction.

10. 5 ÷ 18   **11.** 5 ÷ 6   **12.** 9 ÷ 12

Using Number Lines

Writing to Explain Write an answer for the question.

340   350

13. How can you use this number line to round 347 to the nearest ten?

Multiplying Decimals by 10, 100, or 1,000

$0.45 per lb

What is the rule for multiplying decimals by 10, 100, or 1,000?

A baker buys some of the ingredients he uses in bulk. He needs to purchase 10 lb of pecans and 100 lb of flour. How much will the baker spend for each amount?

Choose an Operation Multiply to join equal groups.

$2.89 per lb

Guided Practice*

Do you know HOW?

In **1** through **8**, use mental math to find each product.

1. 0.009 × 10

2. 0.45 × 100

3. 3.1 × 1,000

4. 7.4 × 10

5. 0.062 × 100

6. 1.24 × 1,000

Do you UNDERSTAND?

7. To find the product of 5.8 × 1,000, move the decimal point ▢ places to the right and annex ▢ zeros.

8. How much will the baker spend if he buys 10 lb of flour? 1,000 lb of flour?

Independent Practice

In **9** through **36**, use mental math to find each product.

9. 4.23 × 1

10. 4.23 × 10

11. 4.23 × 100

12. 4.23 × 1,000

13. 0.0867 × 10

14. 0.0867 × 100

15. 0.0867 × 1

16. 0.0867 × 1,000

17. 63.7 × 10

18. 56.37 × 1,000

19. 0.365 × 100

20. 5.02 × 1,000

21. 94.6 × 1,000

22. 0.9463 × 100

23. 0.678 × 10

24. 681.7 × 100

25. 4.3 × 10

26. 0.32 × 100

27. 5.1 × 100

28. 1.02 × 1,000

29. 0.004 × 1,000

30. 0.001 × 10

31. 6.02 × 100

32. 5.07 × 10

33. 0.063 × 100

34. 7.25 × 1,000

35. 19.212 × 100

36. 0.62 × 10

For another example, see Set A on page 194.

Use the patterns in this table to find 0.45×100 and 2.89×10.

Multiply by	Move the decimal point to the right
1	0 places
10	1 place
100	2 places
1,000	3 places

When you need to move the decimal point beyond the number of digits in the number you are multiplying, *annex* (place) 1 or more zeros.

Cost of flour:
$0.45 \times 100 = 0.45 = 45$

Cost of pecans:
$2.89 \times 10 = 2.89 = 28.9$

The flour will cost $45.00, and the pecans will cost $28.90.

If 100 lb or 1,000 lb of pecans needed to be purchased, the pattern can be continued to find the cost.

$2.89 \times 100 = 2.89 = 289$
$2.89 \times 1,000 = 2.890 = 2,890$

Problem Solving

The table at the right shows the coins saved by Tina and her sister for one year.

37. **Number Sense** Find the total value of each type of coin the girls have saved.

38. **Number Sense** Find the total value for the coins saved by the sisters.

39. The principal of Mountain Middle School has a big glass jar of marbles. The empty jar weighs 40.5 ounces, and each of the 1,000 marbles weighs 1.25 ounces. Find the total weight in ounces of the marbles.

Type of Coin	Number Saved
	1,000
	100
	1,000
	10

40. **Writing to Explain** Marcia and David each multiplied 5.6×10 and 0.721×100. Marcia got 0.56 and 7.21 for her products. David got 56 and 72.1 for his products. Which student multiplied correctly? How do you know?

41. The Parents' Club is trying to decide on favors for International Night. They will need 100 items, and they have a budget of $250. They can choose from 100 baseball hats at $2.45 each, 100 sports bottles at $2.50 each, or 100 flags at $2.75 each. Which item(s) can they afford to buy?

42. **Algebra** In which of the following equations does $n = 1,000$?

A $n \times 0.426 = 42.6$ C $n \times 100 = 630$

B $7.078 \times n = 7,078$ D $5.9 \times n = 0.59$

Multiplying a Decimal by a Whole Number

Understand It!
The steps for multiplying whole numbers by decimals are almost identical to the steps for multiplying whole numbers by whole numbers.

How do you multiply a whole number by a decimal?

The price of admission to a minor league baseball game increased by 0.17 times the amount of last year's admission. If last year's admission was $26, how much is the increase?

Choose an Operation Multiply to find 26 × 0.17.

last year's price

$26.00

BASEBALL
Lions Vs. Rockets
7:00 PM

this year's price

$30.42

Lions Vs. Rangers
7:30 PM

THIS TICKET GOOD FOR ONE ADMISSION

Guided Practice*

Do you know HOW?

Find each product.

1. 9.8
   × 2

2. 0.67
   × 8

3. 0.457 × 3

4. 34 × 5.3

5. 45 × 0.003

6. 34.6 × 21

Do you UNDERSTAND?

7. **Writing to Explain** What is the difference between multiplying a whole number by a decimal and multiplying two whole numbers?

8. Use the information from the example above. How much will admission cost to a minor league game this year?

Independent Practice

Find each product.

9.   34.6
    × 9

10.   56.3
     × 22

11.   405
     × 0.47

12.   9.32
     × 16

13.   12.9
     × 8

14.   27.4
     × 7

15.   336
     × 0.4

16.   88
     × 1.8

17. 84 × 0.005

18. 34,000 × 2.65

19. 64.2 × 20

20. 38.6 × 19

21. 40 × 0.22

22. 57 × 2.3

23. 5.8 × 11

24. 56 × 0.4

25. 0.1 × 22

26. 170 × 0.003

27. 4.02 × 9

28. 514 × 0.4

29. 0.3 × 99

30. 52 × 3.6

31. 105 × 0.4

32. 92 × 0.9

For another example, see Set B on page 194.

Multiply as you would with whole numbers.

```
    1 4
  0. 1 7
 ×   2 6
 ─────────
   1 0 2
   3 4 0
 ─────────
   4 4 2
```

Count the decimal places in both factors, and then place the decimal point in the product the same number of places from the right.

```
    1 4
  0. 1 7    2 decimal places
 ×   2 6    0 decimal places
 ─────────
   1 0 2
   3 4 0
 ─────────
   4. 4 2   2 decimal places
```

The increase from last year's admission is $4.42.

Problem Solving

For **33**, refer to the prices at the right.

33. Mia is shopping and finds a sale. She has $25 in her wallet and a coupon worth $4 off the cost of a dress.

  a How much money will the dress cost if she uses the coupon?

  b Find the total cost of 3 T-shirts.

  c How much change will Mia get back from $25 after she buys the 3 T-shirts?

$7.55

$15.50

34. To determine the tip for a restaurant server, many people multiply the amount of the check by 0.15. Find the amount of the tip on a check of $20.

35. Gary had 10 rosebushes to plant. On Friday, he planted 4 of the bushes. In simplest form, what fraction of the bushes did he plant?

36. The fastest growing flowering plant is the *Hesperoyucca Whipplei*. It was recorded that one of these plants grew at a rate of 25.4 cm per day. How many centimeters did this plant grow in 7 days?

37. The airline that Vince is using has a baggage weight limit of 41 pounds. He has two green bags, each weighing 18.4 pounds, and one blue bag weighing 3.7 pounds. What is the combined weight of his baggage?

  A 22.1 lb   **C** 40.5 lb

  B 38.7 lb   **D** 41 lb

38. Raul, Tim, Yuko, and Joe have to line up according to height from tallest to shortest. Raul is 145.52 cm tall; Tim is 151 cm tall; Yuko is 159.5 cm tall; and Joe is 145.25 cm tall. Who is first in line?

Understand It!
Rounding and compatible numbers can be used to estimate the product of a decimal and a whole number.

Estimating the Product of a Decimal and a Whole Number

What are some ways to estimate products with decimals?

A planner for a wedding needs to buy 16 pounds of sliced cheddar cheese. About how much will the cheese cost?

Estimate 2.15×16.

$2.15 per pound

Another Example How can you estimate products of decimals that are less than 1?

You already know how to estimate products of whole numbers using rounding and compatible numbers. You can use the same methods to estimate products with decimals.

Manuel found the total distance he walks to and from school is equal to 0.75 mile. If Manuel walks to and from school 184 days in one year, about how many total miles will he walk?

Using rounding

184×0.75

$\downarrow \qquad \downarrow$

$200 \times 0.8 = 160.0$

 Tip Be sure to place the decimal point correctly.

Using compatible numbers

184×0.75

$\downarrow \qquad \downarrow$

$180 \times 0.8 = 144.0$

Compatible numbers are close to the actual numbers and are easy to multiply.

Since the compatible numbers are closer to the actual numbers than the rounded numbers, that estimate is closer to the actual product.

Manuel will walk about 144 miles to and from school in one year.

Guided Practice*

Do you know HOW?

In **1** through **6**, estimate each product using rounding or compatible numbers.

1. 0.87×412

2. 104×0.33

3. 9.02×80

4. 0.54×24

5. 33.05×200

6. 0.79×51

Do you UNDERSTAND?

7. Writing to Explain How can estimating be helpful before finding an actual product?

8. About how much money would have to be spent on 18 pounds of cheese if the price is $3.95 per pound?

For another example, see Set C on page 195.

One Way	Another Way
Round each number to the greatest place that has a non-zero digit.	Use compatible numbers that you can multiply with mentally.

One Way

Round each number to the greatest place that has a non-zero digit.

$2.15 × 16
↓   ↓
$2 × 20

$2 × 20 = $40

The cheese will cost about $40.

Another Way

Use compatible numbers that you can multiply with mentally.

$2.15 × 16
↓   ↓
$2 × 15

$2 × 15 = $30

The cheese will cost about $30.

Independent Practice

Estimate each product.

9. $0.12 × 5$

10. $45.3 × 4$

11. $99.2 × 82$

12. $37 × 0.93$

13. $0.667 × 4$

14. $0.6 × 184$

15. $25 × 0.37$

16. $0.904 × 75$

Problem Solving

For **17** and **18**, use the chart.

17. Number Sense About how much money does Stan need to buy 5 T-shirts and 10 buttons?

18. Number Sense Pat has $55. Does she have enough money to buy 4 T-shirts?

Data	Souvenir	Cost
	Button	$1.95
	T-Shirt	$12.50

19. **About the Process** You want to estimate $0.67 × 85$. Which way will give you an estimate that is closest to the actual product?

  A Round 0.67 to 1.0 and 85 to 90, multiply.

  B Round 0.67 to 0.7 and 85 to 90, multiply.

  C Round 0.67 to 70 and 85 to 80, multiply.

  D Round 0.67 to 1.0 and 85 to 80, multiply.

20. Dentalia shells were used by some Native American tribes to make jewelry. Each dentalia shell is 1.25 inches long. If a necklace had been made with 18 dentalia shells, about how long was this necklace? Explain your estimate.

21. Reasoning Will the actual product of $7.69 × 5$ be greater than or less than its estimate of $8 × 5$? Why?

22. Algebra If $n × 4.16$ is about 200, what is a reasonable estimate for n?

Understand It!
The steps for multiplying decimals by decimals are almost identical to the steps for multiplying whole numbers by whole numbers.

Multiplying Two Decimals

How can you multiply two decimals?

Nancy walked 1.7 miles in 1 hour. If she walks at the same rate, how far will she walk in 1.5 hours?

Choose an Operation
Multiply to find 1.7×1.5.

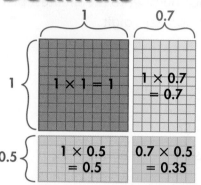

Guided Practice*

Do you know HOW?

For **1** through **6**, estimate first. Then find each product. Check that your answer is reasonable.

1. $\begin{array}{r} 9.3 \\ \times\ 4.1 \\ \hline \end{array}$

2. $\begin{array}{r} 3.02 \\ \times\ 0.6 \\ \hline \end{array}$

3. 0.7×1.9

4. 12.6×0.2

5. 8.3×10.7

6. 2.04×1.8

Do you UNDERSTAND?

7. **Writing to Explain** How is multiplying two decimals different from multiplying one decimal by a whole number?

8. Using the example above, how many miles will Nancy walk in 2.8 hours? Show an estimate first.

Independent Practice

For **9** through **28**, estimate first. Then find each product. Check that your answer is reasonable.

9. $\begin{array}{r} 5.2 \\ \times\ 4.6 \\ \hline \end{array}$

10. $\begin{array}{r} 0.05 \\ \times\ 4.5 \\ \hline \end{array}$

11. $\begin{array}{r} 19.1 \\ \times\ 8.5 \\ \hline \end{array}$

12. $\begin{array}{r} 8.6 \\ \times\ 0.08 \\ \hline \end{array}$

13. 0.6×0.49

14. 32.3×0.7

15. 3.42×4.7

16. 8.11×0.05

17. 3.5×0.4

18. 28.6×0.17

19. 0.21×1.5

20. 1.11×6.1

21. 6.8×7.2

22. 8.3×6.4

23. 9.1×11.6

24. 0.04×15.6

25. 18.1×3.7

26. 0.06×15

27. 0.28×3.7

28. 3.14×6.2

For another example, see Set D on page 195.

Estimate 1.7 × 1.5

2 × 2 = 4

Step 2

Multiply as you would with whole numbers.

$$\begin{array}{r} 1.7 \\ \times\ 1.5 \\ \hline 85 \\ 170 \\ \hline 255 \end{array}$$

Step 3

Count decimal places in *both* factors.

Write the decimal point in the product.

$$\begin{array}{r} 1.7 \leftarrow\ \text{1 decimal place} \\ \times\ 1.5 \leftarrow\ \text{1 decimal place} \\ \hline 85 \\ 170 \\ \hline 2.55 \leftarrow\ \text{2 places} \end{array}$$

Step 4

Check your answer.

Since 2.55 is close to your estimate of 4, the answer is reasonable.

In 1.5 hours, Nancy will walk 2.55 miles.

Problem Solving

29. The fifth-grade planning committee needs to buy items for sandwiches for its annual lunch. Fill in the chart and determine the amount of money they'll need to buy the items for sandwiches.

Item	Amount	Price	Total
	15.5 pounds	$3.50 per pound	
	10.5 pounds	$2.90 per pound	
	12 packages	$2.50 per package	

30. Geometry Karly's bedroom measures 13.2 feet long by 10.3 feet wide. Use the formula Area = length × width to determine the number of square feet for the floor of Karly's bedroom.

31. A bag of grass seed weighs 5.8 pounds. How many pounds would 2.5 bags weigh?

A 14.5

B 13.8

C 8.3

D 3.3

32. Joy drinks 4 bottles of water per day. Each bottle contains 16.5 fluid ounces. She wants to find the total number of fluid ounces she drinks per day. How many decimal places will be in the product?

A One   **C** Three

B Two   **D** Four

33. Mary Ann ordered 3 pens and a box of paper on the Internet. Each pen cost $1.65 and the paper cost $3.95 per box. How much did she spend?

34. An astronaut's Apollo space suit weighs 29.8 pounds on the moon. It weighs approximately 6.02 times as much on Earth. About how much does an Apollo space suit weigh on Earth?

35. Writing to Explain How does estimation help you place the decimal point in a product correctly?

Dividing Decimals by 10, 100, or 1,000

Understand It!
Patterns can be used when mentally dividing decimals by 10, 100, or 1,000.

How can you divide decimals by 10, 100, and 1,000?

Shondra wants to cut a cloth into 10 strips. All the strips should be exactly the same size. How wide will each strip be?

Choose an Operation Divide to find equal parts of a whole.

89.5 cm

Guided Practice*

Do you know HOW?

In **1** through **6**, use mental math to find each quotient.

1. 370.2 ÷ 10

2. 126.4 ÷ 100

3. 684.5 ÷ 1,000

4. 72.5 ÷ 10

5. 28.14 ÷ 100

6. 42.5 ÷ 1,000

Do you UNDERSTAND?

7. Look at the table above. When dividing by 1,000, why was it necessary to place a zero in the tenths place?

8. If Shondra wanted to cut the cloth into 100 strips, how wide would each strip be?

Independent Practice

In **9** through **31**, find each quotient. Use mental math.

9. 23.75 ÷ 1
23.75 ÷ 10
23.75 ÷ 100
23.75 ÷ 1,000

10. 509.3 ÷ 1,000
509.3 ÷ 100
509.3 ÷ 10
509.3 ÷ 1

11. 98.2 ÷ 100
98.2 ÷ 1
98.2 ÷ 1,000
98.2 ÷ 10

12. 13.65 ÷ 10

13. 75.3 ÷ 100

14. 890.1 ÷ 1,000

15. 5.67 ÷ 100

16. 8.74 ÷ 100

17. 32.40 ÷ 1,000

18. 12.33 ÷ 10

19. 0.5 ÷ 10

20. 4.5 ÷ 10

21. 9.78 ÷ 100

22. 7,446.5 ÷ 1,000

23. 234.5 ÷ 10

24. 0.27 ÷ 100

25. 121.6 ÷ 1,000

26. 8.373 ÷ 10

27. 6.9 ÷ 1,000

28. 8.25 ÷ 10

29. 31.8 ÷ 100

30. 0.36 ÷ 1,000

31. 9.47 ÷ 100

*For another example, see Set E on page 196.

Find 89.5 ÷ 10.

The quotient of a number divided by 10, 100, or 1,000 is less than the number.

Moving the decimal point in a number to the left decreases the number's value.

Since place-value is based on 10, dividing by 10, 100, or 1,000 gives the same result as moving the decimal point 1, 2, or 3 places.

Notice the patterns in the table.

Divide by	Examples	Move decimal point to the left
1	12.5 ÷ 1 = 12.5	0 places
10	12.5 ÷ 10 = 1.25	1 place
100	12.5 ÷ 100 = 0.125	2 places
1,000	12.5 ÷ 1,000 = 0.0125	3 places

So, 89.5 ÷ 10 = 8.9.5 = 8.95

Each cloth strip will be 8.95 centimeters wide.

Problem Solving

For **32** through **34**, use the chart.

Pacific Middle School posted the winning times at the swim meet.

50-yard freestyle	22.17 seconds
100-yard backstroke	53.83 seconds
100-yard butterfly	58.49 seconds

32. What was the time per yard of the swimmer who swam the butterfly?

33. If the 50-yard freestyle swimmer could swim the 100-yard freestyle in exactly double his 50-yard time, what would his time per yard be?

34. What was the time per yard of the swimmer who swam the backstroke?

35. Rodella has a jar full of dimes. The total amount of money in her jar is $45.60. How many dimes does she have?

36. Writing to Explain How is dividing 360 by 10 similar to dividing 3,600 by 100? Explain.

37. Helen is saving to buy a Koala Club child's membership to the San Diego Zoo as a present for her brother. The membership fee is $21.50. Helen has 10 weeks in which to save for it. How much money should she save each week?

38. Algebra In which of the following equations does $n = 100$?

A $1946.8 ÷ n = 1.9468$

B $61.5 ÷ n = 0.615$

C $11.73 ÷ n = 0.01173$

D $4.12 ÷ n = 0.412$

39. The dimensions of a room are shown on a blueprint with the measures of 12 inches long and 10 inches wide. The actual room is 12 times as big. How many feet long and wide is the actual room?

Understand It!
The process used to divide whole numbers by whole numbers can be used to divide money amounts and decimals.

Dividing a Decimal by a Whole Number

How do you divide a decimal by a whole number?

The three children in the Diego family are equally sharing the cost of an anniversary gift for their parents. How much will each child pay?

Choose an Operation Divide to find equal shares of the whole price.

$42.45

Other Examples

When do you write more zeros to the right of the decimal point in the dividend?

You know how to divide decimals by 10, 100, or 1,000. Now you will learn to divide decimals by other whole numbers.

Ann hiked for 6 hours on the river trail. She hiked a total of 19.5 miles. How many miles did she hike each hour?

Find 19.5 ÷ 6.

```
      3.25
   6)19.50
     18
     ──
      15
      12
     ──
       30
       30
      ──
        0
```

You can annex a 0 at the end of 19.5 in order to continue dividing.

Ann hiked 3.25 miles each hour.

Ann bought hiking and camping gear for a total of $239.49. She paid for the gear in 5 equal installments. How much was each installment?

Find 239.49 ÷ 5.

```
   $  47.898
  5)$239.490
    20
    ──
     39
     35
    ──
      44
      40
     ──
       49
       45
      ──
        40
        40
       ──
         0
```

Sometimes when you divide with money, there is a remainder after you divide the hundredths.

Annex a zero after the hundredths place of the dividend and continue dividing to determine the thousandths place of the quotient.

Then round the quotient to the nearest hundredth. So, $239.49 ÷ 5 is about $47.90.

Ann paid in installments of $47.90.

Explain It

1. Why must a zero be annexed to the right of the decimal point in the dividend?

2. Why is a quotient that represents money rounded to the nearest hundredth?

Find 42.45 ÷ 3.

Write the decimal point in the quotient directly above the decimal point in the dividend.

$$3 \overline{)\ \$42.45}$$

Divide the same way you would divide whole numbers.

$$
\begin{array}{r}
\$14.15 \\
3\overline{)\$42.45} \\
-3 \\
\hline
12 \\
12 \\
\hline
4 \\
3 \\
\hline
15 \\
15 \\
\hline
0
\end{array}
$$

Use multiplication to check.

$$
\begin{array}{r}
\$14.15 \\
\times\ \ \ \ 3 \\
\hline
\$42.45
\end{array}
$$

Each child will pay $14.15.

Guided Practice*

Do you know HOW?

In **1** through **10**, find each quotient.

1. $4\overline{)\$6.48}$ **2.** $3\overline{)\$7.32}$

3. $5\overline{)4.50}$ **4.** $50\overline{)5.5}$

5. $1.90 \div 19$ **6.** $13.2 \div 11$

7. $5.6 \div 8$ **8.** $12.5 \div 25$

9. $22.1 \div 17$ **10.** $26.52 \div 13$

Do you UNDERSTAND?

11. For $3.6 \div 60$, why do you need to write a zero to the right of the decimal point in the quotient?

12. How is dividing decimals unlike dividing whole numbers?

13. Reasonableness All 5 members of the Diego family went to dinner and shared the bill, which was $78.49, equally. Was each person's share less than $16.50?

Independent Practice

In **14** through **28**, find each quotient.

14. $2\overline{)\$56.84}$ **15.** $6\overline{)\$120.72}$ **16.** $7\overline{)\$35.14}$

17. $9\overline{)36.27}$ **18.** $16\overline{)39.68}$ **19.** $18\overline{)324.18}$

20. $64.33 \div 5$ **21.** $406.2 \div 30$ **22.** $489.6 \div 32$

23. $297.81 \div 9$ **24.** $175.75 \div 25$ **25.** $35.902 \div 58$

26. $432.88 \div 8$ **27.** $28.4 \div 40$ **28.** $1.5 \div 20$

*For another example, see Set F on page 196.

29. If one dozen of the same size avocados weighs 7.2 lb, what does one avocado weigh?

30. Number Sense Without dividing, how do you know that the quotient of $84 \div 17$ will NOT be 14?

31. While traveling in the car, Juanita counted 27 out-of-state license plates, Carol counted 19, and Ramon counted 22. How many more out-of-state license plates did Juanita count than Carol?

32. Cora is saving for a vacation. The total cost of the vacation is $1,800.36, and she has a year to save the money. How much should she save per month so she can meet her goal?

33. Joe took out a $7,200 loan to buy a used car. He will make monthly payments for 4 years. How much will Joe pay each month on his loan?

34. Algebra A college baseball stadium holds 6,000 people. At a recent game only 5,145 seats were filled. Tickets to the game cost $12 each. Write and solve an equation to find how many seats were empty.

35. Think About the Process Tina bought 3 plants at $2.50 each and 3 clay pots at $4.25 each. Which expression shows how to find how much Tina spent on the plants and pots?

A ($2.50 + $4.25) + 3

B (3 + $4.25) × (3 + $2.50)

C (3 × $4.25) + (3 × $2.50)

D 3 × ($4.25 × $2.50)

36. Think About the Process Jill is 4 years older than Keiko. Robert is 2 years older than Keiko. If you know that Keiko is 12 years old, which number sentence can you use to find the sum, s, of the three ages?

A $s = 2 + 4 + 12$

B $s = (12 - 4) + (12 - 2) + 12$

C $s = (12 + 4) + (12 - 2) + 12$

D $s = (12 + 4) + (12 + 2) + 12$

37. Four college friends decided to share an apartment and some expenses equally.

a They plan to paint the apartment before they move in. The cost of paint and supplies is $76.80. What is each person's share?

b They plan to budget $225 for food each month. What is each person's share?

c The telephone service will cost $36.95 per month. What is each person's share?

38. Alyson works as a waitress. Last week she earned a total of $128.60 in tips in 5 days. How much did she earn in tips each day, if she earned the same amount each day?

39. Writing to Explain Why don't the expressions $4 \times 6 + 9$ and $4 \times (6 + 9)$ have the same value?

Find the quotient. Estimate to check if the answer is reasonable.

1. 96 ÷ 4

2. 77 ÷ 8

3. 9)475

4. 805 ÷ 2

5. 3)1,804

6. 6)87

7. 95 ÷ 32

8. 17)35

9. 299 ÷ 74

10. 74)614

11. 608 ÷ 67

12. 23)281

13. 24)984

14. 847 ÷ 84

15. 56)702

16. 600 ÷ 51

17. 728 ÷ 51

Find the difference. Estimate to check if the answer is reasonable.

18. 9,000
    − 486

19. 8,030
    − 6,090

20.   436
    − 85

21. 6,821
    − 5,932

22. 8,005
    − 3,213

Error Search Find each quotient that is not correct.
Write it correctly and explain the error.

23. 47 ÷ 3 = 15 R2

24. 6)606 = 11

25. 629 ÷ 2 = 314 R1

26. 89 ÷ 31 = 2 R27

27. 51)154 = 3

28. 879 ÷ 27 = 31 R42

Number Sense

Estimating and Reasoning Write whether each statement is
true or false. Explain your reasoning.

29. The quotient of 7,528 ÷ 9 is greater than 800.

30. The product of 19 and 487 is closer to 10,000 than 8,000.

31. The sum of 73,342 and 27,120 is less than 100,000.

32. The quotient of 759 ÷ 25 has a remainder that is less than 25.

33. The difference of 57.6 − 12.3 is 0.3 greater than 45.6.

34. The sum of 4.143 and 5.709 is between 9 and 11.

Estimation: Decimals Divided by Whole Numbers

How can you estimate quotients with decimals?

Cheryl is saving $23 every week to buy a digital camera. About how many weeks will it take her to save enough money to buy the digital camera?

Choose an Operation Divide to find equal parts of the price. Estimate $269.95 ÷ $23.

$269.95

Guided Practice*

Do you know HOW?

In **1** through **8**, estimate each quotient.

1. 63.5 ÷ 8

2. 72.8 ÷ 10

3. 19.45 ÷ 4

4. 34.25 ÷ 7

5. 105.8 ÷ 11

6. 245.74 ÷ 83

7. 290.6 ÷ 31

8. 564.9 ÷ 90

Do you UNDERSTAND?

9. When would you estimate a quotient instead of finding a more accurate answer?

10. In the example above, if Cheryl could save $32 every week, about how many weeks would it take her to save enough money to buy the camera?

Independent Practice

In **11** through **13**, choose the best estimate for each quotient.

11. 47.52 ÷ 83

   A 60   **C** 0.6

   B 6   **D** 0.06

12. 18.9 ÷ 21

   A 1   **C** 0.01

   B 0.1   **D** 0.001

13. 36.6 ÷ 40

   A 0.009   **C** 0.9

   B 0.09   **D** 9

In **14** through **28**, estimate each quotient.

14. 270.9 ÷ 3

15. 87.3 ÷ 11

16. 7.75 ÷ 4

17. 556.3 ÷ 61

18. 31.77 ÷ 8

19. 56.4 ÷ 19

20. 976.4 ÷ 47

21. 869.77 ÷ 27

22. 195.6 ÷ 12

23. 91.26 ÷ 2

24. 44.8 ÷ 5

25. 88.34 ÷ 4

26. $15.75 ÷ 9

27. $274.89 ÷ 26

28. $346.95 ÷ 52

For another example, see Set G on page 196.

Round each number to the greatest place that has a nonzero digit.

$$\$269.95 \div 23$$

$$300 \quad \div 20$$

$$300 \div 20 = 15$$

Cheryl will take about 15 weeks to save enough money to buy the digital camera.

Use compatible numbers that you can divide mentally.

$$\$269.95 \div 23$$

$$275 \quad \div 25 = 11$$

Cheryl will take about 11 weeks to save enough money to buy the digital camera.

Problem Solving

29. There are 40 mg of caffeine in a 3-cup teapot of green tea. About how many milligrams of caffeine would be in one cup?

30. Jeremy paid $575 for a plane ticket, including tax of $21 and an airport fee of $12. What was the cost of the ticket before tax and the airport fee?

31. A three-pound package of ground beef costs $11.78. About how much does one pound cost?

32. Kira cycles about 10 miles every day. About how many miles does she cycle in 4 weeks?

33. Writing to Explain Rosa babysits from 10 A.M. until 3 P.M. five days per week during the summer. She watches four children, makes lunch, and drives them to swim practice. Her pay is $380.25 per week. How would you estimate the amount she is paid per hour?

34. Algebra Tickets to a movie cost $9 for an adult. Student tickets cost $5. Which expression shows the cost of tickets for a group, g, of students?

A $5 + g$ **C** $5 \times g$

B $9 + g$ **D** $9 \times g$

35. In science class, a student weighed three samples and found the weights to be 0.098 gram, 0.58 gram, and 0.005 gram. Which sample weighed the most?

36. One route from Cheyenne, Wyoming, to Devil's Tower National Monument is approximately 305.4 miles. If a car is driven between 55 and 60 miles per hour, about how many hours will the trip take?

37. A 300-foot fence has a flag on each post. There are posts at each end and every 6 feet along the fence. How many flags are on the fence?

38. Reasoning Find the pattern in the numbers below, and then write the next three numbers.

$$32, 16, 8, 4, 2, 1, 0.5, \ldots$$

Dividing a Decimal by a Decimal

How can you divide a decimal by a decimal?

Ms. Hendricks bought 0.84 pound of almonds. What is the price per pound of almonds?

Choose an Operation Divide the amount paid by the number of pounds bought to find the price per pound.

ALMONDS
NET WEIGHT 0.84 POUNDS

$3.99

Guided Practice*

Do you know HOW?

In **1** through **6**, find each quotient. Write more zeros in the dividends when needed.

1. 4.2 ÷ 0.7

2. 4.52 ÷ 0.2

3. 0.081 ÷ 0.9

4. 23.28 ÷ 9.7

5. 37.2 ÷ 2.4

6. 25.2 ÷ 0.5

Do you UNDERSTAND?

7. For the example above, how would you check the answer?

8. Mary paid $3.60 for pecans that cost $3.75 per pound. How many pounds of pecans did she buy?

Independent Practice

Leveled Practice In **9** through **12**, find each quotient.

9.
$$0.6\overline{)43.2}$$
  7 .
 42
 ‾‾
  1 2
     ▢▢
     ‾‾
      0

10.
$$0.7\overline{)1.61}$$
  2. ▢
 14
 ‾‾
   ▢▢
   ▢▢
   ‾‾
    0

11.
$$3.9\overline{)7.02}$$
  1. ▢
 3 9
 ‾‾
   ▢▢▢
   ▢▢▢
   ‾‾‾
     0

12.
$$1.5\overline{)4.8}$$
  3. ▢
 ▢▢
 ‾‾
  ▢▢
  ▢▢
  ‾‾
   0

In **13** through **24**, find each quotient.

13. $0.08\overline{)0.104}$

14. $1.3\overline{)6.89}$

15. $0.9\overline{)5.49}$

16. $5.8\overline{)3.48}$

17. 69.09 ÷ 0.7

18. 0.410 ÷ 0.2

19. 91.53 ÷ 0.3

20. 0.804 ÷ 0.4

21. 9.483 ÷ 8.7

22. 0.427 ÷ 6.1

23. 28.14 ÷ 1.2

24. 36.8 ÷ 0.25

*For another example, see Set H on page 197.

Step 1

Find 3.99 ÷ 0.84.

Multiply the divisor by a power of 10 to make it a whole number.

0.84 × 100 = 84

$$0.84.\overline{)3.99}$$

Step 2

Multiply the dividend by the same power of 10.

3.99 × 100 = 399

$$0.84.\overline{)3.99.}$$

Step 3

Place the decimal point in the quotient. Divide as you would with whole numbers.

```
        4.75
  84)399.00
    -336
     630
     588
     420
     420
       0
```

Tip Since the quotient represents money, annex two more zeros in the dividend to show cents.

The almonds cost $4.75 per pound.

Problem Solving

For **25** through **27**, use the chart at the right.

25. How many pounds of apples could you buy for $8.00?

26. How much would a half pound of pears cost?

27. The price of a pound of cherries is how many times the price of a pound of bananas?

The chart below shows a few recent prices at The Farm Stand.

Data

Fruit	Price per Pound
Pears	$1.38
Apples	$1.25
Cherries	$1.17
Bananas	$0.39

28. An overseas phone call costs $57.66 for 31 minutes. How much does the call cost per minute?

29. Jean paid $21.42 for 6.8 gallons of gasoline that she put in the tank of her car. What was the price per gallon?

30. Tom arranged tiles in the pattern below.

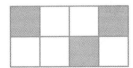

In which pair do both fractions describe the floor tiles that are shaded?

A $\frac{1}{2}, \frac{4}{8}$

B $\frac{3}{8}, \frac{6}{8}$

C $\frac{3}{8}, \frac{6}{16}$

D $\frac{3}{8}, \frac{3}{16}$

31. A quarter horse can run 53.16 miles per hour, and a garden snail can move 0.02 of a mile per hour. How many times as fast does the quarter horse run than the garden snail moves?

32. Writing to Explain How could you use estimation to check the reasonableness of the quotient for 3.99 ÷ 0.84?

Problem Solving

Multiple-Step Problems

John is building 3 boxes. He can buy scrap sheets of plywood at the Use-It-Again store. He needs 6 pieces for each box. How many scrap sheets of plywood does he need?

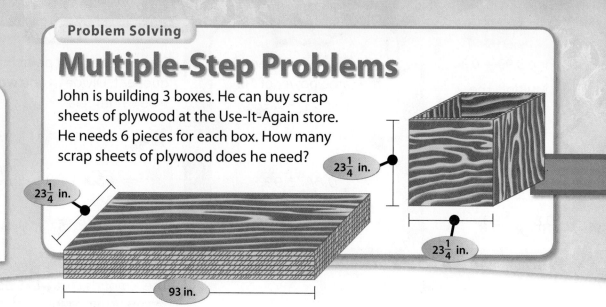

$23\frac{1}{4}$ in.

$23\frac{1}{4}$ in.

$23\frac{1}{4}$ in.

93 in.

Another Example

The Marcos family went on a 2-week trip to San Diego. They drove 575 miles to get there and 627 miles to return home. In San Diego, they drove 121 miles while sightseeing. Their car can travel an average of 31.5 miles on 1 gallon of gas. If the car's gas tank can hold 14 gallons of gas, how many tanks of gas did they use on vacation?

What is one hidden question?

How many miles did the Marcos family drive during their trip?

575 miles + 627 miles + 121 miles = 1,323 miles

The Marcos family drove 1,323 miles on their trip.

What is another hidden question?

How many gallons of gas did they use on their trip?

1,323 miles ÷ 31.5 miles per gallon = 42 gallons

The Marcos family used 42 gallons of gas on their trip.

Divide the number of gallons used by the number of gallons in a full tank of gas.

42 gallons used ÷ 14 gallons in a full tank = 3 full tanks

The Marcos family used 3 tanks of gas on their trip to San Diego.

Explain It

1. Why do you need to find the hidden questions in order to solve the problem?

What do I know?

Six pieces of plywood are needed for each of 3 boxes.

Boxes are $23\frac{1}{4}$ inch cubes.

Each sheet of plywood is $23\frac{1}{4}$ inches wide and 93 inches long

What am I asked to find?

The number of sheets of plywood John needs to buy

Find the hidden question or questions.

1. How many pieces of plywood are needed for three boxes?

$$3 \times 6 = 18$$
boxes · pieces in each · pieces in all

2. How many pieces of plywood can be cut from 1 scrap sheet of plywood?

$$93 \div 23.25 = 4$$

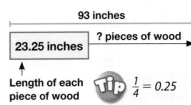

93 inches

23.25 inches · ? pieces of wood

Length of each piece of wood · **Tip** $\frac{1}{4} = 0.25$

3. How many sheets of plywood are needed for three boxes?

$$18 \div 4 = 4 \text{ R2}$$ John needs 5 sheets of plywood.

Guided Practice*

Do you know HOW?

Solve the problem.

1. Tom bought 8 chicken breasts and 5 steaks. Each chicken breast weighed 0.35 pound and each steak weighed 1.25 pound. How many pounds of meat did Tom buy?

Do you UNDERSTAND?

2. What are the hidden questions and answers in Problem 1?

3. **Write a Problem** Write a real-world multiple-step problem that can be solved using multiplication and division.

Independent Practice

In **4** through **7**, write the hidden question or questions. Then solve.

4. Alyssa has a CD that holds 700 megabytes of information. She has saved 53 pictures, each using 2.24 megabytes, to the CD. How much space is left on the CD?

5. Lori bought some plums and 4 peaches. The peaches cost $1.88 in all and the plums cost $0.33 each. She paid $3.86 in all, not including tax. How many plums did she buy?

Stuck? Try this....

- What do I know?
- What am I asked to find?
- What diagram can I use to help understand the problem?
- Can I use addition, subtraction, multiplication, or division?
- Is all of my work correct?
- Did I answer the right question?
- Is my answer reasonable?

For **6**, use the chart at the right.

6. The school cafeteria manager needs to know how many food trays are needed during a week. All of the students eat lunch each school day, and half of all the students eat breakfast. How many trays will be needed in one week?

	Grade	Number of Students	Grade	Number of Students
Data	K	95	3	107
	1	112	4	100
	2	104	5	114

7. Juan used first-class mail to send two baseballs to his grandson. Each baseball weighed 5 ounces. The postage was $0.39 for the first ounce and $0.24 for each additional ounce. How much was the postage?

8. The Meadows Farm has 160 acres. Three times as many acres are used to plant crops as are used for pasture. Draw a picture and write an equation to find how many acres are used for pasture.

9. A youth group charged $6 per car at their car wash to raise money. They raised $858. Of that amount, $175 was given as donations and the rest of the money came from washing cars. Stella estimated that they washed more than 100 cars. Is her estimate reasonable? Explain your reasoning.

10. A hardware store has 5 employees. Each employee works the same number of hours every week, and each one earns $10.50 per hour. Last week they worked a total of 167.5 hours. Draw a picture and write an equation to find how many hours each employee worked.

Think About the Process

11. Matt is saving to buy a skateboard and a helmet. The skateboard costs $57 and the helmet costs $45. Matt has saved $19 so far. Which hidden question needs to be answered before you can find how much more he needs to save?

   A Is the skateboard on sale?

   B How much more does the skateboard cost than the helmet?

   C What is the price of the skateboard minus the price of the helmet?

   D What is the total price of the helmet and the skateboard?

12. Two restaurant waiters share $\frac{1}{4}$ of their tips with the host. On Saturday, one waiter earned $122 in tips, and the other waiter earned $136 in tips. Which expression shows how to find the solution to the hidden question?

   A $122 + 136$

   B $\frac{1}{4} \times 136$

   C $\frac{1}{4} \times 122$

   D $136 - 122$

Find the quotient. Estimate to check if the answer is reasonable.

1. 14.5 ÷ 2.5 **2.** 2.28 ÷ 0.6 **3.** 69.02 ÷ 0.7 **4.** 88.5 ÷ 0.03

5. 0.08 ÷ 0.025 **6.** 3.2 ÷ 0.004 **7.** 15.5 ÷ 6.2 **8.** 2.35 ÷ 4.7

Find the product. Estimate to check if the answer is reasonable.

9.   0.07
   × 0.09

10.   5.6
   × 0.08

11.   6.98
   ×   3.8

12.   1.3
   × 0.04

13.   0.67
   ×   3.6

14.   6.8
   × 9.4

15.   8.88
   × 0.08

16.   0.03
   ×   0.3

Evaluate each expression. Use order of operations.

17. $2 \times 7 + 25 \div 5$ **18.** $(17 - 8) \times 5 + 1$ **19.** $47 - (3 + 6) \times 5 + 1$

Error Search Find each answer that is not correct.
Write it correctly and explain the error.

20. 2.748 ÷ 0.6 = 0.0458 **21.** 7.86 ÷ 6 = 1.31 **22.**   26.82
   ×   3
   ─────
   80.45

23.   5.87
   ×   4.9
   ─────
   287.63

Number Sense

Estimating and Reasoning Write whether each statement is
true or false. Explain your reasoning.

24. The quotient of 4.35 ÷ 6 is closer to 0.7 than 0.8.

25. The expression $8e + 6$ equals 30 when $e = 3$.

26. The product of 5.7 and 8.63 is less than 54.

27. The quotient of 3,467 ÷ 5 is closer to 700 than the quotient of 5,598 ÷ 8.

28. The sum of 99,999 and 3,879 is 1 more than 103,879.

29. The product of 6 and 808 is greater than the product of 8 and 606.

1. Mr. Dodd filled the gas tank on his lawn mower with 3.8 gallons of gas. If he mowed his yard 10 times on the same tank of gas, how much gas did he use each time the lawn was mowed? (7-5)

   A 0.038 gallons

   B 0.38 gallons

   C 38 gallons

   D 380 gallons

2. Lucia scored an 8.65 on her first gymnastics event at a meet. If she scores the same score on each of four events, what will be her total score at the meet? (7-2)

   A 32.48

   B 34.6

   C 34.8

   D 346

3. The table shows the amount of different types of produce Mrs. Cuzalina bought, and the total price she paid for each. What is the price per pound she paid for the apples? (7-8)

Produce	Pounds	Total Price
Apples	3.4	$2.89
Bananas	2.6	$1.27
Grapes	3.7	$2.85

   A $0.09

   B $0.80

   C $0.84

   D $0.85

4. The chef at a restaurant bought 37 pounds of salad for $46.25. How much did she pay for 1 pound of salad? (7-6)

   A $0.125

   B $1.25

   C $1.30

   D $12.50

5. A farmer plants 0.4 of a field with wheat. The field is 3.45 acres in size. How many acres are planted with wheat? (7-4)

   A 0.126

   B 0.138

   C 1.26

   D 1.38

6. If the product of 1,251 and 30 is 37,530, what is the product of 12.51 and 30? (7-2)

   A 3.753

   B 37.53

   C 375.3

   D 3,753

7. Which of the following is the best estimate of 78.4 ÷ 18? (7-7)

   A 740

   B 50

   C 5

   D 4

8.

Notebook Prices

Quantity	Cost
1	$1.29
2	$2.32
5	$4.80
10	$9.00

How much would 10 students save if they bought 10 notebooks as a group rather than individually? (7-9)

A $3.90

B $4.20

C $5.51

D $7.71

9. Which of the following provides the best estimate of the product of 204 and 0.46? (7-3)

A $200 \times 0.5 = 100$

B $250 \times 0.5 = 125$

C $200 \times 1 = 200$

D $250 \times 1 = 250$

10. What is 3.57×4.6? (7-4)

A 3.570

B 13.882

C 16.422

D 164.22

11. What is 0.42×100? (7-1)

A 0.042

B 4.2

C 42

D 420

12. Which step should be taken to find the quotient of $56.8 \div 100$? (7-5)

A Move the decimal point in 56.8 two places to the left.

B Move the decimal point in 56.8 one place to the left.

C Move the decimal point in 56.8 two places to the right.

D Move the decimal point in 56.8 one place to the right.

13. A developer owns 24 acres of land. If he plans to use 1.2 acres of the land for an entrance into a housing development and divide the remaining land into 0.6 acre lots, how many lots will he have? (7-9)

A 42

B 40

C 38

D 2

14. What is $43.68 \div 5.2$? (7-8)

A 8.4

B 8.04

C 7.99

D 0.84

15. Mrs. Frohock bought a watermelon that weighed 10.25 pounds. If she cut it into 5 pieces of equal weight, how many pounds did each piece weigh? (7-6)

A 0.25

B 2.05

C 2.15

D 2.5

Set A, pages 170–171

Use the patterns in this table to find
$8.56 × 10 and 0.36 × 100.

Multiply by	Move the decimal point to the right
1	0 places
10	1 place
100	2 places
1,000	3 places

$8.56 × 10 = $85.6 = $85.60

0.36 × 100 = 36.0 = 36

Remember when you need to move the decimal point beyond the number of digits in the number you are multiplying, annex 1 or more zeros.

Use mental math to solve each problem.

1. 10 × 4.5

2. 100 × 4.5

3. 1,000 × 4.5

4. 10 × 0.89

5. 1,000 × 0.98

6. 10 × 0.0089

7. 3.8 × 1,000

8. 78.6 × 100

Set B, pages 172–173

Find 12 × 0.15.

Step 1

Multiply as you would with whole numbers.

```
    12
×  0.15
─────
    60
+ 120
─────
   180
```

Step 2

Count the decimal places in both factors. Then, place the decimal point in the product the same number of places from the right.

```
    12
×  0.15   2 places
─────
    60
+ 120
─────
  1.80
```

So, 12 × 0.15 = 1.8.

Remember to count the decimal places in both factors before you place the decimal point in the product.

Find each product.

1. 50 × 3.67

2. 5.86 × 5

3. 14 × 9.67

4. 8 × 56.7

5. 11 × 0.006

6. 2.03 × 6

7. 25 × 1.63

8. 5.62 × 75

Set C, pages 174–175

Estimate $4.78 × 18.

One Way

Round each number to the greatest place that has a non-zero digit.

$$\$4.78 \times 18$$
$$\downarrow \qquad \downarrow$$
$$\$5 \quad \times 20$$

$5 × 20 = $100

Estimate 27 × 3.95

Another Way

Use compatible numbers. The numbers 30 and 3 are easy to multiply.

$30 × 3 = 90$

Remember that compatible numbers can also be used to estimate products.

Estimate each product.

1. 24 × 3.67

2. 5.86 × 52

3. 14 × 9.67

4. 8 × 56.7

5. 19 × 9.06

6. 2.03 × 6

7. 3.78 × 9

8. 7.98 × 6

Set D, pages 176–177

Find 3.6 × $2.15.

Estimate: 4 × $2 = $8

Step 1

Multiply as you would with whole numbers.

$$
\begin{array}{r}
\$2.15 \\
\times \quad 3.6 \\
\hline
1290 \\
+ \ 6450 \\
\hline
7740
\end{array}
$$

Step 2

Count the decimal places in both factors. Place the decimal point in the product the same number of places from the right.

$$
\begin{array}{rl}
\$2.15 & 2\ places \\
\times \quad 3.6 & 1\ place \\
\hline
1290 & \\
+ \ 6450 & \\
\hline
\$7.740 &
\end{array}
$$

So, 3.6 × $2.15 = $7.74.

Remember to count the decimal places in both factors before placing the decimal point in the product.

Find each product.

1. 2.4 × 3.67

2. 5.86 × 5.2

3. 8.3 × 10.7

4. 3.42 × 4.7

5. 1.4 × 9.67

6. 11.2 × 9.7

7. 23.3 × 60.5

8. 9.03 × 67.98

Set E, pages 178–179

Find 34.05 ÷ 100.

Dividing by 10 means moving the decimal point one place to the left.

Dividing by 100 means moving the decimal point two places to the left.

Dividing by 1,000 means moving the decimal point three places to the left.

34.05 ÷ 100 = 0.3405 = 0.3405

Remember that when dividing decimals by 10, 100, or 1,000, you may need to use one or more zeros as placeholders: 24.3 ÷ 1,000 = 0.**0**243.

Use mental math to find each quotient.

1. 34.6 ÷ 10   **2.** 64.83 ÷ 100

3. 148.3 ÷ 1,000   **4.** 2.99 ÷ 100

5. 7.07 ÷ 10   **6.** 59.13 ÷ 1,000

7. 8.94 ÷ 100   **8.** 6.34 ÷ 10

Set F, pages 180–182

Find 3.60 ÷ 15.

$$\begin{array}{r} 0.24 \\ 15\overline{)3.60} \\ \underline{3\ 0} \\ 60 \\ \underline{60} \\ 0 \end{array}$$

Place the decimal point in the quotient directly above the decimal point in the dividend. Then divide.

So, 3.60 ÷ 15 = 0.24.

Multiply to check.

0.24 × 15 = 3.60

Remember to write a zero placeholder in the quotient when you cannot divide a place in the dividend.

Find each quotient.

1. 7$\overline{)12.6}$ **2.** 31$\overline{)17.05}$

3. 8$\overline{)51.2}$ **4.** 12$\overline{)60.12}$

5. 199.68 ÷ 64   **6.** 152.5 ÷ 5

7. 47.61 ÷ 23   **8 .** 51.6 ÷ 43

Set G, pages 184–185

Estimate: 25.1 ÷ 11.

Use compatible numbers.

25.1 ÷ 11
↓   ↓
24 ÷ 12 = 2

So, 25.1 ÷ 11 is about 2.

Remember that compatible numbers are numbers that are easy to compute in your head. Rounding can also be used to estimate quotients.

Estimate each quotient.

1. 26.2 ÷ 5   **2.** 31.9 ÷ 3

3. 49.6 ÷ 6   **4.** 163.5 ÷ 80

5. 4,352.9 ÷ 74   **6.** 538.6 ÷ 64

7. 251.6 ÷ 38   **8.** 819.7 ÷ 21

Set H, pages 186–187

Find 57.9 ÷ 0.6.

Since 0.6 has one decimal place, move the decimal point one place to the right in both numbers. Then divide.

```
        96.5
0.6)57.90
     54
     ──
     39
     36
     ──
      30
      30
      ──
       0
```

Annex more zeros in the dividend if needed.

57.9 ÷ 0.6 = 96.5

Remember to place the decimal point in the quotient above the decimal point in the dividend before dividing.

1. 79.36 ÷ 3.2   **2.** 73.44 ÷ 3.6

3. 78.6 ÷ 0.03   **4.** 9.315 ÷ 0.81

5. 0.903 ÷ 2.1   **6.** 4.56 ÷ 0.5

7. 16.4 ÷ 0.8   **8.** 136.5 ÷ 4.2

9. 22.22 ÷ 2.2   **10.** 54.78 ÷ 6.6

11. 71.04 ÷ 7.4   **12.** 40.02 ÷ 8.7

13. 9.6 ÷ 0.03   **14.** 74.48 ÷ 9.8

Set I, pages 188–190

A football coach spent a total of $890.40, including $50.40 tax, for 35 shirts for the team. Each shirt was the same price. What was the price of one shirt?

What is the hidden question or questions?

How much did all of the shirts cost without tax?

$890.40	
$50.40	?

$890.40 − $50.40 = $840.00

What is the price of one shirt?

$840

? ← 35 shirts

price of one shirt

$840 ÷ 35 = $24

The price of one shirt was $24.00.

Remember to answer the hidden question or questions first to solve the problem.

Write and answer the hidden question or questions. Then solve.

1. Royce bought a book for $12.49 and 2 DVDs. Both DVDs were the same price. The tax on all the items is $1.76. He paid a total of $46.23. What was the price of each DVD?

2. Kim bought sandwiches for the football team. Each sandwich cost $3.49. She paid $142.39, including $2.79 tax. How many sandwiches did she buy?

Shapes

1 What geometric ideas are illustrated by the Alamo? You will find out in Lesson 8-1.

2 The Louvre Pyramid serves as the main entrance to the Louvre Museum in Paris, France. How can you classify one of the triangular faces of the pyramid by the lengths of its sides and the measures of its angles? You will find out in Lesson 8-4.

Review What You Know!

Choose the best term from the box.

- algebraic expression
- equation
- variable

1. $3x = 15$ is a(n) __?__.

2. $3x$ is a(n) __?__.

3. In $3x$, x is the __?__.

Rules and Tables

Write a rule for each table using words, and then with a variable.

4.

in	out
36	6
42	7
48	8

5.

in	out
5	12
10	17
15	22

Fractions

Write the fraction. Simplify if necessary.

6. If 2 out of 4 bananas are green, what fraction names the green bananas?

7. If $\frac{5}{6}$ of a loaf of bread is eaten, what part of the loaf is NOT eaten?

Multiplying Factors

Writing to Explain Write an answer for the question.

8. Clint bought 3 T-shirts at $9 each and 2 pairs of shorts at $12 each. Explain how to find the total Clint spent.

3 What shape do these wasps create when they build their hive? You will find out in Lesson 8-3.

4 What kinds of angles are formed by the handles of this basket? You will find out in Lesson 8-2.

Basic Geometric Ideas

How can you describe locations and parts of space?

Points, lines, and planes are basic geometric concepts. Engineers and architects use these concepts in designing streets, buildings, and structures.

Other Examples

	What You Draw	**What You Say**	**What You Write**
A line segment is part of a line and has 2 endpoints.	R •————• S	Line segment *RS*	$\overline{RS}$
A ray is part of a line. It has only one endpoint and extends forever in one direction.	J •———→ K	Ray *JK*	$\overrightarrow{JK}$
Parallel lines never cross and stay the same distance apart.	A, D / V, W	Line *AD* is parallel to line *VW*.	$\overleftrightarrow{AD} \parallel \overleftrightarrow{VW}$
Intersecting lines pass through the same point.	P, C / Q, E	Line *PE* intersects line *QC*.	$\overleftrightarrow{PE}$ intersects $\overleftrightarrow{QC}$
Perpendicular lines are intersecting lines that form square corners.	F, R, H, S	Line *RS* is perpendicular to line *FH*.	$\overleftrightarrow{RS} \perp \overleftrightarrow{FH}$

This symbol means square corner or right angle.

Explain It

1. Are $\overrightarrow{XB}$ and $\overleftrightarrow{YU}$ parallel or intersecting? Explain how you know.

2. Are all perpendicular lines intersecting?
   Are all intersecting lines perpendicular?

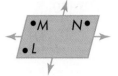
Guided Practice*

Do you know HOW?

In **1** through **4**, use the diagram at the right.

1. Name 4 points.

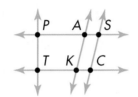

2. Name 3 line segments.

3. Name 2 intersecting lines

4. Name 2 parallel lines.

Do you UNDERSTAND?

In **5** through **7** use the diagram at the left.

5. If $\overleftrightarrow{PS}$ and $\overleftrightarrow{TC}$ are parallel and $\overleftrightarrow{PS}$ is perpendicular to $\overleftrightarrow{PT}$, is $\overleftrightarrow{TC}$ also perpendicular to $\overleftrightarrow{PT}$?

6. Do $\overleftrightarrow{PS}$ and $\overleftrightarrow{SP}$ name the same line?

7. Do $\overrightarrow{PS}$ and $\overrightarrow{SP}$ name the same ray? Explain.

Independent Practice

In **8** through **13**, use the diagram at the right.

8. Name two parallel lines.

9. Name two perpendicular lines.

10. Name two intersecting but not perpendicular lines.

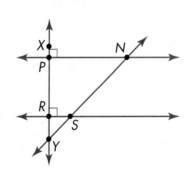

11. Name three line segments.

12. Name a plane.

13. Name three rays.

*For another example, see Set A on page 216.

14. Use the diagram to name each of the following.

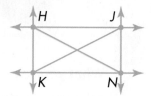

a 2 sets of parallel lines

b 2 sets of perpendicular lines

15. **Think About the Process** Minh bought 2 pounds of apples for $0.50 a pound, and a gallon of milk for $2. Which operations would you use to find Minh's total cost for the apples and milk?

A Multiply and divide

B Add and add

C Multiply and subtract

D Multiply and add

16. **Reasoning** Points *D*, *E*, and *F* lie in plane *DEF*. How many lines in plane *DEF* can you draw that contain both points *D* and *E*?

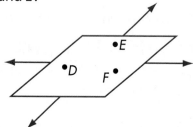

17. **Think About the Process** Joshua bought a basketball for $22 and 3 T-shirts for $9 each. Which expression shows how to find how much Joshua spent?

A $22 + (3 × $9)

B 3 × ($22 + $9)

C (3 × $22) + (3 × $9)

D (3 + $22) × (3 + $9)

18. Rover weighs 5 pounds more than the neighbor's dog. Rover is 7 years old, and the neighbor's dog is 9 years old. Together they weigh 75 pounds. How much does Rover weigh?

19. An airplane is carrying 148 passengers. There are 110 adults and 38 children. If half of the passengers get off the plane at Houston, how many passengers are left on the plane?

20. **Writing to Explain** How are perpendicular lines like intersecting lines? What is the difference between perpendicular and intersecting lines?

For **21**, use the diagram.

22. In how many different ways can you arrange the books shown at the right on a shelf? Make a list of the possible ways.

21. a Name a pair of parallel lines.

b What kind of lines are $\overleftrightarrow{AF}$ and $\overleftrightarrow{DH}$?

Algebra Connections

Shape Patterns

Look at the shapes below. Can you identify a pattern?

The pattern is 1 rectangle, 1 circle, 1 square, and 1 circle.

In **1** through **6**, name the shape asked for in each pattern.

1. What is the 13th shape?

2. What is the 20th shape?

3. What is the 50th shape?

4. What is the 28th shape?

5. What is 11th shape?

6. What is the 50th shape?

Example:

Name the 10th shape in the pattern at left.

Think How many shapes before the pattern repeats itself?

The pattern of 1 rectangle, 1 circle, 1 square, 1 circle repeats after 4 shapes.

$$4 + 4 + 2 = 10$$

The 2nd shape in the pattern is a circle, so the 10th shape is also a circle.

In **7** through **12**, continue the pattern for two more figures.

7.

8.

9.

10.

11.

12.

Measuring and Classifying Angles

Hands-On
protractor

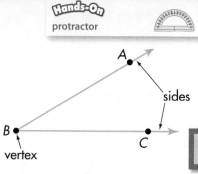

Understand It!
A number can be used to describe the size of an angle's opening.

How can you measure an angle?

An angle is formed by two rays that have the same endpoint. The common endpoint is called the vertex (plural: vertices.)

Angle *ABC* is shown above to the right. We write this as ∠*ABC*. It can also be named ∠*CBA* or just ∠*B*.

Another Example **How can you classify angles?**

An acute angle has a measure between 0° and 90°.

A right angle has a measure of 90°.

An obtuse angle has a measure between 90° and 180°.

A straight angle has a measure of 180°.

Guided Practice*

Do you know HOW?

In **1** and **2**, measure and classify each angle.

1.
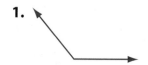

2.

3. Reasoning Give three different names for this angle. Identify the vertex and sides.

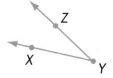

Do you UNDERSTAND?

4. In the figure below, how many angles are formed? What are their measures? Are the angles acute, right, or obtuse?

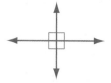

5. Draw an obtuse angle. Label it with 3 points and the angle measure.

DIGITAL
Animated Glossary, eTools
www.pearsonsuccessnet.com

To measure an angle

You use a protractor to measure and draw angles. Angles are measured in degrees. It takes 90° to fill a square corner.

Place the protractor's center on the angle's vertex. Place the 0° mark on one side of the angle. Read the measure where the other side of the angle crosses the protractor.

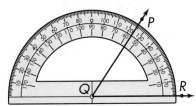

The measure of ∠PQR is 56°.

To draw an angle of 140°

Draw $\overrightarrow{TU}$. Be sure to label the endpoint *T*. Place the protractor's center on *T*. Line up $\overrightarrow{TU}$ with the 0° mark. Place a point at 140°. Label it *W*. Draw $\overrightarrow{TW}$.

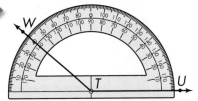

The measure of ∠WTU is 140°.

Independent Practice

In **6** through **8**, classify each angle as acute, right, obtuse, or straight. Then measure each angle.

6.

7.

8.

In **9** through **12**, draw the angles with a protractor. Classify the angles as acute, right, or obtuse.

9. 35°   **10.** 110°   **11.** 90°   **12.** 76°

Problem Solving

13. Reasoning If $\overrightarrow{CB}$ is perpendicular to $\overrightarrow{CD}$, then ∠BCD is

A an acute angle.   **C** an obtuse angle.

B a right angle.   **D** a straight angle.

14. For his birthday, John received the same amount of money from each of his 10 friends, plus $20 from his brother. If John received a total of $120, how much did each friend give him?

15. Angles can be found on the world's largest basket. What kind of angle is ∠ADC? ∠CBD? ∠ADB?

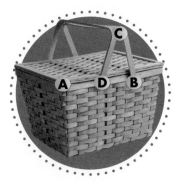

16. Writing to Explain Carlos says that two times the measure of an acute angle will always equal the measure of an obtuse angle. Is he right? Give examples to explain your answer.

Understand It!
Some polygons have special names that tell how many sides the polygon has.

Polygons

How do you name a polygon?

A polygon is a closed plane figure made up of line segments.

A regular polygon has sides of equal length and angles of equal measure.

Guided Practice*

Do you know HOW?

Name the polygon and classify it as regular or irregular.

1.

2.

Do you UNDERSTAND?

3. How many sides and how many vertices does a pentagon have? A hexagon?

4. What type of polygon does each road sign in the example at the top appear to be? Which one is a regular polygon?

Independent Practice

In **5** through **8**, name each polygon. Then write yes or no to tell if it is regular.

5.

6.

7.

8.

Which figures are polygons? If not, explain why.

9.

10.

11.

12.

Animated Glossary
www.pearsonsuccessnet.com

DIGITAL

*For another example, see Set C on page 216.

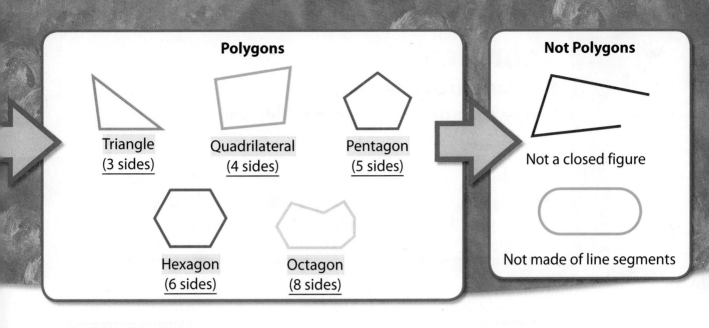

Polygons

Triangle
(3 sides)

Quadrilateral
(4 sides)

Pentagon
(5 sides)

Hexagon
(6 sides)

Octagon
(8 sides)

Not Polygons

Not a closed figure

Not made of line segments

Problem Solving

13. A regular hexagon has six angles that are all equal. If the total measure of the angles is 720°, how many degrees is each angle of the hexagon?

A 40°   **C** 60°

B 90°   **D** 120°

14. Algebra What is the value of k in the equation $k \div 12 = 4$?

A $k = 3$ **C** $k = 60$

B $k = 48$ **D** $k = 72$

15. If each side of a regular pentagon equals 4 feet, what is its perimeter?

16. Divide a square in half by connecting two vertices. What type polygons are formed? Are they regular or irregular?

17. **Think About the Process** Juanita's car gets 28 miles per gallon. Which expression shows how many gallons it will take to drive 720 miles?

A 720×28 **C** $720 + 28$

B $720 \div 28$ **D** $720 - 28$

18. After a party, there was one pizza left. It was divided into 8 pieces. Kip shared it equally among 4 friends. Which shows how many pieces each friend got?

A 8   **C** 4

B 6   **D** 2

19. While driving, Shania saw a No Passing Zone sign and an Interstate Highway sign. Are these polygons? If so, are they regular?

20. Each cell from a wasps' hive has 6 sides. What is the name of this polygon?

Understand It!
Triangles can be classified according to the lengths of their sides or the measures of their angles.

Triangles

How can you classify triangles?

Triangles can be classifed by the length of their sides.

Equilateral triangle
All sides are the same length.

Isosceles triangle
Two sides are the same length.

Scalene triangle
No sides are the same length.

Another Example **How can you find a missing angle measure in a triangle?**

The sum of the measures of the angles of a triangle is 180°. What is the measure of Angle a?

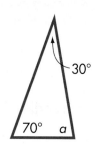

30°

70° a

Step 1 Add the two measures you know.   70° + 30° = 100°

Step 2 Subtract the sum from 180° to find the measure of the third angle.   180° − 100° = 80°

Think

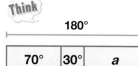

180°		
70°	30°	a

So, Angle a measures 80°.

Explain It

1. If two angles of a triangle measure 35° and 45°, how would you find the measure of the third angle?

Guided Practice*

Do you know HOW?

Classify each triangle by its sides and then by its angles.

1.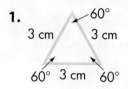
   60°
   3 cm   3 cm
   60° 3 cm 60°

2.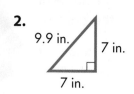
   9.9 in.   7 in.
   7 in.

Do you UNDERSTAND?

3. Can a right triangle have an obtuse angle in it? Why or why not?

4. Can an equilateral triangle have only two sides of equal length? Why or why not?

Animated Glossary
www.pearsonsuccessnet.com

DIGITAL

*For another example, see Set D on page 217.

Triangles can also be classified by the measures of their angles.

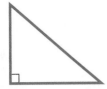

Right triangle
One angle is a right angle.

Acute triangle
All three angles are acute angles.

Obtuse triangle
One angle is an obtuse angle.

Independent Practice

Classify each triangle by its sides and then by its angles.

5.
30°
6 in. 6 in.
75° 75°
3.1 in.

6.
9 yd 12 yd
15 yd

7.
11 cm 60° 11 cm
60° 60°
11 cm

8.
15.1 m
9.2 m 110°
9.2 m

Two angle measures of a triangle are given. Find the measure of the third angle.

9. 48°, 63°

10. 90°, 40°

11. 65°, 50°

12. 130°, 24°

Problem Solving

For **13**, use the picture at the right.

13. The Louvre Museum is located in Paris, France. The Louvre Pyramid serves as an entrance to the museum. Classify the triangle on the front of the Louvre Pyramid by the lengths of its sides and the measures of its angles.

14. Writing to Explain The measures of two angles of a triangle are 23° and 67°. Is the triangle acute, right, or obtuse? Use geometric terms in your explanation.

15. Strategy Focus During a sale at the bookstore, books sold for $3 and magazines sold for $2.50. Jan spent $16 and bought a total of 6 books and magazines. How many of each did she buy? Use Try, Check, and Revise.

Quadrilaterals

How can you classify quadrilaterals?

A quadrilateral is any polygon with 4 sides. Quadrilaterals can be classified by their angles or pairs of sides.

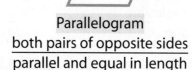

Parallelogram
both pairs of opposite sides
parallel and equal in length

Trapezoid
only one pair
of parallel sides

Another Example **How can you find a missing angle measure in a quadrilateral?**

The sum of the measures of the angles of a quadrilateral is 360°. What is the measure of Angle *Y*?

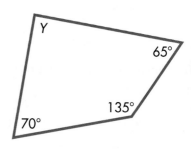

Step 1 Add the known measures. $65° + 135° + 70° = 270°$

Step 2 Subtract 270° from 360° to find the measure of the fourth angle. $360° - 270° = 90°$

So, Angle *Y* measures 90°.

Guided Practice*

Do you know HOW?

In **1** through **4**, classify each quadrilateral.

1.

2.

3.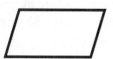

4.

Do you UNDERSTAND?

5. A square and a rhombus both have four sides that are equal in length. How can you tell the difference between the two quadrilaterals?

6. **Writing to Explain** Why can a rectangle also be called a parallelogram?

*For another example, see Set E on page 217.

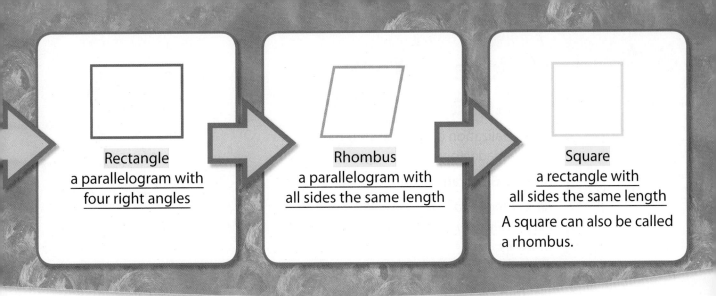

Rectangle
a parallelogram with
four right angles

Rhombus
a parallelogram with
all sides the same length

Square
a rectangle with
all sides the same length

A square can also be called
a rhombus.

Independent Practice

Classify each quadrilateral.

7.

8. 9 ft
9 ft $\square$ 9 ft
9 ft

9. 6 m
9 m 9 m
6 m

10. 3 ft
3 ft $\square$ 3 ft
3 ft

Three angle measures of a quadrilateral are given.
Find the measure of the fourth angle.

11. 54°, 100°, 120°

12. 150°, 30°, 30°

13. 90°, 106°, 117°

Problem Solving

14. Which quadrilateral never has 4 equal sides?

    A Square   **C** Rectangle

    B Trapezoid   **D** Rhombus

15. Draw a quadrilateral that is not a parallelogram.

16. Draw rectangle ABCD. Then draw a diagonal line connecting points B and D. If triangle BCD is a right isosceles triangle, what do you know about rectangle ABCD?

17. **Think About the Process** Hot dog buns come in packages of 12. Which of the following is NOT needed to find out how much you will spend on hot dog buns?

    A The cost of one pack of buns

    B The cost of the hot dogs

    C The number of buns you need

    D All of the information is necessary.

Problem Solving

Make and Test Generalizations

A generalization or general statement
can be made about a rectangle.

Make a Generalization

*All rectangles can be cut in half
diagonally to make two congruent
triangles.*

Guided Practice*

Do you know HOW?

Test the generalization and state whether
it appears to be correct or incorrect. If
incorrect, give an example to support why.

1. All right triangles are scalene triangles.

2. Two congruent equilateral triangles
   can be joined to make a rhombus.

Do you UNDERSTAND?

3. In the exercise above, how was the
   conclusion reached?

4. What is another generalization you can
   make and test about rectangles?

5. **Write a Problem** Write a real-world
   problem that can be solved by making
   and testing a generalization.

Independent Practice

In **6** through **10**, test the generalization and state whether
it appears to be correct or incorrect. If incorrect, give an
example to support why.

6. The sum of the angles of any triangle is 180°.

7. Parallel lines never intersect.

8. All rectangles have four congruent sides.

9. All even numbers are composite.

10. All triangles have at least two acute angles.

Stuck? Try this....

- What do I know?
- What am I asked to find?
- What diagram can I use to help
  understand the problem?
- Can I use addition, subtraction,
  multiplication, or division?
- Is all of my work correct?
- Did I answer the right question?
- Is my answer reasonable?

For another example, see Set F on page 217.

Test Your Generalization

Draw a rectangle with the length at the base.

I can cut this rectangle diagonally to make two congruent triangles.

Test Again if Possible

Draw a different rectangle.

I can also cut this rectangle diagonally to make two congruent triangles.

Conclusion

To prove a generalization incorrect, you need an example of when the test shows the generalization being incorrect.

Based on the results of the tests, this generalization appears to be correct.

---

11. What is the same about all of these polygons?

A B C D

12. One pint of blueberries contains about 80 berries. You have a fruit salad recipe that calls for 20 blueberries per serving. You have all of the other fruit necessary for the salad, but only 1 quart of blueberries. How many servings of the fruit salad can you prepare?

13. What is the best estimate of the shaded portion of the picture shown below?

14. Draw the next figure in the pattern shown below.

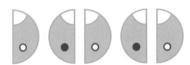

15. Mike weighs 24 more pounds than Marcus. Together, they weigh 250 pounds. How much do they each weigh?

17. Marcia and Tim played Ping-Pong. Marcia won the game with a score of 21. She won by 7 points. Draw a picture and write an equation to find Tim's score.

18. How many whole numbers have exactly two digits? Hint: 99 is the greatest two-digit whole number.

16. Find the missing numbers in each table. Then, write the rule.

a

Days	1	2	4	7
Dollars	$8	▨	$32	▨

b

Team	1	2	4	9
Players	▨	10	20	▨

DIGITAL Animated Glossary
www.pearsonsuccessnet.com

1. Which of the following correctly describes the triangles shown? (8-4)

  A Both triangles have a right angle.

  B Only one triangle has an acute angle.

  C Both triangles have at least two obtuse angles.

  D Both triangles have at least two acute angles.

2. A right triangle has an angle whose measure is 35°. What is the measure of the third angle in the triangle? (8-4)

  A 35°

  B 55°

  C 72.5°

  D 145°

3. Which of the following can be used to describe the shape below? (8-5)

  A Opposite sides are perpendicular.

  B All angles are obtuse.

  C Adjacent sides are parallel.

  D All sides are congruent.

4. What is the relationship between segments *AD* and *BC*? (8-1)

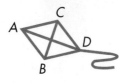

  A They are congruent.

  B They are adjacent.

  C They are perpendicular.

  D They are parallel.

5. Sabra's glasses have lenses that are the shape shown in the picture below. Which of the following could NOT be used to describe the lenses? (8-3)

  A Quadrilateral

  B Regular polygon

  C Hexagon

  D Opposite sides parallel

6. Which of the following appear to be parallel lines in the diagram shown? (8-1)

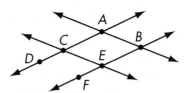

  A $\overleftrightarrow{AB}$ and $\overleftrightarrow{CE}$

  B $\overleftrightarrow{AB}$ and $\overleftrightarrow{FB}$

  C $\overleftrightarrow{CE}$ and $\overleftrightarrow{DA}$

  D $\overleftrightarrow{FB}$ and $\overleftrightarrow{CE}$

7. The figures below are rhombuses. Which generalization is incorrect, based on these figures? (8-6)

    A A square can be a rhombus.

    B A rhombus can be a square.

    C All rhombuses are squares.

    D All squares are rhombuses.

8. A sail on a sailboat is a triangle with two sides perpendicular and no two sides congruent. What two terms could be used to describe the sail? (8-4)

    A Equilateral and right

    B Right and isosceles

    C Scalene and right

    D Isosceles and acute

9. How many degrees is the measure of the fourth angle in the necklace charm shown? (8-5)

    A 45°

    B 135°

    C 180°

    D 360°

10. Which of the following is closest to the measure of the angle shown? (8-2)

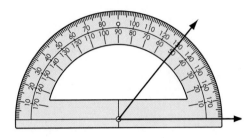

    A 40°

    B 50°

    C 130°

    D 140°

11. Triangle *HJK* is an isosceles triangle. The measures of angles *J* and *K* are equal. The measure of angle *H* is 100°. What is the measure of angle *J*? (8-4)

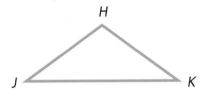

    A 40°

    B 45°

    C 50°

    D 80°

12. Which of the following quadrilaterals must have all four sides of equal length? (8-5)

    A Parallelogram

    B Trapezoid

    C Rectangle

    D Rhombus

Set A, pages 200–202

Geometric ideas are shown in the diagram below.

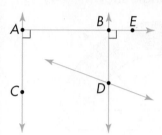

Name one line segment on $\overrightarrow{AE}$. $\overline{AB}$

Name two perpendicular rays. $\overrightarrow{AE}$ and $\overrightarrow{BD}$

Name two parallel lines. $\overleftrightarrow{AC}$ and $\overleftrightarrow{BD}$

Name three points. C, B, A

Remember that intersecting lines pass through the same point. If they form a right angle, they are perpendicular lines.

Use the figure at the left to name each of the following.

1. A ray that intersects two parallel line segments.

2. A vertical ray.

3. A horizontal ray.

4. A line segment that is perpendicular to two rays.

Set B, pages 204–205

Measure the angle below with a protractor and classify it as acute, right, or obtuse.

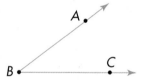

An acute angle measures less than 90°. This angle measures 38°, so this angle is acute.

Remember that you can compare most angles to a right angle and know whether it is greater or less than 90°, or you can measure it with a protractor.

Measure each angle with a protractor and classify it as acute, right, or obtuse.

1.   2.

Set C, pages 206–207

Name the polygon and state whether it is regular or irregular.

The polygon has six sides that are all equal in length and angles that are equal in measure. It is a regular hexagon.

Remember that a regular polygon has sides and angles of equal length and measure.

1.    2.

Set D, pages 208–209

Classify the triangle by the measure of its angles and the length of its sides.

Since one of the angles is right, this is a right triangle. Since two of the sides are the same length, this is an isosceles triangle.

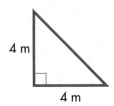

4 m

4 m

Using both terms, this is a right, isosceles triangle.

Remember that right, obtuse, and acute describe the angles of a triangle. Equilateral, scalene, and isosceles describe the sides of a triangle.

Classify each triangle by the size of its angles and the length of its sides.

1.
60°
60° 60°

2.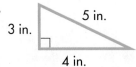
3 in.
5 in.
4 in.

Set E, pages 210–211

Classify the quadrilateral. Then find the missing angle measure.

The quadrilateral has two pairs of parallel sides with all sides the same length. It is a rhombus.

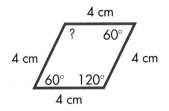

4 cm

4 cm   ?   60°   4 cm

60°   120°

4 cm

The sum of the measures of the angles in a quadrilateral is 360°.

360° − (60° + 60° + 120°) = 120°

So, the missing angle measure is 120°.

Remember that the sum of the angles of a quadrilateral is 360°.

Classify the quadrilateral. Then find the missing angle measure.

1.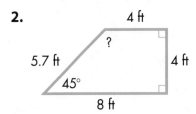
3 cm
110°   ?
70°   110°
6 cm

2.
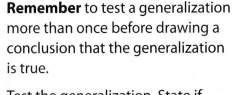
4 ft
?
5.7 ft   4 ft
45°
8 ft

Set F, pages 212–213

Test the following generalization and state whether it appears to be correct or incorrect. If incorrect, give an example to support why.

Generalization
The sum of the angles in any rectangle is 180°.

Test Your Generalization
Draw a rectangle.
Notice that each of the four angles is 90°.
Add to find the sum of the angles.
90° + 90° + 90° + 90° = 360°

Conclusion
The generalization is incorrect.

Remember to test a generalization more than once before drawing a conclusion that the generalization is true.

Test the generalization. State if it appears to be correct or not. If incorrect, give an example to support why.

1. The sum of two prime numbers equals a prime number.

Fractions and Decimals

1

The Great Owlet Moth of Brazil has one of the largest wingspans of all insects. Just how large is it? You will find out in Lesson 9-8.

2

The largest bird egg on record was laid by an ostrich. How can the weight of this egg be expressed as a fraction? You will find out in Lesson 9-9.

Review What You Know!

Vocabulary

Choose the best term from the box.

> • difference   • quotient
> • product   • thousandths

1. In 55 ÷ 5 = 11, the 11 is the __?__.

2. In 0.456, the 6 is in the __?__ place.

3. To find the __?__ between 16 and 4 you subtract.

4. Multiplying is the same as finding the __?__.

Division

Find each answer.

5. 32 ÷ 4   **6.** 97 ÷ 8

7. 69 ÷ 16   **8.** 95 ÷ 10

9. 163 ÷ 31   **10.** 725 ÷ 25

Multiplication

Find each answer.

11. 40 × 8   **12.** 30 × 500

13. 31 × 46   **14.** 92 × 18

15. 319 × 4   **16.** 2 × 25 × 30

Properties of Multiplication

Writing to Explain Write an answer for each question.

17. Explain how you can use the Associative Property to evaluate (7 × 50) × 4.

18. Can you use the Associative Property to evaluate 3 × (4 + 5)?

3

What fraction is equivalent to the weight of this goliath spider? You will find out in Lesson 9-4.

4

How can you write the height of the Long Term Parking Sculpture in France as a mixed number and an improper fraction? You will find out in Lesson 9-3.

Meanings of Fractions

What is the meaning of a fraction?

A <u>fraction</u> describes <u>one or more parts of a whole that is divided into equal parts.</u> The whole can be a region, a set, or a segment.

numerator $\quad 3 \leftarrow$ number of equal parts that are red
denominator $\quad 5 \leftarrow$ total number of equal parts

In the flag shown at the right, $\frac{3}{5}$ of the flag is red.

Part of
a region

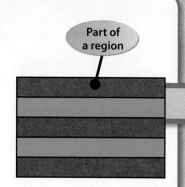

Another Example Does a fraction such as $\frac{1}{2}$ always represent the same amount?

In each figure below, $\frac{1}{2}$ of the figure is shaded. Does $\frac{1}{2}$ represent the same amount for both figures? Explain.

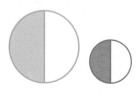

No. Even though $\frac{1}{2}$ of each figure is shaded, the whole in the first figure is much larger than the whole in the second figure. The amount of the whole determines what the fraction represents.

Explain It

1. In each segment, $\frac{3}{4}$ of the segment is shaded. Does $\frac{3}{4}$ of the first segment represent the same amount as $\frac{3}{4}$ of the second? Explain.

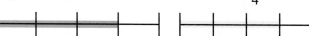

Guided Practice*

Do you know HOW?

In **1** and **2**, write the fraction that names the shaded part.

1.

2.

Do you UNDERSTAND?

3. What fraction names the blue part of the flag at the top?

4. What fraction names the part of the animals that are dogs in the figure at the top?

5. If a quilt has 16 equal parts and 4 of the parts are yellow, what fraction names the part that is yellow? What fraction names the part that is not yellow?

Part of a set

There are 8 animals.

3 out of 8 are cats.

$\frac{3}{8}$ of the animals are cats.

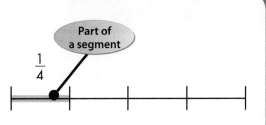

Part of a segment

$\frac{1}{4}$

There are 4 parts to the segment.

1 of the parts is shaded.

$\frac{1}{4}$ of the segment is shaded.

Independent Practice

In **6** through **10**, write the fraction that names the shaded part.

Tip *You can count the number of shaded parts to find the numerator.*

6.

7. ●●○○○○○

8.

9. ▢▢▢▢▢▢▢□□□

10.

In **11** through **14**, write the fraction that names the unshaded part.

11. ♥♥♥♥♥♡♡
♡♡♡♡♡♡♡

12.

13.

14. ★★★★
★★★☆

In **15** through **17**, draw a model to show each fraction.

15. 8 out of 9 as part of a region

16. 6 out of 7 as part of a set

17. 3 out of 5 as part of a segment

18. Ladybugs are easy to identify because they are red with black spots. What fraction of the insects shown below are ladybugs?

19. What fraction of the fruit are pineapples?

20. Write a numerical expression for each word expression:

a fifty-two divided by 2

b the product of twenty-two and two

c five dollars less than eighteen dollars

d eighty increased by 5

21. What fraction of the parking spaces are in use?

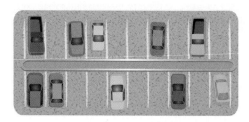

22. John bought a shirt and a CD. The CD cost $13 and the shirt cost $17 more than the CD. How much did John spend in all?

23. Writing to Explain Explain how to round 456 to the hundreds place.

24. If you throw a bowling ball and knock down four pins, what fraction of the total number of pins are still standing?

A $\frac{4}{10}$ **C** $\frac{4}{6}$

B $\frac{6}{10}$ **D** $\frac{4}{5}$

25. **Think About the Process** How could you find the numerator of the fraction that represents the shaded part of the square that is divided into 4 equal parts?

A Count the total parts that are shaded.

B Count the total parts that are unshaded.

C Count the total number of shaded and unshaded parts.

D Subtract the number of unshaded parts from the shaded parts.

26. About 4 square feet out of every 5 square feet of exhibit space at a convention center is used for a yearly auto show. What fraction of the exhibit space represents this estimated space used for the auto show?

Algebra Connections

Properties and Equations

Number properties help you solve equations. Examples of each property are shown.

Commutative Properties

Addition $\qquad 3 + 7 = 7 + 3$

Multiplication $\quad 7 \times 9 = 9 \times 7$

Associative Properties

Addition $\qquad 3 + (7 + 5) = (3 + 7) + 5$

Multiplication $\quad 2 \times (4 \times 3) = (2 \times 4) \times 3$

Identity Properties

Addition $\qquad 10 + 0 = 10$

Multiplication $\quad 13 \times 1 = 13$

Zero Property of Multiplication

$9 \times 0 = 0$

Distributive Property

$3 \times (10 + 4) = (3 \times 10) + (3 \times 4)$

Example:

Solve the following equation.

$8 \times (10 + 2) = (8 \times 10) + (y \times 2)$

Think The Distributive Property means that $8 \times (10 + 2) = (8 \times 10) + (8 \times 2)$

So, $y = 8$

Use the number properties to help you solve each equation.

Tip *Remember that $3 \times m$ can be written as 3m.*

1. $z + 37 = 37 + 4$

2. $38y = 38$

3. $8 + (3 + 9) = (8 + 3) + x$

4. $8y = 0$

5. $21 + z = 21$

6. $17 \times 25 = 25 \times t$

7. $10 \times (3 \times 9) = (10 \times 3) \times z$

8. $16 + (y + 4) = (16 + 3) + 4$

9. $8 \times (10 + 3) = (8 \times 10) + (8 \times y)$

10. $346y = 346$

11. One display in a store has 12 rows of 4 photos. Another display has same number of photos arranged in 4 rows. How many photos are in each row of the second display?

12. Write a Problem Write a real-world problem that can be solved by writing and solving the equation $3 + 10 = x + 3$.

Fractions and Division

How can fractions be used to show division?

Al, Lisa, Nico, and Laura are making a collage. They will share 3 rectangular strips of colored paper. What fraction represents the part of a whole strip of paper each will get?

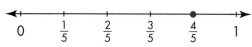

1 whole   1 whole   1 whole

Find $3 \div 4$.

Another Example **How can you use a number line to represent fractions?**

One way to find a point on a number line that represents a fraction is to divide a unit segment (0 to 1) into equal parts. To find $\frac{4}{5}$, divide the segment into 5 equal parts.

Then find the point $\frac{4}{5}$ of the way from 0 to 1.

Explain It

1. Explain how you would find the fraction $\frac{2}{5}$ on the number line above.

2. What fraction is shown by Point A below? Point B?

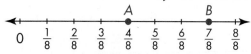

Guided Practice*

Do you know HOW?

Give each answer as a fraction.

1. $1 \div 2$ **2.** $1 \div 4$

3. $9 \div 10$ **4.** $5 \div 8$

5. $3 \div 4$ **6.** $7 \div 9$

7. $7 \div 11$ **8.** $3 \div 6$

Do you UNDERSTAND?

9. How can you represent $\frac{3}{4}$ on a number line?

10. Four friends want to share three loaves of bread. One student suggests that each of the three loaves be divided into 4 equal parts. If each person gets 3 of the parts, how much of a whole loaf does each person get in all?

*For another example, see set B on page 250.

One way to divide 3 wholes into 4 equal parts is to first divide each whole into 4 equal parts. Each part is $\frac{1}{4}$ of a whole.

Rearrange the $\frac{1}{4}$ pieces. Each person gets 3 of the $\frac{1}{4}$ pieces. Each gets $\frac{3}{4}$. So $3 \div 4 = \frac{3}{4}$.

Al   Nico

Lisa   Laura

Independent Practice

In **11** through **14**, write each as a fraction. Then show each on a number line.

11. $1 \div 3$ **12.** $2 \div 3$ **13.** $3 \div 4$ **14.** $1 \div 2$

In **15** through **18**, use the number line to name each point with a fraction.

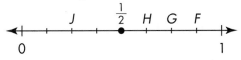

15. *F*   **16.** *G*   **17.** *H*   **18.** *J*

Problem Solving

19. Algebra Which expression represents "30 subtracted from a number"?

A $30n$

B $30 - n$

C $30 + n$

D $n - 30$

21. Which fraction is closer to 1: $\frac{3}{4}$ or $\frac{5}{12}$? Use the number lines below to justify your answer.

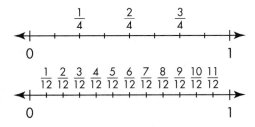

20. **Think About the Process** There are 6 pieces of construction paper for 7 people. Each person needs an equal amount. What is the first step to divide the construction paper?

A Cut each piece of construction paper into 6 equal parts.

B Cut each piece of construction paper into 7 equal parts.

C Cut each piece of construction paper into 13 equal parts.

D Cut each piece of construction paper into 42 equal parts.

Understand It!
Fractions greater than or equal to 1 can be represented by a mixed number.

Mixed Numbers and Improper Fractions

How are mixed numbers and improper fractions related?

Jack has 20 square tiles. He uses them to cover box lids with 3 rows of 3 square tiles. What number can name the total region covered by the tiles?

Guided Practice*

Do you know HOW?

Write each improper fraction as a mixed number or each mixed number as an improper fraction.

1. $\frac{3}{2}$
2. $2\frac{3}{4}$
3. $3\frac{1}{4}$
4. $\frac{7}{6}$
5. $9\frac{1}{10}$
6. $\frac{21}{2}$

Do you UNDERSTAND?

7. What is a general rule for writing a mixed number as an improper fraction?

8. **Writing to Explain** Simone thinks that $\frac{8}{4}$ is not an improper fraction because $8 \div 4 = 2$. Is she correct? Explain.

Independent Practice

In **9** and **10**, write an improper fraction and a mixed number for the model.

9.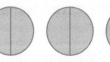

10.

In **11** through **18**, write each improper fraction as a mixed number or each mixed number as an improper fraction.

11. $4\frac{1}{2}$
12. $\frac{3}{2}$
13. $4\frac{9}{10}$
14. $5\frac{3}{4}$

15. $\frac{22}{3}$
16. $\frac{5}{4}$
17. $8\frac{2}{3}$
18. $6\frac{1}{3}$

Animated Glossary
www.pearsonsuccessnet.com

For another example, see Set C on page 250.

A mixed number is a whole number and a fraction. You can write $20 \div 9$ as a mixed number. You know that $20 \div 9 = \frac{20}{9}$.

Divide the numerator by the denominator.

$$9\overline{)20}$$
$$\underline{18}$$
$$2$$

Write the remainder as a fraction. Put the remainder over the divisor.

So, $20 \div 9 = \frac{20}{9}$ or $2\frac{2}{9}$.

An improper fraction is a fraction whose numerator is greater than or equal to its denominator.

Write $2\frac{2}{9}$ as an improper fraction.

Multiply the denominator of the fraction by the whole number. $9 \times 2 = 18$.

Add the numerator of the fraction. $18 + 2 = 20$

Write using the same denominator.

So, $2\frac{2}{9} = \frac{20}{9}$

Problem Solving

19. The Long Term Parking sculpture in France contains 60 cars embedded in concrete. It is 65.6 feet high. How tall is the Long Term Parking sculpture as a mixed number and an improper fraction?

20. Which property tells you that $7 \times 1 = 7$?

21. Reasoning Is $\frac{5}{5}$ an improper fraction? Explain your reasoning.

22. What is the value of the underlined digit 423,1<u>4</u>8,675?

23. The weights in pounds of 4 packages are given below. Order the weights from least to greatest.
0.9   0.03   1.8   0.14

24. Write an improper fraction and mixed number for the shaded portion of the model.

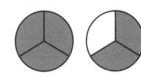

25. A board is $4\frac{2}{3}$ feet long. How could you change $4\frac{2}{3}$ into an improper fraction?

  A Add 4 and $\frac{2}{3}$.

  B Divide 4 by $\frac{2}{3}$.

  C Multiply 4 by 3. Then, add 2. Write that number as a numerator over a denominator of 3.

  D Multiply 4 by 2 and then add 3. Write as a numerator over a denominator of 3.

Understand It!
A part of a whole or a part of a set can be named by equivalent fractions.

Equivalent Fractions

How do you find equivalent fractions?

Out of 12 apples, 8 are red. So, $\frac{8}{12}$ of the apples are red. Hannah says that $\frac{4}{6}$ of the apples are red, and Sam says that $\frac{2}{3}$ are red. Who is correct?

Guided Practice*

Do you know HOW?

In **1** through **6**, find two equivalent fractions for each fraction.

1. $\frac{1}{3}$

2. $\frac{5}{6}$

3. $\frac{2}{5}$

4. $\frac{3}{8}$

5. $\frac{9}{18}$

6. $\frac{8}{10}$

Do you UNDERSTAND?

7. Sam said that $\frac{4}{12}$ of the apples are green. Name two equivalent fractions for $\frac{4}{12}$.

8. **Writing to Explain** Jon said that it would be impossible to write all fractions equivalent to $\frac{1}{2}$. Is he right?

Independent Practice

In **9** through **12**, find the missing nonzero number to make the fractions equivalent.

9. $\dfrac{1 \times \blacksquare = 6}{3 \times \blacksquare = 18}$

10. $\dfrac{17 \div \blacksquare = 1}{34 \div \blacksquare = 2}$

11. $\dfrac{30 \div \blacksquare = 6}{35 \div \blacksquare = 7}$

12. $\dfrac{9 \times \blacksquare = 36}{12 \times \blacksquare = 48}$

In **13** through **16**, find the missing numerator to make the fractions equivalent.

13. $\frac{1}{3} = \frac{\blacksquare}{9}$

14. $\frac{7}{9} = \frac{\blacksquare}{63}$

15. $\frac{30}{40} = \frac{\blacksquare}{8}$

16. $\frac{15}{35} = \frac{\blacksquare}{7}$

In **17** through **24**, find the missing denominator to make the fractions equivalent.

17. $\frac{5}{12} = \frac{10}{\blacksquare}$

18. $\frac{2}{7} = \frac{10}{\blacksquare}$

19. $\frac{14}{80} = \frac{7}{\blacksquare}$

20. $\frac{6}{18} = \frac{3}{\blacksquare}$

21. $\frac{80}{100} = \frac{20}{\blacksquare}$

22. $\frac{12}{\blacksquare} = \frac{3}{16}$

23. $\frac{10}{\blacksquare} = \frac{2}{5}$

24. $\frac{7}{\blacksquare} = \frac{21}{36}$

For another example, see Set D on page 251.

You can multiply or divide the numerator and denominator by the same nonzero number to get equivalent fractions.

Use multiplication.

Multiply 4 and 6 by 2.

$$\frac{4}{6} = \frac{8}{12}$$

$\times 2$

$\times 2$

The fractions $\frac{4}{6}$ and $\frac{8}{12}$ are equivalent fractions.

Use division.

Divide 4 and 6 by 2.

$$\frac{4}{6} = \frac{2}{3}$$

$\div 2$

$\div 2$

The fractions $\frac{4}{6}$ and $\frac{2}{3}$ are equivalent fractions.

So, Hannah and Sam were both correct since $\frac{8}{12}$ is equivalent to $\frac{4}{6}$, and $\frac{2}{3}$ is equivalent to $\frac{4}{6}$.

Problem Solving

25. Ming dropped a package of 8 light bulbs and 2 of the bulbs broke. Write two equivalent fractions to represent the fraction of the bulbs that broke.

26. Marcus spelled 20 out of 25 words correctly. What fraction of the words did he spell correctly? What fraction of the words did he spell incorrectly? Write two equivalent fractions for each.

27. What is the least amount you can spend to buy 7 books?

Sale
2 for $5.50 or
1 for $3.00

28. Writing to Explain Explain why $\frac{6}{15}$ and $\frac{3}{5}$ are NOT equivalent fractions.

29. It rained 0.45 inch on Friday, 2.2 inches on Saturday, and 1.02 inches on Sunday. How much more did it rain on Saturday than on Friday and Sunday combined?

30. It takes about 12 minutes to hard boil an egg. What fraction of an hour is 12 minutes?

   A $\frac{1}{4}$ **C** $\frac{2}{5}$

   B $\frac{1}{5}$ **D** $\frac{2}{3}$

31. A 2-year old goliath bird-eating spider weighs 6 oz, or $\frac{6}{16}$ lb. Which fraction is equivalent to $\frac{6}{16}$?

   A $\frac{1}{4}$

   B $\frac{1}{3}$

   C $\frac{1}{8}$

   D $\frac{3}{8}$

6/16 LBS

32. Maurice ran $\frac{1}{2}$ of a mile, or 2,640 feet in 3 minutes 30 seconds. Which of the following is NOT an equivalent fraction for $\frac{1}{2}$?

   A $\frac{2}{4}$ **C** $\frac{17}{34}$

   B $\frac{10}{20}$ **D** $\frac{16}{30}$

Comparing and Ordering Fractions and Mixed Numbers

How can you compare fractions?

Shawna and Tom walked two different paths in Trout Park. Shawna walked $\frac{5}{6}$ mile. Tom walked $\frac{3}{4}$ mile. Which is greater, $\frac{5}{6}$ or $\frac{3}{4}$?

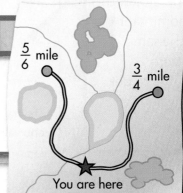

$\frac{5}{6}$ mile

$\frac{3}{4}$ mile

You are here

Another Example How can you order fractions and mixed numbers?

Write $2\frac{5}{12}$, $\frac{11}{12}$, $3\frac{1}{6}$, and $2\frac{1}{3}$ in order from greatest to least.

You know that $\frac{11}{12} < 1$ and all the mixed numbers are greater than 1. So, $\frac{11}{12}$ is the least number.

When comparing mixed numbers, look at the whole number parts. Since $3 > 2$, you know that $3\frac{1}{6}$ is greater than both $2\frac{1}{3}$ and $2\frac{5}{12}$.

Next, compare $2\frac{1}{3}$ and $2\frac{5}{12}$.
Since the whole numbers are the same, compare the fractions.

Compare $\frac{1}{3}$ and $\frac{5}{12}$. Change $\frac{1}{3}$ to $\frac{4}{12}$. $\frac{4}{12} < \frac{5}{12}$.

So, $2\frac{1}{3} < 2\frac{5}{12}$.

From greatest to least, the numbers are $3\frac{1}{6}$, $2\frac{5}{12}$, $2\frac{1}{3}$, $\frac{11}{12}$.

Guided Practice*

Do you know HOW?

Compare. Write $>$, $<$ or $=$ for each $\bigcirc$.

1. $\frac{3}{5} \bigcirc \frac{4}{5}$

2. $\frac{1}{4} \bigcirc \frac{2}{3}$

Order the numbers from least to greatest.

3. $\frac{2}{3}$, $\frac{1}{4}$, $\frac{9}{10}$

4. $1\frac{2}{3}$, $2\frac{1}{4}$, $1\frac{9}{10}$

Do you UNDERSTAND?

5. How do you know that $\frac{5}{12}$ is less than $\frac{1}{2}$?

6. How do you know that $5\frac{1}{12} > 4\frac{1}{2}$ without finding a common denominator for both fraction parts?

*For another example, see Set E on page 251.

One Way

To compare fractions, find a common denominator by writing the multiples of each denominator.

4: 4, 8, (12), 16, 20, . . .

6: 6, (12), 18, 24, . . .

Use 12 as the common denominator.

$$\frac{5}{6} \times \frac{2}{2} = \frac{10}{12} \qquad \frac{3}{4} \times \frac{3}{3} = \frac{9}{12}$$

$$\frac{10}{12} > \frac{9}{12}, \text{ so, } \frac{5}{6} > \frac{3}{4}.$$

Another Way

You can multiply the denominators to find a common denominator.

Compare $\frac{3}{4}$ and $\frac{5}{6}$.

Multiply denominators: $4 \times 6 = 24$.

Use 24 as the common denominator.

$$\frac{5}{6} \times \frac{4}{4} = \frac{20}{24} \qquad \frac{3}{4} \times \frac{6}{6} = \frac{18}{24}$$

$$\frac{20}{24} > \frac{18}{24}, \text{ so, } \frac{5}{6} > \frac{3}{4}.$$

Independent Practice

In **7** through **10**, compare the numbers. Write >, < or = for each $\bigcirc$.

 You can always multiply the denominators to find a common denominator.

7. $\frac{3}{4} \bigcirc \frac{4}{5}$

8. $\frac{9}{10} \bigcirc \frac{18}{20}$

9. $3\frac{6}{7} \bigcirc 3\frac{13}{14}$

10. $1\frac{7}{8} \bigcirc 1\frac{2}{3}$

In **11** and **12**, order the numbers from least to greatest.

11. $\frac{1}{2}, \frac{1}{4}, \frac{5}{6}, \frac{3}{4}$

12. $2\frac{1}{2}, 1\frac{7}{8}, 2\frac{3}{4}, 2\frac{3}{5}$

Problem Solving

13. Birdhouses can provide homes for many different kinds of birds. The size of the opening will determine the kind of bird that can use it. Order the data in the table from least to greatest.

Type of Bird	Size of Birdhouse Opening (in inches)
Screech owl	3
Chickadee	$1\frac{1}{8}$
House wren	1
Tree swallow	$1\frac{1}{2}$

14. Sarah rode her bike $2\frac{1}{2}$ miles on Thursday, $2\frac{7}{10}$ miles on Friday, and $2\frac{5}{8}$ miles on Saturday. Which day did she ride farthest?

15. At the school fair, 157 tickets were sold. The tickets cost $3 apiece. The goal was to make $300 in ticket sales. By how much was the goal exceeded?

A $71

B $171

C $371

D $471

Common Factors and Greatest Common Factor

How can you find the greatest common factor?

A pet store has goldfish and angelfish that have to be put into the fewest number of glass containers. Each container must contain the same number of fish, and each must contain all goldfish or all angelfish.

20 angelfish

30 goldfish

Another Example How can you use prime factorization to find the GCF of two numbers?

Step 1 Find the prime factors of each number.

Step 2 List the prime factors of each number.

$24 = 2 \times 2 \times 2 \times 3$
$18 = 2 \times 3 \times 3$

$$
\begin{array}{cc}
24 & 18 \\
4 \quad \times \quad 6 & 2 \quad \times \quad 9 \\
2 \times 2 \times 2 \times 3 & 2 \times 3 \times 3
\end{array}
$$

Step 3 Circle the prime factors that both numbers share. Here they share the numbers 2 and 3.

$24 = 2 \times 2 \times 2 \times 3$
$18 = 2 \times 3 \times 3$

Step 4 Multiply the common factors. $2 \times 3 = 6$

So, the GCF of 18 and 24 is 6.

Guided Practice*

Do you know HOW?

For **1** through **4**, find the GCF of each pair of numbers.

1. 9 and 12   **2.** 20 and 45

3. 7 and 28   **4.** 18 and 32

Do you UNDERSTAND?

5. If two numbers are prime, what is their GCF?

6. Writing to Explain In the example above, how would the GCF change if there were 40 goldfish?

DIGITAL   Animated Glossary
www.pearsonsuccessnet.com

  *For another example, see Set F on page 252.

Find the greatest common factor (GCF) of 20 and 30 to find the greatest number of fish that could be put into each container.

If a number is a factor of two numbers, it is called a common factor.

The greatest common factor (GCF) of two numbers is the greatest number that is a factor of both numbers.

To find the greatest common factor of 20 and 30, you can list all the factors of each number and circle all the common factors.

20: 1, 2, 4, 5, 10, 20
30: 1, 2, 3, 5, 6, 10, 15, 30

The GCF of 20 and 30 is 10.

So, the store can put 10 fish in each container.

Independent Practice

In **7** through **18**, find the greatest common factor (GCF) of each number using prime factorization or a list of factors.

7. 20 and 35　　**8.** 16 and 18　　**9.** 15 and 6　　**10.** 24 and 36

11. 48 and 30　　**12.** 22 and 77　　**13.** 100 and 96　　**14.** 60 and 32

15. 90 and 81　　**16.** 72 and 27　　**17.** 11 and 15　　**18.** 14 and 21

Problem Solving

19. Rick Hansen holds the record for the longest journey by wheelchair. He wheeled his wheelchair across 4 continents and 34 countries. What is the GCF of 4 and 34?

A 1　　**B** 2　　**C** 4　　**D** 17

20. Which list shows all the common factors of 36 and 54?

A 1, 2, 3, 6　　　　**C** 1, 2, 3, 6, 9, 18
B 1, 2, 3, 6, 9　　**D** 1, 2, 3, 6, 9, 12, 18

21. If you buy a television for $486, including tax, and are allowed to pay for it in 6 equal payments, how much will each payment be?

22. How many pairs of factors does 40 have? List them.

The **Venn diagram** at the right shows the common factors and the GCF of 30 and 42.

23. What does each region of the diagram show?

24. Use a Venn diagram to show the common factors of 48 and 72. What is the GCF?

Factors of 30		Factors of 42
5	1	7
10	2	14
15	3	21
30	6	42

Fractions in Simplest Form

How can you write a fraction in simplest form?

Understand It!
A fraction can be changed to simplest form by dividing the numerator and denominator by their greatest common factor.

A stained glass window has 20 panes. Out of 20 sections, 12 are yellow. So $\frac{12}{20}$ of the panes are yellow. Notice how the picture also shows that $\frac{3}{5}$ are yellow.

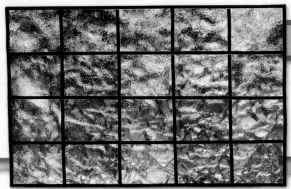

Another Example How can you use the GCF to find the simplest form of a fraction?

There are 36 students in the fifth-grade class. Twenty-seven will go to the mathematics competition. What is the simplest form of the fraction of the class going to competition?

A $\frac{1}{9}$ **B** $\frac{2}{5}$ **C** $\frac{3}{4}$ **D** $\frac{7}{8}$

Factors of 27: 1, 3, 9, 27

Factors of 36: 1, 2, 3, 4, 6, 9, 18, 36.

The GCF of 27 and 36 is 9.

Then, divide the numerator and denominator by the GCF.

$\frac{27 \div 9}{36 \div 9} = \frac{3}{4}$

The simplest form of $\frac{27}{36}$ is $\frac{3}{4}$.

The correct choice is **C**.

Explain It

1. In finding the simplest form in the Another Example, do you get the same answer if you list factor pairs? Explain.

2. John said that he divided the numerator and denominator of $\frac{18}{54}$ by 2, so $\frac{9}{27}$ is the simplest form of the fraction. Do you agree? Explain.

A fraction is in simplest form when its numerator and denominator have no common factor other than 1.

To write $\frac{12}{20}$ in simplest form, find a common factor of the numerator and the denominator. Since 12 and 20 are even numbers, they have 2 as a factor.

Divide both 12 and 20 by 2.

$$\frac{12 \div 2}{20 \div 2} = \frac{6}{10}$$

Both 6 and 10 are even. Divide both by 2.

$$\frac{6 \div 2}{10 \div 2} = \frac{3}{5}$$

Since 3 and 5 have no common factor other than 1, you know that $\frac{3}{5}$ is in simplest form.

Guided Practice*

Do you know HOW?

In **1** through **6**, write each fraction in simplest form.

1. $\frac{16}{32}$ 2. $\frac{10}{14}$

3. $\frac{33}{77}$ 4. $\frac{16}{20}$

5. $\frac{30}{40}$ 6. $\frac{10}{15}$

Do you UNDERSTAND?

7. In the stained glass window pattern above, what fraction in simplest form names the green tiles?

8. **Writing to Explain** Why is it easier to divide the numerator and denominator by the GCF rather than any other factor?

Independent Practice

For **9** through **32**, write each fraction in simplest form.

9. $\frac{300}{400}$ 10. $\frac{55}{60}$ 11. $\frac{3}{6}$ 12. $\frac{75}{100}$

13. $\frac{14}{21}$ 14. $\frac{4}{12}$ 15. $\frac{42}{48}$ 16. $\frac{63}{70}$

17. $\frac{18}{21}$ 18. $\frac{22}{44}$ 19. $\frac{6}{42}$ 20. $\frac{15}{25}$

21. $\frac{9}{81}$ 22. $\frac{12}{100}$ 23. $\frac{7}{21}$ 24. $\frac{16}{30}$

25. $\frac{99}{121}$ 26. $\frac{122}{144}$ 27. $\frac{28}{42}$ 28. $\frac{32}{80}$

29. $\frac{40}{80}$ 30. $\frac{11}{22}$ 31. $\frac{60}{80}$ 32. $\frac{8}{100}$

DIGITAL

Animated Glossary
www.pearsonsuccessnet.com

33. Write a fraction in simplest form that shows the shaded part of the figure.

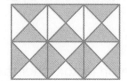

34. Mrs. Lok is planning a 600-mile trip. Her car has an 18-gallon gas tank and gets 29 miles per gallon. Will 1 tank full of gas be enough for the trip?

35. **Writing to Explain** Explain how you know that $\frac{55}{80}$ is not in simplest form.

36. If 5 packages of hot dogs cost $10.25, what is the cost of 1 package?

37. **Writing to Explain** Can you assume that any fraction is in simplest form if either the numerator or denominator is a prime number?

38. A store manager wants to give away the last 84 samples of hand cream. She counts 26 customers in the store. She will give each customer the same number of free samples. How many free samples will each customer get?

39. Mayflies can live at the bottom of lakes for 2 to 3 years before they become winged adults. Mayflies are between $\frac{4}{10}$ inches and 1.6 inches long. If this mayfly is $\frac{4}{10}$ of an inch long, how can you write $\frac{4}{10}$ in simplest form?

A $\frac{1}{6}$

C $\frac{2}{5}$

B $\frac{1}{4}$

D $\frac{8}{20}$

40. **Reasoning** Use divisibility rules to find a number that satisfies the given conditions.

a a number greater than 75 that is divisible by 2 and 5.

b a three-digit number divisible by 3, 5 and 6.

41. **Think About the Process** Rita sells birdhouses for $10 each. She uses $3\frac{1}{2}$ ft of wood for each birdhouse. Which operation would she use to find how much money she will receive if she sells 14 birdhouses?

A Multiplication

B Division

C Addition

D Subtraction

42. **Think About the Process** A parking garage has 4 levels with 28 spaces on each level. If 52 spaces are occupied, which of the following shows a way to find the number of spaces that are unoccupied?

A Add 28 to the product of 52 and 4.

B Add 52 to the product of 28 and 4.

C Subtract 28 from the product of 52 and 4.

D Subtract 52 from the product of 4 and 28.

Mixed Problem Solving

New England Colonies			Middle Colonies			Southern Colonies		
Colony	Year	Reason	Colony	Year	Reason	Colony	Year	Reason
Mass. Bay	1630	Escape religious persecution	New York	1664	Build colony on Dutch land	Virginia	1607	Search for gold
Conn.	1639	Farming, trade, political freedom	New Jersey	1664	Build colony on Dutch land	Maryland	1634	Refuge for Catholics
Rhode Island	1636	Colony for all religions	Penna.	1682	Establish religious colony	North Carolina	1729	Farming
New Hampshire	1679	Trade, fishing	Delaware	1704	Trade, farming	South Carolina	1670	Farming
						Georgia	1733	Military defense, religious refuge, farming

1. What fraction of the colonies were founded for farming?

2. What fraction of the colonies are the Southern Colonies?

3. What fraction of the colonies were founded in 1729?

4. What fraction of the New England Colonies were founded in 1636?

5. James stated that $\frac{1}{3}$ of the colonies were the Middle Colonies. Is he correct? Why or why not?

6. Write a problem using the fraction $\frac{1}{5}$. Use the chart to help you.

7. What fraction tells you how many colonies were founded because of trade?

A $\frac{1}{13}$ **C** $\frac{1}{2}$

B $\frac{3}{13}$ **D** $\frac{3}{4}$

8. What fraction of the colonies are the Middle Colonies and the Southern Colonies together?

A $\frac{1}{2}$ **C** $\frac{8}{13}$

B $\frac{9}{13}$ **D** $\frac{4}{13}$

9. Strategy Focus Solve using the strategy, Draw a Picture and Write an Equation.

How many years passed from the time the first colony was founded until the last one was founded?

Tenths and Hundredths

How can you write a fraction as a decimal?

A fraction such as $\frac{3}{10}$ or $\frac{9}{100}$ can be shown by a model.

$\frac{3}{10}$ $\frac{9}{100}$

Other Examples

How can you use division to write a fraction as a decimal?

Write $\frac{3}{5}$ as a decimal.

$\frac{3}{5} = 3 \div 5$

Divide the numerator by the denominator.

$$\begin{array}{r} 0.6 \\ 5\overline{)3.0} \\ -\ 3\,0 \\ \hline 0 \end{array}$$ Insert a decimal point after 3 and annex zeros as needed.

So, $\frac{3}{5} = 0.6$.

Write $\frac{1}{4}$ as a decimal.

$\frac{1}{4} = 1 \div 4$

$$\begin{array}{r} 0.25 \\ 4\overline{)1.00} \\ -\ 8\downarrow \\ \hline 20 \\ -\ 20 \\ \hline 0 \end{array}$$ Insert a decimal point after 1 and annex zeros as needed.

So, $\frac{1}{4} = 0.25$.

Explain It

1. How can you write $\frac{9}{100}$ as a division problem?

2. In the second example, how many zeros did you need to annex after 1 when you divided 1 by 4?

Guided Practice*

Do you know HOW?

Write each decimal as a fraction and each fraction as a decimal.

1. 0.1

2. 0.02

3. $\frac{9}{10}$

4. $\frac{7}{100}$

5. Use division to change $\frac{11}{20}$ to a decimal.

Do you UNDERSTAND?

6. Describe two ways to write a decimal as a fraction.

7. **Writing to Explain** How is $\frac{3}{10}$ equal to 0.3?

The word name for $\frac{3}{10}$ is three tenths. Three tenths can be shown on a place-value chart,

0.3

So, $\frac{3}{10} = 0.3$.

The word name for $\frac{9}{100}$ is nine hundredths. Nine hundredths can be shown on a place-value chart,

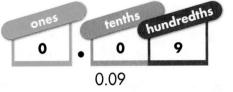

0.09

So, $\frac{9}{100} = 0.09$.

Independent Practice

In **8** through **11**, write a decimal and fraction for the shaded portion of each model.

8.

9.

10.

11.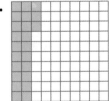

In **12** through **19**, write each decimal as either a fraction or a mixed number.

12. 3.2　　　　**13.** 0.7　　　　**14.** 0.23　　　　**15.** 9.75

16. 7.7　　　　**17.** 0.4　　　　**18.** 0.81　　　　**19.** 2.43

In **20** through **27**, write each fraction or mixed number as a decimal.

20. $2\frac{1}{100}$　　　　**21.** $9\frac{3}{10}$　　　　**22.** $\frac{9}{10}$　　　　**23.** $1\frac{18}{100}$

24. $6\frac{31}{100}$　　　　**25.** $4\frac{1}{10}$　　　　**26.** $\frac{4}{10}$　　　　**27.** $6\frac{6}{100}$

Use division to change each fraction to a decimal.

28. $\frac{2}{5}$　　　　**29.** $\frac{3}{25}$　　　　**30.** $\frac{7}{50}$　　　　**31.** $\frac{9}{20}$

32. What is $\frac{97}{100}$ as a decimal?

    A 97.0   **C** 0.97

    B 9.7   **D** 0.097

33. Kate drives 234 miles in 5 hours. Felix only has to drive one half the distance that Kate does. How many miles does Felix have to drive?

34. What is the value of the underlined digit? 457,1<u>4</u>0,167

35. What is the best estimate for this product? 81 × 409

36. Jorge is packing books into boxes. Each box can hold 16 books. Which expression can be used to find the total number of boxes that he needs in order to pack 96 books?

    A 96 ÷ 16

    B 96 − 16

    C 96 + 16

    D 96 × 16

37. At a high-school graduation, there were 200 students in the class. They were seated in 5 different sections of the auditorium. How many graduates were seated in each section?

    A 40

    B 195

    C 400

    D 1,000

38. *Titanus giganteus* is one of the largest known beetles on Earth.

    a How long is *Titanus giganteus* as a mixed number?

    b How long is *Titanus giganteus* as an improper fraction?

39. The Great Owlet Moth of Brazil has a wingspan of 12.13 inches. Write this number as a mixed number.

40. **Think About the Process** A design is divided into 5 equal parts and $\frac{2}{5}$ are shaded. How would you change $\frac{2}{5}$ to a decimal?

    A Divide 2 by 5.

    B Divide 5 by 2.

    C Multiply 2 by 5.

    D Add 2 and 5.

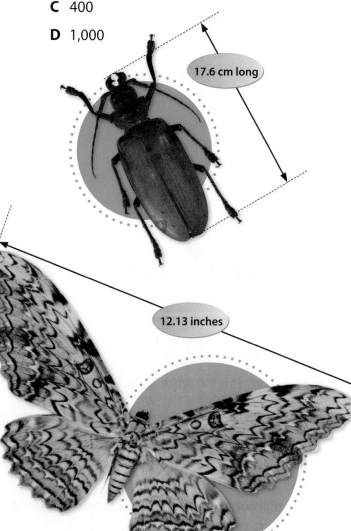

17.6 cm long

12.13 inches

Changing from Fraction to Decimal Form

Write $\frac{17}{50}$ and $\frac{33}{50}$ in decimal form.

Step 1 To write $\frac{17}{50}$ in decimal form, divide 17 by 50.

Press: 17 ÷ 50 **ENTER =**

Display: `.34`

So, $\frac{17}{50} = 0.34$.

Step 2 To write $\frac{33}{50}$ in decimal form, divide 33 by 50.

Press: 33 ÷ 50 **ENTER =**

Display: `.66`

So, $\frac{33}{50} = 0.66$.

When the denominator of a fraction is 50, one way to find the decimal form is to put 2 times the numerator in the tenths and hundredths places. Look at the example above. $2 \times 33 = 66$. Place 66 in the tenths and hundredths places, and the answer is 0.66.

Practice

Write each fraction in decimal form.

1. $\frac{3}{10}$

2. $\frac{7}{10}$

3. $\frac{1}{10}$

4. $\frac{2}{5}$

5. $\frac{4}{5}$

6. $\frac{3}{5}$

7. $\frac{7}{25}$

8. $\frac{9}{25}$

9. $\frac{21}{25}$

10. $\frac{9}{20}$

11. $\frac{11}{20}$

12. $\frac{19}{20}$

13. $\frac{6}{10}$

14. $\frac{8}{10}$

15. $\frac{2}{10}$

16. $\frac{1}{5}$

17. $\frac{5}{5}$

18. $\frac{0}{5}$

19. $\frac{13}{20}$

20. $\frac{15}{20}$

21. $\frac{18}{20}$

Understand It!
A fraction can also be represented by a decimal.

Thousandths
How are fractions related to decimals?

A large box is filled with cubes. There are 1,000 cubes in all. Each cube can be thought of as $\frac{1}{1,000}$ of the whole box.

Think about pulling 3 cubes from the box. Since one cube can be shown as $\frac{1}{1,000}$, this means that 3 cubes could be shown by $\frac{3}{1,000}$. How can you use a decimal to represent this fraction?

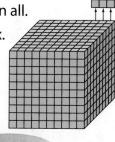

$10 \times 10 \times 10$

Guided Practice*

Do you know HOW?

In **1** through **4**, write each decimal as a fraction or mixed number.

1. 0.003   **2.** 0.050

3. 7.001   **4.** 0.393

In **5** through **8**, write each fraction a decimal.

5. $\frac{389}{1,000}$ **6.** $3\frac{673}{1,000}$

7. $\frac{211}{1,000}$ **8.** $\frac{90}{1,000}$

Do you UNDERSTAND?

9. **Writing to Explain** How is $\frac{3}{10}$ different from $\frac{3}{1000}$ in place value?

10. How would you write the fraction of cubes that are left when 3 cubes are pulled from the box in the model above?

Independent Practice

In **11** through **18**, write each decimal as a fraction or mixed number.

11. 0.007   **12.** 0.008   **13.** 0.065   **14.** 0.900

15. 0.832   **16.** 0.023   **17.** 3.078   **18.** 5.001

In **19** through **26**, write each fraction or mixed number as a decimal.

19. $\frac{434}{1,000}$ **20.** $3\frac{499}{1,000}$ **21.** $\frac{873}{1,000}$ **22.** $\frac{309}{1,000}$

23. $1\frac{17}{1,000}$ **24.** $\frac{9}{1,000}$ **25.** $\frac{990}{1,000}$ **26.** $5\frac{707}{1,000}$

For another example, see Set I on page 253.

The word name for $\frac{3}{1,000}$ is three thousandths. A decimal place-value chart can help you determine the decimal.

ones	.	tenths	hundredths	thousandths
0	.	0	0	3

So, $\frac{3}{1,000}$ can be represented by the decimal 0.003.

Problem Solving

27. A bagel costs $1.25, the cream cheese costs $0.30, and a glass of juice costs $2.25. How much change would you get from $10.00 if you buy all three items?

28. The largest egg on record was laid by an ostrich. The weight was 5.476 pounds. Which digit is in the tenths place?

    A 4   **C** 6

    B 5   **D** 7

29. Write the fractions $\frac{9}{10}$, $\frac{9}{100}$, and $\frac{9}{1,000}$ as decimals.

30. Frank reasoned that $\frac{97}{1,000}$ can be written as 0.97. Is this correct? If not, justify your reasoning.

31. **Writing to Explain** How many cubes are in the box? What fraction of the entire box do the 7 cubes represent? Explain your answer.

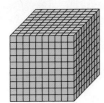

$10 \times 10 \times 10$

32. What part of the entire square is shaded?

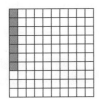

    A 0.007   **C** 0.7

    B 0.07   **D** 7.0

33. Which illustrates the Associative Property of Multiplication?

    A $5 \times 7 = 7 \times 5$

    B $0 \times 8 = 0$

    C $6 \times 1 = 6$

    D $1 \times (2 \times 3) = (1 \times 2) \times 3$

Understand It!
A point on a number line can represent a number that has both a fraction and a decimal name.

Fractions and Decimals on the Number Line

How can you locate fractions and decimals on the same number line?

Jules is playing a game in which she chooses 3 cards. Each is labeled with a fraction or a decimal. Then she must locate a point for each number on a number line that is divided into 10 segments between 0 and 1.

0.9

$\frac{3}{20}$

0.617

Another Example How can you name points on a number line?

What fraction or mixed number can name Point *A*? Point *B*?
What decimal can name Point *A*? Point *B*?

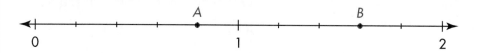

A   B

0   1   2

The segment between 0 and 1 is divided into 5 equal parts. So, Point *A* is named by $\frac{4}{5}$. You could use division to change $\frac{4}{5}$ to 0.8. Point *B* is named by $1\frac{3}{5}$.
Since $3 \div 5 = 0.6$, another name for Point *B* is 1.6.

$$\begin{array}{r} 0.8 \\ 5\overline{)4.0} \\ -40 \\ \hline 0 \end{array} \qquad \begin{array}{r} 0.6 \\ 5\overline{)3.0} \\ -30 \\ \hline 0 \end{array}$$

Explain It

1. Which is farther to the right on the number line, $\frac{1}{4}$ or 0.2? Why?

Guided Practice*

Do you know HOW?

Show each set of numbers on the same number line.

1. $\frac{8}{10}$, 0.2, 0.7

2. $\frac{18}{20}$, 0.1, $\frac{6}{10}$

3. $\frac{11}{10}$, 0.65, 0.311

Do you UNDERSTAND?

4. Is $\frac{9}{10}$ to the left or right of 1 on the number line? Explain.

5. Will 0.617 be to the left or right of $\frac{6}{10}$ on a number line?

6. **Writing to Explain** Explain how you can find 0.311 on the number line.

What You Think

- I know that 0.9 also means $\frac{9}{10}$. I can easily locate $\frac{9}{10}$.

- I know that $\frac{3}{20}$ means $3 \div 20$. I can divide to find $3 \div 20 = 0.15$.

  $0.1 = 0.10$ and $0.2 = 0.20$. So, 0.15 is halfway between 0.1 and 0.2.

- $0.6 = 0.600$ and $0.7 = 0.700$. So 0.617 is between 0.6 and 0.7. It is closer to 0.6 than 0.7.

What You Show

Independent Practice

In **7** through **10**, name the fraction or mixed number and decimal that identifies each point.

Tip *Remember to count over from 0 on the number line to find the number of parts of the whole.*

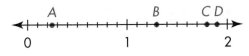

7. Point *A*   **8.** Point *B*   **9.** Point *C*   **10.** Point *D*

Draw a number line to show each set of numbers. Then order the numbers from least to greatest.

11. $\frac{2}{5}$, 0.35, 0.7

12. $\frac{7}{20}$, 0.15, $\frac{12}{25}$

13. $\frac{3}{4}$, 0.1, 0.22

Problem Solving

14. **Number Sense** Nadia has $2\frac{1}{2}$ pounds of tomatoes, 2.7 pounds of chicken, 2.1 pounds of celery, and $2\frac{2}{5}$ pounds of tomatillos. Which food weighs the most?

15. The top three scores in an ice-dancing competition were 60.53, 59.29, and 61.07. Order the scores from least to greatest.

16. If you located the following numbers on a number line, which would be closest to 0?

$$0.2, \frac{2}{100}, \frac{3}{5}, \frac{2}{20}$$

A 0.2   **C** $\frac{3}{5}$

B $\frac{2}{100}$ **D** $\frac{2}{20}$

17. Chris bought an apple for $0.58 with a $1 bill and received $0.42 in change. What is the least number of coins he could have received?

A 4   **C** 6

B 5   **D** 7

Understand It!
Writing to explain can help you when you are asked to explain how you solved a problem.

Writing to Explain

How do you write a math explanation?

The circle graph shows the continents where the 20 most populated countries of the world are located. Estimate the fractional part for each continent. Explain how you decided.

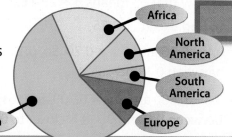

Locations of the 20 Most Populated Countries in the World

Africa
North America
South America
Europe
Asia

Guided Practice*

Do you know HOW?

1. Estimate the fractional part of the square that is shaded. Explain how you decided.

Do you UNDERSTAND?

2. Draw a picture to show $\frac{2}{3}$ as a benchmark fraction.

3. **Write a Problem** Write a real-world problem that involves a benchmark fraction. Your problem should ask for an explanation as part of the solution.

Independent Practice

For **4** and **5**, use the picture below.

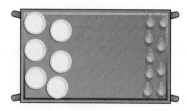

4. Estimate the part of the table that is covered with plates. Explain how you decided.

5. Estimate the part of the table that is covered with glasses. Explain how you decided.

6. Draw a kitchen table. Using plates, show the benchmark fraction, $\frac{3}{4}$. Explain how you decided the number of plates to draw.

Stuck? Try this....

- What do I know?
- What am I asked to find?
- What diagram can I use to help understand the problem?
- Can I use addition, subtraction, multiplication, or division?
- Is all of my work correct?
- Did I answer the right question?
- Is my answer reasonable?

DIGITAL
Animated Glossary
www.pearsonsuccessnet.com

*For another example, see Set K on page 253.

To estimate a fractional amount, use a benchmark fraction that is close to the actual fractional amount.

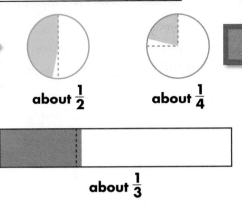

about $\frac{1}{2}$ about $\frac{1}{4}$

about $\frac{1}{3}$

Writing a Math Explanation

Use *words, pictures, numbers,* or *symbols* to write a good math explanation.

Asia: *If you draw a line from the top of the graph to the bottom, you can see this continent is a little more than* $\frac{1}{2}$.

Africa: *This part is a little less than* $\frac{1}{4}$.

Europe and North America: *About 10 of each of these can fill the circle, so this is about* $\frac{1}{10}$.

South America: *This part is less than the part for Europe, so I'll say about* $\frac{1}{20}$.

---

7. Estimate the fractional part of the square that is shaded. Explain how you decided.

8. Estimate the part of the square that is *NOT* shaded. Explain how you decided.

9. Draw a rectangle and shade about $\frac{1}{3}$ of it. Explain how you decided how much to shade.

10. Draw two circles that are different sizes. Shade about $\frac{1}{8}$ of each. Are the shaded parts the same amount? Explain.

11. The Mayfield Little League baseball infield is being covered with a tarp because of rain. Is more or less than $\frac{3}{4}$ of the infield grass covered with the tarp?

12. Cereal can be a good source of protein. How many quarter cups of cereal are there in $6\frac{1}{4}$ cups?

13. A refreshment stand at the fair was open for 3 hours. Four people each took turns working at the stand for the same amount of time. How many minutes did each person work?

For **14**, decide if there is extra or missing information. Solve if possible.

14. Gene's new car gets 35 miles per gallon. Matt's car gets 32 miles per gallon. How many more gallons of gas will Matt's car use than Gene's car to go to the beach?

1. To make a stained glass window, Robert used 16 pieces of glass. Seven of the pieces were red. What fraction of the pieces were red? (9-1)

A $\frac{7}{16}$

B $\frac{9}{16}$

C $\frac{7}{9}$

D $\frac{16}{7}$

2. How can $\frac{12}{18}$ be written in simplest form? (9-7)

A Multiply 12 and 18 by their GCF, 3.

B Multiply 12 and 18 by their GCF, 6.

C Divide 12 and 18 by their GCF, 3.

D Divide 12 and 18 by their GCF, 6.

3. Which fraction represents $3 \div 8$? (9-2)

A $\frac{8}{3}$

B $\frac{3}{8}$

C $\frac{5}{8}$

D $\frac{5}{3}$

4. Jason ran $2\frac{9}{10}$ miles on Monday, $1\frac{4}{5}$ miles on Tuesday, and $1\frac{7}{10}$ miles on Thursday. Which list has the miles Jason ran from least to greatest? (9-5)

A $1\frac{4}{5}, 2\frac{9}{10}, 1\frac{7}{10}$

B $1\frac{4}{5}, 1\frac{7}{10}, 2\frac{9}{10}$

C $1\frac{7}{10}, 2\frac{9}{10}, 1\frac{4}{5}$

D $1\frac{7}{10}, 1\frac{4}{5}, 2\frac{9}{10}$

5. The atomic weight of hydrogen is 1.008. Which of the following mixed numbers is the same as 1.008? (9-9)

A $1\frac{8}{1000}$

B $1\frac{8}{100}$

C $1\frac{8}{10}$

D $1\frac{10}{8}$

6. A store has the floor plan shown. The area of the women's department is 600 ft². Find the best estimate of the total area of the store. (9-11)

A Women's is about $\frac{1}{3}$ of the total area, so the store is about 600×3 or 200 ft².

B Women's is about $\frac{1}{3}$ of the total area, so the store is about 3×600 or 1,800 ft².

C Women's is about $\frac{1}{4}$ of the total area, so the store is about $600 \div 4$ or 150 ft².

D Women's is about $\frac{1}{4}$ of the total area, so the store is about 4×600 or 2,400 ft².

7. To amend the Constitution of the United States, $\frac{2}{3}$ of each house of Congress must approve the amendment. Is $\frac{7}{12}$ of a house's approval enough? (9-5)

A Yes, because $\frac{7}{12} < \frac{2}{3}$

B Yes, because $\frac{7}{12} > \frac{2}{3}$

C No, because $\frac{7}{12} < \frac{2}{3}$

D No, because $\frac{7}{12} > \frac{2}{3}$

8. Which is equal to $5\frac{3}{10}$? (9-3)

A $\frac{53}{50}$

B $\frac{25}{10}$

C $\frac{53}{10}$

D $\frac{15}{10}$

9. About $\frac{2}{5}$ of U.S. households own at least one dog. Which is equal to $\frac{2}{5}$? (9-8)

A 0.6

B 0.4

C 0.2

D 0.04

10. Which point on the number line represents 1.2 or $1\frac{1}{5}$? (9-10)

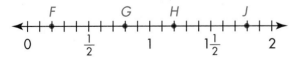

A Point *F*

B Point *G*

C Point *H*

D Point *J*

11. The table shows water fowl that Hong counted at the lake. What fraction of the water fowl listed are Mallards? (9-7)

Water Fowl Type	Number
Canadian geese	5
Crane	3
Mallards	12

A $\frac{3}{5}$

B $\frac{8}{12}$

C $\frac{3}{2}$

D $\frac{5}{3}$

12. Which of the following lists all the common factors of 45 and 60? (9-6)

A 1, 3, 5

B 1, 3, 5, 15

C 1, 2, 3, 5

D 1, 15

13. Which of the following equals $\frac{15}{8}$? (9-9)

A 1.875

B 1.625

C 1.58

D 1.375

14. What number makes the equation true? (9-4)

$$\frac{7}{12} = \frac{\square}{24}$$

A 2

B 12

C 14

D 19

Set A, pages 220–222

You can find the part of the whole, part of the set, or part of a segment using a model.

Write the fraction that names the shaded part.

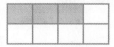

The model shows $\frac{3}{8}$ shaded.

Remember that the numerator tells you how many equal-sized parts are shaded. The denominator tells you the total number of equal-sized parts.

Write fractions for the shaded and unshaded portions of each model.

1.   **2.**

Set B, pages 224–225

José and three friends want to create chalkboard art in three equal-sized spaces on the playground. How much of each space will each student get?

To show 3 ÷ 4, you can use a fraction.

$3 \div 4 = \frac{3}{4}$

Each student will get $\frac{3}{4}$ of one space.

Remember that to show a fraction on the number line, you need to divide the number line into equal parts.

Give each answer as a fraction. Then show each on a number line.

1. 1 ÷ 4   **2.** 2 ÷ 5

Set C, pages 226–227

Write the improper fraction and mixed number.

There are 2 wholes shaded and $\frac{4}{5}$ of 1 whole shaded. You can see that this is $2\frac{4}{5}$ or $\frac{14}{5}$. You can also follow the steps below to write $2\frac{4}{5}$ as an improper fraction.

Step 1	Step 2	Step 3
Multiply the denominator of the fraction by the whole number. $2 \times 5 = 10$	Add the numerator of the fraction to the product of the denominator and the whole number. $10 + 4 = 14$	Write the fraction using the same denominator. $\frac{14}{5}$

So, $2\frac{4}{5} = \frac{14}{5}$.

Remember that an improper fraction and a mixed number can represent the same value.

Write each mixed number as an improper fraction.

1. $3\frac{1}{2}$ **2.** $2\frac{2}{3}$

3. $5\frac{1}{6}$ **4.** $3\frac{4}{5}$

5. $1\frac{1}{5}$ **6.** $9\frac{7}{8}$

Write each improper fraction as a mixed number.

7. $\frac{4}{3}$ **8.** $\frac{3}{2}$

9. $\frac{6}{4}$ **10.** $\frac{12}{9}$

11. $\frac{31}{7}$ **12.** $\frac{46}{5}$

Set D, pages 228–229

Write two fractions equivalent to $\frac{3}{7}$.

To form equivalent fractions, multiply both the numerator and denominator of the given fraction by the same number.

$$\frac{3 \times 4}{7 \times 4} = \frac{12}{28}; \frac{3 \times 5}{7 \times 5} = \frac{15}{35}$$

So, $\frac{12}{28}$ and $\frac{15}{35}$ are equivalent to $\frac{3}{7}$.

Remember that you multiply or divide both the numerator and denominator to find equivalent fractions.

Write two fractions that are equivalent to each of the following.

1. $\frac{1}{2}$ **2.** $\frac{3}{4}$

3. $\frac{2}{3}$ **4.** $\frac{5}{7}$

Set E, pages 230–231

Compare $\frac{4}{16}$ and $\frac{3}{8}$.

To compare numbers, you can find a common denominator. Write multiples of each number.

Circle the common multiple.

16: 16, 32, 48, . . .

8: 8, 16, 24, . . .

Use 16 as the common denominator.

$$\frac{4}{16} = \frac{4}{16} \qquad \frac{3 \times 2}{8 \times 2} = \frac{6}{16}$$

$\frac{4}{16} < \frac{6}{16}$, and so $\frac{4}{16} < \frac{3}{8}$.

Write $\frac{1}{5}, \frac{1}{8}, \frac{3}{10}$, and $1\frac{1}{2}$ in order from least to greatest.

$\frac{1}{8} < \frac{1}{5}$ because both numerators are 1, and $8 > 5$.

$\frac{1}{5} < \frac{3}{10}$ because $\frac{1}{5} = \frac{2}{10}$ and $\frac{2}{10} < \frac{3}{10}$.

$1\frac{1}{2}$ is greater than any of the values because it is greater than 1.

So, the order is $\frac{1}{8}, \frac{1}{5}, \frac{3}{10}, 1\frac{1}{2}$.

Remember that you can always find a common denominator by multiplying the denominators together.

Compare. Write $>$, $<$, or $=$ for each ◯.

1. $\frac{2}{5}$ ◯ $\frac{3}{10}$ **2.** $\frac{9}{12}$ ◯ $\frac{1}{5}$

3. $\frac{7}{12}$ ◯ $\frac{1}{3}$ **4.** $\frac{8}{15}$ ◯ $\frac{20}{45}$

5. $\frac{3}{6}$ ◯ $\frac{4}{7}$ **6.** $\frac{9}{10}$ ◯ $\frac{18}{19}$

Order the numbers from the least to greatest.

7. $\frac{2}{3}, \frac{1}{4}, \frac{2}{5}, \frac{1}{3}$

8. $\frac{2}{7}, \frac{1}{10}, \frac{1}{3}, \frac{5}{6}$

9. $\frac{9}{10}, 1\frac{3}{5}, \frac{4}{7}, \frac{11}{12}$

10. $3\frac{1}{2}, 3\frac{1}{8}, 3\frac{2}{5}, 3\frac{7}{8}$

Set F, pages 232–233

Common factors are factors shared by a group of numbers. The GCF is the largest factor shared by a group of numbers.

12: (1)(2)(3)(4)(6)(12)
60: (1)(2)(3)(4) 5(6) 10, (12) 15, 20, 30, 60

The GCF of 12 and 60 is 12.

Remember to use divisibility rules to help you find factors of a number. List the factors of each pair of numbers, then find the GCF.

1. 15, 45   **2.** 60, 80

3. 12, 14   **4.** 24, 56

Set G, pages 234–236

Write $\frac{21}{36}$ in simplest form.

To express a fraction in simplest form, divide the numerator and denominator by the greatest common factor.

The GCF of 21 and 36 is 3.

$$\frac{21 \div 3}{36 \div 3} = \frac{7}{12}$$

Remember that the simplest form can also be found by dividing by common factors until the common factor is 1.

Write each fraction in simplest form.

1. $\frac{45}{60}$ **2.** $\frac{32}{96}$

3. $\frac{24}{30}$ **4.** $\frac{42}{49}$

Set H, pages 238–240

Write $\frac{60}{100}$ as a decimal.

You can write fractions as decimals using a place-value chart. You read $\frac{60}{100}$ as 60 hundredths.

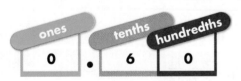

ones	.	tenths	hundredths
0	.	6	0

You can see that $\frac{60}{100} = 0.60$.

Remember that to write a decimal, you need to pay particular attention to the denominator of the fraction.

For **1** through **4**, write each decimal as a fraction.

1. 0.3   **2.** 0.42

3. 0.08   **4.** 8.23

For **5** through **8**, write each fraction or mixed number as a decimal.

5. $1\frac{2}{10}$ **6.** $\frac{9}{100}$

7. $\frac{7}{10}$ **8.** $2\frac{35}{100}$

Set I, pages 242–243

Write $\frac{7}{1,000}$ as a decimal.

You can write fractions as decimals using a place value chart. You read $\frac{7}{1,000}$ as seven thousandths.

You can see that $\frac{7}{1,000} = 0.007$.

Remember that to write a decimal with thousandths place, you need to use three decimal places after the decimal.

Write each decimal as a fraction.

1. 0.192 **2.** 0.042

Write each fraction as a decimal.

3. $\frac{189}{1,000}$ **4.** $\frac{3}{1,000}$

Set J, pages 244–245

You can use a number line to locate fractions and decimals, and compare values.

Locate 0.2, $\frac{18}{20}$, and 0.75 on a number line.

You know that 0.2 also means $\frac{2}{10}$.

You know that $\frac{18}{20}$ also means 18 ÷ 20. Use division to find 18 ÷ 20 = 0.90.

0.7 = 0.70 and 0.8 = 0.80. So, 0.75 is halfway between 0.7 and 0.8.

So the order from least to greatest is 0.2, 0.75, and $\frac{18}{20}$.

Remember to divide the number line into equal sized segments to find the correct location for each fraction or decimal.

In **1** through **4**, name the fraction that identifies each point on the number line.

1. Point A **2.** Point B

3. Point C **4.** Point D

Set K, pages 246–247

When you are asked to explain how you found your answer, follow these steps:

Step 1

Break the process into steps.

Step 2

Use pictures and words to explain.

Step 3

Tell about things to watch out for and be careful about.

Step 4

Write your steps in order using words like *find* and *put*.

Remember to show your work clearly so that others can understand it.

1. Sara's paper airplane flew 8.5 yards. Jason's flew $8\frac{2}{3}$ yards. Michael's flew $8\frac{1}{4}$ yards and Denise's flew $8\frac{1}{6}$ yards. Whose airplane flew the farthest? Explain how you found your answer.

Adding and Subtracting Fractions and Mixed Numbers

1 This Parsons chameleon can extend its tongue up to $1\frac{1}{2}$ times the length of its body. What is the total length of the chameleon when its tongue is fully extended? You will find out in Lesson 10-5.

2 How much smaller is the bumblebee bat than the Etruscan pygmy shrew? You will find out in Lesson 10-6.

Review What You Know!

3

The world's smallest horse is named Thumbelina. How much shorter is Thumbelina than the second shortest horse? You will find out in Lesson 10-6.

4

Native Americans have made baskets like the ones shown below, since the early 1900s. What is the length of one side of a triangle on a basket like this one? You will find out in Lesson 10-3.

Vocabulary

Choose the best term from the box.

- common denominator
- denominator • numerator

1. In the fraction $\frac{7}{15}$, the number 15 is the ___?___.

2. In the fraction $\frac{11}{21}$, the number 11 is the ___?___.

3. Fractions with the same denominator have a ___?___.

Fractions in Simplest Form

Write each fraction in simplest form.

4. $\frac{6}{18}$ 5. $\frac{12}{22}$ 6. $\frac{15}{25}$

7. $\frac{8}{26}$ 8. $\frac{14}{35}$ 9. $\frac{4}{18}$

Common Denominators

Compare. Write >, <, or = for each $\bigcirc$.

10. $\frac{5}{25} \bigcirc \frac{2}{5}$ 11. $\frac{12}{27} \bigcirc \frac{6}{9}$

12. $\frac{11}{16} \bigcirc \frac{2}{8}$ 13. $\frac{2}{7} \bigcirc \frac{1}{5}$

Fractions

Writing to Explain Write an answer for each question.

14. How do you know when a fraction is in simplest form?

15. How can the greatest common factor help you write a fraction in simplest form?

Adding and Subtracting Fractions with Like Denominators

Understand It!
When two fractions have the same denominators, their sum or difference has the same denominator.

How do you add or subtract fractions with like denominators?

If Miguel and Alma ride 2 roller coasters in the morning and 5 in the afternoon, on what fraction of the park's roller coasters will they ride?

Choose an Operation Add to find the total.

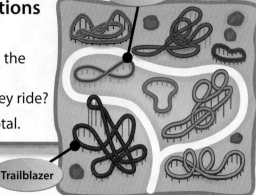

Gold Rush

Trailblazer

Another Example How do you subtract fractions with like denominators?

The Trailblazer has the longest track. It is $\frac{9}{10}$ of a mile. The Gold Rush has only $\frac{3}{10}$ mile of track. How much longer is the Trailblazer's track?

Choose an Operation Subtract to compare two lengths.

What You Show

1
One mile

| $\frac{1}{10}$ | $\frac{1}{10}$ | $\frac{1}{10}$ | $\frac{1}{10}$ | $\frac{1}{10}$ | $\frac{1}{10}$ | $\frac{1}{10}$ | $\frac{1}{10}$ | $\frac{1}{10}$ |
Length of Trailblazer track

| $\frac{1}{10}$ | $\frac{1}{10}$ | $\frac{1}{10}$ |
Length of Gold Rush track

Difference

What You Write

$$\begin{array}{r} \frac{9}{10} \\ -\frac{3}{10} \\ \hline \frac{6}{10} \end{array}$$

The fractions have like denominators.

Subtract the numerators.

Write the difference over the common denominator.

Tip *Fractions have a common denominator when their denominators are the same.*

The Trailblazer's track is $\frac{6}{10}$, or $\frac{3}{5}$, of a mile longer than the Gold Rush's track.

Explain It

1. How do you simplify $\frac{6}{10}$ to $\frac{3}{5}$?

Since there are 8 roller coasters, use 2 eighths to show the morning rides and 5 eighths to show the afternoon rides.

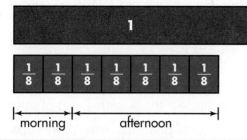

All the roller coasters

Roller coasters they will ride

morning | afternoon

$\dfrac{2}{8}$
$+\dfrac{5}{8}$
$\overline{}$
$\dfrac{7}{8}$

The fractions have like denominators. Add the numerators.

Write the sum over the common denominator.

Miguel and Alma will ride on $\dfrac{7}{8}$ of the roller coasters that day.

Guided Practice*

Do you know HOW?

In **1** through **6**, find each sum or difference. Simplify your answers.

1. $\dfrac{1}{4}$
    $+\dfrac{1}{4}$

2. $\dfrac{5}{6}$
    $-\dfrac{3}{6}$

3. $\dfrac{6}{9}$
    $+\dfrac{2}{9}$

4. $\dfrac{6}{7}+\dfrac{5}{7}$

5. $\dfrac{7}{12}-\dfrac{5}{12}$

6. $\dfrac{4}{5}-\dfrac{2}{5}$

Do you UNDERSTAND?

7. In the example above, why is the sum of $\dfrac{2}{8}$ and $\dfrac{5}{8}$ not equal to $\dfrac{7}{16}$?

8. In the example above, if Miguel and Alma were able to ride only on 3 coasters in the afternoon, on what fraction of the roller coasters will they ride?

Independent Practice

In **9** through **25**, find each sum or difference. Simplify your answers.

9. $\dfrac{1}{2}$
    $+\dfrac{1}{2}$

10. $\dfrac{3}{4}$
     $-\dfrac{1}{4}$

11. $\dfrac{4}{6}$
     $-\dfrac{1}{6}$

12. $\dfrac{3}{10}$
     $+\dfrac{5}{10}$

13. $\dfrac{3}{8}+\dfrac{1}{8}$

14. $\dfrac{6}{7}-\dfrac{3}{7}$

15. $\dfrac{5}{18}+\dfrac{1}{18}$

16. $\dfrac{8}{11}-\dfrac{2}{11}$

17. $\dfrac{1}{3}+\dfrac{1}{3}+\dfrac{1}{3}$

18. $\dfrac{11}{12}-\dfrac{2}{12}-\dfrac{1}{12}$

19. $\dfrac{1}{2}+\dfrac{1}{2}+\dfrac{1}{2}$

20. $\dfrac{12}{20}+\dfrac{5}{20}+\dfrac{2}{20}$

21. $\dfrac{1}{12}+\dfrac{3}{12}+\dfrac{5}{12}$

22. $\dfrac{13}{16}-\left(\dfrac{4}{16}+\dfrac{3}{16}\right)$

23. $\dfrac{5}{9}-\left(\dfrac{1}{9}+\dfrac{1}{9}\right)$

24. $\dfrac{1}{8}+\left(\dfrac{5}{8}-\dfrac{3}{8}\right)$

25. $\left(\dfrac{7}{10}-\dfrac{3}{10}\right)+\dfrac{1}{10}$

26. On a Greatest Rock Bands CD, all-men groups sing $\frac{5}{13}$ of the songs and all-women groups sing $\frac{3}{13}$ of the songs. What fraction of the songs are sung by those two groups combined?

27. Jolene paid $10.50 to bowl 3 games. She also paid $2.50 to rent bowling shoes. How much did Jolene pay per game she bowled?

28. A painter mixes $\frac{1}{4}$ gallon of red paint with $\frac{1}{4}$ gallon of yellow paint. How much paint is in the bucket?

29. Nadia made a snack with $\frac{3}{4}$ cup of raisins and $\frac{1}{4}$ cup of peanuts. How many cups of snack did she make?

For **30**, use the data in the table at the right.

30. a How many students are in the class?

   b What fraction of the class selected surfing or softball?

   c What fraction of the class did not select soccer or football?

Results of Mr. Willis's Class Survey Favorite Sport

Sport	Number of Students
Soccer	7
Basketball	2
Football	3
Softball	2
Surfing	6

31. Writing to Explain Mr. Hughes made 33 birdhouses that he will sell for $28.95 each. If he sells all the birdhouses, will he earn more than $1,000? Explain how to use estimation to find the answer.

32. Tanya has 8 bird posters and 12 reptile posters to display in groups. She wants each group to have the same number of posters and to have one type of animal. What is the greatest number of posters she can put in each group?

33. Brenda spent 0.6 hour practicing the drums. How many minutes did she practice?

34. Reasoning Suppose two fractions are both less than 1. Can their sum be greater than 1? greater than 2?

35. Algebra Which operation should be done first in $(14 - 5) \times 5 + 1$?

36. Think About the Process Mrs. Morales's flowers are starting to bloom. Last week, $\frac{1}{11}$ of the buds bloomed and $\frac{4}{11}$ bloomed this week. Which expression shows how to find the fraction of the buds that have not yet bloomed?

37. Ms. Hall's company pays her $0.32 for each mile she drives for work. How much did she receive for a 621-mile trip?

A $\frac{1}{11} + \frac{11}{11} - \frac{4}{11}$ **C** $\frac{1}{11} + \left(\frac{11}{11} - \frac{4}{11}\right)$

B $\frac{1}{11} - \frac{4}{11} - \frac{11}{11}$ **D** $\frac{11}{11} - \left(\frac{1}{11} + \frac{4}{11}\right)$

Algebra Connections

Fractions and Equations

Remember that an equation uses an equal sign to show that two expressions have the same value.

$$\frac{1}{3} + \frac{1}{3} = \frac{2}{3}$$

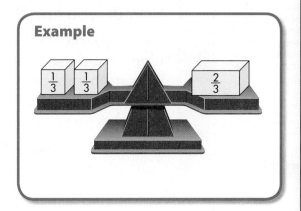

Example

In **1** through **12**, complete each equation by filling in the missing value(s). Check your answers by making sure the expressions in the equations are equal to each other.

1. $\frac{3}{8} + \underline{\quad} = \frac{5}{8}$

2. $\underline{\quad} - \frac{1}{15} = \frac{1}{15}$

3. $\frac{9}{\underline{\quad}} + \frac{4}{\underline{\quad}} = \frac{13}{18}$

4. $\frac{8}{10} - \frac{3}{\underline{\quad}} = \frac{5}{\underline{\quad}}$

5. $\frac{\underline{\quad}}{4} + \frac{\underline{\quad}}{4} = \frac{3}{4}$

6. $\frac{5}{6} - \frac{\underline{\quad}}{\underline{\quad}} = \frac{2}{6}$

7. $\frac{\underline{\quad}}{\underline{\quad}} - \frac{7}{12} = \frac{3}{12}$

8. $\frac{5}{16} + \frac{\underline{\quad}}{\underline{\quad}} = \frac{11}{16}$

9. $\frac{1}{2} - \frac{\underline{\quad}}{\underline{\quad}} = 0$

10. $\frac{4}{9} + \frac{\underline{\quad}}{\underline{\quad}} = \frac{7}{9}$

11. $\frac{1}{4} + \frac{\underline{\quad}}{\underline{\quad}} + \frac{1}{4} = \frac{3}{4}$

12. $\frac{8}{10} - \frac{\underline{\quad}}{\underline{\quad}} - \frac{1}{10} = \frac{6}{10}$

For **13** through **24**, use the number line below to write and solve each equation. Simplify, if possible. The distance between each consecutive label on the number line is the same.

```
←┬──┬──┬──┬──┬──┬──┬─┬──┬──┬──┬──┬→
 0  A  B  C  D  E  F G  H  I  J  K  1
```

13. $A + A = \underline{\quad}$

14. $K - A = \underline{\quad}$

15. $B + D = \underline{\quad}$

16. $F - B = \underline{\quad}$

17. $H + A = \underline{\quad}$

18. $I - C = \underline{\quad}$

19. $J - \underline{\quad} = E$

20. $G + \underline{\quad} = K$

21. $C - \underline{\quad} = 0$

22. $B + B + B = \underline{\quad}$

23. $K - A - \underline{\quad} = \frac{3}{4}$

24. $G + \underline{\quad} + B = \frac{5}{6}$

25. Write a word problem using one of the equations in **13** through **24**.

Common Multiples and Least Common Multiple

Understand It!
Making a list of multiples for two numbers is helpful when trying to determine the least common multiple.

How do you find the least common multiple?

Loren is buying fish fillets and buns for the soccer team dinner. What is the smallest number of fish fillets and buns she can buy to have the same number of each?

Guided Practice*

Do you know HOW?

In **1** through **6**, find the LCM of each pair of numbers.

1. 2 and 4
   2: 2, 4, 6, 8, . . .
   4: 4, 8, 12, 16, . . .

2. 3 and 4
   3: 3, 6, 9, 12, 15, . . .
   4: 4, 8, 12, 16, . . .

3. 3 and 7

4. 8 and 15

5. 12 and 9

6. 6 and 18

Do you UNDERSTAND?

7. In the example above, why is 24 the LCM of 6 and 8?

8. How many packages of each does Loren need to buy to have 24 fish fillets and 24 buns?

Independent Practice

Leveled Practice In **9** through **27**, find the LCM of each pair of numbers.

9. 2 and 4
   2: 2, 4, . . .
   4: 4, 8, . . .

10. 2 and 3
   2: 2, 4, 6, 8, . . .
   3: 3, 6, 9, 12, . . .

11. 5 and 6
   5: 5, 10, 15, 20, 25, 30, 35, 40, . . .
   6: 6, 12, 18, 24, 30, 36, 42, . . .

12. 3 and 5

13. 6 and 8

14. 4 and 5

15. 3 and 10

16. 4 and 9

17. 8 and 20

18. 6 and 9

19. 10 and 12

20. 8 and 12

21. 4 and 6

22. 8 and 16

23. 12 and 16

24. 8 and 9

25. 4 and 12

26. 5 and 10

27. 14 and 21

Animated Glossary
www.pearsonsuccessnet.com

DIGITAL

Find the common multiples of 6 and 8.

Remember that a multiple of a number is a product of a given whole number and another whole number.

A common multiple is a number that is a multiple of two or more numbers.

List the multiples of 6 and 8.

6: 6, 12, 18, 24, 30, 36, 42, 48, 54, …

8: 8, 16, 24, 32, 40, 48, 56, …

Two common multiples of 6 and 8 are 24 and 48.

Find the least common multiple of 6 and 8.

A least common multiple (LCM) is the least number that is a multiple of both numbers.

Both 24 and 48 are common multiples of 6 and 8. So, the LCM of 6 and 8 is 24.

Loren will need to buy 24 fish fillets and 24 buns.

Problem Solving

28. Pecans are sold in 6-oz cans, almonds in 9-oz cans, and peanuts in 12-oz cans. What is the least number of ounces you can buy to have equal amounts of pecans, almonds, and peanuts?

29. Writing to Explain Can you always find the LCM for two numbers by multiplying them together? Why or why not?

30. Number Sense The batting averages of three players are 0.261, 0.267, 0.264. Write the averages in order from least to greatest. Use $<$.

31. A cell phone call costs $0.07 per minute for the first 25 minutes and $0.10 per minute for each additional minute. How much would a 47-minute call cost?

32. a Peter is distributing pamphlets about dog care and samples of dog biscuits. The dog biscuits come in packages of 12 and the pamphlets are in packages of 20. What is the smallest number of samples and pamphlets he needs to distribute without having any left over?

b How many packages of dog biscuits and pamphlets will Peter need?

33. Katie bought dinner at 5 different restaurants. Each dinner cost between $12 and $24. What is a reasonable total cost for all 5 dinners?

A less than $60

B more than $150

C between $24 and $60

D between $60 and $120

34. Julie drank $1\frac{2}{3}$ cups of cranberry juice. Her brother said she drank $\frac{5}{3}$ cups of juice. Is her brother correct? Explain your answer.

35. A factory whistle blows every 30 minutes. The clock tower chimes every 15 minutes. If they both sounded at 1:00 P.M., at what time will you hear them both at the same time again?

Understand It!
To add fractions with unlike denominators, find equivalent fractions with the least common denominator, then add.

Adding Fractions with Unlike Denominators

How can you add fractions with unlike denominators?

Alex rode his scooter from his house to the park. Later, he rode from the park to baseball practice. How far did Alex ride?

Choose an Operation Add to find the total distance Alex rode his scooter.

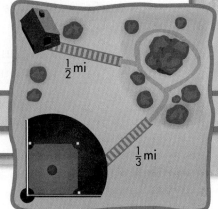

$\frac{1}{2}$ mi

$\frac{1}{3}$ mi

Guided Practice*

Do you know HOW?

In **1** through **4**, find each sum. Simplify, if necessary.

1. $\frac{1}{2} = \frac{9}{18}$
   $+ \frac{2}{9} = \frac{4}{18}$

2. $\frac{2}{6} = \frac{8}{24}$
   $+ \frac{3}{8} = \frac{9}{24}$

3. $\frac{3}{4} + \frac{7}{10}$

4. $\frac{5}{12} + \frac{1}{8}$

Do you UNDERSTAND?

5. **Writing to Explain** In the example above, would you get the same sum if you used 12 as the common denominator?

6. In the example above, if the park was $\frac{4}{5}$ mile from baseball practice, how far would Alex ride his scooter?

Independent Practice

Leveled Practice In **7** through **22**, find each sum. Simplify, if necessary.

7. $\frac{1}{9} = \frac{}{18}$
   $+ \frac{5}{6} = \frac{}{18}$

8. $\frac{1}{12} = \frac{}{12}$
   $+ \frac{2}{3} = \frac{}{12}$

9. $\frac{1}{3} = \frac{}{15}$
   $+ \frac{1}{5} = \frac{}{15}$

10. $\frac{1}{8} = \frac{}{56}$
    $+ \frac{3}{7} = \frac{}{56}$

11. $\frac{2}{9} + \frac{2}{3}$

12. $\frac{5}{8} + \frac{1}{6}$

13. $\frac{3}{4} + \frac{2}{5}$

14. $\frac{1}{6} + \frac{3}{10}$

15. $\frac{7}{8} + \frac{1}{12}$

16. $\frac{11}{16} + \frac{1}{2}$

17. $\frac{5}{6} + \frac{3}{4}$

18. $\frac{7}{12} + \frac{9}{16}$

19. $\frac{1}{2} + \frac{1}{8} + \frac{1}{4}$

20. $\frac{1}{3} + \frac{5}{6} + \frac{4}{9}$

21. $\frac{1}{2} + \frac{1}{3} + \frac{1}{4}$

22. $\frac{1}{2} + \frac{3}{4} + \frac{3}{5}$

DIGITAL
Animated Glossary
www.pearsonsuccessnet.com

*For another example, see Set C on page 274.

Change the fractions to equivalent fractions with a common, or like, denominator.

The least common denominator (LCD) of two fractions is the least common multiple of the denominators.

Multiples of 2: 2, 4, 6, 8, 10, 12, . . .

Multiples of 3: 3, 6, 9, 12, . . .

The LCM is 6, so the LCD is 6.

Write the equivalent fractions.

$$\frac{1}{2} \overset{\times 3}{=} \frac{3}{6} \quad \frac{1}{3} \overset{\times 2}{=} \frac{2}{6}$$

Add. Simplify if necessary.

$$\begin{array}{r} \frac{1}{2} = \frac{3}{6} \\ + \frac{1}{3} = + \frac{2}{6} \\ \hline \frac{5}{6} \end{array}$$

Alex rode his scooter $\frac{5}{6}$ mile.

Problem Solving

23. Cindy added $\frac{7}{8}$ cup of water to $\frac{1}{4}$ cup of juice concentrate. How much juice did Cindy make?

24. Abdul bought 10 packages of string cheese. If each package costs $1.59, how much did Abdul spend?

25. Mr. Perez is building a fence. He wants to bolt together 2 boards. One is $\frac{3}{4}$ inches thick and the other is $\frac{7}{8}$ inches thick. What will be the total thickness of the 2 boards?

26. About $\frac{1}{10}$ of the bones in your body are in your skull. Your hands have about $\frac{1}{4}$ of the bones in your body. What fraction of the bones in your body are in your hands and skull?

27. Number Sense At an auction, the bid for a painting starts at $150,000. The next bid is $170,000. The next 2 bids are $190,000 and $210,000. If the pattern continues, what is the next bid?

28. Dennis spent $\frac{1}{4}$ hour walking his dog. He spent another $\frac{1}{3}$ hour giving it food and water. What fraction of an hour did Dennis spend with the dog?

29. Native Americans made baskets like this one in the early 1900s. If two sides of the triangle shown on the basket measure $\frac{1}{4}$ in., and the third side measures $\frac{3}{8}$ in., what is the perimeter of the triangle?

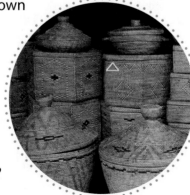

30. A girls' club is selling hats to raise money. They ordered 500 hats that cost $5.15 each. They will sell the hats for $18.50 each. All the hats were sold. Which expression shows how to find the amount of money the club made after expenses?

A $500 \times (18.50 + 5.15)$

B $(500 \times 18.50) + (500 \times 5.15)$

C $(500 \times 5.15) - (500 \times 18.50)$

D $500 \times (18.50 - 5.15)$

Subtracting Fractions with Unlike Denominators

Understand It!
To subtract fractions with unlike denominators, find equivalent fractions with the least common denominator, then subtract.

How can you subtract fractions with unlike denominators?

Linda used $\frac{1}{4}$ yard of the fabric she bought for a sewing project. How much fabric did she have left?

Choose an Operation Subtract to find how much fabric was left.

$\frac{2}{3}$ yard

Guided Practice*

Do you know HOW?

In **1** through **4**, find each difference. Simplify, if necessary.

1. $\frac{5}{6} = \frac{5}{6}$
    $-\frac{1}{2} = \frac{3}{6}$
    _____

2. $\frac{4}{7} = \frac{12}{21}$
    $-\frac{1}{3} = \frac{7}{21}$
    _____

3. $\frac{1}{2} - \frac{3}{10}$

4. $\frac{7}{8} - \frac{1}{3}$

Do you UNDERSTAND?

5. In the example above, is it possible to use a common denominator greater than 12 and get the correct answer? Why or why not?

6. In the example above, if Linda had started with one yard of fabric and used $\frac{5}{8}$ of a yard, how much fabric would be left?

Independent Practice

Leveled Practice In **7** through **24**, find each difference. Simplify, if necessary.

7. $\frac{1}{3} = \frac{\blacksquare}{6}$
    $-\frac{1}{6} = \frac{\blacksquare}{6}$
    _____

8. $\frac{2}{3} = \frac{\blacksquare}{12}$
    $-\frac{5}{12} = \frac{\blacksquare}{12}$
    _____

9. $\frac{3}{5} = \frac{\blacksquare}{15}$
    $-\frac{1}{3} = \frac{\blacksquare}{15}$
    _____

10. $\frac{2}{9} = \frac{\blacksquare}{72}$
    $-\frac{1}{8} = \frac{\blacksquare}{72}$
    _____

11. $\frac{1}{4} = \frac{\blacksquare}{8}$
    $-\frac{1}{8} = \frac{\blacksquare}{8}$
    _____

12. $\frac{2}{3} = \frac{\blacksquare}{6}$
    $-\frac{1}{2} = \frac{\blacksquare}{6}$
    _____

13. $\frac{3}{4} = \frac{\blacksquare}{8}$
    $-\frac{3}{8} = \frac{\blacksquare}{8}$
    _____

14. $\frac{5}{6} = \frac{\blacksquare}{6}$
    $-\frac{1}{3} = \frac{\blacksquare}{6}$
    _____

15. $\frac{5}{8} - \frac{1}{4}$

16. $\frac{9}{16} - \frac{3}{8}$

17. $\frac{1}{5} - \frac{1}{7}$

18. $\frac{7}{10} - \frac{2}{4}$

19. $\frac{5}{6} - \frac{3}{4}$

20. $\frac{2}{3} - \frac{5}{9}$

21. $\frac{4}{5} - \frac{1}{4}$

22. $\frac{5}{8} - \frac{7}{12}$

23. $\frac{6}{7} - \frac{1}{2}$

24. $\frac{5}{12} - \frac{4}{16}$

For another example, see Set C on page 274.

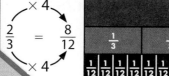

Step 1

Change the fractions to equivalent fractions with a common denominator.

Find the LCM of the denominators

Multiples of 3:
3, 6, 9, 12, . . .

Multiples of 4:
4, 8, 12, . . .

The LCM is 12, so the LCD is 12.

Step 2

Write the equivalent fractions.

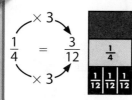

$$\frac{2}{3} = \frac{8}{12}$$

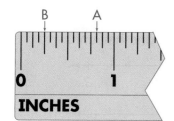

$$\frac{1}{4} = \frac{3}{12}$$

Step 3

Subtract. Simplify if necessary.

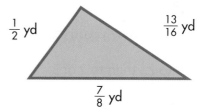

$$\frac{2}{3} = \frac{8}{12}$$
$$-\frac{1}{4} = -\frac{3}{12}$$
$$\overline{\phantom{-\frac{1}{4}=}\frac{5}{12}}$$

Linda has $\frac{5}{12}$ yard of fabric left.

Problem Solving

25. Write a number sentence to name the difference between Point *A* and Point *B*.

B   A

|||||||||||||||||||||||||||||
0   1
INCHES

26. Geometry Find the perimeter of the figure below.

$\frac{1}{2}$ yd $\frac{13}{16}$ yd

$\frac{7}{8}$ yd

27. When Mr. Goldman left on a business trip, his car had $\frac{3}{4}$ of a tank of gas. At the first rest stop, there was only $\frac{1}{2}$ tank left. How much gas had the car used?

28. Mariko's social studies class lasts $\frac{5}{6}$ of an hour. Only $\frac{3}{12}$ of an hour has gone by. What fraction of an hour remains of Mariko's social studies class?

29. Estimation Roy earned $72.50, $59, and $41.75 in tips when waiting tables last weekend. About how much did Roy earn in tips?

30. Nate exercises $\frac{1}{2}$ hour every day. LaDonna exercises $4\frac{1}{4}$ hours each week. Who exercises more in one week? How much more?

31. Writing to Explain Why do fractions need to have a common denominator before you add or subtract them?

32. Algebra Jay saved $300 to buy a new laptop computer. The computer costs $800. Which equation shows how to find the amount Jay still needs to save?

A $300 - n = 800$ **C** $n - 300 = 800$

B $800 + 300 = n$ **D** $n + 300 = 800$

33. Number Sense What is the greatest common multiple of 3 and 4?

Adding Mixed Numbers

How can you add mixed numbers?

Rhoda mixes sand with $2\frac{2}{3}$ cups of potting mixture to prepare soil for her cactus plants. After mixing them together, how many cups of soil does Rhoda have?

Choose an Operation Add to find the total amount of soil.

$1\frac{1}{2}$ cups

Another Example **How can you check for reasonableness?**

You just found that the sum of $2\frac{2}{3}$ and $1\frac{1}{2}$ is $4\frac{1}{6}$. You can use estimation to check that a sum is reasonable.

Estimate $2\frac{2}{3} + 1\frac{1}{2}$.

A number line can help you round mixed numbers to the nearest one-half unit.

$2\frac{2}{3}$ is closer to $2\frac{1}{2}$ than to 2 or 3.

$1\frac{1}{2}$ is halfway between 1 and 2.

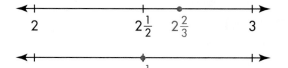

Add: $2\frac{1}{2} + 1\frac{1}{2} = 4$

Since $2\frac{2}{3}$ was rounded to $2\frac{1}{2}$, the answer will be greater than the estimate.

The actual sum, $4\frac{1}{6}$ is reasonable because it is close to the estimate 4.

Guided Practice*

Do you know HOW?

Find each sum. Simplify, if necessary. Estimate for reasonableness.

1. $\begin{array}{r} 1\frac{7}{8} = 1\frac{\ \ }{8} \\ + 1\frac{1}{4} = +1\frac{\ \ }{8} \\ \hline \end{array}$

2. $\begin{array}{r} 2\frac{2}{5} = 2\frac{\ \ }{30} \\ + 5\frac{5}{6} = +5\frac{\ \ }{30} \\ \hline \end{array}$

3. $4\frac{1}{9} + 1\frac{1}{3}$

4. $6\frac{5}{12} + 4\frac{5}{8}$

Do you UNDERSTAND?

5. Reasoning How is adding mixed numbers like adding fractions and whole numbers?

6. Writing to Explain Kyle used 9 as an estimate for $3\frac{1}{6} + 5\frac{7}{8}$. He added and got $9\frac{1}{24}$ for the actual sum. Is his answer reasonable?

*For another example, see Set D on page 275.

Step 1

Find $2\frac{2}{3} + 1\frac{1}{2}$.

Write equivalent fractions with the least common denominator.

$2\frac{2}{3} = 2\frac{4}{6}$

$+ 1\frac{1}{2} = + 1\frac{3}{6}$

Step 2

Add the fractions.

$2\frac{2}{3} = 2\frac{4}{6}$

$+ 1\frac{1}{2} = + 1\frac{3}{6}$

$\overline{3\frac{7}{6}}$

Step 3

Add the whole numbers. Simplify the sum if necessary.

$2\frac{2}{3} = 2\frac{4}{6}$

$+ 1\frac{1}{2} = + 1\frac{3}{6}$

$\overline{3\frac{7}{6}}$

$3\frac{7}{6} = 4\frac{1}{6}$

Rhoda prepared $4\frac{1}{6}$ cups of soil.

Independent Practice

Leveled Practice For **7** through **18**, find each sum. Simplify, if necessary. Estimate for reasonableness.

7. $\quad 3\frac{1}{6} = \quad 3\frac{\boxed{}}{6}$
$\quad + 5\frac{2}{3} = + 5\frac{\boxed{}}{6}$

8. $\quad 11\frac{1}{2} = \quad 11\frac{\boxed{}}{10}$
$\quad + 10\frac{3}{5} = + 10\frac{\boxed{}}{10}$

9. $\quad 9\frac{3}{16}$
$\quad + 7\frac{5}{8}$

10. $\quad 5\frac{6}{7}$
$\quad + 8\frac{1}{7}$

11. $4\frac{1}{10} + 6\frac{1}{2}$

12. $9\frac{7}{12} + 4\frac{3}{4}$

13. $5 + 3\frac{1}{8}$

14. $8\frac{3}{4} + 7\frac{3}{4}$

15. $2\frac{3}{4} + 7\frac{3}{5}$

16. $3\frac{8}{9} + 8\frac{1}{2}$

17. $1\frac{7}{12} + 2\frac{3}{8}$

18. $3\frac{11}{12} + 9\frac{1}{16}$

Problem Solving

19. Arnie skates $1\frac{3}{4}$ miles from home to the lake, then goes $1\frac{1}{3}$ miles around the lake, and then back home. How many miles did he skate?

A $2\frac{1}{12}$ miles

B $3\frac{1}{12}$ miles

C $4\frac{5}{6}$ miles

D $4\frac{5}{12}$ miles

20. a Use the map below to find the distance from the start of the trail to the end.

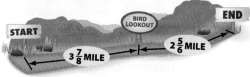

b Louise walked from the start of the trail to the bird lookout and back. Did she walk more or less than if she had walked from the start of the trail to the end?

21. The length of a male Parsons chameleon can be up to $23\frac{1}{2}$ inches. It can extend its tongue up to $35\frac{1}{4}$ inches to catch its food. What is the total length of a male Parsons chameleon when its tongue is fully extended?

Subtracting Mixed Numbers

How can you subtract mixed numbers?

A golf ball measures about $1\frac{2}{3}$ inches in diameter. What is the difference between the diameter of the hole and the golf ball?

Choose an Operation Subtract to find the difference in diameters.

$4\frac{1}{4}$ inches

Another Example How can you check for reasonableness?

You just found that the difference of $4\frac{1}{4}$ and $1\frac{2}{3}$ is $2\frac{7}{12}$. You can use estimation to check that a difference is reasonable.

Estimate $4\frac{1}{4} - 1\frac{2}{3}$.

$4\frac{1}{4}$ is close to 4 or $4\frac{1}{2}$.
You can round to 4.

$1\frac{2}{3}$ is closer to $1\frac{1}{2}$ than to 1 or 2.

Subtract: $4 - 1\frac{1}{2} = 2\frac{1}{2}$.

The actual difference, $2\frac{7}{12}$ is reasonable because it is close to the estimate $2\frac{1}{2}$.

Guided Practice*

Do you know HOW?

Find each difference. Simplify, if necessary. Estimate for reasonableness.

1. $\quad 7\frac{2}{3} = \quad 7\frac{\square}{6} = 6\frac{\square}{6}$
$\quad - 3\frac{5}{6} = -3\frac{\square}{6} = 3\frac{\square}{6}$

2. $\quad 5 = \quad \square\frac{\square}{4}$
$\quad - 2\frac{3}{4} = -2\frac{3}{4}$

3. $6\frac{3}{10} - 1\frac{4}{5}$

4. $9\frac{1}{3} - 4\frac{3}{4}$

Do you UNDERSTAND?

5. In Exercise 2, why do you need to rename 5?

6. **Reasonableness** Could two golf balls fall into the hole at the same time? Explain your reasoning.

Write equivalent fractions with the least common denominator.

$$4\frac{1}{4} = \quad 4\frac{3}{12}$$
$$-\,1\frac{2}{3} = -\,1\frac{8}{12}$$

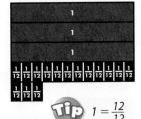

Tip You cannot subtract $\frac{8}{12}$ from $\frac{3}{12}$.

Rename $4\frac{3}{12}$ to show more twelfths.

$$4\frac{3}{12} = \quad 3\frac{15}{12}$$
$$-\,1\frac{8}{12} = -\,1\frac{8}{12}$$

Tip $1 = \frac{12}{12}$

Subtract the fractions. Then subtract the whole numbers. Simplify, if necessary.

$$4\frac{1}{4} = \quad 4\frac{3}{12} = \quad 3\frac{15}{12}$$
$$-\,1\frac{2}{3} = -\,1\frac{8}{12} = -\,1\frac{8}{12}$$
$$\overline{\qquad\qquad\qquad\quad 2\frac{7}{12}}$$

The hole is $2\frac{7}{12}$ inches wider.

Independent Practice

Leveled Practice For **7** through **18**, find each difference. Simplify, if necessary. Estimate for reasonableness.

7. $\quad 8\frac{1}{4} = \quad 8\frac{\square}{8} = 7\frac{\square}{8}$
$\quad -2\frac{7}{8} = -2\frac{\square}{8} = 2\frac{\square}{8}$

8. $\quad 3\frac{1}{2} = 3\frac{\square}{6}$
$\quad -1\frac{1}{3} = 1\frac{\square}{6}$

9. $\quad 4\frac{1}{8}$
$\quad -1\frac{1}{2}$

10. $\quad 6$
$\quad -2\frac{4}{5}$

11. $6\frac{1}{3} - 5\frac{2}{3}$

12. $9\frac{1}{2} - 6\frac{3}{4}$

13. $8\frac{3}{16} - 3\frac{5}{8}$

14. $7\frac{1}{2} - \frac{7}{10}$

15. $15\frac{1}{6} - 4\frac{3}{8}$

16. $13\frac{1}{12} - 8\frac{1}{4}$

17. $6\frac{1}{3} - 2\frac{3}{5}$

18. $10\frac{5}{12} - 4\frac{7}{8}$

Problem Solving

19. The average weight of a basketball is $21\frac{1}{10}$ ounces. The average weight of a baseball is $5\frac{1}{4}$ ounces. How many more ounces does the basketball weigh?

20. As of 2006, the world's shortest horse is Thumbelina. She is $17\frac{1}{4}$ inches tall. The second shortest horse, Black Beauty, is $18\frac{1}{2}$ inches tall. How much shorter is Thumbelina than Black Beauty?

21. The smallest mammals on Earth are the bumblebee bat and the Etruscan pygmy shrew. A length of a bumblebee bat is $1\frac{9}{50}$ inches. A length of an Etruscan pygmy shrew is $1\frac{21}{50}$ inches. How much smaller is the bat than the shrew?

22. **Geometry** How are the parallelogram and the rectangle alike? How are they different?

Understand It!
Learning how and when to *try, check, and revise* can be helpful when solving problems.

Try, Check, and Revise

Which of these square tiles can be used to completely cover the area of this floor without cutting tiles, or combining tiles of different sizes?

2 ft   3 ft

4 ft | Floor

8 ft

4 ft   5 ft

Guided Practice*

Do you know HOW?

1. Which of these tiles can be used to cover a 10 ft × 10 ft floor: 2 × 2 ft, 3 × 3 ft, 4 × 4 ft, or 5 × 5 ft tile?

2. What size rectangular tile floor can be completely covered by using only 2 × 2 ft tiles OR 3 × 3 ft tiles? Remember, you can't cut tiles or combine the two tile sizes.

Do you UNDERSTAND?

3. How do you use *Try, Check, and Revise* to help you find the solution to a problem?

4. **Write a Problem** Write a real-world problem that involves common factors and can be solved using the *Try, Check, and Revise* strategy.

Independent Practice

For **5** through **9**, use *Try, Check, and Revise* to solve.

5. Bert is planning to tile a floor that measures 9 ft × 11 ft. What size square tile can he use to completely cover it?

6. Mrs. Gonzales wants to tile her floor with a pattern that repeats every 3 feet. Can she cover the floor without cutting off part of the pattern? Explain.

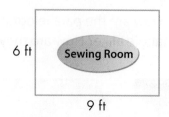

6 ft   Sewing Room

9 ft

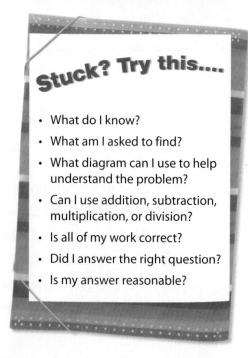

Stuck? Try this....

- What do I know?
- What am I asked to find?
- What diagram can I use to help understand the problem?
- Can I use addition, subtraction, multiplication, or division?
- Is all of my work correct?
- Did I answer the right question?
- Is my answer reasonable?

Use reasoning to make good tries. Then check.

One side of the floor is 4 feet so I think the 4 x 4 ft tile is the only one that works.

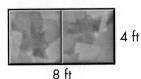

4 ft

8 ft

It works!

Next I'll try the 3 x 3 ft tile.

4 ft

8 ft

3 does not work for the 4 ft width and 8 ft length because 3 is not a factor of 4 or 8.

Revise what you know.

4 works for the 4 ft width.

4 works for the 8 ft length.

5 is not a factor of 4 or 8, so the 5 x 5 ft tile won't work.

2 is a factor of 4 and 8, so the 2 x 2 ft tile will work too.

4 ft

8 ft

7. You buy a baseball and a bat and spend $31. The bat costs $19 more than the baseball. What is the price of the baseball? What is the price of the bat?

8. The difference between the prices of two bikes is $22. The sum of the prices is $328. How much does each bike cost?

For **9**, use the picture at the right.

9. Kyle's mother spent $115 on shirts and pairs of socks for him. If she bought at least 3 shirts, how many pairs of socks and how many shirts did she buy?

$3

$17

$22

For **10**, draw a picture, write an equation, and solve.

10. Each of the 13 members of a basketball team bought a team emblem. The emblems cost the team $78. How much did it cost each member of the team for an emblem?

11. A group of 168 students are going to a ball game. They will travel on buses that hold 36 students. How many buses could be completely filled? How many buses will be needed? How many seats are left on the bus that is not filled?

12. It costs $2 for each person to ride the bus in the city. A transfer costs $0.50. If 10 people get on the bus, and 5 of those people want a transfer, what is the total amount the bus driver collects?

13. A farmer has 9 cows, 10 pigs, and 25 sheep on his farm. Special food for all the animals costs $3 a pound. If the farmer needs to buy 100 pounds of food for each animal, what will his total cost be?

1. Manny used the computer for $\frac{2}{10}$ of his allotted time before school and $\frac{3}{10}$ after school. Which of the following can be used to find how much of his allotted time he used the computer? (10-1)

   A Write $\frac{2+3}{10+10}$ to get $\frac{5}{20}$. Simplify to $\frac{1}{4}$.

   B Write $\frac{2+3}{10+10}$ to get $\frac{5}{20}$. Simplify to $\frac{1}{5}$.

   C Write $\frac{2+3}{10}$ to get $\frac{5}{10}$. Simplify to $\frac{1}{2}$.

   D Write $\frac{2+3}{10+10}$ to get $\frac{5}{0}$.

2. Rick made a paper football that was $1\frac{1}{6}$ inches long. Carly made one $\frac{5}{6}$ of an inch long. How much longer was Rick's paper football than Carly's? (10-6)

   A $1\frac{4}{6}$ inches

   B $1\frac{2}{3}$ inches

   C $\frac{2}{3}$ inch

   D $\frac{1}{3}$ inch

3. What is $4\frac{1}{6} + 3\frac{1}{5}$? (10-5)

   A $7\frac{1}{15}$

   B $7\frac{2}{11}$

   C $7\frac{11}{60}$

   D $7\frac{11}{30}$

4. Which of the following pairs of numbers has a least common multiple of 24? (10-2)

   A 4 and 6

   B 3 and 8

   C 2 and 12

   D 3 and 6

5. In music, a sixteenth note often receives $\frac{1}{4}$ of a beat and an eighth note often receives $\frac{1}{2}$ of a beat. What fraction of a beat would a sixteenth note and an eighth note receive together? (10-3)

   A $\frac{3}{4}$

   B $\frac{3}{8}$

   C $\frac{3}{16}$

   D $\frac{1}{4}$

6. The table lists sizes of packages of school supplies. What is the smallest number of pencils and erasers that Mrs. Deng can buy so that she will have the same number of each? (10-2)

Item	Number in Package
Paper	50
Pencils	12
Erasers	10

   A 24

   B 30

   C 60

   D 120

7. Mrs. Jin said that $\frac{4}{12}$ of the test items are multiple choice, $\frac{5}{12}$ are short answer, and the rest are matching. What fraction of the items are either multiple choice or short answer? (10-1)

   A $\frac{1}{12}$

   B $\frac{1}{4}$

   C $\frac{3}{8}$

   D $\frac{3}{4}$

8. Teri and her friends bought a submarine sandwich that was 28 inches or $\frac{7}{9}$ yards long. They ate 24 inches or $\frac{2}{3}$ of a yard. What part of a yard was left? (10-4)

A $\frac{5}{6}$

B $\frac{5}{9}$

C $\frac{1}{9}$

D $\frac{1}{18}$

9. Casey has $56 to spend on juice and crackers for a party. Juice costs $2 per bottle and crackers cost $3 per box. If Casey would like to buy 2 more boxes of crackers than bottles of juice, how many of each should Casey buy to spend exactly $56? (10-7)

A 12 bottles of juice and 10 boxes of crackers

B 8 bottles of juice and 10 boxes of crackers

C 10 bottles of juice and 12 boxes of crackers

D 8 bottles of juice and 14 boxes of crackers

10. A green snake is about $\frac{8}{9}$ of a yard long. A garter snake is about $\frac{13}{18}$ of a yard. About how much longer is the green snake than the garter? (10-4)

A $\frac{1}{6}$ yard

B $\frac{4}{18}$ yard

C $\frac{5}{18}$ yard

D $\frac{5}{9}$ yard

11. Of the balls shown, $\frac{1}{3}$ are basketballs and $\frac{1}{15}$ are soccer balls. What fraction of the balls are either basketballs or soccer balls? (10-3)

A $\frac{1}{9}$

B $\frac{2}{15}$

C $\frac{1}{5}$

D $\frac{2}{5}$

12. The Jacobys went on a 600 mile trip. On the first day they drove $5\frac{2}{3}$ hours and on the second day they drove $4\frac{3}{5}$ hours. How long did they drive during the first two days? (10-5)

A $10\frac{4}{15}$ hours

B 10 hours

C $9\frac{19}{30}$ hours

D $9\frac{4}{15}$ hours

13. Marie needs $2\frac{1}{4}$ yards of fabric. She already has $1\frac{3}{8}$ yards. How many yards of fabric does she need? (10-6)

A $\frac{3}{4}$ yard

B $\frac{7}{8}$ yard

C $1\frac{1}{4}$ yard

D $1\frac{7}{8}$ yard

14. Which equals $\frac{5}{12} - \frac{3}{12}$? (10-1)

A $\frac{1}{12}$

B $\frac{1}{6}$

C $\frac{8}{12}$

D $\frac{2}{3}$

Set A, pages 256–258

Find $\frac{3}{8} + \frac{7}{8}$.

$\frac{3}{8} + \frac{7}{8} = \frac{10}{8}$ Add the numerators.
Write the sum over the
common denominator.

$= 1\frac{2}{8}$ Simplify the sum.

$= 1\frac{1}{4}$

Remember when adding or
subtracting fractions with like
denominators, the common
denominator does not change.

1. $\frac{2}{7} + \frac{4}{7}$ **2.** $\frac{8}{12} - \frac{3}{12}$

3. $\frac{7}{9} - \frac{4}{9}$ **4.** $\frac{7}{10} + \frac{7}{10}$

5. $\frac{3}{6} + \frac{5}{6}$ **6.** $\frac{3}{4} - \frac{1}{4}$

Set B, pages 260–261

Find the least common multiple (LCM) of 9 and 12.

Make a list of the multiples of each number.

Multiples of 9: 9, 18, 27, 36, 45, …

Multiple of 12: 12, 24, 36, 48, …

Identify the least number that is a multiple of both
9 and 12.

The least common multiple of 9 and 12 is 36.

Remember that the least common
multiple of two numbers is the least
number that is a multiple of both of
the numbers. Multiples do not involve
fractions.

1. 3 and 5   **2.** 4 and 6

3. 5 and 9   **4.** 6 and 10

5. 8 and 12   **6.** 8 and 3

7. 10 and 4   **8.** 6 and 9

Set C, pages 262–265

Find $\frac{5}{6} + \frac{3}{4}$.

 Find the least common multiple (LCM)
of 6 and 4.
The LCM is 12, so the least common
denominator (LCD) is 12.

 Use the LCD to write equivalent
fractions.

$\frac{5}{6} = \frac{5 \times 2}{6 \times 2} = \frac{10}{12}$ $\frac{3}{4} = \frac{3 \times 3}{4 \times 3} = \frac{9}{12}$

 Add the equivalent fractions.
Simplify, if possible.

$\frac{10}{12} + \frac{9}{12} = \frac{19}{12} = 1\frac{7}{12}$

Remember to multiply the numerator
and denominator by the same number
when writing equivalent fractions.

1. $\frac{2}{5} + \frac{3}{10}$ **2.** $\frac{7}{9} + \frac{5}{6}$

3. $\frac{3}{4} - \frac{5}{12}$ **4.** $\frac{7}{8} - \frac{2}{3}$

5. $\frac{5}{16} - \frac{1}{8}$ **6.** $\frac{7}{10} - \frac{1}{6}$

7. $\frac{2}{3} + \frac{3}{4}$ **8.** $\frac{1}{4} + \frac{3}{8}$

9. $\frac{4}{5} - \frac{1}{3}$ **10.** $\frac{5}{8} - \frac{1}{2}$

11. $\frac{2}{3} + \frac{1}{2} + \frac{3}{4}$ **12.** $\frac{7}{10} + \frac{4}{5} + \frac{3}{4}$

Set D, pages 266–267

Find $1\frac{5}{6} + 2\frac{3}{8}$.

$$1\frac{5}{6} = 1\frac{20}{24}$$
$$+ 2\frac{3}{8} = + 2\frac{9}{24}$$
$$\overline{\qquad\quad 3\frac{29}{24} = 4\frac{5}{24}}$$

Step 1 Write equivalent fractions with the LCD.

Step 2 Add the fractions.

Step 3 Add the whole numbers. Simplify the sum, if necessary.

Remember that mixed numbers are added the same way whole numbers and fractions are added.

1. $5\frac{1}{2} + 2\frac{1}{8}$ **2.** $3\frac{1}{4} + 1\frac{5}{6}$

3. $5\frac{7}{10} + 4\frac{2}{5}$ **4.** $7\frac{3}{5} + 6\frac{2}{3}$

5. $8\frac{5}{9} + 9\frac{1}{3}$ **6.** $2\frac{5}{12} + 3\frac{3}{4}$

Set E, pages 268–269

Find $5\frac{1}{5} - 3\frac{1}{2}$.

$$5\frac{1}{5} = 5\frac{2}{10} = 4\frac{12}{10}$$
$$- 3\frac{1}{2} = - 3\frac{5}{10} = - 3\frac{5}{10}$$
$$\overline{\qquad\qquad\qquad\qquad 1\frac{7}{10}}$$

Step 1 Write equivalent fractions with the LCD.

Step 2 Rename $5\frac{2}{10}$ to show more tenths.

Step 3 Subtract the fractions. Subtract the whole numbers. Simplify the difference.

Remember that subtracting mixed fractions may require renaming.

1. $7\frac{5}{6} - 3\frac{2}{3}$ **2.** $2\frac{3}{5} - 1\frac{1}{2}$

3. $5\frac{2}{3} - 4\frac{5}{6}$ **4.** $9 - 3\frac{3}{8}$

5. $3\frac{1}{9} - 1\frac{1}{3}$ **6.** $6\frac{1}{4} - 3\frac{2}{5}$

7. $9\frac{1}{4} - 2\frac{5}{8}$ **8.** $4 - 1\frac{2}{5}$

Set F, pages 270–271

When you *try*, *check*, and *revise* to solve a problem, follow these steps:

Step 1

Make a reasonable first try.

Step 2

Check by using information given to you.

Step 3

Use your first try to make a reasonable second try.

Step 4

Keep checking until you find the answer.

Remember *try*, *check*, and *revise* can help to solve a problem.

1. Mr. Herrera wants to tile his floor with a pattern that repeats every 3 feet. Could he cover the floor without cutting off part of the pattern? Explain.

20 ft.

8 ft.   Living Room

Multiplying Fractions and Mixed Numbers

1 What would a fifth-grader who weighs 96 pounds on Earth weigh on Mars? You will find out in Lesson 11-1.

2 How much silver does this half dollar contain? You will find out in Lesson 11-1.

3 The world's smallest gecko can fit on the face of a dime. How does its length compare to the length of an adult male Western Banded Gecko that is shown below? You will find out in Lesson 11-3.

Review What You Know!

Vocabulary

Choose the best term from the box.

- denominator
- least common multiple
- numerator
- least common denominator

1. The number above the fraction bar is the ___?___.

2. The smallest common multiple of two numbers is called the ___?___.

3. The number below the fraction bar is the ___?___.

4. The smallest common multiple of two denominators is called the ___?___.

Least Common Denominator

Write each pair of fractions with their LCD.

5. $\frac{5}{12}$ and $\frac{1}{4}$

6. $\frac{3}{4}$ and $\frac{1}{6}$

7. $\frac{5}{6}$ and $\frac{3}{8}$

8. $\frac{7}{9}$ and $\frac{1}{2}$

Adding and Subtracting

Find each sum or difference. Simplify, if possible.

9. $\frac{5}{8} + \frac{1}{4}$

10. $\frac{11}{12} - \frac{1}{4}$

11. $\frac{4}{5} + \frac{1}{2}$

12. $\frac{6}{15} - \frac{1}{3}$

Adding Mixed Numbers

13. **Writing to Explain** Write an answer to the question.

How would you find $2\frac{1}{3} + 1\frac{2}{3}$?

4

The Akashi-Kaikyo Bridge in Japan (top) is the longest suspension bridge in the world. How does the length of this bridge compare to the length of the Golden Gate Bridge in San Francisco? You will find out in Lesson 11-3.

Understand It!
Multiplying a whole number by a fraction involves division as well as multiplication.

Multiplying Fractions and Whole Numbers

What are some ways to think about multiplying fractions and whole numbers?

How many cups of orange juice are needed to make 8 batches of fruit drink?

One way to find $8 \times \frac{3}{4}$ is to use repeated addition.

$$8 \times \frac{3}{4} = \frac{3}{4} + \frac{3}{4} + \frac{3}{4} + \frac{3}{4} + \frac{3}{4} + \frac{3}{4} + \frac{3}{4} + \frac{3}{4} = \frac{8 \times 3}{4} = \frac{24}{4} = 6$$

$\frac{3}{4}$ cup of orange juice for each batch

Guided Practice*

Do you know HOW?

In **1** through **4**, find each product.

1. $\frac{1}{7}$ of 14

2. $\frac{3}{7}$ of 14

3. $25 \times \frac{1}{5}$

4. $\left(\frac{5}{6} - \frac{2}{6}\right) \times 40$

Do you UNDERSTAND?

5. How is finding $8 \times \frac{3}{4}$ similar to finding $\frac{3}{4}$ of 8?

6. If you wanted to make 4 batches using the recipe above, how many cups of orange juice would you need?

Independent Practice

In **7** through **38**, find each product.

7. $\frac{1}{4}$ of 40

8. $\frac{1}{3}$ of 15

9. $\frac{1}{5}$ of 40

10. $\frac{1}{7}$ of 28

11. $\frac{2}{9}$ of 90

12. $\frac{2}{5}$ of 40

13. $\frac{1}{2}$ of 50

14. $\frac{5}{8}$ of 32

15. $\frac{3}{4}$ of 12

16. $\frac{6}{7}$ of 49

17. $\frac{3}{5}$ of 25

18. $\frac{2}{7}$ of 35

19. $\frac{5}{8}$ of 24

20. $\frac{3}{7}$ of 21

21. $\frac{8}{9}$ of 81

22. $\frac{7}{8}$ of 56

23. $\frac{2}{3} \times 27$

24. $\frac{3}{8} \times 16$

25. $\frac{5}{6} \times 18$

26. $50 \times \frac{7}{10}$

27. $25 \times \frac{4}{5}$

28. $12 \times \frac{2}{3}$

29. $32 \times \frac{1}{4}$

30. $18 \times \frac{2}{9}$

31. $\frac{2}{5} \times 35$

32. $\frac{8}{9} \times 18$

33. $\frac{4}{7} \times 35$

34. $\frac{5}{8} \times 16$

35. $\frac{3}{8} \times 24$

36. $\frac{7}{9} \times 36$

37. $\left(\frac{3}{4} - \frac{1}{4}\right) \times 24$

38. $\left(\frac{3}{5} - \frac{3}{10}\right) \times 30$

For another example, see Set A on page 292.

To find $8 \times \frac{3}{4}$, you can multiply first and then divide.

$8 \times \frac{3}{4} = \frac{24}{4} = 6$

Another way to think about multiplication of a whole number and a fraction is to find a part of a whole group.

Martin has 8 oranges to make juice. If he uses $\frac{3}{4}$ of the oranges, how many will he use? To find $\frac{3}{4}$ of 8, you can draw a picture.

To find $\frac{3}{4}$ of 8, you can divide first and then multiply.

Think $\frac{1}{4}$ of 8 = 2.

So, $\frac{3}{4}$ of 8 = 3 × 2 or 6.

Remember that $\frac{3}{4}$ of 8 means $\frac{3}{4} \times 8$.

So, $\frac{3}{4} \times 8 = 6$.

Problem Solving

39. Number Sense Explain how you would find $36 \times \frac{3}{4}$ mentally.

40. Lions spend about $\frac{5}{6}$ of their days sleeping. How many hours a day does a lion sleep?

41. Writing to Explain Jo said that when you multiply a nonzero whole number by a fraction less than 1, the product is always less than the whole number. Do you agree?

42. Who ran the most miles by the end of the week? Use the table below.

	Monday	Wednesday	Saturday
Pat	2.75 mi	3 mi	2.5 mi
Toby	2 mi	2.25 mi	3.5 mi

43. On Mars, your weight is about $\frac{1}{3}$ of your weight on Earth. If a fifth grader weighs 96 pounds on Earth, about how much would be his or her weight on Mars?

44. How much change will Stacy get if she buys two CDs and two books and gives the clerk two $20 bills?

Sale: CDs for
$8.25 each

Sale: 2 books
for $10.00

45. A recipe calls for $\frac{1}{2}$ cup of walnuts and $\frac{3}{16}$ cup of dates. Which of the following shows the correct relationship?

A $\frac{1}{2} > \frac{3}{16}$ **C** $\frac{3}{8} < \frac{1}{4}$

B $\frac{1}{2} = \frac{3}{16}$ **D** $\frac{1}{2} < \frac{3}{16}$

46. A 1965 U.S. half dollar contains $\frac{2}{5}$ ounce of silver. How many ounces of silver do 100 of those coins contain?

Understand It!
Using common factors is helpful when multiplying two fractions.

Multiplying Two Fractions

How can you multiply fractions?

Tom has $\frac{3}{4}$ of a pan of lasagna. His friends ate $\frac{2}{3}$ of this amount of lasagna. What fraction of a whole pan of lasagna did his friends eat?

Find $\frac{2}{3}$ of $\frac{3}{4}$.

Another Example ## How can you simplify before you multiply?

A fraction times a fraction

Find $\frac{3}{4} \times \frac{5}{6}$.

Find the GCF of any numerator and any denominator.

The GCF of 3 and 6 is 3.

Divide 3 and 6 by 3.

$$\frac{\overset{1}{\cancel{3}}}{4} \times \frac{5}{\underset{2}{\cancel{6}}} = \frac{1 \times 5}{4 \times 2} = \frac{5}{8}$$

So, $\frac{3}{4} \times \frac{5}{6} = \frac{5}{8}$.

A fraction times a whole number

Find $\frac{2}{3} \times 18$.

Write 18 as an improper fraction.

$$\frac{2}{3} \times 18 = \frac{2}{3} \times \frac{18}{1}$$

The GCF of 3 and 18 is 3.

Divide 3 and 18 by 3.

$$\frac{2}{3} \times 18 = \frac{2}{\underset{1}{\cancel{3}}} \times \frac{\overset{6}{\cancel{18}}}{1} = \frac{12}{1} = 12$$

Explain It

1. To find $\frac{3}{4} \times \frac{5}{6}$ in the first example above, why is the 3 crossed out with a 1 written above it, and why is the 6 crossed out with a 2 written below it?

2. To find $\frac{2}{3} \times 18$ in the second example above, how is the problem changed so that you could multiply a fraction by a fraction?

One Way

Draw a picture to represent $\frac{3}{4}$. Shade 3 of the 4 parts red. Then draw two horizontal lines to show thirds. Use yellow to shade $\frac{2}{3}$ of the whole rectangle. Where the two shadings overlap is orange.

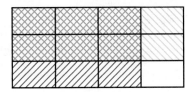

2×3 out of 3×4 parts are shaded orange.

They ate $\frac{6}{12}$ or $\frac{1}{2}$ of the pan of lasagna.

Another Way

Multiply the numerators and denominators. Simplify if possible.

$$\frac{2}{3} \times \frac{3}{4} = \frac{2 \times 3}{3 \times 4} = \frac{6}{12} = \frac{1}{2}$$

Guided Practice*

Do you know HOW?

In **1** through **4**, find each product. Simplify, if necessary.

1. $\frac{3}{4} \times \frac{7}{8}$

2. $15 \times \frac{3}{4}$

3. $\frac{3}{4} \times \frac{1}{4} \times 2$

4. $\left(\frac{2}{3} - \frac{1}{3}\right) \times \frac{5}{8}$

Do you UNDERSTAND?

5. How can you find the product of $\frac{6}{6} \times \frac{3}{8}$ mentally?

6. In the problem above, find the fraction of a whole pan of lasagna that Tom's friends ate if he started with $\frac{7}{8}$ of a pan.

Independent Practice

In **7** through **31**, find each product. Simplify, if necessary.

7. $\frac{3}{5} \times \frac{5}{9}$

8. $13 \times \frac{1}{5}$

9. $\frac{3}{4} \times \frac{1}{3} \times 2$

10. $\frac{2}{3} \times \frac{5}{8} \times 4$

11. $\frac{1}{6} \times \frac{5}{6}$

12. $\frac{1}{3} \times \frac{1}{4} \times \frac{2}{3}$

13. $\frac{1}{7} \times \frac{2}{3} \times 6$

14. $\frac{1}{2} \times \frac{3}{8} \times \frac{3}{4}$

15. $\frac{1}{3} \times \frac{2}{5}$

16. $\frac{7}{8} \times \frac{2}{3}$

17. $\frac{2}{5} \times \frac{3}{4} \times 10$

18. $\frac{1}{8} \times \frac{1}{3} \times 24$

19. $\frac{2}{9} \times \frac{3}{10}$

20. $\frac{3}{7} \times \frac{1}{3}$

21. $\frac{1}{6} \times \frac{3}{5} \times 20$

22. $\frac{1}{2} \times \frac{2}{5} \times 5$

23. $\left(\frac{1}{4} + \frac{1}{4}\right) \times \frac{7}{8}$

24. $\left(\frac{2}{3} - \frac{1}{3}\right) \times \frac{4}{9}$

25. $\left(\frac{3}{8} + \frac{1}{8}\right) \times \frac{2}{5}$

26. $\left(\frac{2}{3} - \frac{1}{4}\right) \times \frac{5}{6}$

27. $\left(\frac{1}{8} + \frac{1}{8}\right) \times \frac{5}{9}$

28. $\left(\frac{3}{4} - \frac{1}{3}\right) \times \frac{3}{5}$

29. $\left(\frac{1}{8} + \frac{1}{4}\right) \times \frac{1}{2}$

30. $\left(\frac{4}{5} - \frac{1}{2}\right) \times \frac{3}{8}$

31. $\left(\frac{1}{2} - \frac{4}{8}\right) \times \frac{3}{7}$

32. In the voting for City Council Precinct 5, only $\frac{1}{2}$ of all eligible voters cast votes. What fraction of all eligible voters voted for Shelley? Daley? Who received the most votes?

Candidate	Fraction of Votes Received
Shelley	$\frac{1}{10}$
Daley	$\frac{2}{8}$

33. Geometry The stained glass shown here is a regular hexagon. How can you use multiplication to find its perimeter?

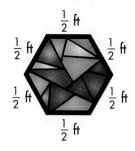

$\frac{1}{2}$ ft
$\frac{1}{2}$ ft $\frac{1}{2}$ ft
$\frac{1}{2}$ ft $\frac{1}{2}$ ft
$\frac{1}{2}$ ft

34. Writing to Explain Will $50 be enough to buy 6 cans of paint?

$8.95

35. Algebra What is the value of n in the equation $\frac{2}{3} \times n = \frac{4}{9}$?

36. Number Sense $\frac{4}{9} \times \frac{7}{8} = \frac{7}{18}$. What is $\frac{7}{8} \times \frac{4}{9}$? How do you know without multiplying?

37. Writing to Explain To amend the U.S. Constitution, $\frac{3}{4}$ of the states must approve the amendment. If 35 of the states approve an amendment, will the constitution be amended?

38. A plumber charges $45 for the first hour and $30 for each additional hour. How much does he charge if it takes him 4 hours to make a repair?

A $165   **C** $120

B $135   **D** $75

39. Naomi has 3 pounds of apples and $2\frac{1}{2}$ pounds of grapes. If she gives $\frac{1}{3}$ of her apples to Christine, how many pounds of apples does she have left?

A $\frac{1}{6}$ pound   **C** 1 pound

B $\frac{1}{2}$ pound   **D** 2 pounds

40. A video rental store has 6,000 movies. One Friday, $\frac{3}{5}$ of the movies were rented. How many movies were rented that Friday night?

41. One lap around the Lincoln School track is $\frac{1}{4}$ mile. If Eddie runs 6 laps around the track and then runs $2\frac{1}{2}$ miles to get home, how far will he run in all?

42. Ben found a recipe that calls for $\frac{3}{4}$ cup of chopped apples. If he wants to make half the recipe, how many cups of chopped apples should he use?

Find each product. Simplify if possible.

1. $\frac{1}{8} \times 6$ **2.** $7 \times \frac{1}{2}$ **3.** $\frac{4}{5} \times 3$ **4.** $5 \times \frac{7}{10}$

5. $8 \times \frac{5}{6}$ **6.** $\frac{2}{3} \times 9$ **7.** $4 \times \frac{5}{12}$ **8.** $\frac{1}{6} \times 12$

Find each product. Simplify if possible.

9. $\frac{2}{3} \times \frac{1}{4}$ **10.** $\frac{3}{5} \times \frac{3}{10}$ **11.** $\frac{1}{2} \times \frac{5}{12}$ **12.** $\frac{1}{4} \times \frac{1}{8}$ **13.** $\frac{2}{3} \times \frac{4}{5}$

14. $\frac{3}{4} \times \frac{1}{3}$ **15.** $\frac{8}{9} \times \frac{1}{2}$ **16.** $\frac{1}{5} \times \frac{1}{5}$ **17.** $\frac{3}{8} \times \frac{5}{6}$ **18.** $\frac{1}{2} \times \frac{1}{2}$

Find each sum. Simplify if possible.

19. $\frac{5}{6} + \frac{1}{12}$ **20.** $\frac{1}{2} + \frac{3}{8}$ **21.** $\frac{1}{3} + \frac{5}{12}$ **22.** $\frac{2}{3} + \frac{1}{9}$ **23.** $\frac{1}{5} + \frac{3}{10}$

Error Search Find each product that is not correct. Write it correctly and explain the error.

24. $\frac{2}{3} \times 3 = 2$ **25.** $\frac{3}{4} \times \frac{2}{5} = \frac{3}{20}$ **26.** $\frac{2}{10} \times \frac{3}{10} = \frac{6}{10}$

Number Sense

Estimating and Reasoning Write whether each statement is true or false. Explain your reasoning.

27. The product of 7 and 4.83 is greater than 35.

28. The sum of 45,752 and 36,687 is greater than 70,000 but less than 90,000.

29. The difference of $\frac{1}{2}$ and $\frac{1}{3}$ equals their product.

30. The product of $\frac{3}{4}$ and 5 is less than 5.

31. The quotient of $534 \div 9$ is greater than 60.

32. The sum of 21.45 and 4.2 is less than 25.

Multiplying Mixed Numbers

How do you find the product of mixed numbers?

A clothing factory has machines that make jackets. The machines operate for $7\frac{1}{2}$ hours each day. How many jackets can each machine make in one day?

Jackets Per Hour	
Machine A	**Machine B**
$2\frac{3}{4}$	$3\frac{1}{3}$

Choose an Operation Use multiplication to find how many jackets each machine can make in a day.

Guided Practice*

Do you know HOW?

In **1** and **2**, estimate the product. Then copy and complete the multiplication.

1. $2\frac{3}{4} \times 8 = \frac{\blacksquare}{4} \times \frac{8}{1}$

2. $4\frac{1}{2} \times 1\frac{1}{4} = \frac{\blacksquare}{2} \times \frac{\blacksquare}{4}$

Do you UNDERSTAND?

3. Explain how you would use improper fractions to multiply $5 \times 2\frac{1}{2}$.

4. How many jackets a day can Machine A make if it can make $4\frac{1}{4}$ jackets an hour?

Independent Practice

In **5** through **10**, estimate the product. Then copy and complete the multiplication.

5. $3\frac{4}{5} \times 5 = \frac{\blacksquare}{5} \times \frac{5}{1}$

6. $1\frac{3}{5} \times 2\frac{1}{4} = \frac{\blacksquare}{5} \times \frac{\blacksquare}{4}$

7. $1\frac{1}{2} \times 3\frac{5}{6} = \frac{\blacksquare}{2} \times \frac{\blacksquare}{6}$

8. $4\frac{2}{3} \times 4 = \frac{\blacksquare}{3} \times \frac{4}{1}$

9. $3\frac{1}{7} \times 1\frac{1}{4} = \frac{\blacksquare}{7} \times \frac{\blacksquare}{4}$

10. $1\frac{1}{3} \times 2\frac{1}{6} = \frac{\blacksquare}{3} \times \frac{\blacksquare}{6}$

In **11** through **22**, estimate the product. Then find each product. Simplify if possible.

11. $2\frac{1}{6} \times 4\frac{1}{2}$

12. $\frac{3}{4} \times 8\frac{1}{2}$

13. $1\frac{1}{8} \times 3\frac{1}{3}$

14. $3\frac{1}{4} \times 6$

15. $5\frac{1}{3} \times 3$

16. $2\frac{3}{8} \times 4$

17. $\left(\frac{1}{3} + 1\frac{4}{9}\right) \times \left(2\frac{3}{4} - 1\frac{1}{2}\right)$

18. $\left(1\frac{2}{9} + 2\frac{1}{3}\right) \times \left(2\frac{3}{4} - 1\frac{1}{8}\right)$

19. $\left(1\frac{1}{8} + 1\frac{1}{2}\right) \times \left(2\frac{2}{5} - 1\frac{1}{10}\right)$

20. $\left(\frac{1}{6} + 2\frac{2}{3}\right) \times \left(1\frac{1}{4} - \frac{1}{2}\right)$

21. $\left(2\frac{4}{9} + \frac{1}{3}\right) \times \left(1\frac{1}{4} - \frac{1}{8}\right)$

22. $\left(1\frac{7}{8} + 2\frac{1}{2}\right) \times \left(1\frac{1}{5} - \frac{1}{10}\right)$

*For another example, see Set C on page 292.

Machine A

Estimate $7\frac{1}{2} \times 2\frac{3}{4}$ is about the same as 8×3, so the answer should be about 24 jackets a day.

Change the mixed numbers to improper fractions.

$$7\frac{1}{2} \times 2\frac{3}{4} = \frac{15}{2} \times \frac{11}{4}$$
$$= \frac{165}{8}$$
$$= 20\frac{5}{8}$$

Machine A makes $20\frac{5}{8}$ jackets each day.

Machine B

Estimate $7\frac{1}{2} \times 3\frac{1}{3}$ is about the same as 8×3, so the answer should be about 24 jackets per day.

$$7\frac{1}{2} \times 3\frac{1}{3} = \frac{\overset{5}{\cancel{15}}}{2} \times \frac{\overset{5}{\cancel{10}}}{\underset{1}{\cancel{3}}}$$
$$= \frac{25}{1} = 25$$

Machine B makes 25 jackets each day.

Problem Solving

For **23** through **25**, use the diagram at the right.

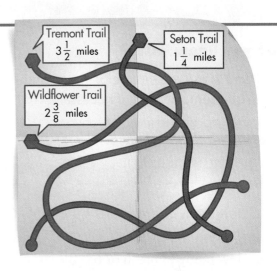

Tremont Trail $3\frac{1}{2}$ miles

Seton Trail $1\frac{1}{4}$ miles

Wildflower Trail $2\frac{3}{8}$ miles

23. Bernie and Chloe hiked the Tremont Trail to the end and back. Then they hiked the Wildflower Trail to the end before stopping to eat lunch. How far did they hike before they ate lunch?

24. Before he ate lunch, Ricardo hiked $2\frac{2}{3}$ times as far as Bernie and Chloe. How far did he hike?

25. The city plans to extend the Wildflower Trail $2\frac{1}{2}$ times its current length in the next 5 years. How long will the Wildflower Trail be at the end of 5 years?

26. Writing to Explain How can you use multiplication to find $3\frac{3}{5} + 3\frac{3}{5} + 3\frac{3}{5}$?

27. The world's smallest gecko is $\frac{3}{4}$ inch long. An adult male Western Banded Gecko is $7\frac{1}{3}$ times longer. How long is a Western Banded Gecko?

28. The Akashi-Kaikyo Bridge in Japan is about $1\frac{4}{9}$ as long as the Golden Gate Bridge in San Francisco. The Golden Gate Bridge is about 9,000 feet long. About how long is the Akashi-Kaikyo Bridge?

29. Patty spent $3\frac{1}{2}$ times as much as Sandy on their shopping trip. If Sandy spent $20.50, how much did Patty spend?

   A $71.75   **C** $100.25

   B $92.20   **D** $143.50

Relating Division to Multiplication of Fractions

How can you divide by a fraction?

Joyce is making sushi rolls. She needs $\frac{1}{4}$ cup of rice for each sushi roll. How many sushi rolls can she make if she has 3 cups of rice?

1 cup   1 cup   1 cup

Understand It!
To divide a whole number by a fraction, multiply the whole number by the reciprocal of the fraction.

Guided Practice*

Do you know HOW?

In **1** and **2**, use the picture below to find each quotient. Simplify, if necessary.

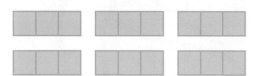

1. How many $\frac{1}{3}$s are in 3? $3 \div \frac{1}{3} = $ ▢

2. How many $\frac{2}{3}$s are in 6? $6 \div \frac{2}{3} = $ ▢

Do you UNDERSTAND?

3. In the example above, if Joyce had 4 cups of rice, how many rolls could she make?

4. **Writing to Explain** In the example above, how does the diagram help to show that $3 \div \frac{1}{4}$ is equal to 3×4?

Independent Practice

In **5** and **6**, use the picture to find each quotient.

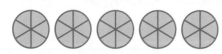

5. How many $\frac{1}{6}$s are in 1? $1 \div \frac{1}{6} = $ ▢

6. How many $\frac{1}{6}$s are in 5? $5 \div \frac{1}{6} = $ ▢

In **7** through **11**, draw a picture to find each quotient.

7. $4 \div \frac{1}{2}$ 8. $8 \div \frac{1}{4}$ 9. $2 \div \frac{1}{8}$ 10. $4 \div \frac{2}{3}$ 11. $6 \div \frac{3}{4}$

In **12** through **16**, use multiplication to find each quotient.

12. $3 \div \frac{1}{5}$ 13. $8 \div \frac{1}{3}$ 14. $3 \div \frac{1}{10}$ 15. $9 \div \frac{3}{8}$ 16. $15 \div \frac{3}{5}$

Animated Glossary
www.pearsonsuccessnet.com

DIGITAL

*For another example, see Set D on page 293.

Draw a diagram.

How many $\frac{1}{4}$s are in 3?

Think $3 \div \frac{1}{4}.$

There are twelve $\frac{1}{4}$s in three whole cups.

So, Joyce can make 12 sushi rolls.

The diagram shows $3 \div \frac{1}{4} = 12$.

You also know that $3 \times 4 = 12$. This suggests that you can also use multiplication to divide by a fraction.

Two fractions whose product is 1 are reciprocals. For example, $\frac{1}{4} \times \frac{4}{1} = 1$, so $\frac{1}{4}$ and $\frac{4}{1}$ are reciprocals. Dividing by a fraction is the same as multiplying by its reciprocal.

$$3 \div \frac{1}{4} = 3 \times \frac{4}{1} = 12$$

So, Joyce can make 12 sushi rolls.

Problem Solving

For **17** and **18**, use the following information.

Bijan is making a banner for his school. Along the bottom edge of the banner is a row of small squares. Each square is 6 inches by 6 inches.

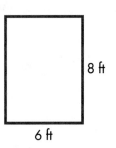

8 ft

6 ft

17. How many small squares can Bijan put along the bottom of the banner?

18. If every fourth square is colored blue, how many blue squares are along the bottom?

19. Reasoning When you divide a whole number by a fraction with a numerator of 1, explain how you can find the quotient.

20. Writing to Explain Write a word problem that can be solved by dividing 10 by $\frac{2}{3}$. Include the answer to the problem.

21. As of 2006, the world's largest leather work boot is 16 feet tall. A typical men's work boot is $\frac{1}{2}$ foot tall. How many times as tall is the largest boot as the height of a typical work boot?

22. Estimation The Nile River is 4,160 miles long. You want to spend three weeks traveling the entire length of the river. Estimate the number of miles you should travel each day.

23. Maria used one bag of flour. She baked two loaves of bread. Each loaf required $2\frac{1}{4}$ cups of flour. Then she used the remaining $6\frac{1}{2}$ cups of flour to make muffins. How much flour was in the bag to begin with?

24. Rudy has 8 yards of twine. If he cuts the twine into equal pieces of $\frac{3}{4}$ feet each, how many pieces can he cut?

A $10\frac{1}{2}$ **C** 32

B 24   **D** $96\frac{1}{2}$

Understand It!
Drawing a picture can help when writing and solving an equation.

Draw a Picture and Write an Equation

The string on Josie's kite is $12\frac{1}{2}$ feet long. Marcus's kite string is 5 times as long as Josie's kite string. How long is the string on Marcus's kite?

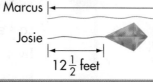

Marcus |←————————— ? —————————→|

Josie

$12\frac{1}{2}$ feet

Guided Practice*

Do you know HOW?

Solve. Draw a picture and write an equation.

1. If one bottle of yogurt contains $6\frac{1}{4}$ ounces, how much yogurt is in a 4-pack of yogurt?

Do you UNDERSTAND?

2. How do you know your answer for Exercise 1 is reasonable?

3. **Write a Problem** Write a real-world problem that you can solve by using multiplication of fractions.

Independent Practice

4. Danielle has a board that is $41\frac{2}{3}$ inches long. It is 5 times as long as the board Gina has. How long is Gina's board? Write an equation, then solve.

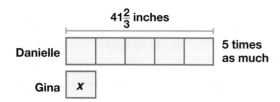

$41\frac{2}{3}$ inches

Danielle

5 times as much

Gina | x |

For **5** through **7**, draw a picture, write an equation, then solve.

5. Phil collected $3\frac{1}{2}$ buckets of shells at the beach. Caleb collected three times as many buckets. How many buckets of shells did Caleb collect?

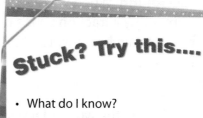

Stuck? Try this....

- What do I know?
- What am I asked to find?
- What diagram can I use to help understand the problem?
- Can I use addition, subtraction, multiplication, or division?
- Is all of my work correct?
- Did I answer the right question?
- Is my answer reasonable?

What do I know?

Josie's kite string is $12\frac{1}{2}$ feet long. Marcus's kite string is 5 times as long.

What am I asked to find?

The length of the string on Marcus's kite

Draw a Picture

n feet

| Marcus | $12\frac{1}{2}$ | $12\frac{1}{2}$ | $12\frac{1}{2}$ | $12\frac{1}{2}$ | $12\frac{1}{2}$ | 5 times as long |

| Josie | $12\frac{1}{2}$ |

Write an Equation

Let n = length of Marcus's kite string

$$12\frac{1}{2} \times 5 = n$$

$$62\frac{1}{2} = n$$

Marcus's kite string is $62\frac{1}{2}$ feet long.

---

6. Josh volunteered at the zoo for 14 hours in one month. This was $3\frac{1}{2}$ times as many hours as Gina volunteered. How many hours did Gina volunteer?

7. Tina is making a sign to advertise the school play. The width of the sign is $2\frac{2}{3}$ feet. If the length is $4\frac{1}{2}$ times as much, then what is the length of the sign?

8. Brown bats sleep for 20 hours each day. How many hours per week are they awake? How many hours per year are they awake?

9. Brenda says a good estimate for $50 \times 31\frac{3}{4}$ is 800. Is she correct? Explain.

10. Wanda needs to buy at least 50 stickers. Will 1 sheet of stickers be enough? How do you know?

11. Jin's friends collected 149 bottles of water for riders going on a bike trip. If each rider needs 4 bottles, how many riders can they supply with water?

12. **Think About the Process** A ticket to Los Angeles costs $390, and a ticket to Hong Kong costs $2\frac{1}{2}$ times as much. Which equation can you solve to show how much the ticket to Hong Kong costs?

A $\$390 + \$390 = c$

B $\$390 \times 2\frac{1}{2} = c$

C $\$390 \div 2\frac{1}{2} = c$

D $(2 \times \$390) + (2 \times \$390) = c$

13. **Think About the Process** Each shelf holds 24 books. There are 8 shelves. Which equation could you solve to find how many books there are in all?

A $24 + 8 = b$

B $24 - 8 = b$

C $24 \times 8 = b$

D $24 \div 8 = b$

1. How many $\frac{3}{4}$s are in 6? (11-4)

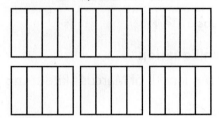

A $4\frac{1}{2}$

B $6\frac{3}{4}$

C 8

D 24

2. Alberto runs $3\frac{1}{4}$ miles each day. Which of the following can be used to find n, the number of miles he will run in a week? (11-5)

			n total miles			
$3\frac{1}{4}$	$3\frac{1}{4}$	$3\frac{1}{4}$	$3\frac{1}{4}$	$3\frac{1}{4}$	$3\frac{1}{4}$	$3\frac{1}{4}$

A $3\frac{1}{4} \times n = 7$

B $7 \times n = 3\frac{1}{4}$

C $7 \times 3\frac{1}{4} = n$

D $3\frac{1}{4} \div 7 = n$

3. If the diameter of a tree trunk is growing $\frac{1}{4}$ inch each year, how many years will it take for the diameter to grow 8 inches? (11-4)

A 2 years

B 8 years

C 24 years

D 32 years

4. Monica lives $\frac{8}{10}$ of a mile from Wally and $\frac{3}{4}$ of this distance from Adam. How far does Monica live from Adam? (11-2)

A $\frac{1}{2}$ mile

B $\frac{3}{5}$ mile

C $\frac{15}{16}$ mile

D $1\frac{11}{20}$ miles

5. Mrs. Webster wants to divide the milk shown into servings that are $\frac{2}{3}$ of a pint in size. How many servings are possible? (11-4)

A 9

B 5

C 4

D 2

6 pints

6. Mary is making a window covering that has 5 sections, each of which is $1\frac{3}{10}$ feet in width. What is the width of the entire window covering? (11-3)

A $6\frac{1}{2}$ feet

B $5\frac{1}{2}$ feet

C $5\frac{3}{10}$ feet

D $3\frac{11}{13}$ feet

7. Which of the following is equal to $\frac{4}{7} \times \frac{14}{3}$? (11-2)

A $\frac{4}{7} \times \frac{3}{14}$

B $4 \times \frac{2}{3}$

C $\frac{7}{4} \times \frac{14}{3}$

D $\frac{2}{7} \times \frac{7}{3}$

8. Tracy took a quiz containing 12 items. If she got $\frac{5}{6}$ of the items correct, how many did she get correct? (11-1)

A 5

B 6

C 9

D 10

9. A retaining wall on the playground is shown below. If $\frac{2}{3}$ of the wall is made from brick, what is the height of the brick portion of the wall? (11-3)

$2\frac{3}{4}$ feet

A $2\frac{1}{2}$ feet

B $1\frac{5}{6}$ feet

C $\frac{7}{12}$ foot

D $\frac{2}{9}$ foot

10. What is $\frac{7}{9} \times 63$? (11-1)

A 14

B 18

C 49

D 81

11. What is $\frac{1}{4} \times \frac{1}{6}$? (11-2)

A $\frac{1}{5}$

B $\frac{1}{10}$

C $\frac{1}{12}$

D $\frac{1}{24}$

12. What product does the diagram show? (11-2)

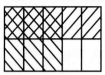

A $\frac{1}{2} \times \frac{3}{5} = \frac{3}{10}$

B $\frac{1}{2} \times \frac{3}{4} = \frac{3}{8}$

C $\frac{1}{3} \times \frac{1}{2} = \frac{1}{6}$

D $\frac{1}{3} \times \frac{3}{5} = \frac{1}{5}$

13. Which equals $4 \div \frac{1}{8}$? (11-4)

A $4 \div 8$

B $4 \times \frac{8}{1}$

C $4 \times \frac{1}{8}$

D $8 \div 4$

14. What is $2\frac{2}{5} \times 3\frac{1}{4}$? (11-3)

A $7\frac{4}{5}$

B $7\frac{7}{10}$

C $6\frac{1}{10}$

D $3\frac{1}{5}$

15. Two-fifths of the students in Mrs. Navares' fifth-grade class ride the bus to school. If there are 25 students in her class, how many ride the bus to school? (11-1)

A 5 students

B 7 students

C 10 students

D 15 students

Set A, pages 278–279

Find $\frac{2}{3}$ of 6.

One Way

$\frac{1}{3}$ of 6 is 2

$\frac{2}{3}$ is twice as much as $\frac{1}{3}$.

So, $\frac{2}{3}$ of 6 is 4.

Another Way

Multiply first, and then divide.

$\frac{2}{3} \times 6 = \frac{2}{3} \times \frac{6}{1} = \frac{12}{3} = 4$

Remember that the fraction line means to divide.

Find each product.

1. $4 \times \frac{1}{2}$

2. $\frac{3}{4}$ of 16

3. $24 \times \frac{1}{8}$

4. $\frac{4}{7}$ of 28

5. $20 \times \frac{1}{4}$

6. $\frac{5}{6}$ of 24

Set B, pages 280–282

Find $\frac{5}{6} \times \frac{2}{3}$.

Multiply.

$\frac{5}{6} \times \frac{2}{3} = \frac{10}{18}$.

Simplify, if possible.

$\frac{10 \div 2}{18 \div 2} = \frac{5}{9}$.

Remember to multiply both the numerator and the denominator.

Find each product. Simplify, if possible.

1. $\frac{3}{5} \times \frac{1}{4}$ 2. $\frac{6}{7} \times \frac{1}{2}$

3. $\frac{4}{9} \times \frac{2}{3}$ 4. $\frac{3}{8} \times \frac{1}{3}$

5. $\frac{2}{3} \times \frac{1}{3}$ 6. $\frac{7}{8} \times \frac{2}{3}$

Set C, pages 284–285

Find $3\frac{1}{2} \times 2\frac{7}{8}$.

Estimate. $3\frac{1}{2} \times 2\frac{7}{8}$ is about 4×3 or 12.

Change mixed numbers to improper fractions and multiply.

$\frac{7}{2} \times \frac{23}{8} = \frac{161}{16} = 10\frac{1}{16}$

The product $10\frac{1}{16}$ is close to the estimate, 12.

Remember to check your answer against your original estimate to be sure your answer is reasonable.

Find each product.

1. $2\frac{1}{3} \times 4\frac{1}{5}$

2. $4\frac{1}{2} \times 6\frac{2}{3}$

3. $7\frac{1}{8} \times 2\frac{3}{4}$

4. $3\frac{3}{5} \times 2\frac{5}{7}$

5. $2\frac{1}{2} \times 2\frac{1}{2}$

Set D, pages 286–287

Find $2 \div \frac{1}{4}$

One Way

Draw a picture.

There are eight $\frac{1}{4}$s in 2.

So, $2 \div \frac{1}{4} = 8$.

Another Way

Use multiplication.
Multiply by the recriprocal of the divisor.

$2 \div \frac{1}{4} = \frac{2}{1} \times \frac{4}{1}$

$\qquad = \frac{8}{1}$

$\qquad = 8$

Remember that you can multiply by the reciprocal of the divisor when you divide by a fraction.

Find each quotient. Simplify, if possible.

1. $2 \div \frac{1}{3}$

2. $6 \div \frac{1}{6}$

3. $8 \div \frac{1}{2}$

4. $4 \div \frac{4}{5}$

5. $2 \div \frac{2}{3}$

6. $10 \div \frac{1}{4}$

Set E, pages 288–289

A 4-foot board is cut into pieces that are $\frac{1}{2}$ foot in length. How many pieces will there be?

Draw a Picture.

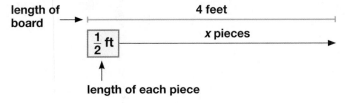

Write an equation: $x = 4 \div \frac{1}{2}$

$\qquad = 4 \times \frac{2}{1}$

$\qquad = \frac{8}{1}$

$\qquad = 8$

Remember to draw a picture to help write an equation.

Draw a picture and write an equation. Then solve.

1. A total of 60 students are being separated into 5 equal teams. How many students are on each team?

2. A 4-pound package of peanuts is divided into $\frac{1}{4}$-pound packages. How many packages will there be?

3. Each bead on a necklace weighs $\frac{1}{2}$ ounce. How many beads will it take to weigh one pound (16 ounces)?

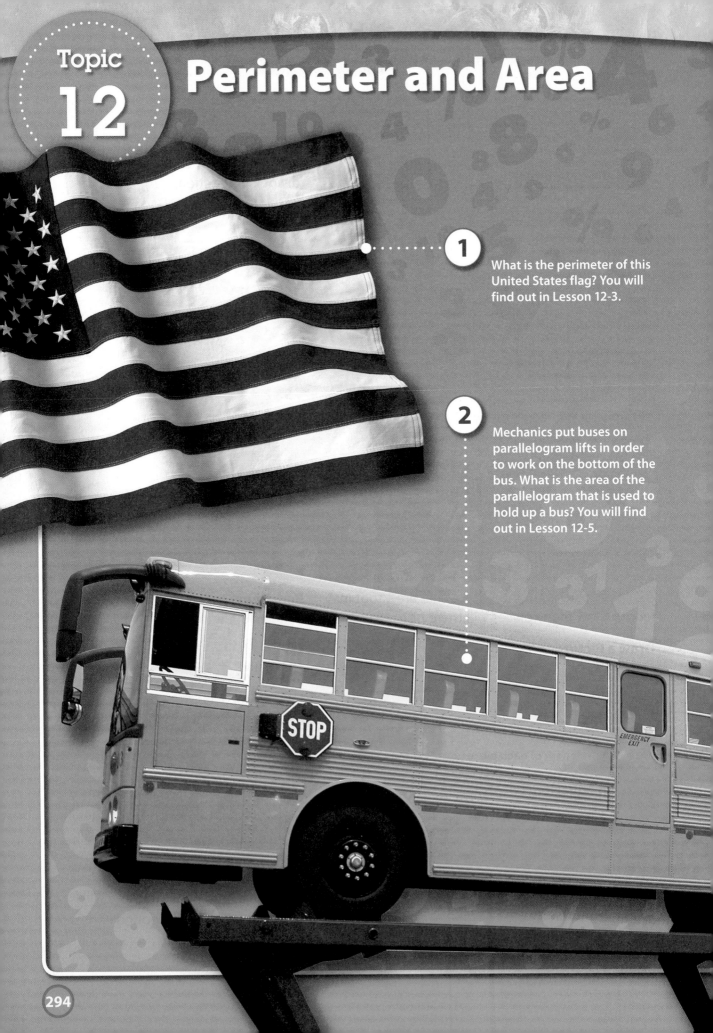

Perimeter and Area

1 What is the perimeter of this United States flag? You will find out in Lesson 12-3.

2 Mechanics put buses on parallelogram lifts in order to work on the bottom of the bus. What is the area of the parallelogram that is used to hold up a bus? You will find out in Lesson 12-5.

Vocabulary

Choose the best term from the box.

- divisor
- hundredths
- quotient
- tenths

1. The number 2.45 has a four in the __?__ place and a five in the __?__ place.

2. In $36 \div 9 = 4$, the 4 is called the __?__, and the 9 is called the __?__.

③ The East Room is the largest room in the White House. What is its area? You will find out in Lesson 12-4.

Multiplying Fractions

Find each product. Simplify if necessary.

3. $\frac{5}{6} \times \frac{3}{4}$ 4. $\frac{14}{21} \times \frac{3}{7}$ 5. $\frac{8}{10} \times \frac{3}{5}$

6. $\frac{2}{13} \times \frac{1}{9}$ 7. $\frac{1}{2} \times \frac{2}{25}$ 8. $\frac{4}{5} \times \frac{5}{4}$

9. $\frac{4}{1} \times \frac{8}{3}$ 10. $\frac{3}{7} \times \frac{12}{3}$ 11. $\frac{3}{5} \times \frac{3}{2}$

④ Cowboys on cattle drives in the 1800s were called to dinner by the ringing of a triangular bell. What is the area of a triangular dinner bell? You will find out in Lesson 12-6.

Evaluating Expressions

Evaluate each expression for $n = 2$.

12. $148 + n$ 13. $(n + 6) \div 4$

14. $\frac{70}{n}$ 15. $51 \times n$

16. $(60 - n) \times 5$ 17. $532 - n$

Properties of Multiplication

Writing to Explain Write an answer to the question.

18. How can the Associative Property of Multiplication be used to compute $14 \times 2 \times 50$ mentally?

12-1

Understand It!
Fractions can be used to express measurements more precisely.

Using Customary Units of Length

Hands-On
inch ruler

How can you use fractions to measure more precisely?

Since an inch is divided into equal parts, you can use fractions to measure lengths. You can estimate the length of this DVD case first. What is the length of the DVD case to the nearest $\frac{1}{8}$ inch?

Guided Practice*

Do you know HOW?

For **1** and **2**, measure each segment to the nearest inch, $\frac{1}{2}$ inch, $\frac{1}{4}$ inch, and $\frac{1}{8}$ inch.

1.

2.

Do you UNDERSTAND?

3. In the example above, why isn't the measurement of the DVD case 8 inches to the nearest inch?

4. **Writing to Explain** Would it be reasonable to measure pieces of lumber needed to build a house only to the nearest inch?

Independent Practice

In **5** through **7**, use a ruler to measure each object to the nearest inch, $\frac{1}{2}$ inch, $\frac{1}{4}$ inch, and $\frac{1}{8}$ inch.

5.

6.

7.

In **8** through **13**, estimate each measure first. Then use a ruler to measure each to the nearest $\frac{1}{4}$ inch and $\frac{1}{8}$ inch.

8. The length of a pencil

9. The width of your foot

10. The length of a piece of chalk

11. The length of your index finger

12. The length of your math book

13. The width of your hand

eTools
www.pearsonsuccessnet.com

For another example, see Set A on page 318.

Your estimate for the length of the DVD case should be about 7 inches. You can use a ruler to find the length to the nearest 1 in., $\frac{1}{2}$ in., $\frac{1}{4}$ in., and $\frac{1}{8}$ in.

$$\frac{1}{8} \quad \frac{1}{4} \quad \frac{1}{2}$$

0   1

INCHES

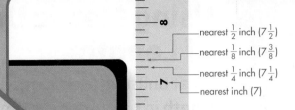

nearest $\frac{1}{2}$ inch $(7\frac{1}{2})$
nearest $\frac{1}{8}$ inch $(7\frac{3}{8})$
nearest $\frac{1}{4}$ inch $(7\frac{1}{4})$
nearest inch (7)

Since the length of the DVD case ends at $7\frac{3}{8}$ inch, this is its length to the nearest $\frac{1}{8}$ inch.

Problem Solving

14. Which line segment measures about $2\frac{1}{2}$ inches long?

A ⊢————————⊣

B ⊢——————⊣

C ⊢——————————⊣

D ⊢—————————⊣

15. **Think About the Process** Mae spent $12 on a new purse, $6 on lunch, and $14 for a book. She had $12 when she got home. Which expression shows how much money Mae started with?

A $12 - 12 + 6 + 14$

B $(2 \times 12) + 14 + 6$

C $12 - 6 - (14 + 12)$

D $2 \times (12 + 12) - 14$

16. **Writing to Explain** When you measure the length of an object, will your measurement ever be exact? Explain.

17. Jan has $49 to spend on poster board. If each poster board costs $3, how many poster boards can she buy?

18. **Estimation** Sheri played 4 computer games in 48 minutes. She scored about 825 points per game. About how many points did she score per minute?

19. **Number Sense** To find $8.3 \times 1,000$, how many places will you move the decimal point to the right? How many zeros will you need to annex? What is the product?

20. The measure of the length of a paper clip to the nearest inch, $\frac{1}{2}$ inch, and $\frac{1}{4}$ inch is 2 inches. How is this possible?

21. **Writing to Explain** Fifteen pounds of meat cost $26.85. Is it reasonable to say that the price per pound is $11? Explain.

Understand It!
The basic unit of length in the metric system is the meter.

Using Metric Units of Length

centimeter ruler

What units are used to measure length in the metric system?

Measurements in the metric system are based on the meter. The chart at the right lists other commonly used metric units and their equivalents.

Metric Equivalents

1 centimeter = 10 millimeters (mm)

1 meter = 100 centimeters (cm)

1 meter = 1,000 millimeters (mm)

1,000 meters = 1 kilometer (km)

Another Example How do you measure length using metric units?

To the nearest centimeter: 12 cm   To the nearest millimeter: 118 mm

---

Guided Practice*

Do you know HOW?

1. Which unit would be most appropriate to measure the length of a kitchen?

2. Measure this segment to the nearest centimeter and nearest millimeter.

Do you UNDERSTAND?

3. What two units can be used to measure the thickness of a stack of 10 dimes?

4. **Writing to Explain** Why is the millimeter not an appropriate unit to measure the distance across a town?

Independent Practice

For **5** through **7**, write mm, cm, m, or km as the most appropriate unit.

5. Thickness of a fingernail   6. Length of a picnic table   7. Length of a road

In **8** through **13**, measure each segment to the nearest centimeter and to the nearest millimeter.

8. ├─────────────┤   9. ├──────┤   10. ├────────┤

11. ├─────┤   12. ├───────┤   13. ├──────────┤

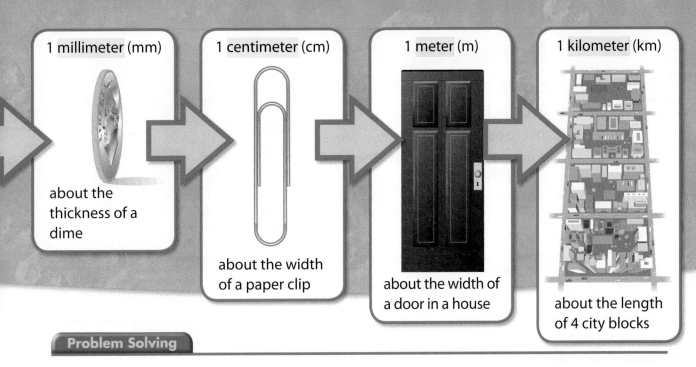

1 millimeter (mm)	1 centimeter (cm)	1 meter (m)	1 kilometer (km)
about the thickness of a dime	about the width of a paper clip	about the width of a door in a house	about the length of 4 city blocks

Problem Solving

14. Which object is 65 millimeters wide?

A

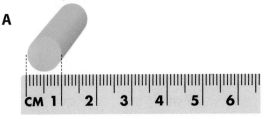

B

C

D

15. Writing to Explain Darcy is estimating how much fabric she will need to make a new jacket. Is estimating reasonable in this situation? Why or why not?

16. Dana ordered 1 medium cheese pizza with 8 slices. She ate 2 pieces. Write 2 equivalent fractions to show the part of the pizza Dana did NOT eat.

17. Choose from the measures listed below to determine the most appropriate lengths.

40 mm	2 m
18 cm	200 km

a The distance between two cities

b The length of a bicycle

c The length of a drinking straw

d The length of a caterpillar

18. Reasoning If a measuring cup has $\frac{1}{4}$ cup milk in it, what fraction represents the amount of milk needed to finish filling the cup?

Perimeter

How can you find the distance around a polygon?

The city wants to build a new fence around the rose garden in the town square. Perimeter is the distance around the outside of any polygon.

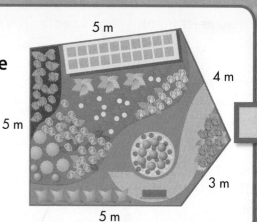

How can you use a formula to find the perimeter of a square and a rectangle?

A formula is a rule that uses symbols.

Use a formula to find the perimeter of the square.

Perimeter = 4 × side
$\quad P = 4 \times s$
$\quad P = 4 \times 29 = 116$ cm

Tip s = side

29 cm
29 cm   29 cm
29 cm

Use either of these formulas to find the perimeter of the rectangle.

One Way

Perimeter = (2 × length) + (2 × width)
$\quad P = (2 \times \ell) + (2 \times w)$
$\quad P = (2 \times 8) + (2 \times 5)$
$\quad P = 16 + 10 = 26$ m

Tip ℓ = length
w = width

8 m
5 m

Another Way

Perimeter = 2 × (length + width)
$\quad P = 2 \times (\ell + w)$
$\quad P = 2 \times (8 + 5)$
$\quad P = 2 \times 13 = 26$ m

Explain It

1. Will the formula for finding the perimeter of a square work for finding the perimeter of a rectangle?

Find the perimeter of the rose garden to find the total length of the new fence needed.

Perimeter is equal to the sum of the side lengths of a polygon.

Add the lengths of the sides.

$P = 5 + 5 + 4 + 3 + 5$
$P = 22 \text{ m}$

The perimeter of the rose garden is 22 m.

Since the longest side lengths are the same, multiplication can be used in the equation.

$P = 5 + 5 + 4 + 3 + 5$
$P = (3 \times 5) + 4 + 3$
$P = \quad 15 \quad + \quad 7$
$P = 22 \text{ m}$

The perimeter of the rose garden is 22 m.

Guided Practice*

Do you know HOW?

In **1** and **2**, find the perimeter of each figure.

1.

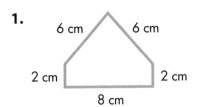

6 cm   6 cm
2 cm   2 cm
8 cm

2.

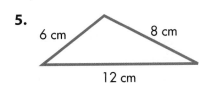

12 in.   12 in.
10 in.

Do you UNDERSTAND?

3. Look at the dimensions of the garden above. If the longest sides of the garden were 9 m, how long would the fence need to be?

4. Writing to Explain In the above example, why can you add the lengths of the sides of the garden in any order to find its perimeter?

Independent Practice

For **5** through **10**, find the perimeter of each figure.

5.

6 cm   8 cm
12 cm

6.

12 m
12 m   12 m
12 m

7.

13 in.
8 in.   8 in.
13 in.

8.

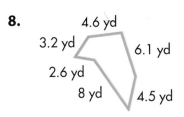

4.6 yd
3.2 yd
6.1 yd
2.6 yd
8 yd   4.5 yd

9.

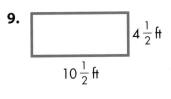

$4\frac{1}{2}$ ft
$10\frac{1}{2}$ ft

10.

42 mm
42 mm   42 mm
42 mm

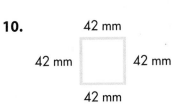 Animated Glossary
www.pearsonsuccessnet.com

DIGITAL

11. Number Sense The perimeter of an equilateral triangle is 51 feet. What is the length of each of its sides?

A 13 ft   **C** 17 ft

B 15 ft   **D** 21 ft

12. Find the perimeter of a parallelogram with sides measuring $3\frac{3}{10}$ m, $8\frac{5}{10}$ m, $3\frac{3}{10}$ m, and $8\frac{5}{10}$ m.

A $23\frac{8}{10}$ m   **C** $24\frac{6}{10}$ m

B $23\frac{3}{5}$ m   **D** 24 m

13. What is the perimeter of the Pentagon near Washington, D.C.?

921 ft   921 ft

921 ft   921 ft

921 ft

14. What is the perimeter of this United States flag?

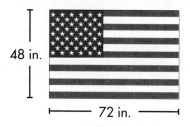

48 in.

72 in.

15. Writing to Explain Alfonso said that the perimeter of this triangle is 66 cm. What was his error? What should the perimeter be? Explain.

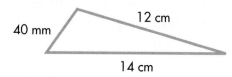

40 mm

12 cm

14 cm

16. Which unit (mm, cm, m, or km) would be the most appropriate for each measurement?

a Distance across Lake Michigan

b Length of a spoon

c Thickness of an envelope

d Height of a building

17. Which is the least common denominator of $\frac{1}{12}$ and $\frac{4}{5}$?

A 5   **C** 30

B 12   **D** 60

18. Reasoning Maria says her pencil is 1.7 meters long. Is this measurement reasonable? Explain.

19. It takes Neptune about 165 Earth years to complete one orbit around the Sun. How many Earth months does it take Neptune to orbit the Sun once?

20. The planet Neptune was discovered in 1846. Neptune's average distance from the Sun is four billion, four hundred ninety-eight million, two hundred fifty-two thousand, nine hundred kilometers. Write this number in standard form.

21. Stan has $2\frac{3}{4}$ pounds of oranges, $1\frac{1}{4}$ pounds of lemons, and $1\frac{3}{4}$ pounds of limes. How many pounds of fruit does Stan have altogether?

Enrichment

Precision in Measurement

Every measurement is approximate and depends on the units on the measuring instrument. The smallest unit on the ruler below is the millimeter. The line segment can be measured to the nearest centimeter or the nearest millimeter.

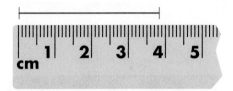

Nearest centimeter: 4 cm
Nearest millimeter: 38 mm

Example: Which measurement is more precise, 19 in. or 2 feet?

The first measurement is measured to the nearest inch. The unit of measure is 1 inch.

The second measurement is measured to the nearest foot. The unit of measure is 1 foot.

Since 1 inch is smaller than 1 foot, the first measurement is more precise than the second.

The smaller the unit of measure, the greater is the **precision** of a measurement. The unit of measure for the first measurement is 1 cm. The unit of measure for the second measurement is 1 mm. Since 1 mm is smaller than 1 cm, the second measurement is more precise than the first.

Some situations require more precise measurements than others. To measure the height of a plant, you might measure to the nearest centimeter. To measure the length of an insect, you might measure to the nearest millimeter.

Practice

Which measurement is more precise?

1. 21 in. or 2 ft

2. 1 kg or 825 g

3. 48 mm or 5 cm

4. 3 m or 278 cm

5. $\frac{1}{2}$ lb or 9 oz

6. 2 gal or 7 qt

7. $2\frac{7}{8}$ in. or 1 ft

8. 7 yd or 255 in.

9. 1 h or 58 min

10. A carpenter is building a garage. Would it be close enough to measure the lumber to the nearest yard? Explain.

11. A landscaper is measuring the distance around a back yard to determine how much sod is needed. Does the landscaper need to measure to the nearest $\frac{1}{8}$ inch? Explain.

Understand It!
Formulas can be used to find areas of squares and rectangles.

Area of Squares and Rectangles

How can a formula be used to find area?

The area of a figure is <u>the amount of surface it covers</u>. What are the areas of the baseball infield and the tennis court?

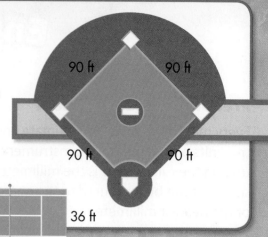

90 ft   90 ft

90 ft   90 ft

36 ft

78 ft

Guided Practice*

Do you know HOW?

In **1** and **2**, find the area of each figure.

1. Find the area of a square with a side that measures 34 cm.

2. Find the area of a rectangle with length 21 m and width 9 m.

Do you UNDERSTAND?

3. Which two dimensions are multiplied when finding the area of a rectangle?

4. **Writing to Explain** In the example above, how can you decide which figure has the greater area, without using the formula?

Independent Practice

For **5** through **10**, find the area of each figure.

5.
   11 in.
   17 in.

6.
   14 ft
   14 ft

7.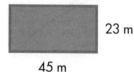
   23 m
   45 m

8.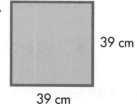
   39 cm
   39 cm

9. A rectangle with length 245 in. and width 167 in.

10. A square with a side that measures 31 yd

*For another example, see Set D on page 319.

The infield is a square, so all of its sides are equal.

Use the formula below to find the area of a square. Area is measured in square units.

Area = side × side
$A = s \times s$
$A = 90 \text{ ft} \times 90 \text{ ft}$
$A = 8{,}100 \text{ ft}^2$

The area of the infield is 8,100 square feet.

The tennis court is a rectangle, so its opposite sides are equal.

Use the formula below to find the area of a rectangle.

Area = length × width
$A = \ell \times w$
$A = 78 \text{ ft} \times 36 \text{ ft}$
$A = 2{,}808 \text{ ft}^2$

The area of the tennis court is 2,808 square feet.

Problem Solving

11. The East Room of the White House is 79 feet long by 36 feet wide. What is the area of the room?

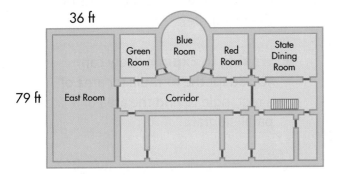

12. Ben's mom wants to buy new carpet for the family room that measures 12 feet by 11 feet. She can purchase the carpet on sale for $6 per square foot including installation. How much will Ben's mom spend to carpet the family room?

A $132

B $791

C $792

D $794

13. Number Sense A set of four postcards cost $1.00. Single postcards cost $0.50. What is the least amount of money you can spend to buy exactly 15 postcards?

14. Which has the greater area: a square with a side that measures 7 meters, or a 6-by-8-meter rectangle? What is the area?

For **15** through **17**, use the drawing at the right.

15. What is the perimeter of an Olympic-size swimming pool?

16. What is the area of the swimming pool?

17. What is the perimeter of each lane?

18. What is the perimeter and area of a square with a side that measures 15 m?

Olympic-Size Pool

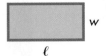

25 m

50 m

2.5 m (×10)

Area of Parallelograms

How can finding the area of a rectangle help you find the area of a parallelogram?

Southwestern rugs often have parallelograms as part of the design. The base of this parallelogram is 8 cm. The height is 4 cm. What is its area?

4 cm   8 cm

Guided Practice*

Do you know HOW?

In **1** and **2**, find the area of each parallelogram.

1.

3 in.

6 in.

2.

5 in.

8 in.

Do you UNDERSTAND?

3. In the example above, which dimensions of the parallelogram correspond to the dimensions of the rectangle?

4. **Writing to Explain** How can you adapt the formula for area of a rectangle to find the area of a parallelogram?

Independent Practice

For **5** through **11**, find the area of each parallelogram.

5.

3 cm

3 cm

6.

7 ft

9 ft

7.

6 cm

9 cm

8.

4 in.

2 in.

9.

10 m

4.5 m

10.

27 m

7 m

11.

5 yd

13 yd

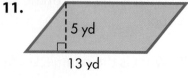

Animated Glossary
www.pearsonsuccessnet.com

*For another example, see Set D on page 319.

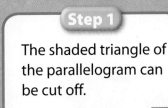

Step 1

The shaded triangle of the parallelogram can be cut off.

4 cm

8 cm

Step 2

The triangle can be placed along the other side to form a rectangle.

4 cm

8 cm

 Think length = base (b)
width = height (h)

Use the formula to find the area of a parallelogram.

Area = base × height
$A = b \times h$
$A = 8 \text{ cm} \times 4 \text{ cm}$
$A = 32 \text{ cm}^2$

The area of the parallelogram is 32 square centimeters.

Problem Solving

12. Parallelogram *A* has a base of 12 ft and a height of 11 ft. Parallelogram *B* has a base of 13 ft and a height of 10 ft. Which parallelogram has the greater area? How much greater is the area?

13. Each morning, Kathie rides the train 9 km to work. The train takes 10 minutes to travel $4\frac{1}{2}$ km. How much time does Kathie spend on the train each day going to and from work?

14. Which of these figures has the greatest area?

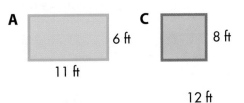

A 6 ft 11 ft

C 8 ft

B 3 ft 7 ft

D 12 ft 5 ft

15. A store display has 36 bottles of perfume on the bottom shelf, 30 bottles on the shelf above that, and 24 on the shelf above that. If this pattern continues, how many bottles will be on the next shelf above?

16. What is the area of the parallelogram lift shown below?

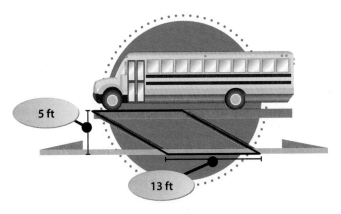

5 ft

13 ft

17. Writing to Explain Kurt bought two items that cost a total of $100. One item cost $10 more than the other. What was the cost of each item? Explain your reasoning.

18. Algebra Paige knows the area of a parallelogram is 54 square inches. The base of this parallelogram is 9 inches, and the height is *h* inches. What is the measure for the height of this parallelogram?

Lesson 12-5   **307**

Area of Triangles

How can you use a parallelogram to find the area of a triangle?

This parallelogram is divided into two congruent triangles. The area of each triangle is equal to half the area of the parallelogram.

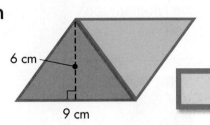

6 cm

9 cm

Guided Practice*

Do you know HOW?

In **1** and **2**, find the area of each triangle.

1.

6 in.

7 in.

2.

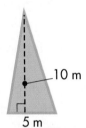

10 m

5 m

Do you UNDERSTAND?

3. Writing to Explain In the example above, how do you know the area of the triangle is equal to half the area of the parallelogram?

4. In the example above, find the area of the red triangle if the base measures 12 cm and the height remains the same.

Independent Practice

In **5** through **10**, find the area of each triangle.

5.

6 in.

5 in.

6.

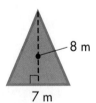

8 m

7 m

7.

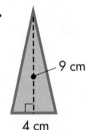

9 cm

4 cm

8.

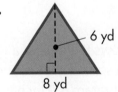

6 yd

8 yd

9.

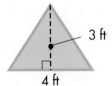

3 ft

4 ft

10.

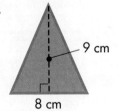

9 cm

8 cm

For another example, see Set D on page 319.

Step 1

Find the area of the red triangle.

Identify the measures of the base and height of the triangle.

base (b) = 9 cm
height (h) = 6 cm

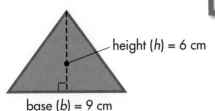

height (h) = 6 cm

base (b) = 9 cm

Step 2

To find the area of a triangle, adapt the formula for the area of a parallelogram—just multiply by $\frac{1}{2}$.

Substitute the values into the formula.

$$\text{Area} = \frac{1}{2} \times \text{base} \times \text{height}$$

$$A = \frac{1}{2} \times b \times h$$

$$A = \frac{1}{2} \times 9 \times 6$$

$$A = 27 \text{ cm}^2$$

The area of the red triangle is 27 square centimeters.

Problem Solving

11. Writing to Explain Jay says that this triangle has an area of 3,000 square inches. Is Jay correct? Explain.

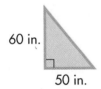

60 in.

50 in.

12. Terry wants to buy one pair of moccasins. She can choose from some that cost $22.50, $27.00, $20.95, and $24.75. How much will Terry save if she buys the least expensive instead of the most expensive pair?

13. Reasoning The difference between the prices of two bikes is $18. The sum of the prices is $258. How much does each bike cost?

14. What is the area of a triangle with a base of 7 inches and a height of 8 inches?

A 15 in²   **C** 56 in²

B 28 in²   **D** 64 in²

15. Which of the following numbers is a composite number?

A 2   **C** 7

B 5   **D** 9

16. Natalie is going to wallpaper her room. Each wall in her bedroom measures 10 ft by 8 ft. How much wallpaper will Natalie need to cover 3 of the bedroom walls?

17. Algebra A lunar module has triangular-shaped windows. The base of each window is 60 cm. The height is h cm. The area of each window is 1,200 square centimeters. Find the height of each window.

18. What is the area of the dinner bell shown at the right?

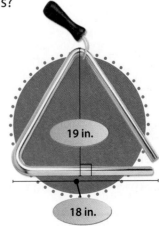

19 in.

18 in.

Understand It!
A circle is a familiar plane figure that is not a polygon.

Circles and Circumference

What are the names of segments and angles related to a circle?

A circle is a closed plane figure made up of all the points that are the same distance from a given point called the center. A circle is named by its center. Circle *O* is shown at the right.

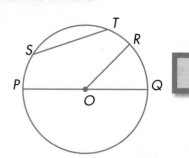

Other Examples

How are the measurements of a circle related to each other?

For any circle, the circumference is always about 3.14 times the diameter. Because this value is always the same, ancient mathematicians gave it a special name, pi (pronounced like *pie*). Pi is represented by the Greek letter π. However, 3.14 is only an approximate value of π. The digits in π actually go on forever: 3.141592 . . . .

Because the relationship between the circumference and the diameter of a circle is always the same, you can use a formula to describe it.

FORMULA FOR CIRCUMFERENCE

Circumference = π × diameter

$C = \pi \times d$

Find the circumference.

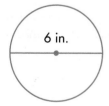

6 in.

Find the circumference.

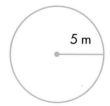

5 m

$C = \pi \times d$
$C \approx 3.14 \times 6$
$C \approx 18.84$ in.

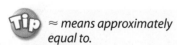 ≈ means approximately equal to.

The diameter of a circle is twice the radius.
$C = \pi \times 2 \times r$, or $C = 2 \times \pi \times r$
$C \approx 2 \times 3.14 \times 5$
$C \approx 31.4$ m

Explain It

1. Why can you use either $C = \pi \times d$ or $C = 2 \times \pi \times r$ to find circumference?

2. **Reasoning** Why do you think people use 3.14 as an estimate for π?

A radius (plural: *radii*) is any line segment that connects the center to a point on the circle. In the circle at the left, $\overline{OR}$ is a radius.

A diameter is any line segment through the center that connects two points on the circle. $\overline{PQ}$ is a diameter.

A chord is any line segment that connects two points on the circle. $\overline{ST}$ is a chord.

A central angle is an angle whose vertex is the center. $\angle ROQ$ is a central angle.

The distance around a circle is called its circumference.

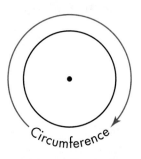

Circumference

Guided Practice*

Do you know HOW?

In **1** through **5**, use the terms above to identify each figure in circle *H*.

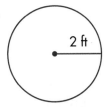

1. Point *H*   2. $\overline{DN}$

3. $\overline{HT}$ 4. $\angle DHT$ 5. $\overline{EF}$

In **6** and **7**, find the circumference. Use 3.14 for π.

6.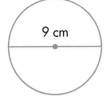
9 cm

7.
2 ft

Do you UNDERSTAND?

8. If you know the radius of a circle, how do you find its diameter?

9. In the circle at the top of page 310, name two radii other than $\overline{OR}$.

10. Explain why a diameter of a circle is also a chord.

11. **Reasoning** In circle *H* at the left, $\angle DHT$ is a central angle. Name two other central angles in circle *H*.

Independent Practice

In **12** through **16**, use circle *A* to identify the following.

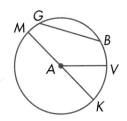

12. the center   13. three radii

14. a diameter   15. a chord

16. three central angles

For another example, see Set E on page 319.

Lesson 12-7

In **17** through **24**, find the circumference. Use 3.14 for π.

17.
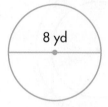
8 yd

18.
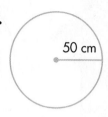
50 cm

19.
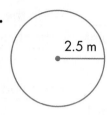
2.5 m

20.
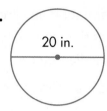
20 in.

21. $d = 6$ cm

22. $r = 7$ ft

23. $d = 1$ in.

24. $r = 11$ mm

Problem Solving

For **25** and **26**, use the fact that the sum of the measures of the central angles of a circle is 360°.

25. Find the missing angle measure in circle P.

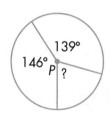
139°
146°
P ?

26. In each wheel shown below, the spokes are evenly spaced. Without measuring, find the measure of $\angle A$, and $\angle B$.

A

B

27. A circular tabletop has a radius of 15 inches. What is its circumference? Use 3.14 for π.

28. Writing to Explain Ana thinks that all radii of a given circle are equal in length. Is she correct? Explain.

29. Estimation The length of the diameter of a circle is 7 centimeters. Is the circumference more or less than 21 centimeters? Explain.

30. A bakery sells muffins for 65¢ apiece and bagels for 49¢ apiece. How much less does it cost to buy two dozen bagels than two dozen muffins?

31. **Think About the Process** Which equation can be used to find the circumference C of a circle with a radius that measures 16 feet?

A $C = \pi \times 8$

B $C = \pi \times 16$

C $C = 2 \times \pi \times 16$

D $C = 2 \times \pi \times 32$

32. A carpenter needs to cut a circular hole in a board. The diameter of the circle must be 6 inches. What will the radius of the circle be?

A 3 inches

B 9.42 inches

C 12 inches

D 18.84 inches

More About Central Angles

A **central angle** of a circle is an angle whose vertex is the center. In the circle below, ∠AOB is a central angle of circle O.

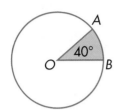

There is a total of 360° around the center of a circle. So you can use the measure of ∠AOB to find what fractional part of the circle's interior is shaded.

Step 1 Write a fraction to show what part of the whole region is shaded.

$\dfrac{40}{360}$ ← number of degrees in the shaded part
← number of degrees in the whole

Step 2 Write the fraction in simplest form.

$$\dfrac{40}{360} = \dfrac{40 \div 40}{360 \div 40} = \dfrac{1}{9}$$

So $\dfrac{1}{9}$ of the circle's interior is shaded.

Example: In the circle below, $\dfrac{2}{5}$ of the interior is shaded. Find the measure of ∠XOY.

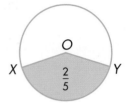

Multiply 360° by the fraction that represents the shaded part.

Think: $\dfrac{2}{5}$ is 2 times as much as $\dfrac{1}{5}$.

$\dfrac{1}{5}$ of 360 is equal to 360 ÷ 5.

360 ÷ 5 = 72

Multiply: $\dfrac{2}{5} \times 360 = 2 \times \left(\dfrac{1}{5} \text{ of } 360\right)$
$= 2 \times 72$
$= 144$

So the measure of ∠XOY is 144°.

Practice

Write a fraction in simplest form to name each shaded part.

1.

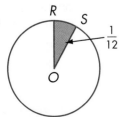

2.

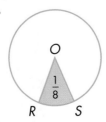

3.

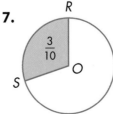

4.

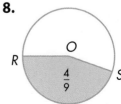

Find the measure of ∠ROS in each circle.

5.

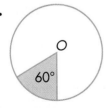

6.

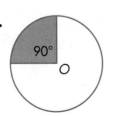

7.

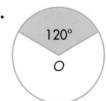

8.

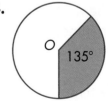

Understand It!
Learning how and when to make an organized list can be helpful when solving problems.

Problem Solving

Draw a Picture and Make an Organized List

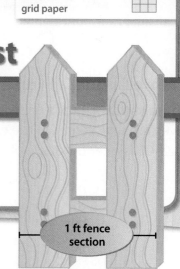

Hands-On
grid paper

The Diaz family has 12 one-foot sections of fence to build a rectangular kennel for their dog. They want the kennel to have a perimeter of 12 ft, and have the greatest possible area. What should the dimensions of the kennel be?

1 ft fence section

Guided Practice*

Do you know HOW?

Draw a picture and make a list to solve.

1. Ali has 18 meters of fence to enclose her garden. She wants this garden to have the greatest possible area. What should the dimensions of Ali's garden be?

2. Eric painted a square picture that has an area of 400 sq cm. He wants to frame it, but needs to know the perimeter. What is the perimeter of Eric's picture?

Do you UNDERSTAND?

3. How does drawing a picture and making a list help you solve these problems?

4. **Write a Problem** Write a real-world problem that can be solved by drawing a picture and making a list.

Independent Practice

In **5** through **9**, draw a picture and make a list to solve.

5. Julie will be making a quilt. If she wants the quilt to have a perimeter of 30 ft, and cover the greatest area possible, what should its dimensions be?

6. A kitchen is 8 feet long and 6 feet wide. If the dimensions of the kitchen are doubled, how will the area change? How will the perimeter change?

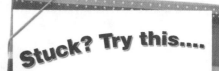

Stuck? Try this....

- What do I know?
- What am I asked to find?
- What diagram can I use to help understand the problem?
- Can I use addition, subtraction, multiplication, or division?
- Is all of my work correct?
- Did I answer the right question?
- Is my answer reasonable?

The length of the kennel cannot be longer than 5 ft because the perimeter needs to be 12 ft.

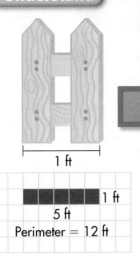

I can draw a picture on grid paper to show this.

1 ft

5 ft
Perimeter = 12 ft

The area is $5 \times 1 = 5$ ft^2

I can draw more pictures and make a list of all possible dimensions and areas.

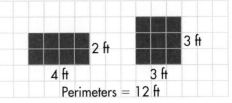

2 ft
4 ft

3 ft
3 ft
Perimeters = 12 ft

$5 \times 1 = 5$ ft^2 $4 \times 2 = 8$ ft^2
$3 \times 3 = 9$ ft^2

The dimensions of the kennel should be 3 ft wide by 3 ft long.

---

7. Mary is designing a geometric picture that will be put on a banner. The parallelogram in the picture has an area of 625 in^2. The square in the picture has the same area as the parallelogram. What are the dimensions of the square?

8. Beth's garden is 6 ft by 3 ft. She wants to plant 6 flowers per square foot.

a How many flowers will she plant?

b How can you check your answer?

9. The length of a rectangular sandbox is 8 ft. The area of the sandbox is 40 ft^2. If the length of the box is extended 2 more feet, how many feet does the width of the box need to be to have a final area of 60 ft^2?

10. Rocio finished 21 pages in a scrapbook. On Monday, she finished half as many pages as on Tuesday. On Wednesday, Rocio finished twice as many pages as on Tuesday. How many pages did Rocio complete each day?

11. Robert has $107.56 in his savings account. He withdraws $30.60. Draw a picture and write an equation that can be solved to find Robert's new balance. Let b = Robert's new balance.

12. **Writing to Explain** Maria says that rectangles with the same perimeter can have different areas. Is Maria correct? Use a drawing to support your explanation.

13. You want to buy 12 comic books. The store sells small and large comics and is having a special. You have $24. Do you have enough money to buy 12 small books? Twelve large books?

3 small for $6

4 large for $12

1. Use a ruler to measure. Which is the measure of the segment to the nearest $\frac{1}{8}$ inch? (12-1)

A 1 in.

B $1\frac{1}{8}$ in.

C $1\frac{2}{8}$ in.

D $1\frac{3}{8}$ in.

2. Which equation shows the perimeter of this rectangle? (12-3)

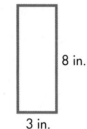

8 in.

3 in.

A $8 \times 3 = 24$ in²

B $2 \times (8 + 3) = 22$ in.

C $8 \times 4 = 32$ in.

D $2 \times (8 \times 3) = 48$ in.

3. Mr. Santiago wants to build a rectangular fence with the greatest area. He wants it to have a perimeter of 40 yards. Which dimensions should he use? (12-8)

A 12 yards by 12 yards

B 15 yards by 5 yards

C 12 yards by 8 yards

D 10 yards by 10 yards

4. Which unit is most appropriate to measure the length of a house? (12-2)

A kilometers

B meters

C centimeters

D millimeters

5. Which of the following can be used to find the area in square meters of a parallelogram whose base measures 20 meters and height measures 12 meters? (12-5)

A $A = (2 \times 20) + (2 \times 12)$

B $A = \frac{1}{2} \times 20 \times 2$

C $A = 20 \times 12$

D $A = 20 + 12$

6. Maria glued sequins around the outside of each of her party invitations. If the invitations are 5 inches wide and 2.5 inches tall, what is the perimeter of the invitations? (12-3)

A 7.5 in.

B 12.5 in.

C 15 in.

D 20 in.

7. Use a ruler to measure. Which is closest to the height of the treble clef shown? (12-1)

A $\frac{1}{4}$ inch

B $\frac{3}{4}$ inch

C $\frac{5}{6}$ inch

D $\frac{7}{8}$ inch

8. The diameter of a circle is 4 feet. What is the circumference of the circle? Use 3.14 for π. (12-7)

A 7.14 feet

B 11.14 feet

C 12.56 feet

D 25.12 feet

9. The area of the rectangle is 120 yd². Which of the following can be used to find the area of the shaded triangle? (12-6)

A 120

B $\frac{1}{2} \times 120$

C 120 − 40

D 120 − (2 × 40)

10. A rectangular window measures 36 inches wide by 48 inches tall. What is the area of the window? (12-4)

A 1,728 in²

B 1,488 in²

C 864 in²

D 168 in²

11. Which shows the area of the parking lot? (12-6)

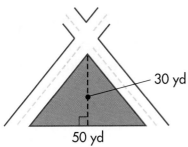

30 yd

50 yd

A 750 yd

B 750 yd²

C 1,500 yd

D 1,500 yd²

12. Which piece of yarn has a length of 6 centimeters? (12-2)

13. What is the missing measure? (12-3)

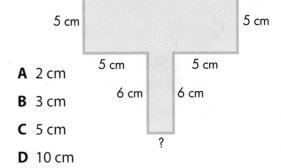

12 cm

5 cm   5 cm

5 cm   5 cm

6 cm   6 cm

?

A 2 cm

B 3 cm

C 5 cm

D 10 cm

14. Which of the following can be used to find the area of the square shown? (12-4)

A A = 4 × 4

B A = 16 × 16

C A = 4 × 16

D A = 2 × 16

16 m

15. Which of the following best describes $\overline{AB}$ in the circle shown? (12-7)

A Chord

B Radius

C Diameter

D Circumference

A   B

C

Set A, pages 296–297

Find the length to the nearest inch, $\frac{1}{2}$ inch, $\frac{1}{4}$ inch, and $\frac{1}{8}$ inch.

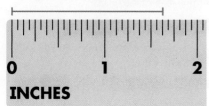

To the nearest

inch: 2 in.

$\frac{1}{4}$ inch: $1\frac{3}{4}$ in.

$\frac{1}{2}$ inch: $1\frac{1}{2}$ in.

$\frac{1}{8}$ inch: $1\frac{5}{8}$ in.

Remember to write your measurements in fractions using simplest form. Use a ruler.

1. Find the length to the nearest $\frac{1}{4}$ inch and $\frac{1}{2}$ inch.

2. Find the length to the nearest inch and $\frac{1}{8}$ inch.

Set B, pages 298–299

Choose a reasonable metric unit for the length of a driveway.

The meter is the most reasonable unit.

The millimeter and centimeter are too small and the kilometer is too large.

Remember the shortest to longest units of length are millimeter (mm), centimeter (cm), meter (m), and kilometer (km).

Write mm, cm, m, or km as the most appropriate unit.

1. length of a calculator

2. distance from Chicago to Denver

Set C, pages 300–302

Find the perimeter.

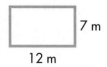 7 m

12 m

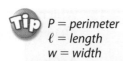 *P* = perimeter
ℓ = length
w = width

Use a formula:

Perimeter = (2 × length) + (2 × width)
$\qquad P = (2 \times \ell) + (2 \times w)$
$\qquad P = (2 \times 12) + (2 \times 7)$
$\qquad P = 24 + 14 = 38 \text{ m}$

Add the side lengths:

$P = 12 + 7 + 12 + 7 = 38 \text{ m}$

Remember that perimeter is the distance around the outside of any polygon.

Find each perimeter.

1.

7 m

2. 23.2 in. 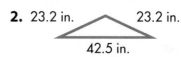 23.2 in.

42.5 in.

3.

6 m

11 m

Set D, pages 304–309

Use a formula to find each area.

7 ft

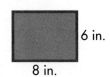
6 in.
8 in.

Use $A = s \times s$.
$A = 7 \times 7 = 49 \text{ ft}^2$

Use $A = \ell \times w$.
$A = 8 \times 6 = 48 \text{ in}^2$

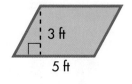
3 ft
5 ft

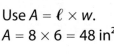
8 m
11 m

Use $A = b \times h$.
$A = 5 \times 3 = 15 \text{ ft}^2$

Use $A = \frac{1}{2} \times b \times h$
$A = \frac{1}{2} \times 11 \times 8 = 44 \text{ m}^2$

Remember to use the appropriate area formula for each polygon.

Find each area.

1.

8 m

2.
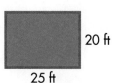
20 ft
25 ft

3.
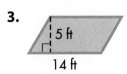
5 ft
14 ft

4.

6 m
10 m

5.
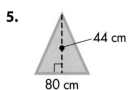
44 cm
80 cm

6.
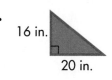
16 in.
20 in.

Set E, pages 310–312

Find the circumference of the circle.

14 yd

Use $C = \pi \times d$.
$C \approx 3.14 \times 14$
≈ 43.96

The circumference is 43.96 yards.

Remember that the diameter of a circle is twice the radius.

Find each circumference. Use 3.14 for π.

1.

20 m

2.

5 ft

Set F, pages 314–315

When you are asked to draw a picture and make a list to solve a problem, follow these steps:

Step 1 Read and understand the problem.

Step 2 Make a plan by creating a list of different possible solutions.

Step 3 Test each of the items in your list to find a solution.

Step 4 Look back and check your work.

Remember that drawing a picture can help you make a list.

1. Cristina has 16 square feet of material to make a rectangular quilt. She wants the quilt to have the least possible (minimum) perimeter. If Cristina uses all 16 square feet, what dimensions should she use for the quilt?

Solids

1 How can you find the surface area of the outer walls and roof of one of these pueblo houses? You will find out in Lesson 13-3.

2 What kinds of solid figures can you find in this Tori Gate? You will find out in Lesson 13-1.

Review What You Know!

Vocabulary

Choose the best term from the box.

- quadrilateral • square
- triangle

1. A polygon with only 3 sides is a __?__.

2. Every rectangle is a __?__.

3. A rectangle with all sides the same length is a __?__.

Area

Find the area of each figure.

4.

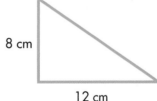

10 ft 6 ft

5.

8 cm 12 cm

Multiplication

Find each product.

6. $10 \times 8 \times 5$

7. $20 \times 40 \times 5$

8. $15 \times 15 \times 15$

9. $\frac{1}{2} \times 10 \times 8$

Geometry

10. Writing to Explain How are parallel lines different from intersecting lines?

3

Some antique boxes, like this one, were made from special cuts of wood and included intricate carvings. How can you find the volume of this box? You will find out in Lesson 13-5.

Understand It!
Solids can be described by their shape and by faces, edges, and vertices.

Solids

What is a solid figure?

A solid figure has 3 dimensions and takes up space. One solid is the cube. It has 6 flat surfaces or faces. All the faces are squares. Each pair of faces intersects in a segment called an edge, and three or more edges intersect at a point called the vertex. The plural of vertex is vertices.

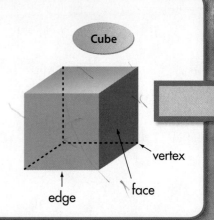

Cube

vertex

edge

face

Other Examples

Some solid figures have curved surfaces, while others have all flat surfaces.

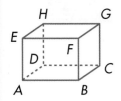

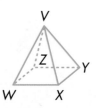

Prism
Solid with two congruent parallel bases and faces that are parallelograms.

Cylinder
Solid with two circular bases that are congruent and parallel.

Cone
Solid with one circular base. The points on this circle are joined to one point outside the base.

Pyramid
Solid with a base that is a polygon. The edges of the base are joined to a point outside the base.

Naming the parts of a solid

Name the vertices, edges, and faces of the triangular prism.

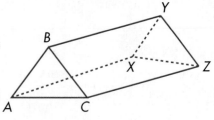

Vertices: *A*, *B*, *C*, *X*, *Y*, and *Z*

Edges: $\overline{AB}$, $\overline{AC}$, $\overline{BC}$, $\overline{XY}$, $\overline{XZ}$, $\overline{YZ}$, $\overline{AX}$, $\overline{BY}$, and $\overline{CZ}$

Faces: triangles *ABC* and *XYZ*, quadrilaterals *ABYX*, *CBYZ*, and *AXZC*

Explain It

1. How many faces, vertices, and edges are there in the triangular prism above?

2. Name other objects in the real world that have similar shapes to the solids described above.

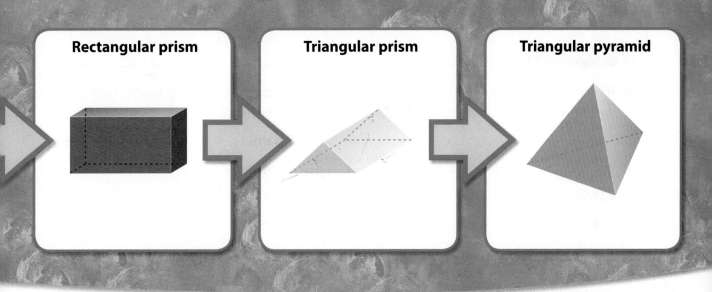

| Rectangular prism | Triangular prism | Triangular pyramid |

Guided Practice*

Do you know HOW?

For **1** through **3**, use the solid at the right.

1. Name the vertices.

2. Name the faces.

3. Name the edges.

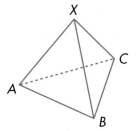

Do you UNDERSTAND?

4. What is the name of the solid figure at the left?

5. Which of the solid figures in Other Examples have curved surfaces?

6. How many faces does a triangular prism have?

Independent Practice

For **7** through **9**, tell which solid figure each object resembles.

7.

8.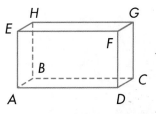

9.

For **10** through **12**, use the drawing to the right.

10. Name the faces.

11. Name the vertices.

12. Name the edges.

*For another example, see Set A on page 344.

Lesson 13-1

13. Which of the following decimals is equivalent to 12.45?

   A 12.0045

   B 12.0450

   C 12.4500

   D 124.5000

14. Which of the following solids has a curved surface?

   A Pyramid

   B Cube

   C Prism

   D Cone

15. Luke's tent weighs $6\frac{1}{2}$ pounds. His fishing tackle weighs $5\frac{1}{2}$ pounds. What is the total weight of both items?

16. **Reasoning** A certain kind of prism has 9 edges and 5 faces. What kind of prism is it?

17. One week, Mary worked for 29 hours. She earned $6 per hour. How much did Mary earn for the time she worked?

18. Wei made two square pyramids and glued the congruent bases together. How many faces does her figure have?

19. Before Andy went shopping, he added $5 he had earned to the money that was already in his wallet. He bought a backpack for $19 and a headset for $12. After he paid for the items, Andy had $8.25 left. How much money did Andy have in his wallet before adding the $5?

20. Which of the following is NOT a rectangular prism?

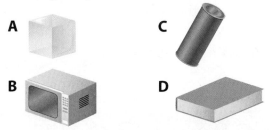

  A   **C**

  B   **D**

21. Tori gates are often found in Japan where they originated. What kinds of solids can you find in a Tori gate?

22. **Algebra** Fillmore Park had 75 spruce trees. Volunteers planted 39 more of these trees. Solve $75 + 39 = t$ to find the total number of spruce trees in the park now.

23. **Reasoning** Another solid figure is the sphere. It has a point that is exactly in the center. What do you know about the distance from any point on the sphere to the center?

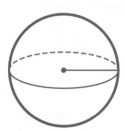

Going Digital

Polygon Patterns

Use  **tools**

Geometry Drawing

Arrange triangles in a pattern with no gaps and no overlap.

Step 1 ⚠️ Go to the Geometry Drawing eTool. Click on the triangle drawing tool. Then click, drag, and click again in the workspace to draw a triangle like the ones shown below. Use the pull-down menu at the top of the page to toggle off the display of points. Use the erase tool if you make a triangle you do not want.

Step 2 Click on the copy tool and then on a side of the selected figure to make a copy. Make 6 copies, so that you have 7 triangles in all. Use the arrow tool to select a triangle and move it. Arrange 3 triangles in a row. Select another triangle. On the Select/Transform tool palette, click the button next to the flip tool to expand the tool palette.

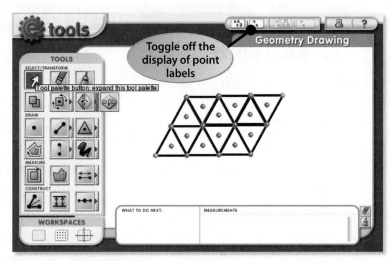

Then select the flip vertical tool and click on the selected triangle. Use the copy tool to copy it 5 times, so that you have 6 flat-side-down triangles and 6 flipped triangles. Use the arrow tool to select and move each triangle to create the pattern shown in the illustration. This arrangement is called a tessellation.

Practice

Arrange each polygon in a pattern with no gaps and no overlap. If it isn't possible, say so.

1.

2.

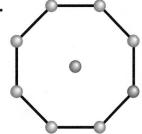

Understand It!
Nets can be used to visualize and construct solids.

Relating Shapes and Solids

How can you use a two-dimensional shape to represent a three-dimensional solid?

A net is a <u>plane figure</u> <u>which, when folded,</u> <u>gives a solid figure.</u>

How can you draw a net for this solid figure?

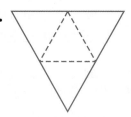

Guided Practice*

Do you know HOW?

Predict what solid each net will make.

1.

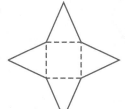

2.

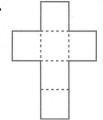

Do you UNDERSTAND?

3. Writing to Explain How did you make your predictions in Exercises 1 and 2?

4. A solid may have different nets. Draw a different net for the solid you identified in Exercise 2.

Independent Practice

For **5** through **7**, predict what solid each net will make.

5.

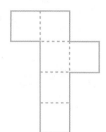

6.

7.

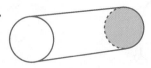

In **8** and **9**, draw a net for each solid.

8.

9.

For another example, see Set B on page 344.

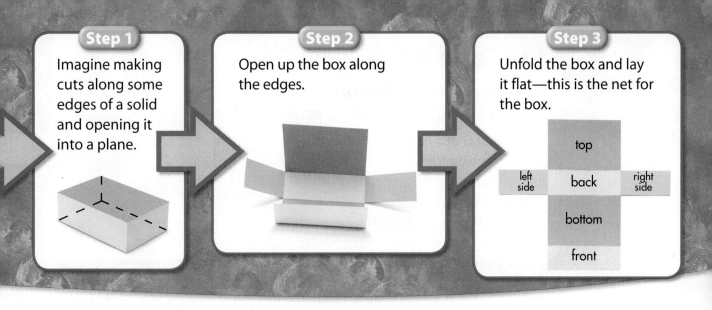

Step 1
Imagine making cuts along some edges of a solid and opening it into a plane.

Step 2
Open up the box along the edges.

Step 3
Unfold the box and lay it flat—this is the net for the box.

top

left side   back   right side

bottom

front

Problem Solving

10. A net has 4 large rectangles and 2 small rectangles. What solid figure might it make?

A Rectangular prism

B Square pyramid

C Triangular prism

D Rectangular pyramid

11. Molly spent $120 on two items. One cost $10 more than the other. Which shows the correct cost for each?

A $70, $50

B $50, $60

C $60, $70

D $55, $65

12. Strategy Focus When some rock music is played unamplified its sound has been measured at 62 decibels. Sound for amplified music can be measured at 124 decibels. Draw a picture and write an equation to find the difference between the number of decibels measured.

13. One company offers customers an Internet coupon to get a $2 discount off a purchase from their Web site. If the value of the coupons downloaded so far is $6,000, how many coupons have been downloaded?

14. Algebra Diane is thinking of a number. She doubles it and adds 10. Her result is 50. Which equation could you use to find Diane's number?

A $(2 \times n) - 10 = 50$

B $2 \times 10n = 50$

C $2 \times n = 50$

D $(2 \times n) + 10 = 50$

For **15**, use the table below.

Temperature

Day	1	2	3	4	5	6	7
Temperature °F	34°	45°	37°	39°	48°	29°	36°

15. In what fraction of the days was the temperature between 30°F and 40°F? In what fraction was the temperature greater than 40°F?

Understand It!
The areas of polygons can be added to find the surface area of a rectangular prism.

Surface Area

Hands-On
grid paper

How can you find the surface area of a rectangular prism?

Remember that a net is a plane figure which when folded gives a solid figure. The surface area (SA) of a rectangular prism is <u>the sum of the area of all its faces.</u>

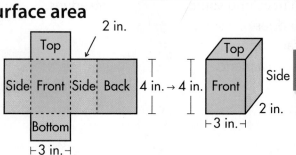

Guided Practice*

Do you know HOW?

Copy the following net on grid paper. Make each rectangle the size shown by the labels. Then cut out the net and fold it to make a rectangular prism.

1.

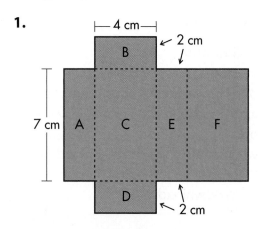

Do you UNDERSTAND?

2. List the congruent faces in the net in Exercise 1.

3. Find the surface area of the solid you built in Exercise 1.

4. For which type of rectangular prism could you find the surface area by finding the area of 1 face and multiplying by 6?

5. What is the surface area of a cube with an edge that measures 3 cm?

Independent Practice

In **6** through **8**, find the surface area of each solid.

6.

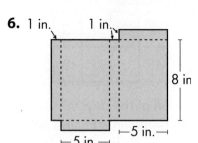

7.

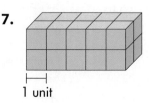

8.

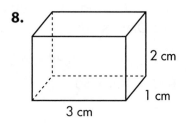

DIGITAL   Animated Glossary, eTools
www.pearsonsuccessnet.com

For another example, see Set B on page 344.

Notice that the solid figure has 6 faces that are rectangles.

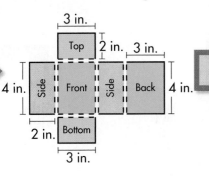

Add the areas of all the faces to find the surface area (SA).

$$\text{SA} = \underset{\downarrow\,\text{side}}{(4 \times 2)} + \underset{\downarrow\,\text{side}}{(4 \times 2)} + \underset{\downarrow\,\text{front}}{(4 \times 3)} + \underset{\downarrow\,\text{back}}{(4 \times 3)} + \underset{\downarrow\,\text{top}}{(3 \times 2)} + \underset{\downarrow\,\text{bottom}}{(3 \times 2)}$$

$$= 8 + 8 + 12 + 12 + 6 + 6$$

$$= 52 \text{ square inches (in}^2)$$

The surface area of the rectangular prism is 52 in².

Problem Solving

For **9** through **11** use the diagram at the right.

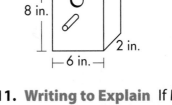

9. Draw a net to represent Mylah's birdhouse. Find the surface area.

10. If Mylah buys paint to cover 76 square inches, will she have enough paint to cover the surface area of the bird house? Explain.

11. Writing to Explain If Mylah puts a ribbon around the base of the birdhouse, would she need to find the perimeter or the area of the base?

12. What transformation is shown below?

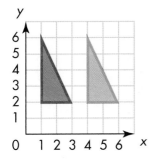

13. Morgan received a parcel that was 4 ft by 2 ft by 3 ft. Kenley received a parcel that was 3 ft by 1 ft by 5 ft. Whose package had the greater surface area? Explain.

For **14**, use the diagram at the right.

14. The Pueblo tribe of New Mexico lived in houses that looked like boxes stacked on top of one another. What would the surface area of the outer walls and roof of a pueblo house be if it had the dimensions shown?

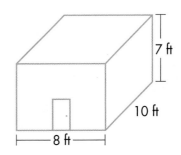

Understand It!
Sketches can be drawn for the front, top, and side views of a solid that is made of unit cubes.

Views of Solids

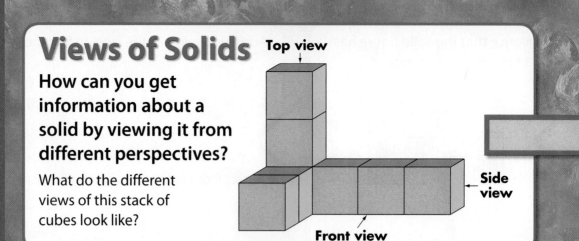

How can you get information about a solid by viewing it from different perspectives?

What do the different views of this stack of cubes look like?

Guided Practice*

Do you know HOW?

1. Sketch the front, top and side views of the solid figure below.

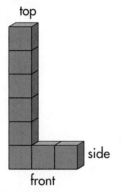

Do you UNDERSTAND?

2. How many blocks are not visible in the diagram at the left?

3. Which two views would be the same for the solid shown below?

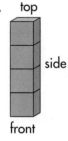

Independent Practice

In **4** through **9**, draw front, side, and top views of each stack of unit blocks.

4.

5.
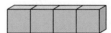

6.

7.
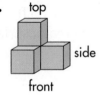

8.
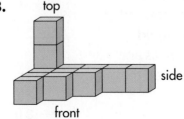

9.
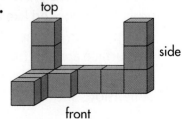

For another example, see Set C on page 344.

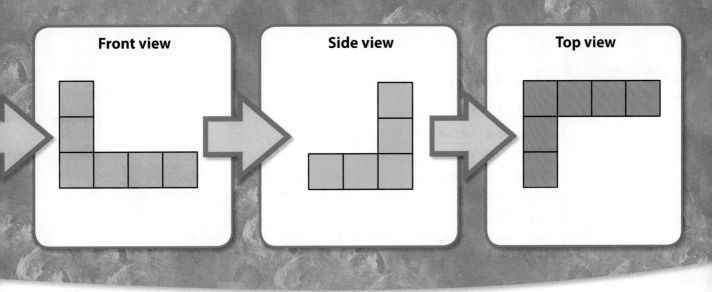

| Front view | Side view | Top view |

10. Beth, Toby, Juan, and Patricia walked 6 miles to raise money. Beth and Patricia each raised $3.50 for each mile walked. Toby raised $3 for each mile walked, and Juan raised $22 in all. Who raised the most money?

A Beth   **C** Juan

B Toby   **D** Patricia

11. Hina bought 21 stickers and 7 rope bracelets. She wants to make small gift packs for her friends. Each gift pack has 3 stickers and 1 rope bracelet. Stickers cost $1.50 each, and bracelets cost $2 each. How much does it cost Hina to make each gift pack?

A $45.50   **C** $3.50

B $6.50   **D** None of the above

12. Draw the front, side, and top views of this stack of cubes and cylinders.

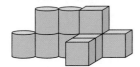

13. A bag contains 5 red marbles, 1 green marble, and 1 yellow marble. If you choose one marble, describe the chance of drawing a red marble.

A Certain   **C** Likely

B Impossible   **D** Unlikely

14. How many blocks are not visible from the top view?

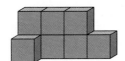

15. In the figure below, which face is parallel to face *ABCD*?

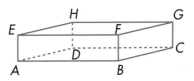

A *BCGF*   **C** *EFGH*

B *ADHE*   **D** *DCGH*

16. If 10 cubes are stacked vertically, how many cubes are not visible from the top view?

Understand It!
Understanding how to find area can be helpful when finding the volume of solid figures.

Volume

How do you find the volume of a prism?

Volume is the number of cubic units needed to fill a solid figure.

A cubic unit is the volume of a cube that measures 1 unit on each edge. Each cube is 1 cubic unit, or 1 unit³.

Find the volume of the rectangular prism.

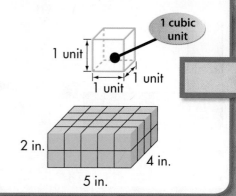

1 cubic unit

1 unit

1 unit
1 unit

2 in.

4 in.

5 in.

Another Example **How do you use a formula to find volume?**

If the measurements of a prism are given in length ℓ, width w, and height h, then use this formula to find volume V:

$$\text{Volume} = (\text{length} \times \text{width}) \times \text{height}$$
$$V = (\ell \times w) \times h$$

Use a formula to find the volume of the prism.

$$V = (\ell \times w) \times h$$
$$V = (5 \times 3) \times 4$$
$$V = 60 \text{ ft}^3$$

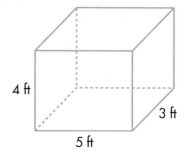

4 ft

3 ft

5 ft

The volume of the prism is 60 ft³.

Sometimes the area of the base will be given.

If a rectangular prism has a base area B and a height h, use this formula:

Tip *Base area is the same as $\ell \times w$*

$$\text{Volume} = \text{base area} \times \text{height}$$
$$V = B \times h$$

Find the volume of a rectangular prism with a base area of 49 cm² and a height of 6 cm.

$$V = B \times h$$
$$V = 49 \times 6$$
$$V = 294 \text{ cm}^3$$

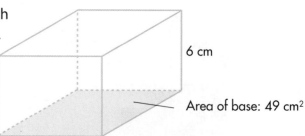

6 cm

Area of base: 49 cm²

Explain It

1. How is counting cubes related to the formulas for finding volume?

2. How do you know which formula for volume to use?

Count cubes to find volume.

If the cubic units are shown, you can count the cubes inside the rectangular prism. Begin with the base layer of the prism. It has 5 cubes each in 4 rows.

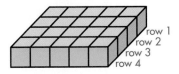

row 1
row 2
row 3
row 4

There are 20 cubic units in the base layer of the prism.

There are two layers.

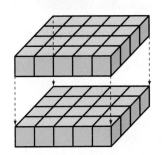

20 cubes × 2 layers = 40 cubic units

The measures are in inches, so the volume of the rectangular prism is 40 cubic inches (in³).

Guided Practice*

Do you know HOW?

In **1** through **3**, find the volume of each rectangular prism.

1.
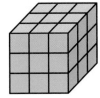

2.
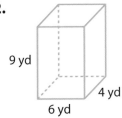

9 yd

4 yd

6 yd

3. Base area: 26 m²
height: 4 m

Do you UNDERSTAND?

4. In the example above, how do you know both of the layers are the same?

5. A cereal box measures 6 in. by 10 in. by 2 in. Draw a rectangular prism and label it. What is the volume of the figure you drew?

6. Writing to Explain How can you use different methods to find the volumes of the prisms in Exercises 1–3?

Independent Practice

In **7** through **12**, find the volume of each rectangular prism.

7.
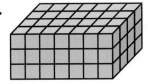

8.
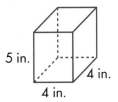

5 in.

4 in.

4 in.

9.
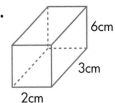

6cm

3cm

2cm

10.
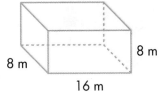

8 m

8 m

16 m

11.

12.
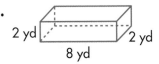

2 yd

2 yd

8 yd

DIGITAL

Animated Glossary
www.pearsonsuccessnet.com

For **13** through **15**, find the volume of each rectangular prism.

13. Base area: 56 in²
height: 5 in.

14. Base area: 100 ft²
height: 17 ft

15. Base area: 72 yd²
height: 8 yd

Problem Solving

For **16** through **18**, use the information below.

Sixty-four students are planning a field trip to the Art Museum.
Each student will pay $9. Each van can hold 7 students and 1 driver.

16. How much money will be collected if all the students attend?

17. How many vans will be needed if all the students travel to the museum?

18. The school pays each driver $50 to drive the van. If the round trip takes 4 hours, how much does each driver make per hour?

19. Estimation A rectangular prism measures 6.7 in. by 4.2 in. by 2.5 in. Round each measure to the nearest whole number to estimate the volume.

20. Only 3 students per event can win medals at the track meet. If 9 students are competing in an event, what fraction of the students will win a medal?

21. What is the perimeter of this figure?

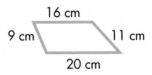

16 cm

9 cm   11 cm

20 cm

22. Algebra Last week 22 people worked a total of 1,100 hours. Each person worked the same number of hours. Which equation represents this information?

A $1{,}100h = 22$ **C** $h \div 1{,}100 = 22$

B $22 \div h = 1{,}100$ **D** $22h = 1{,}100$

23. Writing to Explain Harry is in line at the store. He has 3 items that cost $5.95, $4.25, and $1.05. Explain how Harry can add the cost of the items mentally before he pays for them.

24. Estimation Lisa and Ranjan are going on a trip. The trunk they are using is 4.5 feet wide, 1.75 feet high, and 2 feet deep. What is the estimated volume of the trunk?

26. Algebra Find $3c - 17$ if $c = 20$.

25. Think About the Process Which expression can be used to find the volume of this antique box?

3 in.   4 in.

6 in.

A $(6 \times 4) \times 3$ **C** 6×4

B $(6 \times 4) + 3$ **D** $2 \times (6 \times 4 \times 2)$

Find the product. Estimate to check if the answer is reasonable.

1. 19.38
   × 7

2. 4.25
   × 9

3. 9.345
   × 12

4. 7.43
   × 10

5. 0.076
   × 9

6. 0.0089
   × 100

7. 23.89
   × 6

8. 12.0005
   × 1,000

Find the quotient. Estimate to check if the answer is reasonable.

9. 5)7.75

10. 4.35 ÷ 5

11. 3)10.53

12. 9.24 ÷ 6

13. 8)8.24

14. 0.08 ÷ 4

15. 3)12.48

16. 28.56 ÷ 2

17. 1.28 ÷ 8

18. 2)15.42

19. 60.06 ÷ 6

20. 9)28.8

Error Search Find each answer that is not correct.
Write it correctly and explain the error.

21. 182
    3)547

22. 4,879
    + 236
    4,643

23. 3,193
    − 3,094
    101

24. 52.03
    + 21.67
    73.70

25. 56.7
    × 2.1
    11.907

Number Sense

Estimating and Reasoning Write whether each statement is
true or false. Explain your reasoning.

26. The product of 50 × 8.58 is between 400 and 450.

27. The sum of 45.69 and 10.92 is 0.08 less than 56.69.

28. The expression 18 − 6 + 5 × 2 equals 34.

29. The quotient of 3,216 ÷ 8 is 2 more than 400.

30. The expression $\frac{10k}{5}$ equals 12 when $k = 6$.

31. The quotient 15.89 ÷ 2 is greater than 8.

Irregular Shapes and Solids

How can you find the area of an irregular shape?

A garden has the irregular shape shown at the right. What is the area of the garden?

You can find the area of an irregular shape by separating it into familiar shapes, and then adding the areas of those shapes.

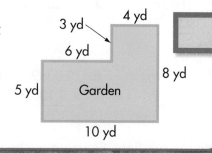

3 yd   4 yd

6 yd

5 yd   Garden   8 yd

10 yd

Another Example ## How can you find the volume of an irregular solid?

You can also find the volume of an irregular solid by separating it into familiar parts.

Find the volume of the solid shown at the right.

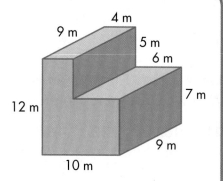

4 m
9 m
5 m
6 m
12 m
7 m
9 m
10 m

Separate the solid into two rectangular prisms. Identify the length, width, and height of each prism.

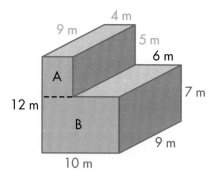

4 m
9 m
5 m
6 m
A
7 m
12 m
B
9 m
10 m

Use the formula $V = \ell \times w \times h$ to find the volume of each rectangular prism.

Volume of Prism A	Volume of Prism B
$V = \ell \times w \times h$	$V = \ell \times w \times h$
$= 9 \times 4 \times 5$	$= 9 \times 10 \times 7$
$= 180 \text{ m}^3$	$= 630 \text{ m}^3$

Add to find the total volume.

$$180 + 630 = 810$$

The volume of the solid is 810 m³.

Explain It

1. Why was the solid separated into rectangular prisms?

2. Why do you add the volumes of the rectangular prisms?

Separate the shape into two rectangles. Identify the length and width of each rectangle.

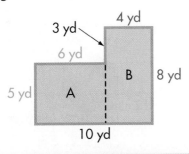

Use the formula $A = \ell \times w$ to find the area of each rectangle.

Area of Rectangle A	Area of Rectangle B
$A = \ell \times w$	$A = \ell \times w$
$= 6 \times 5$	$= 8 \times 4$
$= 30 \text{ yd}^2$	$= 32 \text{ yd}^2$

Add to find the total area.

$30 + 32 = 62 \text{ yd}^2$

The area of the garden is 62 yd².

Guided Practice*

Do you know HOW?

1. Find the area of the irregular shape.

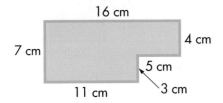

2. Find the volume of the irregular solid.

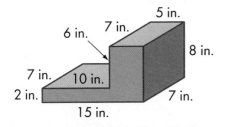

Do you UNDERSTAND?

In **3** and **4**, use the irregular solid below. The dashed line separates it into two rectangular prisms, A and B.

3. What are the length, width, and height of prism A?

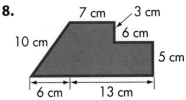

4. What is the volume of prism B?

5. **Draw a Picture** Show a different way to separate the garden, from the example above, into two rectangles.

Independent Practice

In **6** through **8**, find the area of each irregular shape.

6.

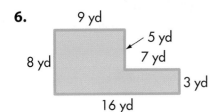

7.

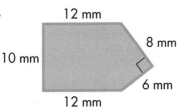

8.

7 cm 3 cm
10 cm 6 cm
5 cm
6 cm 13 cm

In **9** through **11**, find the volume of each irregular solid.

9.

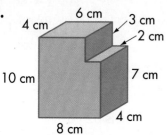

6 cm
4 cm
3 cm
2 cm
10 cm
7 cm
4 cm
8 cm

10.

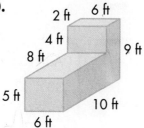

2 ft 6 ft
4 ft
8 ft 9 ft
5 ft
6 ft 10 ft

11.

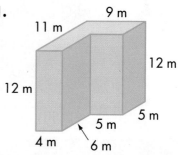

9 m
11 m
12 m
12 m
5 m
4 m 5 m
6 m

In **12** and **13**, use the diagram of a city park shown at the right.

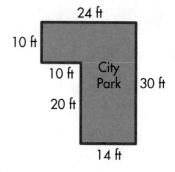

24 ft
10 ft
10 ft City Park 30 ft
20 ft
14 ft

12. It will cost $2 per square foot to plant grass in the park. What will be the total cost of planting the grass?

13. The cost of installing iron fencing is $12 per foot. What will be the total cost of installing an iron fence that covers the entire perimeter of the park?

14. Draw a Picture Join these two rectangles to make an irregular shape. Label the lengths of all the sides. What is the area of the shape you drew?

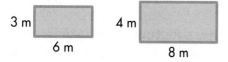

3 m
6 m
4 m
8 m

15. Writing to Explain How do you find an area or volume of an irregular shape or solid? Explain each step.

16. The figure below shows a net that can be folded to form a triangular prism. What is the area of the net?

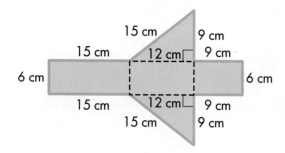

15 cm 9 cm
15 cm 12 cm 9 cm
6 cm 6 cm
15 cm 12 cm 9 cm
15 cm 9 cm

17. What is the volume of this irregular solid?

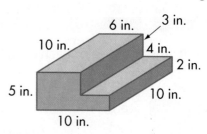

6 in. 3 in.
10 in. 4 in.
2 in.
5 in. 10 in.
10 in.
10 in.

A 50 in³

B 260 in³

C 380 in³

D 500 in³

Enrichment

Estimating Area and Volume

Sometimes it is not possible to separate an irregular shape into familiar shapes. In these cases, you can estimate the area of the shape by placing it on a grid and counting square units.

Example: Estimate the area of the irregular shape shown below.

Step 1

Count the whole square units that lie in the interior of the shape.

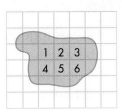

There are 6 whole square units.

Step 2

Count the partial square units that lie in the interior of the shape.

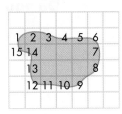

There are 15 partial square units.

Step 3

Add the number of whole square units to half the number of partial square units.

$$6 + \left(\frac{1}{2} \times 15\right) = 6 + 7\frac{1}{2}$$

$$= 13\frac{1}{2}$$

The area is about $13\frac{1}{2}$ square units.

Practice

Estimate the area of each irregular shape.

1.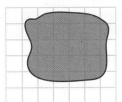

2.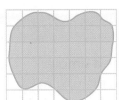

3.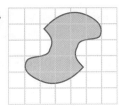

Sometimes you need to estimate the volume of irregular solids. Estimate the volume of each solid in cubic units.

Tip *Think of rearranging the cubes into a familiar solid of about the same size. Remember that some cubes are not visible.*

4.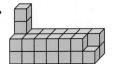

5.

6.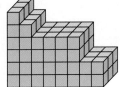

Understand It!
Learning how and when to use objects to solve a simpler problem can be helpful when solving problems.

Use Objects and Solve a Simpler Problem

Hands-On
cubes

Shown at the right are 27 cubes that were glued together to form a larger cube. Then, all 6 faces of the larger cube were painted. How many of the 27 cubes have paint on 1 face? On 2 faces? Use cubes to make a model.

Guided Practice*

Do you know HOW?

1. Use cubes and the example of the simpler problem above to build a larger cube with 4 layers. Each layer will have 4 rows of 4 cubes. How many cubes will the larger cube contain?

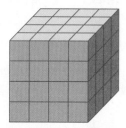

Do you UNDERSTAND?

2. Think of gluing the cubes together for the 4 × 4 × 4 cube you made. Then, think of painting the outside faces. How many cubes will have paint on 1 face? On 2 faces? On 3 faces?

3. **Write a Problem** Write a real-world problem that involves using objects to help solve a simpler problem.

Independent Practice

In **4** through **9**, use objects to help you solve a simpler problem. Use the solution to help you solve the original problem.

4. Alicia uses wood timbers to build steps. The pattern is shown for 1, 2, 3, and 4 steps. How many timbers will she need to build 10 steps?

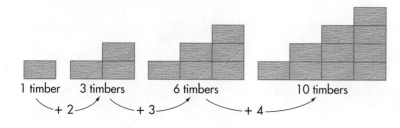

1 timber   3 timbers   6 timbers   10 timbers
— + 2 —   — + 3 —   — + 4 —

Stuck? Try this....

- What do I know?
- What am I asked to find?
- What diagram can I use to help understand the problem?
- Can I use addition, subtraction, multiplication, or division?
- Is all of my work correct?
- Did I answer the right question?
- Is my answer reasonable?

For another example, see Set F on page 345.

How many cubes have paint on 1 face?

The center cube on each of the 6 faces of the larger cube has paint on 1 face.

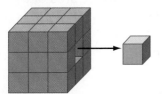

Six of these cubes have paint on 1 face.

How many cubes have paint on 2 faces?

Only 1 cube on each of the 12 edges of the larger cube has paint on 2 faces.

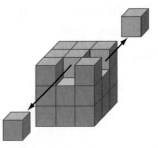

Twelve of these cubes have paint on 2 faces.

5. Four people can be seated at a table. If two tables are put together, six people can be seated. How many tables are needed to make a long table that will seat 20 people?

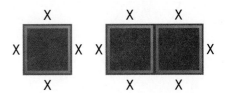

6. Jeremiah wants to make a display of CD boxes. He wants a single box on the top layer. Layers that are below the top layer must form a square, with each layer being 1 box wider than the layer above it. The display can only be 4 layers high. How many total boxes will be in the display? Use cubes.

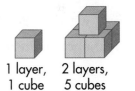

1 layer, 1 cube   2 layers, 5 cubes

7. Katherine is constructing a patio using the design shown at the right.

a How many total blocks will she need in order to have 5 blocks in the middle row?

b How many total blocks will she need in order to have 6 blocks in the middle row?

c What do you notice about the number of blocks in the middle row compared to the total number of blocks?

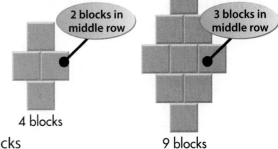

2 blocks in middle row

3 blocks in middle row

4 blocks

9 blocks

8. An artist wants to cut 1 flat sheet of copper into 16 equal pieces. Before he cuts, he will draw segments on the sheet of copper showing where to make the cuts. How many horizontal and vertical segments will he need to draw?

9. There are 24 balls in a large bin. Two out of every three are basketballs. The rest are footballs. How many basketballs are in the bin?

eTools
www.pearsonsuccessnet.com

DIGITAL

1. Which solid has two bases that are parallel, congruent circles? (13-1)

  A Cone

  B Pyramid

  C Cube

  D Cylinder

2. What solid can be made with the net shown? (13-2)

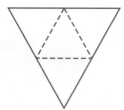

  A Triangular Pyramid

  B Triangular Prism

  C Rectangular Pyramid

  D Cube

3. What is the volume of the step stool shown? (13-6)

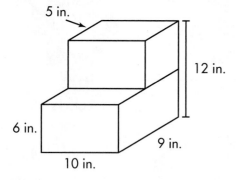

5 in.

12 in.

6 in.

9 in.

10 in.

  A 320 in³

  B 790 in³

  C 840 in³

  D 1,080 in³

4. What is the surface area of the prism formed by the net shown? (13-3)

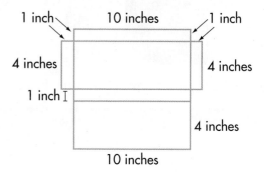

1 inch   10 inches   1 inch

4 inches   4 inches

1 inch

4 inches

10 inches

  A 44 in²

  B 100 in²

  C 108 in²

  D 120 in²

5. Nita stacked some crates to make a bookshelf as shown. Which of the following is the top view of the crates? (13-4)

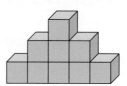

  A

  B

  C

  D

6. Todd's mother is setting up a business renting storage units. She is arranging the units in an L-shape. If she puts 3 units on each side of the L, she has 5 units in all, as shown. How many units does she have if she puts 8 units on each side of the L? (13-7)

A 13

B 15

C 16

D 17

7. Which trunk has a volume of 30 cubic feet? (13-5)

A

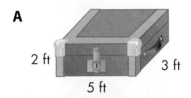

2 ft   3 ft   5 ft

B

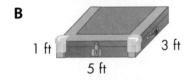

1 ft   3 ft   5 ft

C

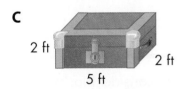

2 ft   2 ft   5 ft

D

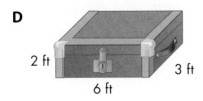

2 ft   3 ft   6 ft

8. What is the surface area of the trunk shown? (13-3)

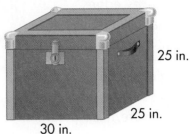

25 in.
25 in.
30 in.

A 320 in²

B 3,000 in²

C 4,250 in²

D 18,750 in²

9. What is the volume of the bale of hay? (13-5)

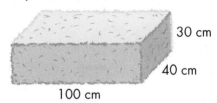

30 cm
40 cm
100 cm

A 120,000 cm²

B 120,000 cm³

C 12,000 cm²

D 12,000 cm³

10. A patio has the irregular shape shown. What is the area of the patio? (13-6)

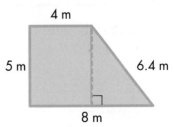

4 m
5 m   6.4 m
8 m

A 20 m²

B 23.4 m²

C 25.6 m²

D 30 m²

Set A, pages 322–324

Solids are classified by their shape and their faces, edges, and vertices. What solid figure is represented at the right?

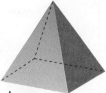

Faces: All triangles, except for the base. They have a common meeting point not on the base. Therefore, it is a pyramid.

Base: A square, so it is a square pyramid

Remember A prism has two congruent parallel bases, but a pyramid has only one base.

1. Classify the solid. List the edges and vertices.

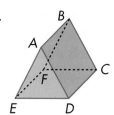

Set B, pages 326–329

A net is a plane figure which, when folded, gives a solid figure. The net below folds to make a rectangular prism.

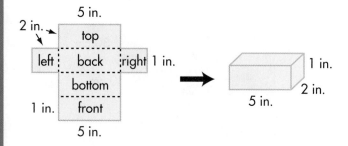

Find the surface area of the prism.

$SA = (5 \times 2) + (5 \times 2) + (2 \times 1) +$
$(2 \times 1) + (1 \times 5) + (1 \times 5) = 34$ in²

Remember that surface area is always measured in square units, such as m².

1. What figure will the net make?

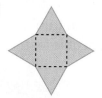

2. What is the surface area of the prism?

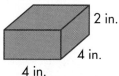

Set C, pages 330–331

Draw the front, top, and side views of the solid made from stacked cubes.

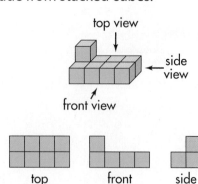

Remember to consider blocks hidden from your view.

1. Draw the front, top, and side views of the solid made from stacked cubes.

Set D, pages 332–334

Find the volume of this rectangular prism.

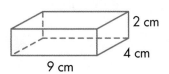

2 cm
4 cm
9 cm

Volume = length × width × height

$V = \ell \times w \times h$

$V = 9 \text{ cm} \times 4 \text{ cm} \times 2 \text{ cm}$

$V = 72 \text{ cm}^3$

Remember If you know the base area of a rectangular prism, use the formula $V = B \times h$, where B is the base area.

Find each volume.

1. Base area = 42 m²
   height = 3 meters

2.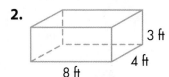

   3 ft
   4 ft
   8 ft

Set E, pages 336–338

Find the area of the irregular shape.

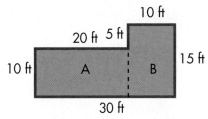

10 ft
20 ft 5 ft
10 ft   A   :   B   15 ft
30 ft

Separate the figure into two rectangles (as shown by the dashed line). Use the formula $A = \ell \times w$ to find the area of each rectangle.

Rectangle A   **Rectangle B**

$A = 20 \times 10$ $A = 10 \times 15$

$\quad = 200$ $\quad = 150$

Add to find the total area: 200 + 150 = 350

The total area is 350 ft².

Remember that some irregular shapes and solids can be separated into regular shapes or solids.

1. Find the area.

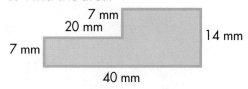

   7 mm
   20 mm
   7 mm
   14 mm
   40 mm

2. Find the volume.

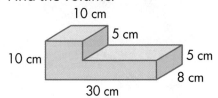

   10 cm
   5 cm
   10 cm
   5 cm
   30 cm
   8 cm

Set F, pages 340–341

To solve a simpler problem, follow these steps:

Step 1

Break apart or change problem into one that is simpler to solve.

Step 2

Use objects to solve the simpler problem.

Step 3

Use the answers to the simpler problem to solve the original problem.

Remember that objects can be used to see patterns or relationships.

1. After folding a piece of paper one time, there are two sections. How many sections are there after 2 folds? After 3 folds? If you fold the paper 5 times, how many sections would you have?

Topic 14

Measurement Units, Time, and Temperature

1 The original Aztec calendar, Sun Stone, was based on a 13-day week. If you visit Mexico to see the stone, when will you leave, if you know the arrival time and the elapsed time of your visit? You will find out in Lesson 14-7.

2 Big Ben not only tells time, but signals when a session of Parliament begins. What time of the day did a session of Parliament end? You will find out in Lesson 14-6.

Review What You Know!

Choose the best term from the box.

- customary
- metric
- perimeter

1. A kilogram is a ___?___ unit of mass.

2. A foot is a ___?___ unit of length.

3. The ___?___ is the distance around a polygon.

Multiplication

Find each product.

4. 60×6 5. 24×3

6. 7×13 7. 12×7

8. 60×34 9. 10×6

Order of Operations

Evaluate each expression.

10. $1 + 4 \times 7$

11. $(8 + 5) + 3 \times 2$

12. $9 \times 15 - 4$

13. $(5 + 7) \times 3 - 5 + (3 \times 5)$

14. $(\frac{1}{2} \times 8) \times 12$

Operations

Writing to Explain Write an answer for the question.

15. How can multiplication be used to check the quotient of a division problem?

③ Over 1.6 million one-inch-square glass tiles cover the walls of the Outer Bay exhibit. What is an estimate for the volume of the main viewing window of this exhibit? You will find out in Lesson 14-3.

④ A bee hummingbird's nest is about the size of a thimble. What is the capacity of this nest? You will find out in Lesson 14-2.

Understand It!
The capacity of a container can be measured using customary units.

Customary Units of Capacity

How can you measure capacity in customary units?

Capacity is the volume of a container measured in liquid units. Common units of capacity are the gallon (gal), quart (qt), pint (pt), cup (c), and fluid ounce (fl oz).

gallon

quart

pint

cup

Guided Practice*

Do you know HOW?

In **1** and **2**, choose a reasonable unit of capacity. Use fl oz, c, pt, qt, or gal.

1.

2.

Do you UNDERSTAND?

3. In the gallon container above, how many cups are in one gallon?

4. Which unit of capacity would be reasonable to measure the capacity of a kitchen sink?

5. Writing to Explain Why is $\frac{1}{8}$ c equal to one fl oz?

Independent Practice

In **6** through **9**, give the capacity of each container.

6.
1 gal

qt

pt

7.
1 c

fl oz

pt

8.
1 pt

c

qt

9.
1 qt

pt

gal

Which unit(s) of capacity would be reasonable to measure each capacity?

10. drinking glass

11. gas tank of car

12. medicine bottle

Animated Glossary
www.pearsonsuccessnet.com

DIGITAL

*For another example, see Set A on page 370.

1 gal = 4 qt   1 qt = 2 pt   1 pt = 2 c   1 c = 8 fl oz

$1\ qt = \frac{1}{4}\ gal$ $1\ pt = \frac{1}{2}\ qt$ $1\ c = \frac{1}{2}\ pt$

Problem Solving

For **13** through **15**, use the drawing at the right.

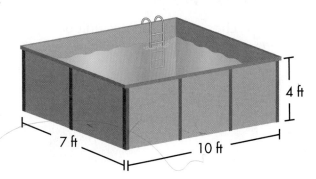

13. What is the perimeter of the base of the swimming pool?

14. The pool is above ground and its height is 4 feet. What is the volume of the pool?

15. Which unit of capacity would be appropriate to find the pool's capacity?

For **16** through **18**, and **20**, use the table. Prices include tax.

Camping Supplies	Cost per Item
5-gallon water jug	$ 7.99
Sleeping bag	$46.50
Compass	$ 5.00
2-quart canteen	$14.80
Backpack	$76.75
Small tent	$49.97

16. How much more does the tent cost than the sleeping bag?

17. David bought a backpack and a canteen. How much change will he receive from $100?

18. Lorelei bought the 5-gallon water jug and a 2-quart canteen. How much change will she receive from $50?

19. Writing to Explain Lorelei filled her 5-gallon jug with water. How many times could she fill her 2-quart canteen with water from the jug?

20. Nathan has $75. Which three supplies does he have enough money to buy?

    A sleeping bag, tent, 5-gallon water jug   **C** tent, 2-quart canteen, compass

    B compass, 5-gallon water jug, backpack   **D** backpack, 2-quart canteen, sleeping bag

Understand It!
The capacity of a container can be measured using metric units.

Metric Units of Capacity
How can you measure capacity in metric units?

Two common metric units of capacity are the milliliter (mL) and the liter (L).

$$1 L = 1,000 mL$$
$$1 mL = 0.001 L$$

A milliliter is about 20 drops of water.

A liter is a little more than a quart

Guided Practice*

Do you know HOW?

In **1** and **2**, choose a reasonable unit of capacity. Use mL or L.

1.

2.

Do you UNDERSTAND?

3. Which is the greater capacity: 200 mL or 2 L?

4. Writing to Explain Look again at the picture of the aquarium in the example above. How can you determine its capacity in milliliters?

Independent Practice

In **5** through **7**, give the capacity of each container.

5.

1 L

____ mL

6.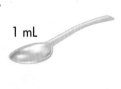

1 mL

____ L

7.

4 L

____ mL

In **8** through **11**, which capacity is more reasonable for each object?

8. cup of soup
200 mL or 2 L

9. soup spoon
1 L or 10 mL

10. Thermos bottle
1.5 L or 15 L

11. barrel of water
170 mL or 170 L

*For another example, see Set B on page 370.

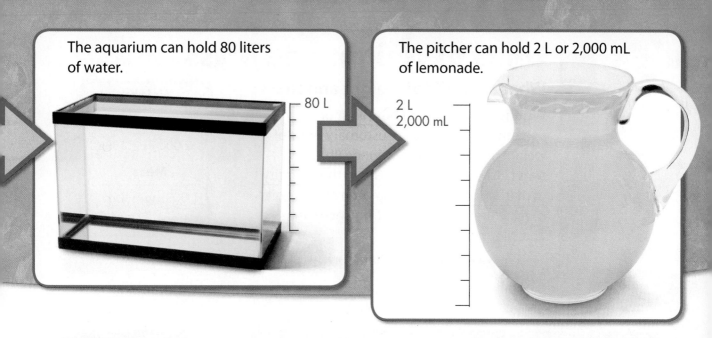

The aquarium can hold 80 liters of water.

80 L

The pitcher can hold 2 L or 2,000 mL of lemonade.

2 L
2,000 mL

Problem Solving

12. Use the following information to answer the questions.

Shawna found 48 tomatoes in her garden. One-eighth of the tomatoes were green and one-fourth were bruised. Only half of the tomatoes were fully ripe and ready for picking.

a Were there more bruised or unripe tomatoes? Explain.

b How many tomatoes were good to eat?

13. **Think About the Process** An electric guitar costs $650. Randy has already saved $375, and saves $75 each month. Which expression shows how to find how many more months it will take Randy to buy the guitar?

A $(650 \times 75) - 375$

B $(650 - 375) \div 75$

C $650 + 75 + 375$

D $650 + 375 - 75$

14. You are filling a 2 L bottle with liquid from a full 125 mL container. How many containers will it take to fill the 2 L bottle?

A 4   **C** 12

B 8   **D** 16

15. One cubic centimeter will hold 1 mL of water. How many milliliters will an aquarium hold if it is 40 cm long, 20 cm wide, and 30 cm high?

16. The nest of a bee hummingbird has a capacity that is about the size of a thimble. Is 3 mL or 3 L more reasonable to express this capacity?

18. Stephan had 8 balloons. He sold $\frac{3}{4}$ of them for $2.00 each. How much money did Stephan collect?

17. What fraction or decimal does NOT name the shaded part?

A $\frac{3}{10}$

B 0.03

C $\frac{30}{100}$

D 0.3

Units of Weight and Mass

What are units of weight and mass?

Understand It!
Weight is measured using customary units. Mass is measured using metric units.

Weight is a measure of how light or heavy something is. Common customary units of weight are ounces (oz), pounds (lb), and tons (T). Mass is the measure of the quantity of matter in an object. Common metric units of mass are the milligram (mg), gram (g), and kilogram (kg).

Weight
16 oz = 1 lb
2,000 lb = 1 ton

Mass
1,000 mg = 1 g
1,000 g = 1 kg

Guided Practice*

Do you know HOW?

In **1** and **2**, which customary unit is best to measure the weight of each object?

1. bulldozer   **2.** envelope

In **3** and **4**, which metric unit of mass would be best for measuring each object?

3. nail   **4.** car

Do you UNDERSTAND?

5. Writing to Explain Would it be better to measure the mass of a person in milligrams, grams, or kilograms?

6. Estimation A kilogram is a little more than 2 pounds. If a boy weighs 100 pounds, about how much is his mass in kilograms?

Independent Practice

In **7** through **10**, which customary unit is best to measure the weight of the object?

7. truck   **8.** bar of soap   **9.** pencil   **10.** dog

In **11** through **14**, which metric unit is best to measure the mass of each object?

11. watermelon   **12.** safety pin   **13.** button   **14.** penguin

In **15** through **22**, which mass or weight is more reasonable for each?

15. kitten
1 g or 1 kg

16. horse
1 ton or 50 lb

17. button
1 kg or 1 mg

18. book
1 kg or 1 g

19. pear
1 kg or 1 mg

20. mug
5 kg or 5 g

21. computer
25 lb or 25 oz

22. dolphin
1 lb or 1 ton

DIGITAL
Animated Glossary
www.pearsonsuccessnet.com

*For another example, see Set C on page 370.

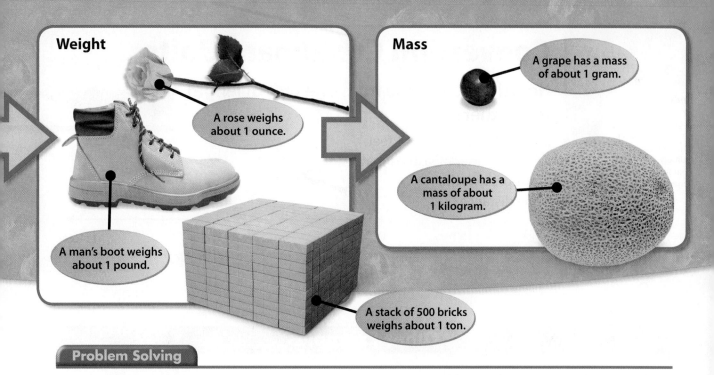

Weight

A rose weighs about 1 ounce.

A man's boot weighs about 1 pound.

A stack of 500 bricks weighs about 1 ton.

Mass

A grape has a mass of about 1 gram.

A cantaloupe has a mass of about 1 kilogram.

For **23** and **24**, use the table at the right.

Akira is volunteering at the Information Center at Big Bend this summer.

23. Which trails should Akira suggest for a visitor who wants to hike at least 2 miles but not more than 3 miles?

Big Bend Trail	Length (in miles)
Lost Mine Trail	4.8
Hot Springs Historic Trail	2
Window View Trail	0.3
Grapevine Hills Trail	2.2
Santa Elena Canyon Trail	1.7

24. A hiker wants to hike a distance of about 4 miles. Which two trails should Akira suggest?

25. What is the volume of an object with a length of 5 in., a width of 7 in., and a height of 8 in.?

26. Marissa has 51 baseball cards. Her brother has x fewer. Which expression shows how many baseball cards Marissa's brother has?

  A $51x$ **C** $x - 51$

  B $51 - x$ **D** $51 + x$

27. The world's largest cowboy boots are over $4\frac{1}{2}$ feet tall. Which customary unit would you use to weigh the world's largest cowboy boots?

  A ounce   **C** pound

  B fluid ounce   **D** ton

28. Estimation The Outer Bay exhibit at Monterrey Bay has a viewing window that is 56.5 feet long, 17 feet tall, and 13 inches thick. Estimate its volume in cubic feet. HINT: 13 inches is about 1 foot.

29. One of the world's heaviest hailstones weighed 2.2 pounds. Which is more reasonable to express its mass, 1 kg or 1 g?

Converting Customary Units

How do you change from one unit of length to another?

Some frogs can jump 11 feet. What are other measures that can represent the same distance?

0

11 feet

Other Examples

5 lb = ▩ oz

Think 1 lb = 16 oz

Find 5 × 16.

5 lb = 80 oz

20 qt = ▩ gal

Think 4 qt = 1 gal

Find 20 ÷ 4.

20 qt = 5 gal

Length
1 foot = 12 inches (in.)
1 yard = 3 feet (ft) = 36 in.
1 mile (mi) = 1,760 yd
          = 5,280 ft

Capacity
1 gallon = 4 quarts (qt)
1 quart = 2 pints (pt)
1 pint = 2 cups (c)
1 cup = 8 fluid ounces (fl oz)

Weight
1 ton (T) = 2,000 pounds (lb)
1 lb = 16 ounces (oz)

Guided Practice*

Do you know HOW?

In **1** through **3**, convert each measurement.

1. 9 ft = ▩ yd

2. 9 lb = ▩ oz

3. 12 fl oz = ▩ c ▩ fl oz

Do you UNDERSTAND?

4. If you want to convert feet to miles, do you multiply or divide?

5. **Writing to Explain** Why would you convert 4 gal 5 qt to 5 gal 1 qt?

Independent Practice

In **6** through **23**, convert each measurement.

6. 36 pt = ▩ qt

7. 2 mi = ▩ ft

8. 6,000 lb = ▩ T

9. 3 yd = ▩ in.

10. 32 pt = ▩ gal

11. 32 oz = ▩ lb

12. 1 qt = ▩ gal

13. 8 oz = ▩ lb

14. 18 yd = ▩ in.

To change larger units to smaller units, multiply.

11 ft = ▮ in.

Think 1 foot = 12 inches.

11 ft

| 12 in. | 12 in. | 12 in. | 12 in. | 12 in. | 12 in. | 12 in. | 12 in. | 12 in. | 12 in. | 12 in. |

↑
1 ft

Find 11 × 12.

11 × 12 = 132

11 feet = 132 inches

To change smaller units to larger units, divide.

11 ft = ▮ yd ▮ ft

Think 3 feet = 1 yard.

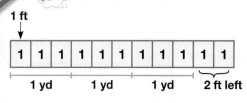
1 ft
↓

| 1 | 1 | 1 | 1 | 1 | 1 | 1 | 1 | 1 | 1 | 1 |

1 yd   1 yd   1 yd   2 ft left

Find 11 ÷ 3.

11 ÷ 3 = 3 R2

11 feet = 3 yards, 2 feet

15. 1 T = ▮ oz

16. 440 yd = ▮ mi

17. 5 gal = ▮ c

18. 12 ft 7 in. = ▮ in.

19. 30 qt = ▮ gal ▮ qt

20. 52 ft = ▮ yd ▮ ft

21. 4 qt 1 pt = ▮ pt

22. 4 yd 2 ft = ▮ in.

23. 1 gal 1 c = ▮ fl oz

Problem Solving

24. Sue is making punch. She needs 3 cups of orange juice and 6 pints of lemonade. How many fluid ounces of orange juice and how many quarts of lemonade does she need?

25. Kirk packed 6 bushels of corn. A bushel of corn weighs 35 pounds. How many ounces of corn did he pack in each bushel? How many ounces did he pack in all?

26. The world's longest known venomous snake is the king cobra, which measures about 18 feet. The world's shortest known venomous snake is the dwarf adder, which measures about 8 inches. What is the difference in length?

27. One tablespoon (tbsp) equals 3 teaspoons (tsp), and 1 fluid ounce equals 2 tablespoons. A recipe calls for 3 tablespoons of pineapple juice. A jar of pineapple juice has 12 fluid ounces. How many teaspoons of juice are in the jar?

28. Don drives a truck that weighs 1 ton. He picked up 2 tons of patio stones. Which is the number of pounds the truck and the patio stones weigh together?

  A 60 lb   **C** 6,000 lb

  B 600 lb   **D** 60,000 lb

29. **Think About the Process** Hector has a roll of craft wire. There are 36 yards of wire on the roll. Which expression can Hector use to find the number of inches of wire that are on the roll?

  A (36 × 3) × 12   **C** (36 × 3) ÷ 12

  B (36 ÷ 3) × 12   **D** (36 ÷ 3) ÷ 12

Converting Metric Units

How do you convert metric units?

You know the following relationships among commonly used metric units of measurement.

You can use these relationships to convert metric units.

Length	Capacity
1 cm = 10 mm	1 L = 1,000 mL
1 m = 100 cm	**Mass**
1 m = 1,000 mm	1 kg = 1,000 g
1 km = 1,000 m	1 g = 1,000 mg

wingspan: up to 1.52 m long

mass: as much as 1,800 g

Other Examples

2,350 mL = ▮ L

Think 1,000 mL = 1 L

Find 2,350 ÷ 1,000.

2,350 ÷ 1,000 = 2.35

2,350 mL = 2.35 L

2.5 kg = ▮ g

Think 1 kg = 1,000 g

Find 2.5 × 1,000.

2.5 × 1,000 = 2,500

2.5 kg = 2,500 g

Guided Practice*

Do you know HOW?

In **1** through **6**, convert each measurement.

1. 80 mm = ▮ cm   **2.** 5 L = ▮ mL

3. 3,000 g = ▮ kg   **4.** 140 cm = ▮ m

5. 0.06 g = ▮ mg   **6.** 23.8 m = ▮ km

Do you UNDERSTAND?

7. Writing to Explain Explain how to convert 4,300 milliliters to liters.

8. Which is the greater length: 1 km or 137,000 mm?

Independent Practice

In **9** through **20**, convert each measurement.

9. 45 m = ▮ cm

10. 12,000 mg = ▮ g

11. 780 mm = ▮ cm

12. 650 L = ▮ mL

13. 3.9 kg = ▮ g

14. 0.4 cm = ▮ mm

15. 1.45 g = ▮ mg

16. 18 mL = ▮ L

17. 62.9 m = ▮ km

18. 522 mL = ▮ L

19. 522 L = ▮ mL

20. 1,320 mg = ▮ g

*For another example, see Set E on page 371.

Convert 1.52 meters to centimeters.

To change from larger units to smaller units, multiply.

1.52 m = ▭ cm

Think 1 m = 100 cm

Find 1.52 × 100.

1.52 × 100 = 152   Use mental math.

1.52 m = 152 cm   Move the decimal point 2 places to the right.

Convert 1,800 grams to kilograms.

To change from smaller units to larger units, divide.

1,800 g = ▭ kg

Think 1,000 g = 1 kg

Find 1,800 ÷ 1,000.

1,800 ÷ 1,000 = 1.8   Use mental math.

1,800 g = 1.8 kg   Write 1,800 as 1,800.0 and move the decimal point 3 places to the left.

In **21** through **26**, compare the measurements. Use <, >, or = for each ◯.

21. 2,000 g ◯ 3 kg

22. 680 mm ◯ 68 cm

23. 0.91 L ◯ 91 mL

24. 7.24 m ◯ 7,240 cm

25. 56 mL ◯ 0.056 L

26. 94 g ◯ 9,400 mg

Problem Solving

27. The instructions for a science experiment call for 227 milligrams of potassium. What is the difference between this amount and 1 gram?

28. A drink pitcher holds 4.5 liters of lemonade. If there are 250 milliliters in a serving, how many servings does the pitcher hold?

29. **Estimation** As of 2006, the longest car ever built is 30.5 meters long. A meter is a little longer than a yard. Estimate the length of this car in feet.

30. The width of a cruise ship called the *Canberra* was 102 feet. What was the width of the *Canberra* in yards?

31. **Writing to Explain** Shayla says that one kilometer is equal to one million millimeters. Is she correct? Explain.

32. The area of a rectangular garden is 240 square feet. If the length of the garden is 20 feet, what is its width?

33. The longest mammal is the blue whale. Its length has been reported to reach 31 meters. How many centimeters is this?

   A 3.1 cm

   B 310 cm

   C 3,100 cm

   D 31,000 cm

34. Think About the Process How can you convert kilograms to grams?

   A Divide by 100.

   B Multiply by 100.

   C Divide by 1,000.

   D Multiply by 1,000.

Understand It!
Units of time can be added and subtracted.

Elapsed Time

How can you find how much time passes between two events?

Elapsed time is the difference between two times.

A plane flies from Seattle to San Francisco. How long is the flight time?

Find the elapsed time between 8:55 A.M. and 11:05 A.M.

Seattle 8:55 A.M. Departure

San Francisco 11:05 A.M. Arrival

Other Examples

How can you use elapsed time to find when an event began or ended?

A plane from Chicago arrived in Nashville at 7:10 P.M. The flight time was 1 hour 25 minutes. What time did the plane leave Chicago?

You can **subtract** to find the start time.

End Time − Elapsed Time = Start Time

$$
\begin{array}{c}
6 \text{ h } 70 \text{ min} \\
\cancel{7 \text{ h } 10 \text{ min}} \\
- \ 1 \text{ h } 25 \text{ min} \\
\hline
5 \text{ h } 45 \text{ min}
\end{array}
$$

25 min > 10 min
Rename to subtract.

The plane left Chicago at 5:45 P.M.

Shaylun's flight left at 4:40 P.M. and took 2 hours 45 minutes. What time did the plane land?

A 5:25 P.M.   **C** 7:25 P.M.

B 6:25 P.M.   **D** 8:25 P.M.

You can **add** to find the end time.

Start time + Elapsed Time = End Time

$$
\begin{array}{c}
4 \text{ h } 40 \text{ min} \\
+ \ 2 \text{ h } 45 \text{ min} \\
\hline
6 \text{ h } 85 \text{ min} \\
= \ 7 \text{ h } 25 \text{ min}
\end{array}
$$

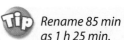 Rename 85 min as 1 h 25 min.

Shaylun's flight arrived at 7:25 P.M.

Explain It

1. How could you count on a number line to solve the first Other Example?

2. How could you check the subtraction used to find the start time in the first Other Example?

3. In the second Other Example, why is 85 minutes renamed as 1 hour 25 minutes?

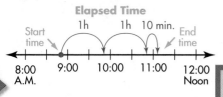

One Way

Count on a number line.

Elapsed Time

$$1 h + 1 h + 10 min = 2 h 10 min$$

The elapsed time of the flight is 2 hours 10 minutes.

Another Way

Subtract.

End Time − Start Time = Elapsed Time

The end time, or the time the flight ended, is 11:05 A.M.

The start time, or the time the flight began, is 8:55 A.M.

$$
\begin{array}{r}
10 \text{ h } 65 \text{ min} \\
\cancel{11 \text{ h } 05 \text{ min}} \\
- 8 \text{ h } 55 \text{ min} \\
\hline
2 \text{ h } 10 \text{ min}
\end{array}
$$

55 min > 5 min
Rename to subtract.

The elapsed time of the flight is 2 hours 10 minutes.

Guided Practice*

Do you know HOW?

For **1** through **6**, find each elapsed time.

1. 3:00 A.M. to 11:24 A.M.

2. 3:46 P.M. to 8:59 P.M.

3. 2:12 P.M. to 6:23 P.M.

4. 6:39 A.M. to 9:14 A.M.

5.

6.

Do you UNDERSTAND?

7. Writing to Explain In order to subtract 6 h 43 min from 12 h 32 min, do you need to rename 12 h 32 min? Why?

8. A flight from El Paso to Austin takes 1 hour 30 minutes. The flight arrives at 5:16 P.M. At what time did the flight leave El Paso?

9. A flight from Minneapolis to Dallas takes 2 hours 32 minutes. The flight departs at 8:47 A.M. At what time does the flight arrive?

10. If you subtract the start time from the end time, what will the difference be?

Independent Practice

For **11** through **14**, find each elapsed time.

11. 2:34 A.M. to 8:20 A.M.

12. 11:00 P.M. to 11:34 P.M.

13.

14.

Animated Glossary
www.pearsonsuccessnet.com

*For another example, see Set F on page 372.

For **15** through **18**, use the elapsed time to find the start time or the end time.

15. Start Time: 7:36 A.M.   Elapsed Time: 3 h 10 min

16. End Time: 7:55 P.M.   Elapsed Time: 2 h 45 min

17. Start Time: 1:45 P.M.   Elapsed Time: 3 h 53 min

18. End Time: 10:00 P.M.   Elapsed Time: 1 h 47 min

Problem Solving

19. **Number Sense** Listed at right are the activities that Javad wants to complete on Saturday.

Javad plans to start his activities at 9:00 A.M. He also wants to schedule 30 minutes of spare time between each activity. Prepare one possible schedule for Javad using the information provided.

Activity	Amount of Time Required
🚲	1 h 10 min
🪁	1 h 30 min
📖	2 h
🍲	1 h

20. A video-store owner reports that $\frac{2}{5}$ of the movies rented yesterday were new releases. The store has 4,000 movies in stock. If 35 movies were rented yesterday, how many rented movies were new releases?

21. The light above Big Ben's clock went on at 9:00 A.M. to signal that a session of Parliament began. Parliament was in session for $10\frac{1}{2}$ hours. At what time did Parliament's session end?

A 5:30 P.M.   **C** 7:30 P.M.

B 6:30 P.M.   **D** 8:30 P.M.

22. **Think About the Process** Alvira needs to find the elapsed time from 5:00 P.M. to 9:30 P.M. How many whole hours will she count?

A 4   **B** 7   **C** 9   **D** 11

23. **Writing to Explain** Sometimes you need to rename to subtract time. Explain the steps to rename 5 hours 18 minutes.

24. A plane leaves New York with a flight time of 2 hours 25 minutes. The plane arrives at Orlando at 4:15 P.M. What time did it leave New York?

25. **Think About the Process** Which expression names the greatest common factor of 16 and 82?

A 2   **C** $2 \times 2 \times 2$

B 2×2 **D** $2 \times 2 \times 2 \times 2$

Mixed Problem Solving

This map of the United States shows the six different time zones.

Pacific Mountain Central Eastern

Alaska

Anchorage, AK

Hawaii

Honolulu, HI

Seatle, WA

Denver, CO

Santa Fe, NM

Houston, TX

Miami, FL

1. In which time zone are you located?

3. What time does your school start in the morning? What time is it in each of the other time zones? Draw clock hands to show each time.

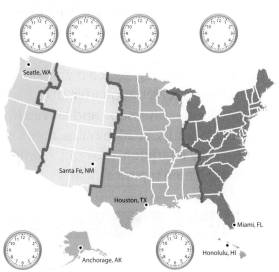

Seatle, WA

Santa Fe, NM

Houston, TX

Miami, FL

Anchorage, AK

Honolulu, HI

4. Your favorite television program is scheduled for 7:00 P.M. Eastern Time. What time does that program start in each of the following time zones?

  a Pacific   **c** Alaska

  b Hawaii   **d** Mountain

2. The President gave a speech in Denver, CO, at 7:30 P.M. It was broadcast live in each of the other time zones. The speech lasted 2 hours 15 minutes. Determine when the President's speech began and ended in each of the following cities:

  a Seattle, WA: Start _____
                        End _____

  b Santa Fe, NM: Start _____
                        End _____

  c Houston, TX: Start _____
                        End _____

  d Miami, FL: Start _____
                        End _____

  e Honolulu, HI: Start _____
                        End _____

  f Anchorage, AK: Start _____
                        End _____

5. **Strategy Focus** Solve using the strategy, Write an Equation. Theo earns $7 an hour washing cars. How many hours will he need to work to earn $847?

Let h = the number of hours of work.

Elapsed Time in Other Units

How can you find how much time passes between events on consecutive days?

Understand It!
Units of time can be added and subtracted.

The Hernandez family took a train that left Washington, D.C., on Tuesday and arrived in Maysville, Kentucky, on Wednesday. How long was the train trip?

 Tip *Quarter to 2 is the same as 1:45.*

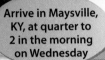

Arrive in Maysville, KY, at quarter to 2 in the morning on Wednesday

Leave Washington, D.C., at 1:05 P.M. on Tuesday

Guided Practice*

Do you know HOW?

In **1** and **2**, find the elapsed time.

1. 4:00 P.M. to 2:00 A.M.

2. 7:10 P.M. to 4:05 A.M.

In **3** and **4**, find the start or end time.

3. Start: 5:12 P.M.
Elapsed: 8 h 10 min

4. End: 10:45 P.M.
Elapsed: 12 h 35 min

Do you UNDERSTAND?

5. Writing to Explain Suppose a train trip starts at 4:00 P.M. on a Wednesday and ends at 1:30 P.M. the next day. What is the elapsed time? Explain how you found it.

6. The Urban family took a train that left St. Paul, MN, at quarter after 2 on Monday afternoon and arrived in Longview, TX, at 20 minutes after 5 on Tuesday afternoon. How much time did the train trip take?

Independent Practice

For **7** through **9**, find each elapsed time.

7. Quarter to 7 in the evening to 11:22 A.M.

8. 1:23 P.M. to 4:00 A.M.

9. Quarter after 11 in the morning to 6:23 P.M.

In **10** through **15**, find the start or end time.

10. Start: 1:23 P.M.
Elapsed: 13 h 12 min

11. End: 3:36 A.M.
Elapsed: 6 h 2 min

12. Start: 11:00 A.M.
Elapsed: 14 h 12 min

13. End: 12:06 P.M.
Elapsed: 10 h 7 min

14. End: 1:58 P.M.
Elapsed: 3 h 58 min

15. Start: 6:36 A.M.
Elapsed: 1 h 42 min

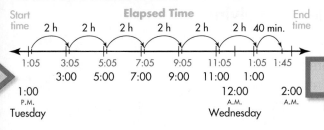

One Way

Count on a number line.

Start time | Elapsed Time | End time
2 h   2 h   2 h   2 h   2 h   2 h   40 min.

1:05   3:05   5:05   7:05   9:05   11:05   1:05 1:45
   3:00   5:00   7:00   9:00   11:00   1:00

1:00 P.M.   12:00 A.M.   2:00 A.M.
Tuesday   Wednesday

2 h + 2 h + 2 h + 2 h + 2 h + 2 h + 40 min
= 12 h 40 min

The train trip took 12 hours 40 minutes.

Another Way

Find the elapsed time before midnight and the elapsed time after midnight.

Before midnight	After midnight
11 h 60 min ~~12 h 00 min~~ – 1 h 05 min ――― 10 h 55 min	1:45 A.M. is 1 hour 45 minutes after midnight.

Add to find the total elapsed time.

   10 h 55 min
+   1 h 45 min
―――――――
11 h 100 min = 12 h 40 min

The train trip took 12 hours 40 minutes.

Problem Solving

16. Use the table below. Find the elapsed time between stations for the *Texas Eagle* train.

City	Schedule	Elapsed Time
Chicago, IL	Depart 3:20 P.M.	-----------
St. Louis, MO	Arrive 8:55 P.M. Depart 9:05 P.M.	
Longview, TX	Arrive 10:20 A.M.	

17. A train from Trenton, New Jersey, leaves at 8:10 A.M. and travels 11 hours 35 minutes to Charlotte, North Carolina. What time will the train arrive in Charlotte?

18. When Tyler's grandparents retired they took a driving trip across the country. They left home on August 4 and returned 2 weeks and 4 days later. What date did they return?

19. Sun Stone, the original Aztec calendar, is a famous symbol of Mexico. Suppose you visit Mexico City to see the stone. If you arrive on Sunday at 11:00 A.M. and stay 48 hours, what time and day will you leave Mexico City?

  A 10:00 A.M. Tuesday

  B 11:00 A.M. Tuesday

  C 12:00 P.M. Tuesday

  D 11:00 A.M. Monday

20. **Think About the Process** A family took a car trip to a cousin's house as shown on the clocks below.

START   FINISH

How many hours and minutes did the car trip take?

  A 4 h

  B 4 h 40 min

  C 4 h 43 min

  D 4 h 54 min

21. Sandy says that 5 × 4 = 4 × 5 is an example of the Associative Property of Multiplication. Is she correct? Why or why not?

Understand It!
Changes in temperature can be expressed in degrees Celsius and degrees Fahrenheit.

Temperature Change

How do you solve problems involving changes in temperature?

Jarusz checked the temperature at three different times. At 8:00 P.M., the temperature had dropped 20°F, or about 11°C, since 2:00 P.M. What was the temperature change from 8:00 A.M. to 2:00 P.M.? What was the temperature at 8:00 P.M.?

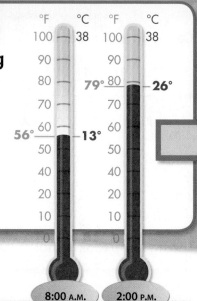

Guided Practice*

Do you know HOW?

For **1** through **4**, find each change in temperature.

1. 103°F to 88°F   **2.** 5°C to 18°C

3. 42°F to 96°F   **4.** −2°C to 18°C

For **5** and **6**, find the temperature after the change.

5. Start: 62°F   Change: 23°F decrease

6. Start: 15°C   Change: 3°C increase

Do you UNDERSTAND?

7. Use the information from the example above. Jarusz checked the temperature at noon. It was 66°F. What was the temperature change from 8:00 A.M. to noon?

8. What operation do you use to find the temperature after the change if you know the temperature increase?

9. For Exercise 4, why is the answer 20°C, not 16°C?

Independent Practice

For **10** through **15**, find each change in temperature.

10. −5°F to 20°F   **11.** 9°C to −3°C   **12.** 82°F to 25°F

13. 17°C to 32°C   **14.** 29°F to 71°F   **15.** 21°C to 13°C

For **16** through **19**, find the temperature after the change.

16. Start: 102°F   Change: 28°F decrease   **17.** Start: 11°C   Change: 14°C decrease

18. Start: −5°F   Change: 14°F increase   **19.** Start: 22°C   Change: 17°C increase

*For another example, see Set H on page 373.

Temperature can be expressed in different units.

In the customary system, temperature is read in degrees Fahrenheit (°F).

In the metric system, temperature is read in degrees Celsius (°C).

Find the temperature change in degrees Fahrenheit from 8:00 A.M. to 2:00 P.M.

79°F − 56°F = 23°F

Find the temperature change in degrees Celsius from 8:00 A.M. to 2:00 P.M.

26°C − 13°C = 13°C

The temperature increased from 8:00 A.M. to 2:00 P.M. by 23°F, or 13°C.

Find the temperature at 8:00 P.M. in degrees Fahrenheit and degrees Celsius.

79°F − 20°F = 59°F
26°C − 11°C = 15°C

The temperature was 59°F, or 15°C, at 8:00 P.M.

Problem Solving

20. Use the following table to answer Problems **a** through **c**.

Clothing	Number of Items	Price per Item
	5	$2
	2	$12
	4	$14

  a How much did all of the clothes cost?

  b Maria's mother will pay for all of the blouses. What is Maria's share of the total cost?

  c What fraction of the clothes are skirts?

23. Reasoning Which is greater, a change of 10°C or a change of 10°F? Explain.

25. A record high temperature of 128°F was set in Lake Havasu City, Arizona, in June 1994. The lowest temperature, −40°F, recorded in Arizona occurred in January, 1971, in Hawley Lake, Arizona. What is the temperature increase from −40°F to 128°F?

  A 88°F **B** 128°F **C** 168°F **D** 124°F

21. Find the change in temperature.

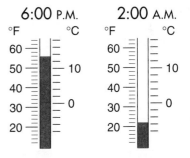

22. Think About the Process One day, at dawn, the temperature was 45°F. At noon, the temperature was 60°F. Which expression gives the temperature increase from dawn to noon?

  A 45°F − 60°F   **C** 2 × 45°F

  B 60°F − 45°F   **D** 60°F − 60°F

24. The average high temperature on a winter day in Minneapolis, Minnesota, is 25°F. The average low temperature for a winter day is 9°F. What is the change in average temperature?

26. Number Sense In Problem 25, did you add or subtract to find the change in temperature? Explain.

Understand It!
Learning how and when to make a table can be helpful when solving problems.

Make a Table

An airline schedules flights to leave from Washington, D.C., to Boston every 45 minutes beginning at 1:25 P.M. The last flight departs at 8:10 P.M. Flights departing before 3:00 P.M. have flight times of 1 hour 20 minutes. Flights departing after 3:00 P.M. have flight times of 1 hour 25 minutes. Which flight would arrive in Boston the closest to 6 P.M.?

Guided Practice*

Do you know HOW?

1. Make a table to solve the problem.

   The temperature in Cody's backyard was 86°F at 6 P.M. If the temperature dropped 2 degrees each hour until midnight, what was the temperature at midnight?

Do you UNDERSTAND?

2. In the example above, what are the headings for the table on page 367?

3. **Write a Problem** Write a real-world problem that can be solved using the table from the example above.

Independent Practice

For **4** and **5**, make a table to solve each problem.

4. Mark is recording the sunrise times this month. The sun rose at 5:18 A.M. the first day of the month. Mark noticed that the sun rose 1 minute later each day, except for every third day when it rose 2 minutes later. Copy and continue the table below to find the sunrise time for the 15th day of the month.

Day of Month	Sunrise
1	5:18 A.M.
2	5:19 A.M.
3	5:20 A.M.
4	5:22 A.M.
5	5:23 A.M.

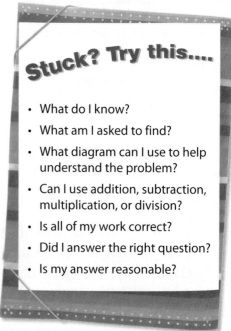

Stuck? Try this....

- What do I know?
- What am I asked to find?
- What diagram can I use to help understand the problem?
- Can I use addition, subtraction, multiplication, or division?
- Is all of my work correct?
- Did I answer the right question?
- Is my answer reasonable?

*For another example, see Set I on page 373.

What do I know?

- First flight leaves at 1:25 P.M.
- Flights depart every 45 minutes.
- Flights departing before 3 P.M. take 1 hour 20 minutes.
- Flights departing after 3 P.M. take 1 hour 25 minutes.

What am I asked to find?

Which flight arrives in Boston the closest to 6:00 P.M.

Make a table of departure and arrival times.

	Departures	Flight Time	Arrivals
Data	1:25 P.M.	(1 h 20 min)	2:45 P.M.
	2:10 P.M.	(1 h 20 min)	3:30 P.M.
	2:55 P.M.	(1 h 20 min)	4:15 P.M.
	3:40 P.M.	(1 h 25 min)	5:05 P.M.
	4:25 P.M.	(1 h 25 min)	5:50 P.M.
	5:10 P.M.	(1 h 25 min)	6:35 P.M.

The flight departing at 4:25 P.M. arrives the closest to 6:00 P.M.

---

5. Ernie's oven takes 2 minutes to heat to 100°F. Then, the oven heats an additional 50°F with each additional minute. How many minutes will it take the oven to heat to 350°F? To 400°F?

6. Delia's play rehearsal was 23 minutes longer than usual. Usually rehearsal lasts 2 hours 30 minutes. If her rehearsal started at 3:30 P.M., what time did it end? Explain how you found your answer.

7. Santino took a survey of his 21 classmates. He asked them how many minutes they spent on the telephone one night. His survey results show the minutes spent on the phone.

20 35 0 65 30 45 50
10 25 60 45 15 20 40
0 40 25 30 0 25 20

Did most of his classmates spend 0 to 25 minutes, 26 to 45 minutes, or over 46 minutes on the telephone?

8. Angelo earns $8.00 per hour delivering pizzas in the summer. His weekly schedule is shown below. How much does Angelo earn each week delivering pizzas?

Friday	5:00 P.M. to 9:00 P.M.
Saturday	11:00 A.M. to 7:00 P.M.
Sunday	1:00 P.M. to 6:00 P.M.

A $128.00   **C** $144.00

B $136.00   **D** $152.00

For **9** and **10**, use the table at the right.

9. Toby wants to take the train from Greenleaf to Main in as little time as possible. Which train should he take?

10. How many minutes does Train C take to go from Newtown to Main?

Train	A	B	C
Greenleaf	6:40	7:10	7:30
Newtown	---	7:20	7:40
Fort Young	7:00	---	8:10
Castle Point	---	---	---
Main	7:20	7:47	8:30

1. Which is most reasonable for the capacity of a water pitcher? (14-2)

   A 2 milliliters

   B 20 milliliters

   C 2 liters

   D 20 liters

2. Which metric unit would be best to measure the mass of a piano? (14-3)

   A Liter

   B Milligram

   C Gram

   D Kilogram

3. Which object would most likely weigh about 50 pounds? (14-3)

   A Elephant

   B Suitcase

   C Car

   D Book

4. Which unit is most appropriate to measure a dose of cough syrup? (14-2)

   A Liter

   B Milliliter

   C Meter

   D Millimeter

5. Which unit of capacity would be best to measure the amount of water in a hot water tank? (14-1)

   A Quart

   B Ounce

   C Gallon

   D Cup

6. Which of the following could NOT be the elapsed time between the two times shown on the clocks? (14-7)

   A 2 hours 25 minutes

   B 8 hours 25 minutes

   C 14 hours 25 minutes

   D 26 hours 25 minutes

7. Bailey watched one movie that was 1 hour 25 minutes in length and another movie that was 1 hour 55 minutes in length. Together the movies were 2 hours 80 minutes in length. Which of the following is equal to 2 hours 80 minutes? (14-6)

   A 2 hours 50 minutes

   B 3 hours 50 minutes

   C 3 hours 20 minutes

   D 3 hours 60 minutes

8. If the temperature on a thermometer reads −5°C and the wind is blowing at 30 miles per hour, the wind-chill factor is −22°C. Which of the following is true? (14-8)

   A The wind-chill factor is 17 degrees colder than the actual temperature.

   B The wind-chill factor is 27 degrees colder than the actual temperature.

   C The wind-chill factor is 17 degrees warmer than the actual temperature.

   D The wind-chill factor is 27 degrees warmer than the actual temperature.

9. The tail of a Boeing 747 airplane is 63 feet 8 inches tall. How many inches tall is the tail? (14-4)

A 71 in.

B 748 in.

C 756 in.

D 764 in.

10. Which distance is equivalent to the length Jake swam? (14-5)

Student	Distance Swam
Alex	1 km 200 m
Santo	1,100 m
Jake	1,300 m
Savannah	1 km 500 m

Data

A 130 km

B 13 km

C 1 km 3,000 m

D 1 km 300 m

11. Mason made 5 quarts of salsa. Which of the following can be used to find the number of cups Mason made? (14-4)

A $5 \times 2 \times 2$

B $5 \times 4 \times 4$

C $5 \div 2 \div 2$

D $5 \times 4 \times 2$

12. The mass of a longhorn bull is about 600 kilograms. What is the mass of this type of bull in grams? (14-5)

A 600,000

B 60,000

C 6,000

D 60

13. Gary finished reading the last chapter of his book in 34 minutes. If he started at 12:48 P.M., what time did he finish? (14-6)

A 1:12 P.M.

B 1:22 P.M.

C 1:34 P.M.

D 2:12 P.M.

14. On average, the temperature inside a car parked in the sun will rise 16°F every 25 minutes. Geraldo's car is parked in the sun and has a temperature of 79°F at 12:30 P.M. Make a table to find the expected time for his car to reach 127°F. (14-9)

A 12:55 P.M.

B 1:20 P.M.

C 1:40 P.M.

D 1:45 P.M.

15. Mrs. Johns is making strawberry jam. If the candy thermometer shown is the current temperature, what temperature change is needed for the jam to reach 220°F? (14-8)

A 305°F increase

B 305°F decrease

C 135°F increase

D 135°F decrease

Set A, pages 348–349

Give the capacity of the container.

1 gal = 4 qt
1 qt = 2 pt
1 pt = 2 c
1 c = 8 fl oz

1 qt

2 pints = 1 quart

$\frac{1}{4}$ gallon = 1 quart

Remember that capacity can be measured in fractional units.

Give the capacity of each container.

1. 1 cup

2.

1 gal

▢ fl oz   ▢ qt

▢ c   ▢ gal

Set B, pages 350–351

Which capacity is more reasonable?

MILK

250 mL
or
2 L

Since one liter is a little more than a quart, 250 mL is the more reasonable capacity.

Remember that one milliliter is about 20 drops of water and that 1,000 mL = 1 L.

Which capacity is more reasonable?

1. water bottle   **2.** bucket of water

   400 mL or 4 L   7 L or 18 L

Set C, pages 352–353

Weight is a measure of how light or how heavy something is. Common customary units of weight are the ounce, pound, and ton.

A book might weigh 3 pounds.

Mass is a metric measure of the quantity of matter in an object. Common units of mass are the milligram, gram, and kilogram.

A pencil might have a mass of 8 grams.

Weight	**Mass**
16 oz = 1 lb	1,000 mg = 1 g
2,000 lb = 1 ton (T)	1,000 g = 1 kg

Remember that a flower weighs about 1 ounce. A man's shoe weighs about 1 pound, and a grape has a mass of about 1 gram.

Which customary unit is best to measure the weight of each object?

1. eraser   **2.** bicycle

3. cookie   **4.** car

Which metric unit is best to measure the mass of each object?

5. chair   **6.** stamp

7. book   **8.** carrot

Set D, pages 354–355

Convert each customary measurement.

A. 24 ft = ▨ in.

To convert from larger units to smaller, **multiply**.

Think 1 foot = 12 in.

Find 24 × 12.

24 ft = 288 in.

B. 12,000 lb = ▨ T

To convert from smaller units to larger, **divide**.

Think 1 ton = 2,000 lb

Find 12,000 ÷ 2,000.

12,000 lb = ▨ T

Remember that customary units can be used to measure length, weight, and capacity.

Convert each measurement.

1. 4 yd = ▨ in.

2. 7 gal = ▨ qt

3. 48 oz = ▨ lb

4. 5 mi = ▨ ft

5. 18 pt = ▨ cups

6. 20 qt = ▨ gal

7. 144 in. = ▨ ft

8. 16 fl oz = ▨ cups

9. 108 in. = ▨ yd

10. 40 qt = ▨ pt

Set E, pages 356–357

Convert each metric measurement.

A. 2.4 m = ▨ mm

To convert from larger units to smaller, **multiply**.

Think 1 m = 10 mm

Find 2.4 × 10.

2.4 m = 2.4 = 24 mm

B. 8,000 mL = ▨ L

To convert from smaller units to larger, **divide**.

Think 1 L = 1,000 mL

Find 8,000 ÷ 1,000.

8,000 mL = 8.000 = 8 L

Remember that the decimal point moves to the right when you multiply by 10, 100, or 1,000 and to the left when you divide by 10, 100, or 1,000.

Convert each measurement.

1. 6 kg = ▨ g

2. 1.4 L = ▨ mL

3. 240 mm = ▨ cm

4. 2.6 km = ▨ m

5. 38 m = ▨ cm

6. 2.9 kg = ▨ g

7. 114 mg = ▨ g

8. 250 mL = ▨ L

9. 350 mm = ▨ m

10. 36.7 m = ▨ km

Set F, pages 358–360

Find the elapsed time in hours and minutes.

2:54 A.M. to 8:08 A.M.

Subtract the start time from the end time.

```
        7 h 68 min
    8 h  8 min    Rename.
  – 2 h 54 min
    5 h 14 min
```

The elapsed time is 5 hours 14 minutes.

Remember that there are 60 minutes in 1 hour.

Find the elapsed time in hours and minutes.

1. 8:36 P.M. to 9:30 P.M.

2. 1:47 P.M. to 10:16 P.M.

3. 3:43 A.M. to 6:35 A.M.

4. 9:24 A.M. to 11:34 A.M.

5. 10:27 A.M. to 12:21 P.M.

Set G, pages 362–363

Find the elapsed time.

Start time P.M.   End time A.M.

Step 1 Find the time elapsed before midnight.

```
            11 h 60 min
        12 h 00 min    Rename.
      – 10 h 20 min
         1 h 40 min
```

The elapsed time before midnight is 1 hour 40 minutes.

Step 2 The elapsed time after midnight is 8 hours 25 minutes.

Step 3 Add to find the total elapsed time.

```
       1 h 40 min
    +  8 h 25 min
       9 h 65 min    Rename 65 minutes as
    = 10 h  5 min    1 hour 5 minutes.
```

The total elapsed time is 10 hours 5 minutes.

Remember to subtract to find the elapsed time before midnight and then add the amount of time after midnight to find the total elapsed time.

Find the elapsed time.

1. Start: 6:00 P.M.
End: 6:06 A.M.

2. Start: 9:30 P.M.
End: 5:56 A.M.

Find the start or end time.

3. Start: 3:45 P.M.
Elapsed: 14 hours 45 minutes

4. Start: 2:00 A.M.
Elapsed: 4 hours 45 minutes

5. End: 2:30 A.M.
Elapsed: 3 hours 30 minutes

6. End: 5:45 P.M.
Elapsed: 7 hours 30 minutes

7. Start: 4:10 P.M.
Elapsed: 5 hours 17 minutes

Set H, pages 364–365

Find the change in temperature in °F.

10:00 A.M.　　　3:30 P.M.

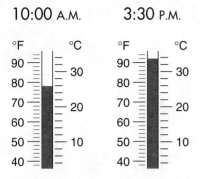

What was the change in temperature?

92°F − 78°F = 14°F

Was this an increase or a decrease in temperature?

The temperature increased because it went from 78°F at 10:00 A.M. to 92°F at 3:30 P.M.

Remember that Fahrenheit and Celsius are two different scales used for measuring temperature.

Find the change in temperature.

1. 5°C to 21°C

2. 85°F to 44°F

3. 28°F to 51°F

4. 15°C to 0°C

5. 15°C to −5°C

6. 22°F to 88°F

7. 5°C to −7°C

8. 17°F to 56°F

9. 3°C to 24°C

Set I, pages 366–367

Mark is training for a race. For every 4 minutes he runs, he walks for 5 minutes. Yesterday, he walked for 35 minutes. How many minutes did he run?

A table can help you organize the information. To make a table, follow these steps:

Step 1 Set up the table with the correct labels.

Step 2 Enter known data into the table.

Step 3 Look for a pattern. Extend the table.

Step 4 Find the answer in the table.

Minutes Running	4	8	12	16	20	24	28
Minutes Walking	5	10	15	20	25	30	35

Mark ran for 28 minutes.

Remember to read the problem carefully and make sure the information in your table is correct.

1. Katie is on a softball team. For every 10 minutes she practices fielding, she takes 5 minutes of batting practice. Yesterday, she took 20 minutes of batting practice. How many minutes did she practice fielding? Make a table to show how you found the answer.

Solving and Writing Equations and Inequalities

1

One of the tallest trees in the world is a sequoia known as General Grant. How many times taller is General Grant than the height of a typical oak tree? You will find out in Lesson 15-2.

2

How much taller is a full-grown male giraffe than a fifth-grade student? You will find out in Lesson 15-2.

3 How many members of the U.S. Senate were women in 2005? You will find out in Lesson 15-1.

4 The area of Lake Victoria, in Africa, is 26,828 square miles. How does the area of Lake Victoria compare to the area of Lake Michigan, in the United States? You will find out in Lesson 15-1.

Review What You Know!

Vocabulary

Choose the best term from the box.

> • equality • operations
> • inverse • variable

1. Addition, subtraction, multiplication, and division are all __?__ .

2. When both sides of an equation have the same value, they have __?__ .

3. A(n) __?__ is a letter or symbol that is used to represent an unknown value.

4. Operations that undo each other are called __?__ operations.

Multiplying Decimals

5. 7.1×8 6. 6.5×9.2 7. 4.8×8

8. 3.6×9.3 9. 9.9×9.8 10. 12.3×4.7

Estimation

Estimate each product, sum, or difference.

11. $13 + 24$ 12. $81 - 19$ 13. 37×3

14. $68 - 31$ 15. 27×2 16. $17 + 59$

Problem Solving

Writing to Explain Write an answer for the question.

17. Lin went to the store with $10.00. She bought a toothbrush for $4.59 and a tube of toothpaste for $3.29. Explain what you could do to find out how much change Lin will receive when she checks out.

Understand It!
Properties of equality and inverse operations are helpful when solving equations.

Solving Addition and Subtraction Equations

How can you use addition and subtraction to solve equations?

In January 2005, there were 83 women in Congress. How many women were serving in the U.S. Senate?

Members of U.S. Congress	
January, 2005	
U.S. Senate	
Men	86
Women	
U.S. House of Representatives	
Men	367
Women	69

Data

Other Examples

Addition Property of Equality:
You can add the same number to both sides of an equation and the sides remain equal.

Example:
$$9 - 4 = 5$$
$$9 - 4 + 2 = 5 + 2$$

Subtraction Property of Equality:
You can subtract the same number from both sides of an equation and the sides remain equal.

Example:
$$8 + 6 = 14$$
$$8 + 6 - 3 = 14 - 3$$

Operations that undo each other are inverse operations.
Addition and subtraction have an inverse relationship.

Guided Practice*

Do you know HOW?

In **1** and **2**, what would you do to get each variable by itself on one side of the equation?

1. $x - 45 = 90$ **2.** $n + 23.4 = 36.9$

In **3** through **6**, use inverse operations and a property of equality to solve these equations.

3. $x + 13 = 42$ **4.** $x - 12 = 37$

5. $a + 8 = 37$ **6.** $b - 9 = 25$

Do you UNDERSTAND?

7. What could you do to check the answer in the example at the top of the page?

8. When finding the number of women in the Senate, why must 69 be subtracted from both sides of the equation?

9. Write a subtraction equation for the problem in the example at the top of the page.

DIGITAL

Animated Glossary
www.pearsonsuccessnet.com

*For another example, see Set A on page 392.

Since Congress includes the Senate plus the House, you can write an addition equation. An equation is a number sentence that uses an equal sign to show that two expressions have the same value.

83	
x	69

Let x = the number of women in the Senate.

Equation: $x + 69 = 83$.

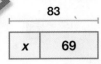

To solve the equation, get the variable alone.

$$x + 69 = 83$$
$$x + 69 - 69 = 83 - 69$$
$$x = 83 - 69$$
$$x = 14$$

You can subtract 69 from both sides of the equation and the quantities on each side of the equal sign are still equal.

There were 14 women serving in the U.S. Senate in January 2005.

Independent Practice

In **10** through **18**, solve each equation.

10. $d - 14 = 13$

11. $p + 31 = 52$

12. $c - 68 = 78$

13. $n + 70 = 265$

14. $y - 28 = 98$

15. $746 + t = 947$

16. $91 = 19 + m$

17. $75 = n - 39$

18. $k + 22.5 = 30$

Problem Solving

19. If there are 57 students in the school band and 29 of them are boys, how many girls are in the band?

20. Writing to Explain Why will the equations $x + 14 = 37$ and $x - 14 = 37$ have different solutions for x?

21. Draw It Draw a diagram to represent the equation $y + 18 = 73$.

22. Mr. Kugel's class raised $213 from different class projects and collected $27 in donations. How much more money is needed to pay for a $500 class picnic?

23. Think About the Process Which operation would you use to solve the equation $x - 17 = 23$?

    A Add 17.   **C** Multiply by 17.

    B Subtract 17.   **D** Divide by 1.

24. The Johnson family shared a spinach quiche for breakfast. Mom ate $\frac{1}{4}$, Dad ate $\frac{1}{3}$, and Julia ate $\frac{1}{4}$ of the quiche. How much of the quiche was not eaten?

25. The area of Lake Victoria in Africa is 26,828 square miles. The area of Lake Michigan in the U.S. is 22,539 square miles. Solve the equation $22,539 + x = 26,828$ to find how much larger Lake Victoria is than Lake Michigan.

Understand It!
Properties of equality and inverse operations are helpful in solving equations.

Solving Multiplication and Division Equations

How can you use multiplication and division to solve equations?

Keef's scoutmaster is buying model cars for his troop. The cars are sold by the case. How many cases should the scoutmaster buy for 32 boys?

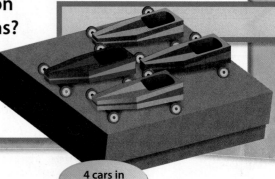

4 cars in each case

Other Examples

Multiplication Property of Equality:
You can multiply both sides of an equation by the same nonzero number and the sides remain equal.

Example:

$$\frac{14}{2} = 7$$

$$\frac{14}{2} \times 2 = 7 \times 2$$

Division Property of Equality:
You can divide both sides of an equation by the same nonzero number and the sides remain equal.

Example:

$$6 \times 5 = 30$$

$$\frac{6 \times 5}{5} = \frac{30}{5}$$

Operations that undo each other are inverse operations.
Multiplication and division have an inverse relationship.

Guided Practice*

Do you know HOW?

In **1** and **2**, what would you do to get each variable alone on one side of the equation?

1. $24n = 120$　　　**2.** $\frac{b}{7} = 42$

In **3** through **6**, use inverse operations and a property of equality to solve these equations.

3. $y \div 9 = 12$　　　**4.** $3m = 63$

5. $85 = 17r$　　　**6.** $24 = \frac{c}{3}$

Do you UNDERSTAND?

7. What could you do to check the answer in the example at the top of the page?

8. Write a division equation for the problem at the top of the page.

9. In the example above, if there were 6 cars in a case, how many cases would the scoutmaster need to buy to be sure every scout had a car?

Animated Glossary
www.pearsonsuccessnet.com

*For another example, see Set B on page 392.

Let c = the number of cases needed.

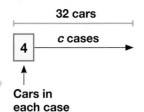

32 cars

c cases

4

Cars in each case

Since each case contains 4 cars, you can write the equation

$4c = 32$

To solve the equation, get the variable alone.

$4c = 32$

$\dfrac{4c}{4} = \dfrac{32}{4}$

$c = 8$

You can divide both sides of the equation by 4 and the quantities on each side of the equal sign are still equal.

Tip *Remember that $\dfrac{4c}{4}$ is the same as $4 \times c \div 4$.*

The scoutmaster should buy 8 cases of cars.

Independent Practice

In **10** through **17**, solve each equation.

10. $14d = 56$

11. $\dfrac{c}{8} = 64$

12. $45y = 135$

13. $184 = 23p$

14. $\dfrac{m}{5} = 12$

15. $8 = \dfrac{k}{30}$

16. $72 = 12t$

17. $14 = \dfrac{w}{7}$

Problem Solving

18. Geometry Each side of a pentagon measures 11 inches. What is the perimeter of the pentagon?

19. Reasoning Randy divides 48 by 6 to solve an equation for y. One side of the equation is 48. Write the equation.

20. Martin is going on a 216-mile trip. If his car gets 24 miles per gallon, how many gallons of gas will he need for his trip?

21. Writing to Explain How could you use mental math to find m in the equation $279\left(\dfrac{m}{279}\right) = 72$?

22. Daria measured the length of three ants in science class. They were $\dfrac{2}{3}$ inch, $\dfrac{3}{5}$ inch, and $\dfrac{1}{4}$ inch. Which ant is the longest?

23. **Think About the Process** Which operation would you use to solve the equation $17x = 255$?

   A Add 17.   **C** Multiply by 17.

   B Subtract 17.   **D** Divide by 17.

24. Giraffes can grow to about 20 feet tall. Some fifth-grade students can be about 5 feet tall. Solve the equation $5x = 20$ to find how many times as tall a giraffe can be as a fifth-grade student.

25. General Grant, a sequoia tree, is 273 feet tall. A typical Red Oak tree is about 70 feet tall. Solve the equation $70x = 280$ to find about how many times as tall the General Grant is as a typical Red Oak.

Inequalities and the Number Line

How can you graph an inequality?

An inequality is a mathematical sentence that contains one of the symbols $>$, $<$, $\geq$, or $\leq$. A solution of an inequality is any number that makes the inequality true.

You can graph the solutions of an inequality, such as $x > 3$, on a number line.

How do you graph $x > 3$?

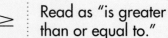

$\geq$: Read as "is greater than or equal to."

$\leq$: Read as "is less than or equal to."

Another Example How do you graph an inequality that involves addition or subtraction?

Graph $y + 5 \leq 12$.

First, solve $y + 5 = 12$.

Think What number plus 5 equals 12?

$7 + 5 = 12$
$12 = 12$

So $y = 7$.

Next, graph $y \leq 7$.

Draw a closed circle at 7 to show that 7 is included in the solution. Then repeat Step 2 in the example above.

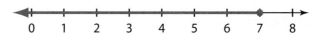

Guided Practice*

Do you know HOW?

Name three solutions of each inequality. Then graph each inequality on a number line.

1. $c < 5$

2. $m \geq 12$

3. $r + 8 > 9$

4. $n - 6 \leq 10$

Do you UNDERSTAND?

5. Writing to Explain Is it possible to make a list of all the solutions of $x > 3$? Explain.

6. How would the graph of $y + 5 < 12$ be different from the graph of $y + 5 \leq 12$?

Independent Practice

Name three solutions of each inequality. Then graph each inequality on a number line.

7. $k \leq 8$

8. $w > 2$

9. $t < 14$

10. $p \geq 18$

11. $d + 6 < 15$

12. $s - 1 \geq 4$

13. $q - 3 \leq 3$

14. $z + 3 > 3$

Animated Glossary, eTools
www.pearsonsuccessnet.com

Step 1

On the number line, draw an open circle at 3. The open circle shows that 3 is not included in the solution.

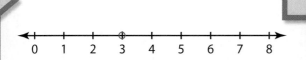

Step 2

Locate three solutions of $x > 3$ on the number line. Start at the open circle and shade a thick line over the numbers. Shade the arrow to show there are infinitely many solutions.

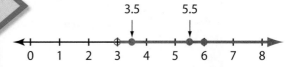

Problem Solving

For **15** through **18**, write an inequality for each graph.

15.

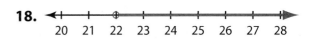

16.

17.

18.

19. Vida is training for a race. Her goal is to run at least 20 miles each week. Let *m* equal the number of miles. On a number line, graph $m \geq 20$ to show the number of miles per week Vida will run.

20. On a city street, you are allowed to drive at a speed of 35 miles per hour or less. Use the variable *s* to represent the speed in miles per hour. Write an inequality that describes the allowed speeds.

21. Writing to Explain How do you know whether to use an open circle or a closed circle when graphing an inequality?

22. Sam is 6 years older than his sister Natalie. The sum of their ages is 30 years. What is Natalie's age?

23. The inequality $w \leq 2$ describes the allowed weight in tons for a vehicle that is crossing a bridge. List three weights that are allowed.

24. Is 7 a solution of the inequality $y + 4 \leq 7$? Explain.

25. Estimation Rosa needs $2\frac{1}{4}$ yards of fabric to make a jacket and $1\frac{7}{8}$ yards of fabric to make a matching skirt. The fabric costs $8.95 per yard. About how much will it cost to buy the fabric for the jacket and the skirt?

26. Which inequality is graphed on the number line below?

A $m = 29$ **C** $m < 29$

B $m \leq 29$ **D** $m \geq 29$

Understand It!
Rules and tables can be used to show how one quantity is related to another.

Patterns and Equations

How can you find a rule for a pattern and complete a table?

Dots were used to draw the figures below.

How many dots would be in the 20th figure?

Which figure would have 100 dots?

| Figure 1 | Figure 2 | Figure 3 | Figure 4 |

Another Example How can you find a rule?

Which equation gives a rule that states the relationship between each pair of values in the table below?

x	22	34	35	40	
y	11	23	24		47

A $y = \frac{x}{2}$ **B** $y = x + 11$ **C** $y = x - 11$ **D** $y = 2x$

Step 1 State the relationship between the first pair of numbers.
y is half of x or y is 11 less than x.

Step 2 Which relationship is also true for the second pair of numbers?
y is 11 less than x.

Step 3 Check that the relationship is also true for other pairs of numbers.

Step 4 The equation for Choice **C** gives a rule for the relationship between x and y in the table.
$y = x - 11$

Explain It

1. If a rule describes the relationship for one pair of numbers in a table, does it always describe every pair in the same table? Explain your answer.

2. If you know a rule for a table, how can you add pairs of numbers to the table?

Make a table.

Figure number (n)	Total number of dots (d)
1	4
2	8
3	12
4	16
20	
	100

Look for a pattern in the relationship between the figure number and the total number of dots in the figure.
Express the pattern as a rule.

Multiply the figure number by 4.

Express the pattern as an equation.

$d = 4n$ 4n means $4 \times n$.

Use the equation to find the missing numbers in the table.

$d = 4 \times 20$

$d = 80$

Figure 20 has 80 dots.

$100 = 4 \times n$

$\dfrac{100}{4} = \dfrac{4 \times n}{4}$

$25 = n$

Figure 25 has 100 dots.

Guided Practice*

Do you know HOW?

x	2	4	6	8	
y	14	28	42		70

1. Write a rule for this table in words.

2. Write an equation for the rule.

3. What is a missing y-value?

4. What is a missing x-value?

Do you UNDERSTAND?

5. In the example above, how do you know the table of values is represented by the equation $d = 4n$?

6. If the n-value in the table above is 36, what is the d-value?

7. Write and solve equations to find the missing numbers in the table in Another Example.

Independent Practice

In exercises **8** through **11**, find a rule for each table. Write an equation for each rule.

8.

x	y
0	16
20	36
36	52
42	58

9.

x	y
25	17
32	24
46	38
59	51

10.

x	y
6	2
12	4
24	8
33	11

11.

x	y
5	30
3	18
9	54
7	42

*For another example, see Set D on page 393.

In **12** through **15**, write an equation for each table and find the missing values for *x* and *y*.

12.

x	y
12	6
10	4
8	■
13	7
■	13

13.

x	y
48	96
30	60
25	50
■	64
14	■

14.

x	y
30	3
80	8
170	17
■	25
320	■

15.

x	y
3	17
7	21
6	■
9	23
■	26

16. **Number Sense** In the equation $y = 12x$, if *y* is to equal 0, what is the value of *x*?

17. Write an equation that will give the answer $y = 3$ when $x = 7$.

18. The Autobahn is a freeway system in Germany. Along most of the Autobahn, there is an advised speed limit of 130 km/h. How many hours would a car need to travel at the advised speed limit to go 520 km?

19. **Geometry** The triangle below is an isosceles triangle. What is the perimeter of the triangle?

x   18

12

For **20** through **22**, use the table at the right.

20. During which month was the electric bill the highest?

21. During which month was the electric bill the lowest?

22. What was the total cost of electricity for the 12 months?

Data	Month	Electric Bill ($)	Month	Electric Bill ($)
	January	58	July	89
	February	52	August	88
	March	46	September	74
	April	47	October	63
	May	44	November	63
	June	75	December	57

23. **Number Sense** In the equation $y = x - 6$, which positive numbers would you use for *x* if you wanted $y < 0$?

24. Which pair of values could appear in a table of values for the equation $y = 2x$?

A $x = 2, y = 5$ **C** $x = 5, y = 10$

B $x = 4, y = 6$ **D** $x = 0, y = 2$

Find the sum. Estimate to check if the answer is reasonable.

1.	1,247 + 997	**2.**	9,012 + 3,993	**3.**	55,391 + 73,428	**4.**	19,601 + 993

5.	14,823 + 16,762	**6.**	36,228 + 44,634	**7.**	88,692 + 608	**8.**	19,832 + 16,588

Find the product. Estimate to check if the answer is reasonable.

9.	6,078 × 91	**10.**	516 × 545	**11.**	7,938 × 68	**12.**	515 × 5	**13.**	123 × 123

14.	5,004 × 28	**15.**	3,333 × 44	**16.**	8,332 × 8	**17.**	605 × 706	**18.**	422 × 381

Error Search Find each answer that is not correct.
Write it correctly and explain the error.

19.	4,000 − 2,745 2,255	**20.**	13.05 × 5 65.05	**21.**	8,605 + 2,503 6,108	**22.**	4.55 2)9.1	**23.**	513 R34 36)18,502

Number Sense

Estimating and Reasoning Write whether each statement is
true or false. Explain your reasoning.

24. The expression $12 ÷ 3 + 8 ÷ 2$ equals 6.

25. The product of 4.8 and 3 is between 12 and 15.

26. The sum of 4,863 and 3,990 is 10 less than 8,863.

27. The quotient of $6,598 ÷ 9$ is greater than 700.

28. The expression $20 − 8m$ equals 24 when $m = 2$.

29. The difference of 74,132 and 26,873 is greater than 50,000 and
less than 60,000.

Draw a Picture and Write an Equation

Understand It!
Drawing a picture can be helpful when writing and solving an equation.

At an art fair, Dean sold different types of paintings. The price of a portrait is $125 more than the price of a still-life painting. What is the price of a still-life painting?

Still Life
$?

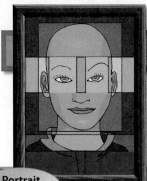

Portrait
$210.00

Landscape
$135.00

Another Example

Dean also sold 8 pen-and-ink sketches at the art fair. All the sketches were the same price. He made $196 on the sale of the sketches. What was the price for each sketch?

Read and Understand

What do you know?　　　Dean sold 8 sketches and made $196.

What are you trying to find?　The price of one sketch

Plan

What strategy will you use?　Write an equation. A diagram can help to picture how the information is related.

Let n = the price of one sketch.

$196

n	n	n	n	n	n	n	n

$8 \times n = 196$
$(8 \times n) \div 8 = 196 \div 8$
$n = 24.50$

Divide both sides of the equation by 8 to get n alone on one side of the equation.

Each sketch was sold for $24.50.

Explain It

1. **Reasonableness** Is $24.50 for each sketch a reasonable answer?

2. How does the diagram above show the information in the problem?

Choose a variable for the unknown quantity.

Let p = the price of a still-life painting.

Use a diagram to picture the relationship between the prices.

$210

p	$125

Write an equation.

$p + 125 = 210$

Solve the equation.

$$p + 125 = 210$$
$$p + 125 - 125 = 210 - 125$$
$$p = 85$$

Subtract 125 from both sides to get the variable alone.

The price of a still-life painting is $85.

Estimate to see if the answer makes sense.

Round 85 to 100.

$100 + 125 = 225$, which is close to 210.

The price of $85 is reasonable.

Guided Practice*

Do you know HOW?

1. Use the picture to write and solve an equation.

34

s	18

Do you UNDERSTAND?

2. Write a Problem Write a real-world problem that you can solve by drawing a picture and writing an addition or subtraction equation.

Independent Practice

In **3** through **5**, use each picture to write and solve each equation.

3. Alice read 5 more pages today than she did yesterday. Today she read 42 pages. How many pages did Alice read yesterday?

42 pages

p	5

4. Dan biked 27 miles yesterday. If he biked 3 times as far as Joe, how far did Joe bike?

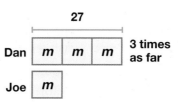
27

Dan | m | m | m | 3 times as far

Joe | m |

5. Max is saving $15 per month to buy a desk that costs $285. How many months will he need to save?

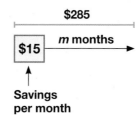
$285

$15 | m months

Savings per month

Stuck? Try this....

- What do I know?
- What am I asked to find?
- What diagram can I use to help understand the problem?
- Can I use addition, subtraction, multiplication, or division?
- Is all of my work correct?
- Did I answer the right question?
- Is my answer reasonable?

For **6** through **8**, draw a picture, and write and solve an equation for each problem.

6. Kieko and Linda sold a total of 124 calendars. Kieko sold 57 of them. How many calendars did Linda sell?

7. Carmen has saved $13 to buy a DVD that costs $29. How much more money does Carmen need to save?

8. Jonathan loaned his brother $22 and had $126 left. How much money did Jonathan have before he loaned the money?

9. Writing to Explain Caryn drew this picture and wrote this equation to represent the problem below.

A zoo has 19 more species of fish than birds. There are 152 species of fish. How many species of birds does the zoo have?

$$b - 19 = 152$$

Is Caryn correct? Explain your answer.

10. Camille used a coupon to pay for a movie ticket. The original cost of the ticket was $6.50, but Camille only paid $4. Write an equation and solve it to find how much the coupon was worth.

11. Orlando saved $520 in 1 year. He saved $330 in the last 4 months. Write and solve an equation to find how much Orlando saved in the first 8 months.

12. Dean also does abstract paintings. He charges $85 less than the price of a portrait. He charges $210 for a portrait. Write and solve an equation to find the price of one of Dean's abstract paintings.

13. Forests once covered about $\frac{1}{2}$ of Earth's land surface. Today, about $\frac{2}{5}$ of Earth's original forest areas remain untouched and undisturbed. What fraction of Earth's land surface are covered by forests today?

Think About the Process

14. A total of 44 adults are going on a field trip with the class. If 14 of the adults are men, how many are women? Which of the following equations gives the number of women?

A $14 + 44 = w$

B $w - 14 = 44$

C $14 + w = 44$

D $w - 44 = 14$

15. Tony is running a 10-kilometer race. He just reached the 4-kilometer marker. Which of the following equations can you use to find out how many more kilometers he needs to run?

A $k - 4 = 10$

B $4 + k = 10$

C $4 - k = 10$

D $10 + 4 = k$

Algebra Connections

Solution Pairs

Remember that an equation is a number sentence that uses an equal sign to show that two expressions have the same value.

When two variables occur in an equation, each variable can be replaced with a different number. When the two replacements make a true equation, the two replacements form a **solution pair**.

> **Example**: Do $x = 12$ and $y = 8$ form a solution pair for $x = y + 4$?
>
> Substitute the given values for x and y into the equation.
>
> Replacing x with 12 and y with 8 gives $12 = 8 + 4$, or $12 = 12$. The equation is true.
>
> So, $x = 12$ and $y = 8$ form a solution pair for $x = y + 4$.

For **1** through **15**, use the table of values at the right. For each equation, determine if the given replacements form a solution pair. Write yes or no.

1. $y + z = 10$

2. $b = x + 15$

3. $b = a + 15$

4. $a + x = 40$

5. $40 - c = x$

6. $c - x = 6$

7. $b - y = 43$

8. $b = 99 - z$

9. $60 - y = b$

10. $63 = b - c$

11. $20 + z = c$

12. $10 - y = z$

13. $20 = x + y$

14. $b + c = 58$

15. $a + b = 85$

Table of Values
$a = 30$
$b = 45$
$c = 18$
$x = 12$
$y = 8$
$z = 2$

For **16** through **17**, refer to the table at the right.

16. The cost of an adult ticket is equal to twice the cost of a child's ticket.
So, $a = 2 \times c$. Find two different pairs of values for a and c to make the equation true.

17. An adult ticket costs $3 more than a student ticket.
So $a = s + 3$. Find two different pairs of values for a and s to make the equation true.

Cost of Museum Tickets	
Ticket	**Price**
Child	c
Adult	a
Student	s
Early Bird	e

1. On average, residents of the United Kingdom have 28 vacation days each year, 14 fewer than the average in Italy. Solve the equation $n - 14 = 28$ to find n, the average number of vacation days in Italy. (15-1)

   A $n = 2$

   B $n = 14$

   C $n = 42$

   D $n = 49$

2. Which equation could be used to represent the table shown? (15-4)

n	m
10	0
12	2
15	5
19	9

   A $m = \dfrac{n}{10}$

   B $m = 10 - n$

   C $m = n + 10$

   D $m = n - 10$

3. An African elephant can eat up to 4,200 pounds of food in a week. Solve the equation $7n = 4,200$ to find n, the pounds of food it can eat in a day. (15-2)

   A $n = 60$

   B $n = 600$

   C $n = 700$

   D $n = 29,400$

4. Which equation could be used to represent the table shown? (15-4)

x	y
20	40
13	26
12	24
5	10

   A $y = 2x$

   B $y = x + 20$

   C $y = \dfrac{x}{2}$

   D $y = 3x$

5. Which of the following is a solution of the inequality $m + 3 > 9$? (15-3)

   A $m = 3$

   B $m = 5$

   C $m = 6$

   D $m = 8$

6. On a trip to the United Kingdom, Kameko exchanged currency as shown in the table. How many British pounds could Kameko get for 38 U.S. dollars? (15-4)

U.S. Dollars	British Pounds
8	4
14	7
20	10

   A 19

   B 28

   C 34

   D 76

7. Which inequality represents the graph shown? (15-3)

   A $x \geq 4$

   B $x > 4$

   C $x < 4$

   D $x \leq 4$

8. What step can be taken to get the x by itself on one side in the equation $x - 13 = 102$? (15-1)

A Add 13 to both sides of the equation.

B Subtract 13 from both sides of the equation.

C Multiply both sides of the equation by 13.

D Divide both sides of the equation by 13.

9. What step can be taken to get the variable m alone on one side of the equation $\frac{m}{5} = 25$? (15-2)

A Add 5 to both sides of the equation.

B Subtract 5 from both sides of the equation.

C Multiply both sides of the equation by 5.

D Divide both sides of the equation by 5.

10. Which of the following describes how to draw the graph of $n \leq 16$ on a number line? (15-3)

A Place an open circle at 16 and draw an arrow pointing to the left.

B Place a closed circle at 16 and draw an arrow pointing to the left.

C Place an open circle at 16 and draw an arrow pointing to the right.

D Place a closed circle at 16 and draw an arrow pointing to the right.

11. For his recital, Alberto chose a song with 112 measures. The song was divided into 7 movements, or parts, each with the same number of measures. Which of the following can be used to find, m, the number of measures in each movement? (15-5)

112 measures

m	m	m	m	m	m	m

↑
Measures in each movement

A $m + 7 = 112$

B $m - 7 = 112$

C $7m = 112$

D $\frac{m}{7} = 112$

12. The table shows the total number of lawns, L, that Saul has mowed after w weeks. Which equation could be used to represent the relationship in the table? (15-4)

Number of weeks, w	Number mowed, L
1	14
2	28
3	42

A $L = \frac{14}{w}$

B $L = \frac{w}{14}$

C $L = w + 13$

D $L = 14w$

Set A, pages 376–377

Solve $x + 15 = 32$.

Since 15 was added to x, *subtract* 15.

$$x + 15 = 32$$
$$x + 15 - 15 = 32 - 15 \quad \text{Subtract 15 from both sides.}$$
$$x = 17$$

Remember that additon and subtraction undo each other.

Solve each equation.

1. $a - 17 = 9$

2. $57 + c = 93$

3. $27 = m - 65$

4. $d + 32 = 97$

5. $m - 14 = 49$

Set B, pages 378–379

Solve $16x = 32$.

Since x was multiplied by 16, *divide* by 16.

$$16x = 32$$
$$\frac{16x}{16} = \frac{32}{16} \quad \text{Divide both sides by 16.}$$
$$x = 2$$

Remember that multiplication and division undo each other.

Solve each equation.

1. $3n = 36$

2. $\frac{x}{4} = 19$

3. $18b = 108$

4. $12b = 144$

5. $\frac{m}{10} = 12$

Set C, pages 380–381

Name three solutions that make the inequality $x - 5 < 2$ true. Then graph the inequality on a number line.

First, solve $x - 5 = 2$

$$x - 5 + 5 = 2 + 5 \quad \text{Add 5 to both sides.}$$
$$x = 7$$

Draw an open circle at 7 to show that 7 is not a solution. Locate 3 solutions of $x < 7$ on the number line, for example 2, 3, and 4. Start at the open circle and draw a thick line over the numbers. Draw an arrow to show there are infinitely many solutions.

Remember that an inequality is a mathematical sentence that contains one of the symbols $>$, $<$, $\geq$, or $\leq$.

Name three solutions of each inequality. Then graph each inequality on a number line.

1. $x > 4$

2. $x \leq 5$

3. $y + 2 < 5$

4. $n - 1 \geq 1$

Set D, pages 382–384

Write an equation for the table.

x	y
4	12
8	16
12	20
16	24

What can be done to x to get y?

$x + 8 = y$, or $3x = y$

$x + 8 = y$, or $2x = y$

$x + 8 = y$

$x + 8 = y$

The equation $x + 8 = y$ is true for all of the pairs in the table.

Choose the equation that matches the table.

x	y
2	8
3	12
4	16
5	20

A $x + 6 = y$

B $y + 6 = x$

C $4x = y$

D $4y = x$

Replace x with the given values to see which equation gives the correct y-values.

The equation $4x = y$ matches the table.
Choice **C** is correct.

Remember that the same equation must be true for each pair of numbers in the table.

Write an equation for each table.

1.

x	y
16	4
20	8
24	12
36	24

2.

x	y
8	1
16	2
24	3
32	4

3. Choose the equation that matches the table.

x	y
2	6
4	12
6	18
8	24

A $x + 4 = y$

B $y + 4 = x$

C $3x = y$

D $3y = x$

Set E, pages 386–388

A flower shop has 98 roses arranged in 7 vases. How many roses are in each vase?

Draw a diagram.

Let r = roses in each vase.

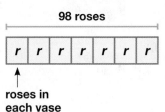

98 roses

roses in each vase

Write and solve an equation.

$$7r = 98$$
$$(7 \times r) \div 7 = 98 \div 7$$
$$r = 14$$

There are 14 roses in each vase.

Remember that a diagram or equation can help you.

Solve.

1. The 5 members of the Wyler family paid $112.50 for admission to a water park. What was the price of each ticket?

2. Tom gave his sister $25 and had $45 left. How much did he have before he gave her the money?

Topic 16

Ratio and Percent

1

Farmers grow almonds for use in food products such as nut mixes. How can you find the ratio of almonds to walnuts in a bowl of mixed nuts? You will find out in Lesson 16-1.

2

Some of the tallest buildings in the world are located in the United States. What percent of the 20 tallest buildings are located in the U. S.? You will find out in Lesson 16-4.

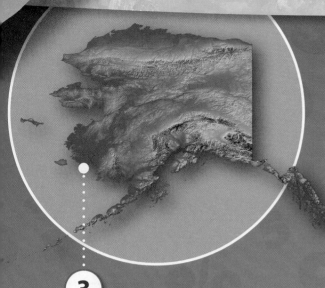

Review What You Know!

Vocabulary

Choose the best term from the box.

- equivalent fractions
- fraction
- mixed numbers

3

Alaska has the greatest amount of land area in the U.S. How can you express this amount as a decimal, fraction, and percent? You will find out in Lesson 16-3.

1. Numbers that include a whole number and a fraction are called __?__.

2. A(n) __?__ can be used to name part of a whole.

3. Two different fractions that represent the same amount are called __?__.

Simplest Form

Write each fraction in simplest form.

4. $\frac{2}{4}$ 5. $\frac{16}{4}$ 6. $\frac{7}{21}$

7. $\frac{5}{25}$ 8. $\frac{9}{6}$ 9. $\frac{8}{10}$

4

Fenway Park is located in Boston, Massachusetts. Opened in 1912, the stadium is the home of the Boston Red Sox. What is the total seating capacity of this ballpark? You will find out in Lesson 16-4.

Decimals and Fractions

Write each decimal as a fraction or as a mixed number in simplest form.

10. 0.25   11. 0.4   12. 0.01

13. 0.72   14. 4.5   15. 2.75

Fractions

Writing to Explain Write an answer for each question.

16. How can you find a fraction equivalent to a given fraction?

17. How can you change a fraction to a decimal?

FENWAY PARK

Understanding Ratios

What are ratios and when are they equal?

Todd is using a recipe to make fruit salad. What is the ratio of cups of cantaloupe to cups of apples? Cups of peaches to cups of fruit in the salad?

If Todd has 2 cups of strawberries, how many cups of cantaloupe should he use?

Fruit Salad
6 c cantaloupe
4 c strawberries
3 c apples
2 c blueberries
3 c peaches

Another Example **How can you find equal ratios?**

Equal ratios show the same comparison.

You can find equal ratios by multiplying or dividing both terms by the same number.

Use multiplication.

		6×2	6×3
Cups of cantaloupe	6	12	18
Total cups of fruit	18	36	54
		18×2	18×3

Equal ratios: $\dfrac{6}{18} = \dfrac{12}{36} = \dfrac{18}{54}$

Use division.

		$6 \div 2$	$6 \div 3$	$6 \div 6$
Cups of cantaloupe	6	3	2	1
Total cups of fruit	18	9	6	3
		$18 \div 2$	$18 \div 3$	$18 \div 6$

Equal ratios: $\dfrac{6}{18} = \dfrac{3}{9} = \dfrac{2}{6} = \dfrac{1}{3}$

Guided Practice*

Do you know HOW?

In **1** through **4**, write each ratio. Then write two other ratios that are equal to each ratio.

1. circles to squares

2. triangles to circles

3. all shapes to squares

4. circles to all shapes

Do you UNDERSTAND?

5. **Writing to Explain** Is the ratio 6 to 3 the same as the ratio 3 to 6? Why or why not?

6. If Todd wanted to double the cups of apples, how many cups of cantaloupe would he need to keep the same ratio of fruit?

DIGITAL

Animated Glossary
www.pearsonsuccessnet.com

*For another example, see Set A on page 408.

A ratio is a comparison where for every *x* units of one quantity there are *y* units of another quantity. A ratio can compare a part to a part, a part to a whole, or the whole to a part.

The ratio of cups of cantaloupe to cups of apples can be written as 6 to 3, 6:3, or $\frac{6}{3}$.

The ratio of cups of peaches to cups of fruit in the salad can be written as 3 to 18, 3:18, or $\frac{3}{18}$.

The recipe calls for 4 cups of strawberries to 6 cups of cantaloupe.

For 2 cups of strawberries, 3 cups of cantaloupe are needed.

Todd should use 3 cups of cantaloupe for 2 cups of strawberries.

Independent Practice

In **7** through **16**, give two other ratios that are equal to each ratio.

7. $\frac{3}{4}$ **8.** 5 to 8   **9.** 12:16   **10.** 10:25   **11.** $\frac{5}{1}$

12. 6:9   **13.** $\frac{4}{5}$ **14.** 16 to 6   **15.** $\frac{15}{27}$ **16.** 3:12

Problem Solving

In **17** and **18**, use the survey results at the right.

17. What is the ratio of people who prefer the fresh mint flavor to those who took the survey? Write another ratio equal to that ratio.

18. The report stated that two out of five people preferred the tasty cinnamon flavor. Is that correct? Explain.

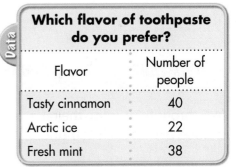

Data

Which flavor of toothpaste do you prefer?	
Flavor	Number of people
Tasty cinnamon	40
Arctic ice	22
Fresh mint	38

19. In a bowl of mixed nuts, there are 96 peanuts, 34 cashews, 28 almonds, and 35 walnuts. What is the ratio of almonds to walnuts in that bowl of mixed nuts? Write another ratio equal to that ratio.

20. Ms. Graham gathered maps for a geography lesson. She had 8 maps of California, 6 maps of Arizona, and 5 maps of Illinois. What is the ratio of maps of Arizona to maps of California?

    A $\frac{5}{8}$ **B** $\frac{3}{4}$ **C** $\frac{4}{3}$ **D** $\frac{8}{6}$

21. **Geometry** What is the ratio of the number of sides of a quadrilateral to the number of sides of a pentagon?

22. **Number Sense** Are the ratios 6 to 20 and 7 to 20 equal? Explain.

Understand It!
A percent is a special type of ratio where a part is compared to a whole, and the whole is 100%.

Understanding Percent

What does percent mean?

The floor plan for a discount store is shown at the right. It is divided into 100 equal parts.

Write the amount of space each department occupies as a ratio and as a percent.

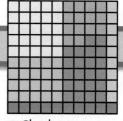

■ Checkout   □ Men's Clothing

□ CDs & DVDs   ■ Children's Clothing

□ Women's Clothing   ■ Toys

Guided Practice*

Do you know HOW?

In **1** through **3**, write the ratio and the percent that is represented by the shaded part of each 100-grid.

1.   **2.**   **3.**

Do you UNDERSTAND?

4. Number Sense If all 100 squares in a 10-by-10 grid are shaded, what percent represents the shaded part?

5. Could the floor space in the store be divided this way: Women's clothing 25%, Children's clothing 25%, Men's clothing 25%, Toys 14%, CDs and DVDs 9%, and checkout counter 10%? Explain your answer.

Independent Practice

In **6** through **10**, write the ratio and the percent that is represented by the shaded part of each 100-grid.

6.   **7.**   **8.**   **9.**   **10.**

In **11** through **15**, write each ratio as a percent.

11. 47 out of 100   **12.** $\frac{50}{100}$ **13.** 76 to 100   **14.** $\frac{9}{100}$ **15.** 35:100

16. Writing to Explain Is 75% the same as the ratio 3 to 4? Why or why not?

Animated Glossary
www.pearsonsuccessnet.com

A percent is a ratio in which the first term is compared to 100.

Percent means *per hundred*.

The percent symbol is %.

Toys occupy 14 out of 100 parts, or 14%.

14% is read "fourteen percent."

Written as a ratio, 14% is 14 to 100, or 14:100, or $\frac{14}{100}$.

Floor space occupied by the departments:

Women's clothing:	25 out of 100, or 25%
Men's clothing:	20 out of 100, or 20%
Children's clothing:	22 out of 100, or 22%
Toys:	14 out of 100, or 14%
CDs and DVDs:	9 out of 100, or 9%
Checkout counter:	10 out of 100, or 10%

Problem Solving

17. In a group of 100 people, 37 people wear glasses. What percent of the people in the group wear glasses?

18. Both triangles below have 50% of their area shaded. Why are the shaded areas not the same amount?

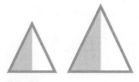

19. A florist is preparing 10 vases of flowers. Each vase will contain 3 roses and 8 carnations. How many of each type of flower will be needed?

20. The Glenview Orchestra contains 100 members. The conductor shaded the grid shown below to represent the members in each section. What percent of the members are in each section?

　a strings

　b woodwinds

　c brass

　d percussion

　e keyboards

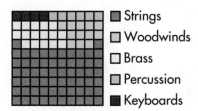

21. Algebra What is the value of *n* in the equation $12n = 180$?

　A 12　　　　　**C** 20

　B 15　　　　　**D** 9

22. Estimation Some zoo employees gathered data one day and found that 153 people entered the zoo in 10 minutes. Based on that data, estimate the number of people who would enter the zoo in 1 hour.

23. Ashley spent $5.75 for camera film and $17.49 for a CD. She also bought lunch. She started the day with $30. If she had $2.35 left, how much did she spend for lunch?

Percents, Fractions, and Decimals
How are percents related to fractions and decimals?

Many states charge sales tax on items you buy. Sales tax is often named as a percent. It compares an amount to the 100 cents in a dollar.

How is Indiana's sales tax expressed as a fraction and as a decimal?

Indiana sales tax 6%

Guided Practice*

Do you know HOW?

In **1** through **3**, write the percent, decimal, and fraction in simplest form represented by the shaded part of each 100-grid.

1.   **2.**   **3.**

Do you UNDERSTAND?

4. Writing to Explain If $\frac{2}{8} = \frac{1}{4} = 25\%$, then how can you find what $\frac{1}{8}$ is as a percent?

5. The sales tax in Chicago is 9%. Write that percent as a decimal and as a fraction in simplest form.

Independent Practice

In **6** through **10**, write the percent, decimal, and fraction in simplest form represented by the shaded part of each 100-grid.

6.   **7.**   **8.**   **9.**   **10.**

In **11** through **20**, write each percent as a decimal and as a fraction in simplest form.

11. 65% **12.** 5% **13.** 23% **14.** 72% **15.** 1%

16. 2% **17.** 45% **18.** 100% **19.** 125% **20.** 200%

Percent means *per hundred.*

So, 6% means 6 out of 100.

The ratio 6 out of 100 can be written as the fraction $\frac{6}{100}$.

In simplest form, $\frac{6}{100}$ can be written as $\frac{3}{50}$.

$$6\% = \frac{6}{100} = \frac{3}{50}$$

The ratio 6 out of 100 can be written as a decimal in hundredths.

$$6\% = \frac{6}{100} = 0.06$$

Tip *Remember to write zeros in a decimal when needed.*

Indiana Sales Tax

As a percent: 6%

As a fraction:

$$\frac{6}{100} = \frac{3}{50}$$

As a decimal: 0.06

For every dollar a person spends, an additional $0.06 is paid for sales tax.

Problem Solving

21. Fill in the missing equivalent values.

percent			33%	
fraction		$\frac{19}{20}$		$1\frac{1}{2}$
decimal	0.3			

22. **Think About the Process** What would you do first to order the following numbers from least to greatest?

$$25\%, \frac{1}{3}, 0.64, \frac{7}{8}, 0.8$$

A Convert the decimals to percents.

B Order the decimals.

C Convert all numbers to decimals or fractions.

D Order the fractions.

23. If there are 4 juice boxes in 50% of a package, how many juice boxes are in a whole package?

24. About 16% of the total U.S. land area is in Alaska. Write 16% as a decimal and as a fraction in simplest form.

25. Only 15% of the class did a science project on birds. What fraction did not do a project on birds?

26. Sally traveled 550 miles on vacation. She traveled 330 of those miles in Nevada. What percent of the trip did she travel in Nevada? (Hint: Write a fraction and find an equivalent fraction with a denominator of 100.)

27. Melanie counted and identified birds that came near her home. The table at the right shows her observations. For each type of bird, find the ratio of the number of birds of that type to the total number of birds. Write each ratio as a percent, a decimal, and a fraction in simplest form.

a Robins

c Cardinals

b Wrens

d Blue Jays

Bird Types	
Robins	15
Cardinals	12
Blue Jays	9
Wrens	24

Finding Percent of a Whole Number

Store	Discount
#1	50%
#2	10%
#3	35%
#4	20%

How can you find a percent of a given number?

Four different stores have included a backpack with a regular price of $25 in their back-to-school sales. What is the amount of the discount at each store?

$25

Guided Practice*

Do you know HOW?

In **1** through **4**, find the percent of each number.

1. 3% of 200

2. 25% of 48

3. 90% of 85

4. 75% of 44

Do you UNDERSTAND?

5. What is an easy way to find 25% of a number?

6. In the example above, what would the amount of the discount be if the backpack were discounted 40%?

Independent Practice

In **7** through **18**, find the percent of each number.

7. 43% of 350

8. 87% of 210

9. 5% of 46

10. 100% of 37

11. 30% of 66

12. 10% of 230

13. 20% of 400

14. 15% of 90

15. 50% of 75

16. 12% of 100

17. 33% of 300

18. 77% of 10

19. Find 1% of 235. How many decimal places in 235 did the decimal point move to the left in the answer?

20. What is an easy way to find 2% of 660?

21. **Writing to Explain** What is an easy way to find 11% of a number? Use 11% of 70 to explain.

*For another example, see Set D on page 409.

Find 50% of 25.	Find 10% of 25.	Find 35% of 25.	Find 20% of 25.

Find 50% of 25.

50% = 0.5

Multiply 25 by 0.5.

$$\begin{array}{r} 25 \\ \times\ 0.5 \\ \hline 12.5 \end{array}$$

Notice that 50% of 25 is the same as 25 ÷ 2.

The discount at store #1 is $12.50.

Find 10% of 25.

10% = 0.1

Multiply 25 by 0.1.

$$\begin{array}{r} 25 \\ \times\ 0.1 \\ \hline 2.5 \end{array}$$

Notice that the decimal point moved one place to the left.

The discount at store #2 is $2.50.

Find 35% of 25.

35% = 0.35

Multiply 25 by 0.35.

$$\begin{array}{r} 25 \\ \times\ 0.35 \\ \hline 8.75 \end{array}$$

The discount at store #3 is $8.75.

Find 20% of 25.

20% = 0.2

Multiply 25 by 0.2.

$$\begin{array}{r} 25 \\ \times\ 0.2 \\ \hline 5.0 \end{array}$$

The discount at store #4 is $5.00.

Problem Solving

22. The total seating capacity at Fenway Park in Boston, Massachusetts, is about 36,000. About how many baseball fans would be seated if the park were filled to 85% of its capacity?

23. Marcia had dinner at a restaurant and wants to leave a 20% tip. Explain how she could calculate the tip using mental math.

Use the information from the chart to answer **24** through **26**.

Meat	Ounces	Cost
Ham	14	$5.74
Turkey	11	$4.07
Pastrami	5	$4.85
Roast Beef	8	$6.56

24. What is the cost of 2 ounces of turkey?

25. Which costs more per ounce, roast beef or pastrami?

26. What is the total cost of 14 ounces of ham and 5 ounces of pastrami?

27. Algebra Jordan bought a $35 jacket and a $40 pair of shoes at a 25% discount. Write an equation to find the total amount of the discount on the items. Solve the equation.

28. Reasoning Write these numbers in order from least to greatest.

60%, $\frac{1}{4}$, 0.75, 28%, $\frac{1}{2}$, 0.55

29. The price of a computer is $1,450, and a monitor costs $350. The sales tax is 6%. What is the total amount of sales tax on both items?

30. Of the 20 tallest buildings in the world, 20% are located in the United States. How many of the world's 20 tallest buildings are in the U.S.?

31. Critical Thinking The price of a new bike is $90. The store is advertising a 30% discount and the sales tax is 7%. Explain how to find the cost of the bike.

Understand It!
Learning how and when to make a table and look for a pattern is helpful in solving problems.

Problem Solving

Make a Table and Look for a Pattern

Kiesha and Sheryl play on the school basketball team. The statistics from the last game are shown at the right.

If they continue at the same rate, what percent of their shots would each player make?

Guided Practice*

Do you know HOW?

Find the percent by completing the table.

1. 4 free throws out of 16 were made

Free throws made	4			
Free throws attempted	16	8	4	

Do you UNDERSTAND?

2. How can a table help you to find a percent?

3. **Write a Problem** Write a real-world problem that you can solve using a table to find a percent.

Independent Practice

In **4** through **7**, find each percent by completing each table.

4. 8 pass completions out of 20 attempts

Pass completions	8				
Pass attempts	20	40	60	80	100

5. 6 out of 30 days were cloudy

Cloudy days	6			
Total days	30	10	50	100

Stuck? Try this....

- What do I know?
- What am I asked to find?
- What diagram can I use to help understand the problem?
- Can I use addition, subtraction, multiplication, or division?
- Is all of my work correct?
- Did I answer the right question?
- Is my answer reasonable?

Make a table and look for patterns to get a comparison with 100. Begin with the numbers you know and find equal ratios.

Kiesha

Baskets made	5				
Shots attempted	20	40	60	80	100

Sheryl

Baskets made	7			
Shots attempted	25	50	75	100

Complete each table and look for patterns.

Kiesha

Baskets made	5	10	15	20	25
Shots attempted	20	40	60	80	100

Sheryl

Baskets made	7	14	21	28
Shots attempted	25	50	75	100

Kiesha might make 25 out of 100, or 25%, of her shots.

Sheryl might make 28 out of 100, or 28%, of her shots.

6. 10 of the 25 fossils are shells.

Shell fossils	10	▪	▪	▪
Total fossils	25	50	75	▪

7. 54 of the 75 votes were for Fred.

Votes for Fred	54	▪	▪	▪
Total votes	75	150	300	▪

8. Rodrigo wants to wrap a package with paper. Find the least amount of paper he will need.

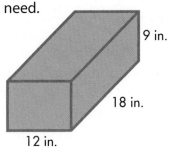

9 in.

18 in.

12 in.

9. Mr. Perez bought 8 souvenir mugs to give as gifts. Mrs. Perez bought 7 souvenir mugs. How much did each person spend? If the tax was 10%, what was their total bill?

$3 each

10. Draw a net to represent the package Rodrigo is wrapping.

11. Luciana made 45 hits out of 150 times at bat. What is that as a percent?

12. Brett plans to walk 16 miles this weekend. On Saturday, he walked 12 miles. What percent of his goal has Brett walked?

13. Tessa used 24 minutes of an 80-minute CD. What percent of the CD has *not* been used? How many minutes is that?

14. **Writing to Explain** Fran estimated 45% of 87 by finding 50% of 90. Will her estimate be greater than or less than the exact answer? Why?

15. Nicole's digital camera has a 360-picture memory. She has taken 162 pictures. Make a table and find a pattern. What percent of the camera's memory has she used?

1. The table shows the number of animals in an animal shelter. What is the ratio of dogs to total animals in the shelter? (16-1)

Animal Type	Number
Cat	18
Dog	12
Rabbit	3

A 12 : 33

B 12 : 21

C 21 : 12

D 33 : 12

2. What is 61 out of 100 as a percent? (16-2)

A 100%

B 61%

C 39%

D 6.1%

3. Which of the following can be used to find 65% of 80? (16-4)

A Multiply 0.65 by 80.

B Multiply 0.65 by 0.8.

C Multiply 80 by 100.

D Multiply 65 by 80 and 100.

4. Which of the following ratios is equal to 15 to 10? (16-1)

A 10 to 15

B 20 to 15

C 3 to 5

D 3 to 2

5. A football team won 75% of their games. If they played 12 games, how many games did they win? (16-4)

A 7

B 8

C 9

D 10

6. Five out of 25 students are absent. What percent of the students are absent? (16-5)

Students Absent	5			
Total Students	25	50	75	100

A 5%

B 10%

C 15%

D 20%

7. About 85% of Americans have Rh positive blood. What is the ratio of Americans that are Rh positive to all Americans? (16-2)

A $\frac{15}{85}$

B $\frac{85}{100}$

C $\frac{100}{85}$

D $\frac{15}{100}$

8. Which of the following represents the shaded area as a percent, a decimal, and a fraction? (16-3)

A 21%, 0.21, $\frac{21}{100}$

B 42%, 0.42, $\frac{21}{100}$

C 42%, 0.42, $\frac{21}{50}$

D 21%, 0.21, $\frac{21}{50}$

9. What is the ratio of shaded circles to shaded squares? (16-1)

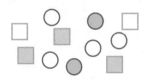

A 3 : 11

B 2 : 11

C 3 : 2

D 2 : 3

10. Which is equal to 20%? (16-3)

A $\frac{2}{100}$

B 20 : 50

C $\frac{1}{5}$

D 2 out of 100

11. Which is 60% written as a decimal and a fraction? (16-3)

A 0.06, $\frac{60}{100}$

B 0.6, $\frac{60}{100}$

C 0.6, $\frac{6}{100}$

D 0.06, $\frac{6}{100}$

12. In a particular hospital during one month, the ratio of the number of girls born to the number of boys born was 24 to 15. Which of the following ratios is equal to 24 to 15? (16-1)

A 5 to 8

B 8 to 5

C 3 to 5

D 19 to 10

13. The United States consumes 27% of all commercially harvested wood in the world. What fraction equals 27%? (16-3)

A $\frac{27}{100}$

B $\frac{73}{100}$

C $\frac{27}{73}$

D $\frac{73}{27}$

14. What percent is represented by the shaded part of the grid? (16-2)

A 0.8%

B 8%

C 18%

D 80%

15. What is 80% of 150? (16-4)

A 80

B 100

C 120

D 130

Set A, pages 396–397

Write the ratio of squares to circles in three ways.

The ratio can be written as
4 to 5, 4:5, or $\frac{4}{5}$.

Write two ratios equal to 4:12.

Multiply or divide both terms by the same number.

$$\frac{4 \times 2}{12 \times 2} = \frac{8}{24} \qquad \frac{4 \div 2}{12 \div 2} = \frac{2}{6}$$

4:12 = 8:24 = 2:6

Remember that the order of the terms is important.

Use the shapes at the left. Write each ratio.

1. triangles to circles

2. all shapes to triangles

3. circles to all shapes

Write two other ratios equal to each ratio.

4. $\frac{9}{12}$ 5. 6 to 7

6. 14:28   7. 27:9

8. 15 to 12   9. $\frac{35}{40}$

10. 5 to 3   11. 18:24

12. $\frac{21}{49}$ 13. $\frac{15}{21}$

Set B, pages 398–399

Write the ratio that compares the shaded squares to all the squares.

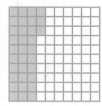

The ratio can be written as
33 to 100, 33:100, or $\frac{33}{100}$.

Write that ratio as a percent.

$\frac{33}{100}$ = 33%

Remember that a percent is a ratio in which a number is compared to 100.

Write the ratio that compares the shaded squares to all the squares for each grid. Write each ratio as a percent.

1.    2.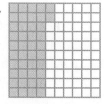

3. 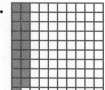   4.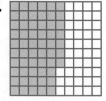

Set C, pages 400–401

Write 24% as a decimal and as a fraction in simplest form.

24% means 24 out of 100.

To write a decimal: Write the ratio as a decimal in hundredths.

24% = 0.24

To write a fraction: Write as a ratio with 100 as the second term and find the simplest form.

$$\frac{24}{100} = \frac{24 \div 4}{100 \div 4} = \frac{6}{25}$$

Remember to write zeros when more decimal places are needed.

Write each percent as a decimal and as a fraction in simplest form.

1. 50%   **2.** 40%

3. 25%   **4.** 5%

5. 36%   **6.** 70%

7. 94%   **8.** 100%

Set D, pages 402–403

Find 40% of 80.

Change 40% to a decimal.   40% = 0.40 or 0.4

Multiply 80 by 0.4.

$$\begin{array}{r} 80 \\ \times\ 0.4 \\ \hline 32.0 \end{array}$$

40% of 80 is 32.

Remember that in order to find the percent of a number, multiply the number by the decimal form of the percent.

Find the percent of each number.

1. 75% of 56   **2.** 10% of 32

3. 50% of 36   **4.** 90% of 60

Set E, pages 404–405

A hockey player attempted 15 shots on goal and made 9 goals. What percent of the shots did she make?

Write the ratio in a table. Find equal ratios to get the second term to be 100. Write the percent.

	ratio	÷3	×4	×5
Goals made	9	3	12	60
Shots attempted	15	5	20	100

Remember that $\frac{60}{100} = 60\%$.

The hockey player made goals on 60% of her shots.

Remember that to find a ratio equal to another ratio, both terms of the ratio must be multiplied or divided by the same number.

Make a table to find each percent.

1. A baseball player was up to bat 40 times and got 14 hits. What percent of the times at bat did he get a hit?

2. The weather report stated that rain fell on 9 of the 30 days last month. On what percent of the days last month did it rain?

Equations and Graphs

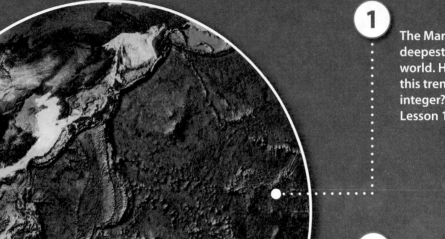

1 The Mariana Trench is the deepest ocean trench in the world. How can the depth of this trench be expressed as an integer? You will find out in Lesson 17-1.

2 A chess board is set up similar to a coordinate plane. Where on the board are the white knights located at the beginning of a game? You will find out in Lesson 17-2.

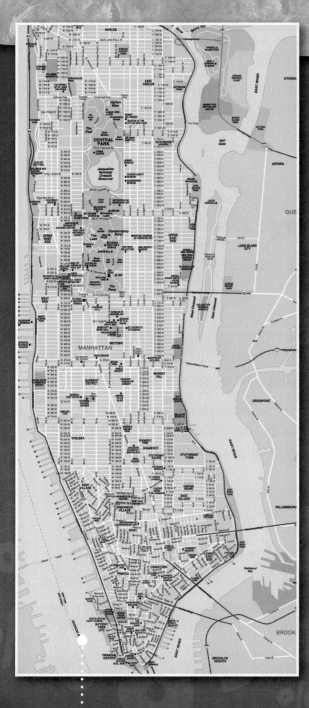

Review What You Know!

Vocabulary

Choose the best term from the box.

- Associative
- estimate
- divisible
- edge

1. A(n) __?__ is a line segment where two faces of a solid figure meet.

2. A number is __?__ when it can be divided by another number without a remainder.

3. A(n) __?__ is an approximate value rather than an exact answer.

4. The __?__ Property of Addition states that addends can be regrouped and the sum remains the same.

Number Sense

Compare the numbers. Use < or > for each ◯.

5. 512 ◯ 521

6. 0.379 ◯ 0.38

7. $\frac{3}{4}$ ◯ $\frac{1}{3}$

8. $2\frac{1}{5}$ ◯ $2\frac{1}{4}$

Number Lines

Write the number for each point.

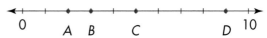

9. C   10. A   11. B   12. D

Fractions and Decimals

Writing to Explain Write an answer to the question.

13. What can you do to make comparing $\frac{3}{4}$ and 0.6 easier?

3

Many cities in the United States are laid out like a coordinate grid. How can this be helpful when finding locations in places such as New York City? You will find out in Lesson 17-2.

Understand It!
A number line can be used to identify and represent integers.

Understanding Integers

What are integers and what situations can integers represent?

The highest point in Louisiana is Driskill Mountain at five hundred thirty-five feet above sea level. The lowest point is New Orleans at eight feet below sea level.

How can you write those highest and lowest points with integers?

535 feet above sea level

Driskill Mountain

New Orleans

Sea level

8 feet below sea level

Guided Practice*

Do you know HOW?

In **1** through **4**, write an integer for each word description.

1. Ten degrees below zero

2. Seventy degrees above zero

3. Two hundred thirty feet above sea level

4. Fifty-two feet below sea level

Do you UNDERSTAND?

5. In the example above, what is the opposite elevation of Driskill Mountain, written as an integer?

6. How far away from sea level is 512 feet below sea level?

7. How would you show sea level represented as an integer?

Independent Practice

In **8** through **12**, use the number line to identify the integer at each point.

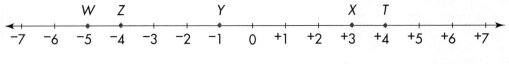

8. T

9. W

10. X

11. Y

12. Z

In **13** through **20**, write an integer for each word description.

13. A withdrawal of $20

14. A deposit of one hundred dollars

15. A gain of three inches

16. A loss of six yards

17. A loss of 7 pounds

18. A temperature drop of 2 degrees

19. 6 steps forward

20. 10 seconds before blastoff

Animated Glossary
www.pearsonsuccessnet.com

*For another example, see Set A on page 426.

Distance above sea level is greater than zero. It is represented by a positive integer. $^{+}535$

Distance below sea level is less than zero. It is represented by a negative integer. $^{-}8$

Integers name magnitude (distance) and direction from 0.

0

$^{-}8$ $^{+}535$

The magnitude of $^{-}8$ is 8.   The magnitude of $^{+}535$ is 535.
The direction is negative.   The direction is positive.

Integers are <u>the whole numbers and their</u> <u>opposites; 0 is its own opposite.</u>

Numbers that are opposites of each other have the same magnitude (distance from 0).
$^{-}5$ and $^{+}5$ are the same distance from 0.

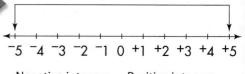

Negative integers are less than zero.	Positive integers are greater than zero.
$^{-}5$ is read "negative five."	$^{+}5$ is read "positive five."

$^{-}2$ is the opposite of $^{+}2$.
$^{+}4$ is the opposite of $^{-}4$.

Problem Solving

21. A football team started at the 20-yard line. In the first two plays, the team lost 4 yards and gained 4 yards. Where did they end up?

22. Adam has $1\frac{1}{2}$ feet of aluminum wire, 1.29 feet of copper wire, and $1\frac{5}{8}$ feet of steel wire. Adam has the most of which kind of wire?

23. A movie company announced that one of its releases lost two million, eight hundred fifty-seven thousand, nine hundred dollars. Write that number in integer form.

24. At midnight, the temperature was 2 degrees. It went down 5 degrees, then it went up 3 degrees, and then dropped 2 degrees. What was the final temperature? Show your answer on a number line.

25. Number Sense Julie needs to select an integer that is two less than $^{-}11$. What number should she pick? How did you find the number?

26. The Mariana Trench is located in the floor of the western North Pacific Ocean. It is 35,798 feet below sea level. Express this depth as an integer.

27. Think About the Process Pam made $168.75 at a craft fair. She sold 75 of the 125 book covers she made. Which expression can you use to find the price she charged for each book cover?

   A $168.75 ÷ 75

   B $168.75 ÷ (125 + 75)

   C $168.75 ÷ 125

   D $168.75 ÷ (125 − 75)

28. Writing to Explain Describe how to find the surface area of the rectangular prism shown below. Then find the surface area.

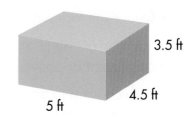

3.5 ft
4.5 ft
5 ft

Understand It!
An ordered pair of numbers is used to locate a point on a coordinate grid.

Ordered Pairs

How can you locate points on a coordinate grid?

A coordinate grid makes it easy to locate a point on a map. Start at 0. Go 3 blocks east and then 2 blocks north. You will be at the bank.
An ordered pair names a point on a coordinate grid. The bank is at (3, 2).

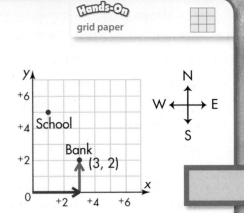

Another Example How do you graph a point on a coordinate plane?

You know that graphs represent data. Now you will see how ordered pairs of numbers can represent points on a coordinate plane.

Graph Point R at (⁻4, ⁻5)

Step 1 Draw and label the x-axis and y-axis on grid paper.

Step 2 Move 4 units to the left of the origin. Then, move 5 units down.

Step 3 Mark a point and label it R.

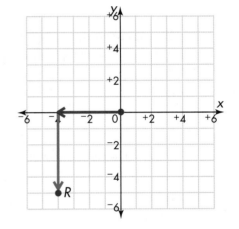

Explain It

1. How would you locate the point (⁺4, ⁻5) on a coordinate grid?

2. If the location of point R above were changed to (⁻4, ⁺5), would the point be above or below its current position?

3. Suppose you want to graph the point (0, ⁺5) on graph paper. When you start from the origin, do you move right 5 units or move up 5 units?

A coordinate plane extends to include both positive and negative numbers. It has a horizontal x-axis and a vertical y-axis. The point at which the x-axis and y-axis intersect is called the origin.

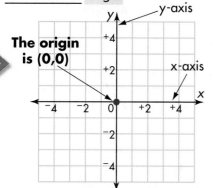

The origin is (0,0)

The first number in an ordered pair, the *x*-coordinate, names the distance to the right or left from the origin along the *x*-axis. The second number, the *y*-coordinate, names the distance up or down from the origin along the *y*-axis.

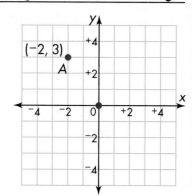

The ordered pair for Point *A* is (⁻2, 3).

Guided Practice*

Do you know HOW?

In **1** through **4**, write the ordered pair for each point. Use the grid at the right.

1. *A*
2. *B*
3. *C*
4. *D*

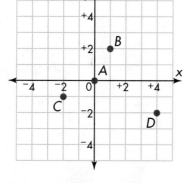

Do you UNDERSTAND?

5. **Writing to Explain** Describe how to plot the ordered pair (⁻3, ⁺4).

6. What ordered pair names the origin of any coordinate plane?

7. In the example above, name the ordered pair for a point that is 3 units directly above Point *A*.

Independent Practice

In **8** through **13**, write the ordered pair for each point. Use the grid at the right.

8. *M*   9. *N*   10. *P*

11. *R*   12. *S*   13. *T*

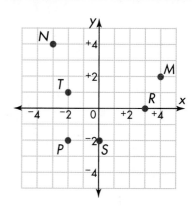

In **14** through **19**, graph and label each point on a grid.

14. *H* (2, ⁺1)   15. *J* (⁺5, ⁺1)   16. *K* (0, ⁺5)

17. *E* (⁺1, ⁻3)   18. *F* (⁺4, ⁻5)   19. *G* (⁻3, ⁻4)

Animated Glossary, eTools
www.pearsonsuccessnet.com

For another example, see Set B on page 426.

Lesson 17-2

Geometry For **20** through **24**, complete the table by listing the ordered pair for each vertex of the pentagon at the right.

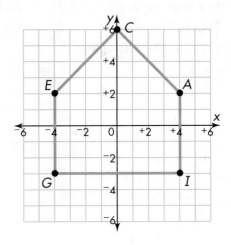

	Label	Ordered Pair
20.	A	
21.	C	
22.	E	
23.	G	
24.	I	

25. Algebra Which equation shows the relationship of the values in the table?

x	y
9	6
8	5
7	4
6	3
3	0

A $y = x + 3$

B $x = y - 3$

C $y = x - 3$

D $y = x$

26. A chess board is similar to a coordinate grid. The pieces that look like horses are called knights. What letter-number combinations name the locations of the white knights?

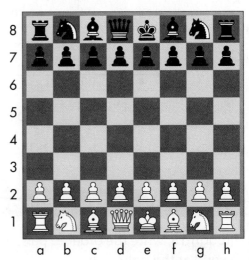

27. Writing to Explain The streets in many cities in the United States are laid out in a coordinate grid. How is this helpful when finding locations such as in New York City?

28. In a class of 25 students, 15 are girls. Which does NOT show the part of the class that are girls?

A $\frac{3}{5}$ **C** 60%

B 0.6   **D** 0.3

Enrichment

Adding Integers

In two plays, a team had a loss of 7 yards and a gain of 6 yards. What was their total gain or loss? You can find $^-7 + {}^+6$.

To find $^-7 + {}^+6$, think of walking along a number line.

> **Adding Integers on the Number Line**
> Always start at 0 and face the **positive integers**. Work forward for positive integers and backward for **negative integers**.

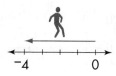

Example: Find $^-4 + {}^-5$.

Start at 0. Face the positive integers. Move backward 4 units.

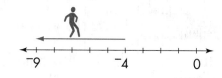

Then move backward 5 units.

$^-4 + {}^-5 = {}^-9$

 Step 1 Start at 0. Face the positive integers. Walk backward 7 steps for $^-7$.

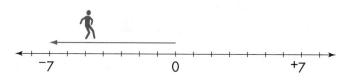

Step 2 Then walk forward 6 steps for $^+6$,

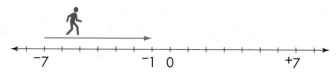

You stop at $^-1$. So, $^-7 + {}^+6 = {}^-1$.

Practice

Add. Use a number line.

1. $^+6 + {}^-4$ **2.** $^+1 + {}^-9$ **3.** $^-7 + {}^-2$ **4.** $^-4 + {}^-4$

5. $^+1 + {}^-5$ **6.** $^+7 + {}^-7$ **7.** $^+3 + {}^-9$ **8.** $^+1 + {}^-9$

9. $^-7 + {}^-2$ **10.** $^+6 + {}^-4$ **11.** $^+7 + {}^+3$ **12.** $^-1 + {}^-2$

13. On Monday, the temperature at 6 A.M. was $^-3°$ F. By noon the temperature was 8 degrees warmer. What was the temperature at noon?

Distances on Number Lines and the Coordinate Plane

How do you find a distance on a number line?

The temperature at midnight was ⁻2°F. By noon, the temperature rose to 4°F. What was the amount of the increase in temperature?

You can think of the two temperatures as integers on a number line.

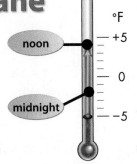

Another Example How do you find a distance on the coordinate plane?

Find the distance between the points named by (⁻2, ⁺5) and (⁻2, ⁺2).

Graph the points on the coordinate plane.

If two points lie along the same grid line, you can find the distance between them by counting grid units.

The distance between the points named by (⁻2, ⁺5) and (⁻2, ⁺2) is 3 units.

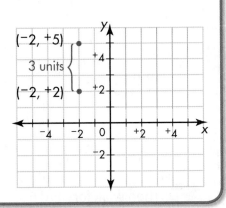

Guided Practice*

Do you know HOW?

In **1** through **3**, find the distance between each pair of integers on a number line.

1. ⁻4, ⁺3   **2.** ⁻5, ⁻1   **3.** ⁺4, ⁺7

4. Find the distance between the points named by (⁻5, ⁻1) and (⁺3, ⁻1) on the coordinate plane.

Do you UNDERSTAND?

5. Find the distance between ⁻3 and ⁺7 without drawing a number line. What is this distance?

6. Writing to Explain Can you count grid units to find the distance between the points named by (⁻3, ⁺2) and (⁺4, ⁺5)? Explain.

Independent Practice

In **7** through **14**, find the distance between each pair of integers on a number line.

7. ⁻6, ⁻4   **8.** ⁺1, ⁺5   **9.** ⁻2, ⁺7   **10.** ⁻7, ⁺2

11. ⁺3, ⁺4   **12.** ⁻2, 0   **13.** 0, ⁺6   **14.** ⁻5, ⁺5

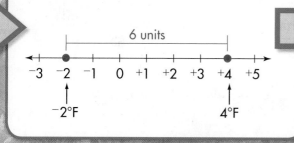

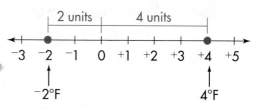

One Way

Count the units between the integers.

6 units

−2°F   4°F

Another Way

Count the units between each integer and 0.

2 units   4 units

−2°F   4°F

Add the distances: 2 units + 4 units = 6 units

The amount of the increase was 6°F.

In **15** through **20**, find the distance between the points named by each set of ordered pairs on the coordinate plane.

15. ($^-$4, $^+$3), ($^+$1, $^+$3)

16. ($^+$2, $^-$4), ($^+$2, $^-$5)

17. ($^-$1, $^+$4), ($^-$1, $^-$3)

18. ($^-$5, $^-$5), ($^-$2, $^-$5)

19. ($^+$4, $^-$2), ($^+$4, 0)

20. (0, $^+$1), (0, $^-$5)

Problem Solving

For **21** through **23**, use the coordinate plane shown at the right.

21. Which point is exactly 7 units from Point *N*?

22. Which is greater: the distance from Point *B* to Point *N*, or the distance from Point *A* to Point *E*?

23. Name all the points that are exactly 3 units from Point *H*.

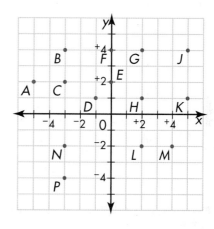

24. Elena, Tran, and Lee live along the same straight road. Lee lives between Elena and Tran. Tran lives 6 miles from Elena and 2 miles from Lee. What is the distance between Elena's house and Lee's house?

25. On the coordinate plane, what is the distance between the points named by ($^+$3, $^-$5) and ($^-$4, $^-$5)?

  A 1 unit   **C** 7 units

  B 5 units   **D** 10 units

26. What two integers on a number line are exactly 3 units from $^-$2?

27. What integer on a number line is the same distance from 0 as $^+$6?

Understand It!
Ordered pairs can be used to graph equations on a coordinate plane.

Graphing Equations

Hands-On
grid paper

How do you graph an equation on a coordinate grid?

Amy can walk 3 miles in 1 hour. At that speed, how far would she walk in 7 hours?

An equation whose graph is <u>a straight line is called a</u> <u>linear equation.</u>

END

7 hours
? miles

1 hour
3 miles

START

Another Example **How do you graph linear equations?**

Carl is four years older than Jamal. How can you graph this situation?

Step 1

Write an equation.

Carl is four years older than Jamal.

Carl's age = Jamal's age + 4

$\quad y \quad = \quad x \quad + 4$

Tip When making a table of values for a linear equation, use at least three values for x.

Step 2

Make a table of values.

Jamal x (years)	Carl y (years)
2	6
4	8
6	10

Step 3

Plot the ordered pairs and connect the points.

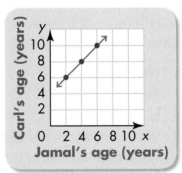

Guided Practice*

Do you know HOW?

In **1** through **4**, find the values of y when x = 2, 4, and 6. Then, name the ordered pairs.

1. $y = x + 3$ **2.** $y = 2x$

3. $y = x - 1$ **4.** $y = 4x$

For **5**, graph the equation.

5. $y = x + 4$

Do you UNDERSTAND?

6. Reasonableness Does the line for $y = x - 4$ include the point (4, 0)?

7. A lion can run about four times faster than a squirrel. What equation represents that relationship? How would you graph it?

DIGITAL

Animated Glossary, eTools
www.pearsonsuccessnet.com

| Step 1 | Step 2 | Step 3 |

Step 1

Write an equation.

Amy walks 3 miles each hour.

miles = 3 × hours

Let y be the number of miles and x be the number of hours.

$y = 3x$

Step 2

Make a table of x- and y- values to show how x and y relate and satisfy the equation.

$y = 3x$

x	y
1	3
3	9
5	15

Step 3

Label the axes on a coordinate grid. Plot the ordered pairs and connect the points to graph the equation.

Extend the line. The y value when $x = 7$ shows that Amy walked 21 miles.

Independent Practice

In **8** through **11**, name the ordered pairs. Let $x = 0, 2,$ and 4.

8. $y = 6x$ **9.** $y = x + 3$ **10.** $y = x + 7$ **11.** $y = x - 0$

In **12** through **15**, make a table of values for each equation and then graph each equation. Use $x = 1, 2,$ and 3.

12. $y = x - 1$ **13.** $y = 2x$ **14.** $y = x + 1$ **15.** $y = x$

Problem Solving

16. Reasoning If the points (1, 3), (1, 7), (1, 12), and (1, 25) were graphed, they would form a vertical line. Do you think the equation for this line would be $x = 1$ or $y = 1$? Explain.

17. Writing to Explain How do you know that the point (4, 8) will appear on graphs for both of the equations $y = 2x$ and $y = x + 4$?

18. Complete the table of values for the equation: $y = x - 6$.

x	6	7		11
y	0		2	

19. Reasoning Will the point (5, 10) be included on a graph for the equation $y = 2x$? Explain your answer.

20. Which ordered pair will be included on the graph for $y = 3 + x$?

A (13, 16)   **C** (1, 3)

B (9, 6)   **D** (9, 3)

Problem Solving

Work Backward

Arnie, Brad, Caren, and Danica sold nature photographs to raise money for their hiking club. Brad raised twice as much money as Arnie. Caren raised $100 more than Brad, and Danica raised half as much as Caren. How much money did each person raise?

BRAD
SALES R

DANICA
SALES REPORT

Total Sales $110

Guided Practice*

Do you know HOW?

You can solve this problem by working backward. Check your work.

1. The Penguins' hockey practice ended at 7:00 P.M. The team began practice by stretching for $\frac{1}{4}$ hour. Then they practiced skating and shooting for $\frac{1}{2}$ hour. During the last $\frac{3}{4}$ hour, the team played a scrimmage game. What time did practice start?

Do you UNDERSTAND?

2. **Writing to Explain** Describe what you did to check your solution to Problem 1.

3. In the problem above, why is Danica's $110 multiplied by 2 to find the amount that Caren raised?

4. **Write a Problem** Write a real-world problem that you can solve by working backward.

Independent Practice

Solve.

5. On a winter night, the temperature dropped 15°F between midnight and 6:00 A.M. By 11:00 A.M., the temperature had gone up 7°F. By 3:00 P.M. the temperature went up another 9°F, making the temperature 25°F. What was the temperature at midnight?

6. Mel spent $9 at the movies, earned $24 mowing lawns, and bought a magazine for $5. He had $21 left. How much money did he have at the start?

Stuck? Try this....

- What do I know?
- What am I asked to find?
- What diagram can I use to help understand the problem?
- Can I use addition, subtraction, multiplication, or division?
- Is all of my work correct?
- Did I answer the right question?
- Is my answer reasonable?

For another example, see Set E on page 427.

I know:

Danica raised $110.

Danica raised half as much as Caren.

Caren raised $100 more than Brad.

Brad raised twice as much money as Arnie.

Plan

I know how much each person made compared to someone else.

Arnie   Brad   Caren   Danica
$ 110

× 2   + 100   ÷ 2

Solve

I can start with the amount Danica raised and work backward.

Arnie   Brad   Caren   Danica
$ 110

÷ 2   − 100   × 2

Caren raised 2 × $110 = $220.
Brad raised $220 − 100 = $120.
Arnie raised $120 ÷ 2 = $60.

---

7. The numbers show how many shells are in each drawer. Meg has a total of 156 shells. She organizes them by size. How many shells are in drawer 1?

35
45
63

8. Mary is knitting a scarf that will be 36 inches long. She knitted 5 inches on the second day, 8 inches on the third day, and 10 inches on the fourth day. She needs to knit 3 inches more to finish the scarf. How much did she knit on the first day?

9. A baby gains about $2\frac{1}{5}$ pounds each month for the first three months after birth. When he was 3 months old, Tyler weighed $14\frac{1}{10}$ pounds. About how much did Tyler weigh at birth?

10. Briana has $1\frac{1}{4}$ cups of sesame seeds left in the bag she bought for baking. She used the sesame seeds to make muffins, bread, and bagels to sell at a bake sale. How many cups of sesame seeds were in the bag she bought?

11. Geometry What is the area of a square garden with a side that measures 18 feet?

$\frac{2}{3}$ cup used $\frac{1}{2}$ cup used $2\frac{1}{3}$ cups used

12. Reasoning Donna, Pam, and Mike worked at a school car wash. Donna washed half as many cars as Mike did. Pam washed 9 more than Donna. Mike washed 5 fewer than Pam. If Mike washed 8 cars, how many cars did Pam and Donna wash? What was the total number of cars washed?

13. Workers need 6 weeks to resurface 15 miles of road. They resurfaced $2\frac{1}{2}$ miles the fourth week, 3 miles the fifth week, and $4\frac{1}{2}$ miles the sixth week. How many miles did they resurface during the first three weeks?

A 5 miles   C 10 miles

B 6 miles   D 11 miles

1. The map shows the approximate placement of some of the Smithsonian museums located on the National Mall. Which museum is located at $(0, {}^-1)$? (17-2)

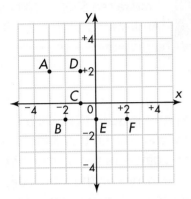

> A = American History Museum
> B = Freer
> C = Smithsonian Castle
> D = Natural History Museum
> E = Hirshhorn Museum
> F = Air and Space Museum

A Hirshhorn Museum

B Freer

C Smithsonian Castle

D Air and Space Museum

2. Find the missing value for y in the table of ordered pairs for the equation $y = x - 5$. (17-4)

x	y
12	7
10	5
8	
5	0

A 1

B 2

C 3

D 13

3. Which of the following can be used to represent a deposit of $132? (17-1)

A $^+132$

B $^+1$

C 0

D $^-132$

4. After a fundraising dinner, a charity has a balance of $2,530. They spent $700 to host the dinner. If they made $1,400 on the event and another $300 afterwards from a private donation, how much money did the charity have before hosting the dinner? (17-5)

A $130

B $1,530

C $2,130

D $3,530

5. What is the distance between $^-3$ and $^+4$ on a number line? (17-3)

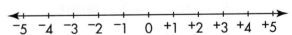

A 1 unit

B 3 units

C 4 units

D 7 units

6. What is the integer at Point L? (17-1)

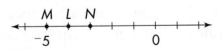

A $^-6$

B $^-5$

C $^-4$

D $^-3$

7. Which ordered pair is located on the line for the equation $y = x + 3$? (17-4)

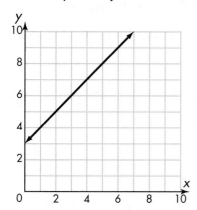

A (1, 4)

B (4, 1)

C (0, 4)

D (4, 0)

8. Martina drew the graph shown. Which equation did she graph? (17-4)

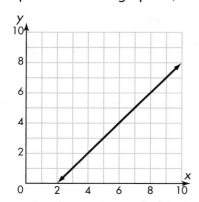

A $y = x - 2$

B $y = x - 1$

C $y = x + 2$

D $y = x + 1$

9. The lowest temperature ever recorded in the United States was in Alaska in 1971. It was about $^-80°$ Fahrenheit. What is the opposite of $^-80$? (17-1)

A $^-80$

B $^-79$

C $^+80$

D $^+81$

10. On a map, Sylvia's house has coordinates ($^+5$, $^-1$) and her school has coordinates ($^+5$, $^+4$). What is the distance between the points that represent the location of Sylvia's house and her school? (17-3)

A 2 units

B 3 units

C 4 units

D 5 units

11. What is the ordered pair for Point X on the graph? (17-2)

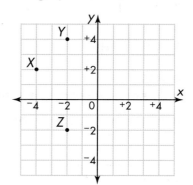

A ($^+2$, $^-4$)

B ($^-4$, $^+2$)

C ($^+4$, $^-2$)

D ($^-2$, $^+4$)

Set A, pages 412–413

Write an integer for each point.

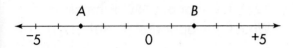

Point *A* is three units from zero and to the left of zero. Point *A* is at ⁻3.

Point *B* is two units from zero and is to the right of zero. Point *B* is at ⁺2.

Remember that the + and − signs name a direction from zero.

Write an integer for each description.

1. Two degrees below zero.

2. Fifty-seven feet above sea level.

Write an integer for each point.

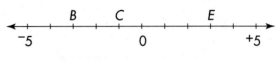

3. *C*   **4.** *E*   **5.** *B*

Set B, pages 414–416

What ordered pair names Point *A*?

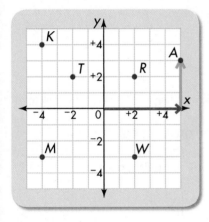

Start at the origin. Move 5 units to the right along the *x*-axis, then 3 units up. Point *A* is at (⁺5, ⁺3).

Remember to name a point on a coordinate grid, first find the *x*-coordinate. Then find the *y*-coordinate. Write the coordinates in (*x*, *y*) order.

1. Which point is located at (⁻4, ⁻3)?

2. Which point is located at (⁺2, ⁺2)?

3. What ordered pair names Point *T*?

4. What ordered pair names Point *W*?

Set C, pages 418–419

Find the distance between ⁻2 and ⁺4 on a number line.

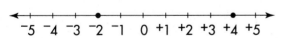

There are 6 units between ⁻2 and ⁺4 on the number line.

Remember that you can also count units to find the distance between points on a coordinate plane.

Find the distance between each pair of integers on a number line.

1. ⁻3 and ⁺5   **2.** ⁻7 and ⁻1

Use a coordinate grid. Find the distance between the points named by each pair of ordered pairs.

3. (⁺3, ⁻2) and (⁺3, ⁻5)

4. (⁻1, ⁺4) and (⁻5, ⁺4)

Set D, pages 420–421

Graph the equation $y = x + 2$.

Choose values for x and find the values for y.

x	y
1	3
4	6
7	9

$y = x + 2$

$3 = 1 + 2$

$6 = 4 + 2$

$9 = 7 + 2$

Use grid paper to draw a coordinate grid.

Label and number the axes.

Plot the ordered pairs and connect the points.

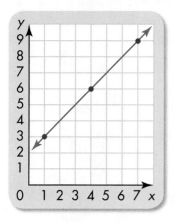

Remember to choose at least three values for x. The values for x and y must satisfy the equation.

Make a table of values for each equation. Then graph the equations on a coordinate grid.

1. $y = x - 4$

x	y
4	
6	
8	

2. $y = 3x$

x	y
0	
1	
2	

3. $y = x + 5$

x	y
0	
3	
4	

4. $y = x$

x	y
0	
2	
4	

Set E, pages 422–423

Rocio worked on her science fair project for 35 minutes. Then she spent 20 minutes working on math homework. After that, Rocio spent 45 minutes on the computer. If she logged off the computer at 8:10 P.M., what time did Rocio begin working on her science fair project?

You can draw a picture to help you work backward. Use inverse operations for each change.

Rocio began her science project at 6:30 P.M.

Remember that addition and subtraction are inverse operations.

Solve.

1. Barb has $3\frac{1}{4}$ ft of ribbon left over. She used $2\frac{1}{4}$ ft to wrap a gift and $\frac{3}{4}$ ft to decorate a picture frame. She then used $1\frac{3}{4}$ ft for hair ribbons. How many feet of ribbon did Barb start with?

Topic 18

Graphs and Data

1 In the 2006 Rubber Duck Derby in Lake Lanier, Georgia, 13,000 rubber ducks raced. Other locations in the U.S. had derbies that same year. Which derby had more ducks than the one in Georgia? You will find out in Lesson 18-2.

2 More than 4,000,000 people visited the Statue of Liberty in 2005. What was the median number of visitors during May through September of that year? You will find out in Lesson 18-8.

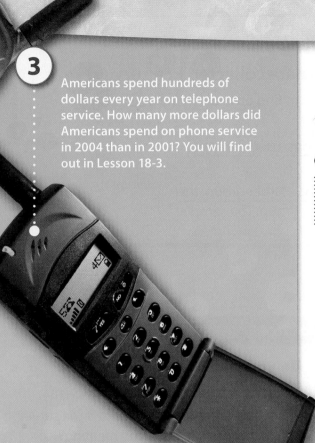

3 Americans spend hundreds of dollars every year on telephone service. How many more dollars did Americans spend on phone service in 2004 than in 2001? You will find out in Lesson 18-3.

4 Cities are located on a globe by using ordered pairs of latitude and longitude. What city is located at the coordinates (30, 30)? You will find out in Lesson 18-3.

Review What You Know!

Vocabulary

Choose the best term from the box.

> • axis   • point
> • ordered pair

1. A(n) _?_ is either of two perpendicular lines on a graph.

2. A(n) _?_ is an exact location in space.

3. A pair of numbers used to locate a point on a graph is called a(n) _?_ .

Number Lines

Use the number line to answer **4** through **6**.

0   1   *A*   *B*   *C*   2

4. Which point is halfway between 1 and 2?

5. Which point is closer to 1 than to 2?

6. Which point is closer to 2 than to 1?

Writing Fractions

7. If 3 out of 6 marbles are red, what fraction, in simplest form, names the red marbles?

8. If 1 out of 5 apples is green, what fraction names the part of the apples that are NOT green?

Division Patterns

Writing to Explain Write an answer to the question.

9. How is the number of zeros in the quotient of 45,000 ÷ 9 related to the number of zeros in the dividend?

Data from Surveys

How can you display the data collected in a survey?

Your teacher might take a survey to find out how many pets students have at home.

A survey is a question, or questions, used to gather information called data.

When people surveyed represent a larger group, the people are a sample of the larger group. The sample should be selected randomly.

Guided Practice*

Do you know HOW?

Mr. Willis's students got the following scores on a 20-word spelling test.

16 18 17 19 18 20 18 17
20 19 17 18 19 15 17 16

1. What are the highest and lowest spelling scores?

2. Make a line plot to display the data.

Do you UNDERSTAND?

3. How might the results shown in the above example be different if the survey were taken at a pet club meeting?

4. **Writing to Explain** A fifth-grade class was surveyed about their favorite type of music. Does this survey represent a sample of the entire population of our country? Why or why not?

Independent Practice

In **5** through **8**, use the line plot at the right to answer the questions.

5. How many people responded to the survey?

6. How many people have 2 or more brothers and sisters?

7. Make a frequency table that shows the same results as the line plot.

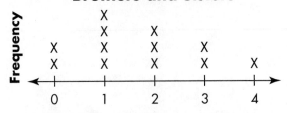

Brothers and Sisters

8. Which is better for displaying a large amount of data, a frequency table or a line plot?

9. **Writing to Explain** Describe how you might choose a sample of 30 people that represent all the students in your entire school.

Animated Glossary
www.pearsonsuccessnet.com

*For another example, see Set A on page 458.

A good survey question is worded clearly.

Question: How many pets do you have at home?

Survey results can be shown by a line plot. A line plot uses Xs to show each response.

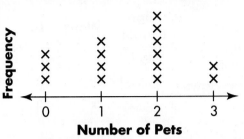

Number of Pets at Home

A frequency table uses numbers to show how many times a response occurs.

Pets at Home	
Number of Pets	Number of Students
0 pets	3
1 pet	4
2 pets	6
3 pets	2

Of the people surveyed, most have 2 pets.

For **10** through **12**, use the frequency table.

10. How many people responded to the survey?

11. How many people own more than 7 CDs?

12. Make a line plot that shows the same information.

Number of CDs Owned	
6 CDs	5
7 CDs	6
10 CDs	8
9 CDs	12

13. An adult has 206 bones. There are 27 bones in each hand. What fraction of the total bones is made up of the bones in both hands combined? Write in simplest form.

14. Algebra The base of a rectangular prism has a length of 8 m and a width of 4 m. If the volume is 64 cubic meters, what is the height of the prism?

15. Estimation If 4 pounds of birdseed cost $6.95, about how much does 1 ounce cost?

    A About $0.01   **C** About $1.00

    B About $0.10   **D** About $1.01

16. Mrs. Dugan plans to serve 100 barbecue sandwiches at the company picnic. How many packages of barbecue buns will she need if buns come in packages of 8? Packages of 12?

17. Algebra Janet had $9.25 this morning. She spent $4.50 for lunch and then spent $3.50 on school supplies. Write an expression to show how much money she had at the end of the day.

18. Geometry Draw and label a rectangle with an area of 32 square inches.

Bar Graphs and Picture Graphs

How can you make and interpret bar graphs?

Understand It!
Bar graphs and picture graphs show comparisons of numerical data. Two sets of similar data can be shown in a double-bar graph.

A bar graph uses rectangles (bars) to show and compare data that tells how many or how much. A double-bar graph uses two different-colored or shaded bars to show two similar sets of data.

Display the softball win-loss records for these three schools in a double-bar graph.

Softball Tournament Records		
High School	**Won**	**Lost**
North	‖‖‖ I	‖‖
Central	‖‖‖ ‖‖	‖‖‖‖
South	‖‖‖	‖‖‖

Another Example How can you make and interpret picture graphs?

Sonya gathered data about the number of ducks in some of the 2006 rubber duck derbies. Sonya listed the data in a frequency table. Then she drew a picture graph to display the data.

Rubber Duck Derbies, 2006				
Location	Congaree River, SC	Lake Lanier, GA	St. Louis Riverfront, MO	Meinig Memorial Park, OR
Number of Rubber Ducks	5,000	13,000	15,000	1,000

A picture graph uses pictures or symbols to represent data. Each picture represents a certain amount in the data.

Rubber Duck Derbies, 2006

Location	Number of Rubber Ducks
Congaree River, SC	🦆 🦆 🦆 🦆 🦆
Lake Lanier, GA	🦆 🦆 🦆 🦆 🦆 🦆 🦆 🦆 🦆 🦆 🦆 🦆 🦆
St. Louis Riverfront, MO	🦆 🦆 🦆 🦆 🦆 🦆 🦆 🦆 🦆 🦆 🦆 🦆 🦆 🦆 🦆
Meinig Memorial Park, OR	🦆

Key: 🦆 = 1,000 rubber ducks

Explain It

1. Which is easier to interpret, a picture graph or a frequency table? Explain.

Step 1
- List the schools along one axis.
- Choose an interval, the difference between adjoining numbers on an axis.

Step 2
- Along the other axis mark the scale, the series of numbers at equal distances. Begin the scale with 0. Include the least and greatest numbers of wins and losses. Label both axes.

Step 3
- Choose colors and make a key to show what each color represents. Graph the data by drawing bars for each value of data.

Step 4
- Title the graph.

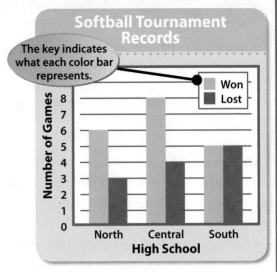

The key indicates what each color bar represents.

Interpret the Graph

Central High School won the most tournament games. North High School lost the fewest tournament games.

Guided Practice*

Do you know HOW?

In **1** and **2**, decide if a bar graph or picture graph would better present the data.

1. The number of cats, dogs, and pet birds in a neighborhood

2. The number of cattle on three ranches

Do you UNDERSTAND?

3. Could the data in the example of the double-bar graph above be presented in a picture graph? Explain.

4. How are bar graphs and picture graphs similar? How are they different?

Independent Practice

In **5** through **8**, answer the questions about the double-bar graph at the right.

5. How many students in Grade 6 get to school by bus? In Grade 7?

6. In which grade do the most students get to school by bus?

7. In which grade do fewer students get to school by bus than other ways?

8. Which grade has the greatest difference between students who get to school by bus and by other ways?

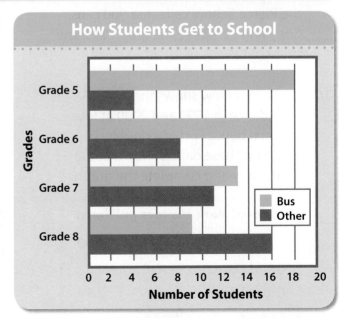

DIGITAL — Animated Glossary, eTools
www.pearsonsuccessnet.com

*For another example, see Set B on page 458.

Lesson 18-2

433

In **9** through **12**, answer the questions about the picture graph at the right.

9. How many people are represented by each picture?

10. What is the difference in populations between the second most populated city and the least populated city?

11. About how many people live in the two most populated cities?

12. Can this data be presented in a bar graph? Explain.

Top 5 U.S. Cities by Population

New York	
Los Angeles	
Chicago	
Houston	
Philadelphia	

Key: = 1 million people

In **13** through **15**, use the partially completed picture graph at the right.

13. What amount does each symbol on the picture graph represent?

14. How many cans did students at the Adams School collect?

15. The students at the Douglas School collected 1,200 cans. The students at the Pierce School collected 900 cans. Copy and complete the graph to show these data.

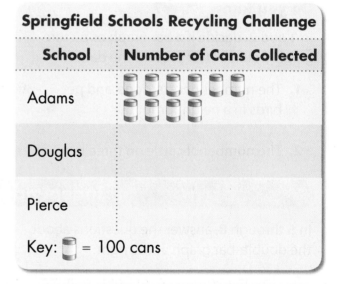

Springfield Schools Recycling Challenge

School	Number of Cans Collected
Adams	
Douglas	
Pierce	

Key: = 100 cans

16. The table below shows the annual attendance in 1990 and 2000 at four national parks. Part of a double-bar graph for these data is shown at the right. Copy and complete the graph.

National Park Visitors (millions)

Park	1990	2000
Grand Canyon	3.8	4.5
Grand Teton	1.6	2.6
Olympic	2.8	3.3
Yellowstone	2.8	2.8

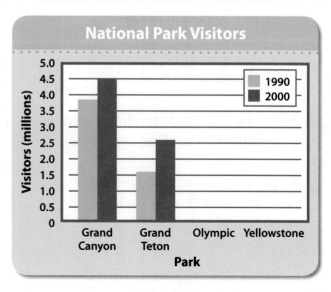

National Park Visitors

In **17** through **20**, use the bar graph.

17. What interval was used for the scale?

18. About how many more eagle pairs were there in 1994 than in 1990?

19. **Writing to Explain** Based on the graph, do you think the number of pairs of eagles increased or decreased after 1994? Explain.

20. Between which 2 years did the number of pairs of eagles increase the most?

Estimated Number of Bald Eagle Pairs in U.S.

In **21** through **23**, use the frequency table.

21. If you were to draw a bar graph for this frequency table, what scale would you use?

22. How many more U.S. residents visited France than Italy in 2004?

23. Why do you think more residents went to Mexico and Canada than the other destinations?

Top 5 Destinations of U.S. Residents, 2004	
Destination	Number of Travelers
Mexico	19,360,000
Canada	15,056,000
United Kingdom	3,692,000
France	2,407,000
Italy	1,915,000

24.  Julio bought 3 dozen eggs. He had 13 eggs left after making egg salad for the picnic. Which shows how to find how many eggs Julio used?

  A $(13 - 12) \times 3$ **C** $(13 \times 12) - 3$

  B $(12 - 3) - 13$ **D** $(3 \times 12) - 13$

26. Point *A* represents which mixed number on this number line?

$$\overset{}{\underset{9}{|}} \qquad \overset{}{\underset{A}{|}} \quad \overset{\bullet}{} \quad \overset{}{\underset{10}{|}}$$

25. **Think About the Process** A school has 12 soccer teams with 10 students on each team. The school wants to have only 8 soccer teams. Which shows how to find the number of students that would be on each team if there were only 8 teams?

  A Multiply 10 by 8.

  B Divide 120 by 8.

  C Divide 8 by 120.

  D Multiply 12 by 8.

Line Graphs

How can data be represented?

A line graph is often used to show a trend or general direction in data.

This table shows the growth of a plant over a period of several days.

The data can be displayed in a line graph.

Hands-On
metric ruler
grid paper

Day 9, 14 cm

Plant Growth	
Day	**Height (cm)**
1	4
3	8
5	10
7	11
9	14

Another Example **How can you read data from line graphs?**

To use data from a graph, locate a point on the graph, and read the values on both axes. To estimate a value not on a graph, interpret the data to determine a trend. The graph below shows Sasha's reading log.

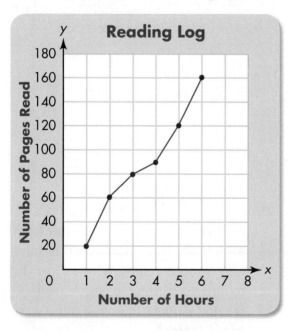

Reading Log	
Hours	**Pages Read**
1	20
2	60
3	80
4	90
5	120
6	160

Explain It

1. Based on the data, how many pages had Sasha read after 2 hours? After 4 hours?

2. If the trend continues, about how many hours will Sasha take to finish a 190-page book?

3. Using the graph, between what two hours was Sasha reading page 140?

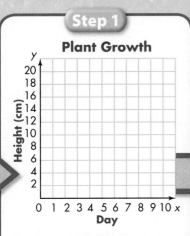

Plant Growth

Draw a coordinate grid, use an appropriate scale, and label each axis. Title the graph.

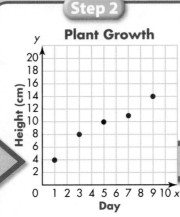

Plant Growth

Plot each ordered pair from the table.

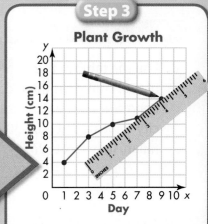

Plant Growth

Use a ruler to connect the points.

Guided Practice*

Do you know HOW?

1. Use grid paper to make a line graph. Plot the ordered pairs from the table of values. Use an interval of 2, and a ruler to connect each point.

Sam's Reading Log

Minutes	Pages
2	4
4	6
6	10
8	10

Data

Do you UNDERSTAND?

2. In the problem above, between which two days was the plant growth the greatest?

3. If the line connecting the points for several days in a row is horizontal, how much taller did the plant grow during those days?

4. **Writing to Explain** How can you determine information from a line graph for a point that is not plotted?

Independent Practice

For **5** through **7**, use the information from the line graph at the right.

5. When were the most DVDs sold?

6. How many more DVDs were sold during Week 3 than Week 5?

7. Based on the trend, estimate the number of DVDs sold during Week 7.

DVD Sales

8. Use the table at the right. On a globe, latitude is the *x*-coordinate. Longitude is the *y*-coordinate. What city is located at (30°, 30°)? Where is Milan, Italy located?

City	Approx. Degrees Latitude	Approx. Degrees Longitude
Cairo, Egypt	30	30
London, U.K.	50	0
Bordeaux, France	45	30
Milan, Italy	45	10

For **9** and **10**, use the line graph at the right.

9. Look for a trend. How many inches do you predict the plant will have grown by the end of Week 5?

10. How many more inches did the plant grow from the end of Week 2 to the end of Week 4?

Plant Growth

Height (in in.) vs. Weeks Passed

11. Use the table below. How much more did Americans spend on telephone service in 2004 than in 2001?

Annual Household Expenditures for Telephone Service					
Year	2000	2001	2002	2003	2004
Amount	$877	$914	$957	$956	$984

12.  **Think About the Process** If a line graph shows an upward trend in population growth for the past five years, what do you know about the population size during that time?

A The population decreased.

B The population inceased and then decreased.

C The population stayed the same.

D The population increased.

For **13** and **14**, use the table at the right. The table shows how far a group of hikers hiked for 4 days.

13. Make a line graph of the data. Use a scale from 0 to 12 and an interval of 2 for the miles hiked. Write a sentence about the trends represented on the graph.

14. During which day did the hikers hike the greatest distance?

Four-day Hike				
By End of Day	1	2	3	4
Total Miles Hiked	2	6	8	11

Animated Glossary, eTools
www.pearsonsuccessnet.com

Line Graphs

Use ⚙ tools

Spreadsheet/Data/Grapher

Draw a line graph of the data in the table.

Step 1 ↗ Go to the Spreadsheet/Data/Grapher eTool. Use the arrow tool to select 6 rows and 2 columns. Set the number of decimal places at zero using the .00 pull-down menu. Type in the data shown in the table to the right.

Data

Elementary (K-8) Students in the United States	
Year	**Millions of Students**
1950	19
1960	27
1970	33
1980	28
1990	30
2000	34

Step 2 ↗ ⎌ Use the arrow tool to select the data. Click on the line graph tool. Enter the title and labels shown in the table. "Millions of Students" should be the Y-Axis Label and "Year" should be the X-Axis Label. Set the interval at 5, the minimum at 0, and the maximum at 40. Click OK.

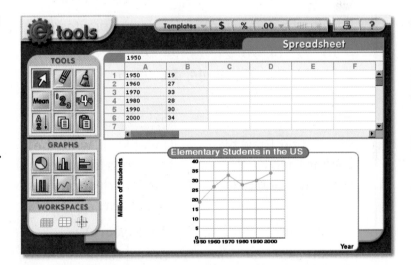

Practice

Use the line graph you created to answer the following questions.

1. Which year showed the only decrease in the number of elementary students?

2. Between which two years did the largest increase take place?

3. Based on the trend in the graph, how many elementary students would you predict in 2010?

4. How many more elementary students were enrolled in the United States in 1960 than in 1950?

Stem-and-Leaf Plots

How do you read a stem-and-leaf plot?

Franco and Gianna have a dog-grooming business. The table at the right shows the number of dogs they groomed in each of the past eight weeks.

What is another way to organize the data?

Number of Dogs Groomed Each Week (for 8 Weeks)

20	29	14	52
34	45	30	48

Another Example How do you make a stem-and-leaf plot?

The table at the right shows the ages of the first twenty people who entered a library in the morning. Make a stem-and-leaf plot of the data.

Ages (in years) of Twenty Library Users

21	12	31	23	20
14	58	35	78	34
50	24	28	10	44
25	29	39	58	36

Step 1

Rewrite the data in order from least to greatest.

10, 12, 14, 20, 21, 23, 24, 25, 28, 29, 31, 34, 35, 36, 39, 44, 50, 58, 58, 78

Step 2

Write a title. Draw two columns and label them *Stem* and *Leaf*.

Ages (years)

Stem	Leaf

Step 3

Under *Stem*, write the tens digits from the data in order from least to greatest.

Ages (years)

Stem	Leaf
1	
2	
3	
4	
5	
6	
7	

Step 4

Under *Leaf*, next to each tens digit, write the ones digits for each data value from least to greatest. Write a key at the bottom.

Ages (years)

Stem	Leaf
1	0 2 4
2	0 1 3 4 5 8 9
3	1 4 5 6 9
4	4
5	0 8 8
6	
7	8

KEY: 1 | 0 = 10

Explain It

1. Why are there two 8s as leaves next to the stem 5?

2. Why do you think the plot includes 6 as a stem?

A stem-and-leaf plot is a convenient way to organize data using numerical order and place value.

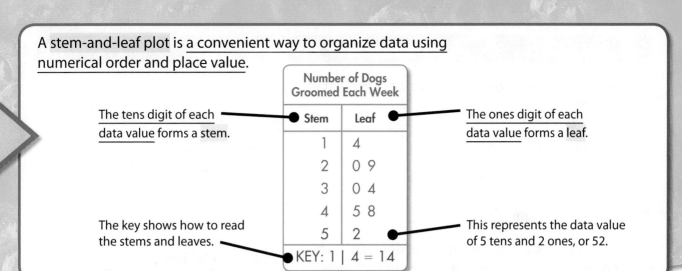

The tens digit of each data value forms a stem.

The ones digit of each data value forms a leaf.

Number of Dogs Groomed Each Week

Stem	Leaf
1	4
2	0 9
3	0 4
4	5 8
5	2

KEY: 1 | 4 = 14

The key shows how to read the stems and leaves.

This represents the data value of 5 tens and 2 ones, or 52.

Guided Practice*

Do you know HOW?

1. Use the stem-and-leaf plot to the right. What is the least number of points scored? The greatest?

Points Scored

Stem	Leaf
1	2 5 8 9
2	0 4 7
3	0 4 6 6 8
4	3 5

KEY: 1 | 2 = 12

2. Make a stem-and-leaf plot of the data.

Ages of People in a Store (years)

27 13 64 46 18 39 10 22
41 70 16 32 15 46 60 17

Do you UNDERSTAND?

3. In the example above, compare the table to the stem-and-leaf plot. Why is the stem-and-leaf plot a better way to display the dog-grooming data?

4. **Writing to Explain** What is the meaning of this key at the bottom of a stem-and-leaf plot?

KEY: 1 | 7 = 17

5. Why should the data from a table be written in numerical order before making a stem-and-leaf plot?

Independent Practice

For **6** through **9**, use the stem-and-leaf plot at the right. It shows points scored by an NBA basketball player in 12 games of a season.

6. What is the greatest number of points scored? The least number?

7. Which point value occurs most often?

8. How many point values are less than 29 points?

9. How many point values are greater than 35 points?

Points Scored in 12 Games

Stem	Leaf
1	8
2	1 6 7 8 9
3	0 5 5
4	1 4 6

KEY: 1 | 8 = 18

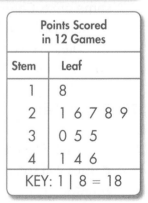

Animated Glossary, eTools
www.pearsonsuccessnet.com

DIGITAL

For **10** and **11**, make a stem-and-leaf plot of the data.

10. Prices of Sweaters (dollars)

33 18 26 37 22
42 26 30 19 27

11. Weights of Pumpkins (pounds)

35 29 50 49 32 16 55 38
57 43 21 72 56 44 49 40

Problem Solving

For **12** through **14**, use the table at the right. Officials at a dog competition record the weight of each dog entered. The data in the table shows the weights of 13 dogs.

12. Make a stem-and-leaf plot of the data.

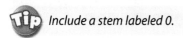 *Include a stem labeled 0.*

13. Refer to the stem-and-leaf plot that you made for Exercise 12. Which stem (or stems) have 3 or more leaves? Which have no leaves?

14. Does the stem-and-leaf plot show that more large dogs or small dogs were entered in the show?

15. Reasoning Suppose there are 15 leaves on a stem-and-leaf plot. How many values are in the data set?

16. Writing to Explain How do you find the least and greatest data values on a stem-and-leaf plot?

Weights (in pounds) of 13 Dogs in a Show	
Breed	**Weight**
Beagle	20
Boxer	71
Chihuahua	7
German Shepherd	81
Golden Retriever	75
Labrador Retriever	67
Miniature Dachshund	20
Miniature Poodle	13
Standard Dachshund	27
Standard Poodle	75
Toy Poodle	10
Shih Tzu	17
Yorkshire Terrier	7

17. At a discount store, all CDs have the same price. Chan bought 6 CDs and paid a total of $62.87, including sales tax. If the sales tax was $2.99, what was the cost of one CD?

18. Think About the Process Which data value occurs most often in this stem-and-leaf plot?

A 6

B 20

C 26

D 36

Hours Spent Volunteering Last Month	
Stem	Leaf
1	6 7 9
2	0 6 6 7 9
3	1 5 6 7
KEY: 1	6 = 16	

19. Terri makes flower bouquets with exactly 3 roses and 5 daisies in each bouquet. She has 72 roses. How many daisies will she need to make the bouquets?

Choosing an Appropriate Graph

Choosing the appropriate type of graph to display a set of data can help you analyze the data.

Example: The graphs below show the favorite colors of several people who answered a survey. Which graph is more appropriate to use to answer the question, "What color is the favorite of the greatest number of people?"

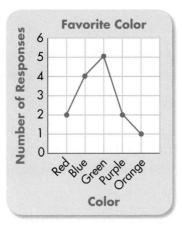

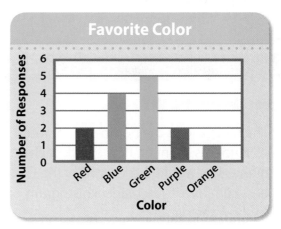

The line graph implies that data exists between the colors, but there is no such data.

The bar graph shows each individual color and the number of people who chose it.

The bar graph is the appropriate graph.

Practice

Tell what type of graph would be most appropriate to represent each set of data.

1. Amount of ticket sales at a movie theater for each day in a week

2. Hourly temperature readings throughout a day

3. A student's growth from birth to 11 years of age

4. A class survey of students' favorite pets

5. A survey was taken to find the number of siblings for each student in a class. Kara made a line graph to show the results. Why is a line graph NOT appropriate to show the data?

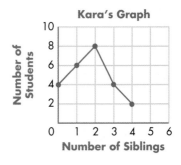

Histograms

Understand It!
A histogram is a bar graph that uses equal intervals on the horizontal axis.

How do you make and interpret a histogram?

A radio station recorded the ages of 25 callers in a phone survey.

This data can be shown by a histogram, a bar graph that groups data into equal intervals shown on the horizontal axis. There is no space between the bars.

Make a histogram to show the frequency of data in each age interval.

Age	Frequency
0–19	6
20–39	12
40–59	5
60–79	2

Guided Practice*

Do you know HOW?

1. The table shows the number of minutes 25 students spent on homework each night. How would the lengths of the bars compare if you made a histogram to show the data?

Number of Minutes	Frequency
0–29	5
30–59	10
60–89	5
90–119	5

Do you UNDERSTAND?

2. According to the histogram in Exercise 1, what fraction of the students surveyed spent 30–59 minutes on homework each night?

3. In the phone-survey example above, how can you tell that $\frac{1}{5}$ of the people surveyed were in the 40–59 age group?

Independent Practice

4. The table shows the results of a class survey about the amount of time students spend on their cell phones each day. Copy and complete the histogram shown at the right.

Amount in Minutes	Frequency
0–9	6
10–19	8
20–29	10
30–39	6

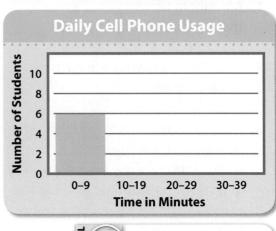

Daily Cell Phone Usage

Animated Glossary
www.pearsonsuccessnet.com

*For another example, see Set E on page 460.

Step 1 List the age intervals along the horizontal axis.

Step 2 Along the vertical axis, mark the scale. List the greatest and least numbers in the survey results. Choose an interval. Label the axes.

Step 3 Graph the data by drawing bars of the correct height. Title the graph.

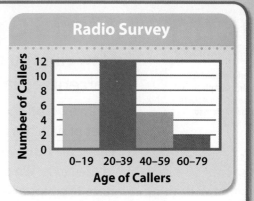

Step 4 Interpret the graph. Twice as many people were in the 20–39 age group as in the 0–19 age group. Most people were in the 20–39 age group.

The group with the least number was the 60–79 age group.

Problem Solving

One class took a survey of the amount of money they spent on CDs over 3 months and made a histogram of the results. The histogram is shown at the right.

5. **a** How many students were surveyed?

  b What fraction of students spent between 0 and $9.99 on CDs?

  c In which range of money spent did twice as many students buy CDs than in the $20–$29.99 range?

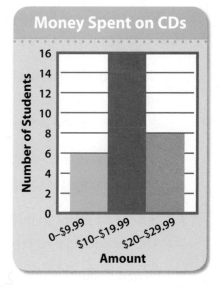

6. **Reasoning** Selma says that a histogram shows that 4 times as many people in the 21–25 age group answered a survey than in the 36–40 age group. How does she know this from looking at the histogram?

7. On a coordinate grid, Sue drew a path starting at (6, 2). She moved 2 spaces to the right and 3 units up. What is the ordered pair for the point where she stopped?

8. On a class trip, Harry spent $28. Nate spent $6 less than Harry. Which expression could you use to find how much both boys spent?

  A 28 + 28 + 6   **C** 28 − (28 + 6)

  B 28 + (28 − 6)   **D** 28 − 28 − 6

9. At 6 A.M., the temperature was ⁻5°F. By noon, the temperature had increased by 12°F. What was the temperature at noon?

  A 17°F   **C** ⁻7°F

  B 7°F   **D** ⁻12°F

Circle Graphs

How can you use fractions and percents to label a circle graph?

A circle graph shows how all (100%) of a set of data has been divided into parts. Each part is shown by a wedge (sector) of the circle. What fraction and percent does the part of each circle that is shaded represent?

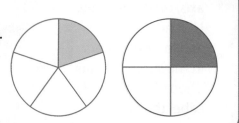

Another Example How can you make a circle graph to display data?

Sixty students were asked to name their favorite sport. How could you use a circle graph to show the results?

Favorite Sport	
Baseball	30
Football	15
Soccer	6
Other	9

Step 1 Use fractions to find what part of the circle should represent each category. Baseball was chosen by 30 out of 60, and $\frac{30}{60}$ is $\frac{1}{2}$ or 50%. So, the wedge for baseball is half the circle.

Football was chosen by 15 out of 60, and $\frac{15}{60}$ is $\frac{1}{4}$ or 25%. So, the wedge for football is $\frac{1}{4}$ of the circle.

Soccer was chosen by 6 out of 60, and $\frac{6}{60}$ is $\frac{1}{10}$ or 10%. The remaining part represents students who chose "other". It is $\frac{9}{60}$ or $\frac{3}{20}$ or 15% of the circle.

Favorite Sport

Football 25%
Baseball 50%
Soccer 10%
Other 15%

Step 2 Draw a circle with sectors for $\frac{1}{2}$, $\frac{1}{4}$, and $\frac{1}{10}$. The remaining sector represents $\frac{3}{20}$. Label the sectors to show what each part of the circle represents. Often circle graphs are labeled with a percent.

Explain It

1. If 20 out of 60 students in the survey had chosen baseball, what fraction would represent the part of the circle that should be shaded to show the part of the students who chose baseball? What percent is equivalent to the fraction?

2. In the circles at the top of the next page, how many of the 12.5% wedges would it take to equal a $\frac{1}{4}$ wedge?

3. In the circle graph at the right, how many wedges should be shaded to show 40%?

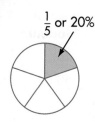

In the first circle graph, $\frac{1}{5}$ or 20% is shaded. In the second circle, $\frac{1}{4}$ or 25% is shaded.

$\frac{1}{5}$ or 20% $\frac{1}{4}$ or 25%

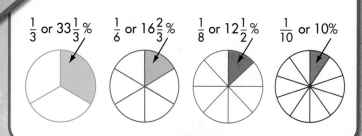

Some other useful fractions for circle graphs are $\frac{1}{3}$, $\frac{1}{6}$, $\frac{1}{8}$, and $\frac{1}{10}$.

$\frac{1}{3}$ or $33\frac{1}{3}$% $\frac{1}{6}$ or $16\frac{2}{3}$% $\frac{1}{8}$ or $12\frac{1}{2}$% $\frac{1}{10}$ or 10%

Guided Practice*

Do you know HOW?

Use the circle below to answer **1** and **2**.

1. If 4 parts of the circle were shaded, what fraction and percent would be represented?

2. If only 1 part were shaded, what fraction and percent would be represented?

Do you UNDERSTAND?

3. In a survey, 20 people out of 80 chose apple as their favorite fruit. If you made a circle graph, which sector shown in the example above would represent apple?

4. Use the data below. Copy and label the graph. Label each sector with the correct color.

Favorite Color	
Blue	3
Green	3
Red	6

Data

Independent Practice

A restaurant offers four main course choices on their dinner menu. One evening the following choices were chosen by 20 customers: chicken, 10; beef, 5; turkey, 3; ham, 2.

5. Copy and complete the table at the right.

6. Copy the circle graph at the right and label each sector with the correct main course.

	Fraction	Percent
Chicken	▨	▨
Beef	▨	▨
Turkey	▨	▨
Ham	▨	▨

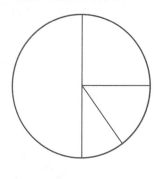

DIGITAL   Animated Glossary
www.pearsonsuccessnet.com

For another example, see Set F on page 460.

Lesson 18-6

In two different surveys, students were asked to name their favorite type of movie. The results are shown in the table at the right.

Favorite Type of Movie		
	Survey of 50 Students	Survey of 100 Students
Comedy	10	25
Animated	20	50
Adventure	20	25

7. In which survey did $\frac{1}{5}$ of the students pick comedy?

8. In which survey did $\frac{1}{2}$ or 50% of the students choose animated movies?

9. Copy each circle graph. Use the survey results to label each sector with the type of movie and the percent. You can remove the dashed lines in your final graph.

Survey of 50 Students   Survey of 100 Students

10. **Number Sense** A circle graph is divided into three sections. One section equals 50%. The other two sections are equal in size. What percent of the circle does each of the other two sections represent?

11. A triangle has a height of 16 mm and a base of 6.4 mm. What is the area of the triangle?

A 22.4 mm²   **C** 51.2 mm²

B 44.8 mm²   **D** 102.4 mm²

12. **Think About the Process** Sonya spent $18 for a book and $22 for a DVD. She paid $2.40 in tax and received $7.60 in change. Which expression shows how to find the amount of money Sonya gave the clerk?

A 18 + 22 + 2.40

B 18 + 22 − 7.60

C 18 + 22 + 2.40 − 7.60

D 18 + 22 + 2.40 + 7.60

13. Renee mixed $\frac{3}{4}$ cup of lime juice, $\frac{7}{8}$ cup of water, and $\frac{1}{2}$ cup of ice to make a limeade. Which is a reasonable total for the amount she mixed?

A Less than 1 cup

B Between $1\frac{1}{2}$ cups and $2\frac{1}{2}$ cups

C More than $2\frac{1}{2}$ cups

D Less than 2 cups

14. A survey asked 200 people to name their favorite type of fruit. The results were as follows: apple, 100; banana, 50; orange, 25; other, 25. Which graph best represents the data?

A 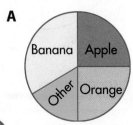   **B** 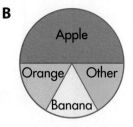   **C** 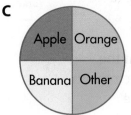   **D**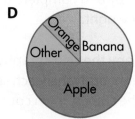

Enrichment

More About Circle Graphs

Each sector of a circle graph includes a central angle of the circle. When you draw a circle graph, it often is helpful to know the measures of the central angles.

If you know the percent for a sector, such as 35%, you can use multiplication to find the degree measure of the central angle. Remember that the sum of the measures of the central angles of a circle is 360°.

Step 1 Write the percent as a decimal.

$$35\% = 0.35$$

Step 2 Multiply 360 by the decimal.

$$\begin{array}{r} 360 \\ \times\ 0.35 \\ \hline 126.00 \end{array}$$

So the measure of the central angle for a sector of 35% is 126°.

Example: Find the measure of each central angle in the circle graph below.

Opinion Poll

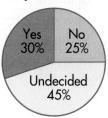

Write each percent as a decimal.

$$30\% = 0.3 \quad 25\% = 0.25 \quad 45\% = 0.45$$

Multiply 360 by each decimal.

$$\begin{array}{r} 360 \\ \times\ 0.3 \\ \hline 108.00 \end{array} \qquad \begin{array}{r} 360 \\ \times\ 0.25 \\ \hline 90.00 \end{array} \qquad \begin{array}{r} 360 \\ \times\ 0.45 \\ \hline 162.00 \end{array}$$

So the measures of the central angles are 108° for *Yes*, 90° for *No*, and 162° for *Undecided*.

Practice

Find the measure of each central angle in the circle graphs below.

1. Class Election Results

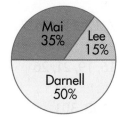

2. Favorite Sports

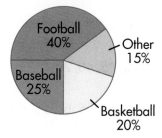

3. Family Budget

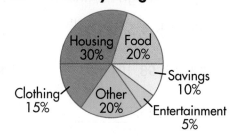

4. A group of 300 students answered a survey about their favorite flavor of ice cream. The results were vanilla, 135; chocolate, 75; strawberry, 45; chocolate chip, 30; other, 15. Suppose you made a circle graph of these data. What would be the measure of the central angle for each category of the graph?

Mean

How can data be described by a single number?

Understand It!
A single number can be used to describe what is typical about a set of data.

How can Carla find the average final score of five bowlers?

The **mean**, or **average**, is <u>the sum of all the numbers in a set of data divided by the number of numbers in the set.</u>

9	10	FINAL SCORE
86 $\lfloor$7$\rfloor$2	95 $\lfloor$6$\rfloor$3 –	95
80 $\lfloor$4$\rfloor$2	87 $\lfloor$7$\rfloor$0 –	87
77 $\lfloor$5$\rfloor$1	84 $\lfloor$4$\rfloor$3 –	84
74 $\lfloor$2$\rfloor$4	81 $\lfloor$5$\rfloor$2 –	81
75 $\lfloor$3$\rfloor$3	83 $\lfloor$6$\rfloor$2 –	83

Guided Practice*

Do you know HOW?

In **1** through **7**, find the mean for each set of data.

1. 5, 4, 4, 9, 8

2. 19, 55, 34, 16

3. 101, 105, 103

4. 8, 2, 11, 6, 8

5. 85, 70, 84, 91, 88, 92

6. 205, 204, 398, 405, 894, 102

7. 28, 32, 36, 40, 42, 57, 58, 59

Do you UNDERSTAND?

8. Another team had 6 bowlers. Would the mean automatically decrease as the number of bowlers increases?

9. In the example above, how could the mean be raised to 90?

10. Writing to Explain Dave said that the mean of 1, 2, 3, 4, and 5 is 8. How do you know this is incorrect without finding the mean?

Independent Practice

In **11** through **22**, find the mean for each set of data.

11. 2, 5, 4, 5

12. 5, 4, 6, 9, 11

13. 6, 17, 12, 11, 4, 6, 7

14. 89, 98, 101

15. 17, 30, 45, 46, 27

16. 13, 16, 19, 21, 26

17. 35, 45, 70

18. 40, 41, 54, 55, 66, 79, 43

19. 164, 198, 301

20. 7.6, 6.2, 6.0, 7.8, 7.4

21. 11, 8.3, 9.0, 3.7

22. 129, 8,002, 1,003, 866

Animated Glossary
www.pearsonsuccessnet.com

For another example, see Set G on page 461.

Add the final scores in the set of data.

$$
\begin{array}{r}
95 \\
87 \\
84 \\
81 \\
+\ 83 \\
\hline
430\ \text{sum}
\end{array}
$$

Divide the <u>sum</u> by the <u>number of numbers</u> in the set.

$$430 \div 5 = 86$$

$$
\begin{array}{r}
86 \\
5\overline{)430} \\
-\ 40 \\
\hline
30 \\
-\ 30 \\
\hline
0
\end{array}
$$

The average, or mean, score for the 5 bowlers is 86.

Problem Solving

Meredith recorded her score for each game of miniature golf she played. Use her scorecard for **23** through **25**.

23. What was Meredith's mean golf score?

24. If Meredith had scored a 50 for the eighth game, how much would her mean score change?

Miniature Golf Scores

Game	1	2	3	4	5	6	7	8
Score	52	56	49	51	54	52	60	58

25. In miniature golf, the lower the score is, the better the game. Meredith wants to find the mean golf score of her four best games. What is this mean score?

26. Geometry Which can be modeled by light beaming from a lighthouse?

A Point

C Ray

B Plane

D Segment

27. Scientists have recorded the lengths of different species of hammerhead sharks. The lengths that have been recorded are 20 ft, 14 ft, 11 ft, and 7 ft. What is the mean length of the hammerhead shark?

A 12.5 ft

C 17 ft

B 13 ft

D 52 ft

29. Reasoning A data set consisting of 3 numbers has a mean of 24. If two of the numbers are 23 and 25, what is the third number?

28. Estimation What is the approximate mean height of the 7 tallest peaks in Texas listed below?

Peaks in Texas	Height in Feet
Guadalupe Peak	8,749
Bush Mountain	8,631
Shumard Peak	8,615
Bartlett Peak	8,508
Mount Livermore	8,378
Hunter Peak	8,368
El Capitan	8,085

Median, Mode, and Range

How can data be described by one number?

Trey listed, in order, the playing times for the best-selling CD of each music type.

How can he describe the data with one number?

CD Playing Times	
Minutes	**Music Type**
59	Popular
61	Country
63	Blues
63	Sound track
64	Gospel
67	Jazz
72	Classical

Guided Practice*

Do you know HOW?

In **1** through **3**, identify the median, mode, and range for each set of data.

1. 5, 7, 5, 4, 6, 3, 5

2. 21, 21, 23, 32, 43

3. 13, 14, 14, 16, 17, 19

 Tip *For an even number of values, the median is the number halfway between the two middle values.*

Do you UNDERSTAND?

4. What operation is used to find the range?

5. In the example at the top, how would the median and mode change if the playing time for the Blues CD changed to 61 minutes?

6. What would the range of playing times be if the 72–minute CD were removed from the list?

Independent Practice

In **7** through **9**, use the table at the right.

7. What are the median, mode, and range for the data?

8. What would happen to the range if the temperature were 82°F on Monday?

9. If the data for Friday were removed from the table, what would the median, mode, and range be?

5-day Weather Forecast	
Day	**Temperature**
Monday	80°F
Tuesday	80°F
Wednesday	82°F
Thursday	84°F
Friday	78°F

Animated Glossary
www.pearsonsuccessnet.com

*For another example, see Set G on page 461.

Find the median.

List the data from least to greatest.

59, 61, 63, 63, 64, 67, 72

Identify the median, or the middle data value in an odd numbered, ordered set of data.

The median of the number of minutes of playing time is 63.

Find the mode.

59, 61, 63, 63, 64, 67, 72

Identify the mode, or the data value that occurs most often in the data set.

The mode of the number of minutes of playing time is 63.

Find the range.

59, 61, 63, 63, 64, 67, 72

Identify the range, or the difference between the greatest and least values.

72 − 59 = 13

The range of the number of minutes of playing time is 13.

Problem Solving

10. Ricardo kept a record of the 7 hottest days of the summer. Use the list below to find the median, mode, and range of the temperatures.

98°F   102°F   100°F   99°F

103°F   98°F   101°F

11. Writing to Explain How can you tell the difference between the net for a triangular prism and the net for a triangular pyramid?

12. Reasoning For each statistical measure (mean, median, mode, and range) tell whether that number is always, sometimes, or never one of the numbers in the data set.

13. **Think** **About the Process** One side of a rectangular garden is 13 feet and the other side is 3 feet. Which expression shows how to find the perimeter?

A $(2 \times 13) + (2 \times 3)$ **C** $2 \times 13 \times 3$

B 13×3 **D** $3 + 13$

For **14** through **17**, use the table.

14. What was the median number of visitors to the Statue of Liberty from May to September in 2005?

15. What is the range of the data?

16. How many months had over 500,000 visitors?

17. Writing to Explain Why do you suppose there had been many fewer visitors in September, than in July or August?

Visitors to the Statue of Liberty	
2005	**Visitors**
May	430,235
June	492,078
July	589,166
August	542,292
September	367,441

Understand It!
Learning how and when to make a graph can help you solve problems.

Make a Graph

Hands-On
grid paper

Data for a company's sales of mountain bicycles and skateboards are shown in the table. Write two statements that compare the sales of bicycles and skateboards.

Make a line graph for each set of data to help you analyze the data.

Year	Number of Bicycle Sales	Number of Skateboard Sales
2003	800	200
2004	900	400
2005	1,000	800
2006	1,000	999
2007	1,100	1,100

Guided Practice*

Do you know HOW?

1. In a survey, students were asked to name their favorite pet. Copy the circle below to make a circle graph to show the data.

Dog	Cat	Bird	Other
12	6	4	2

2. Make a bar graph to show the data in Exercise 1.

Do you UNDERSTAND?

3. In the example above, if the trend continues, what can you say about the sales of both bicycles and skateboards in 2008?

4. **Write a Problem** Write a real-world problem that can be solved by making a graph.

Independent Practice

5. Mr. Lauer surveyed his students to find out what kind of field trip they preferred. Make a bar graph to show the data. Which field trip is most popular?

Field Trip	Number of Votes
Zoo	12
Aquarium	9
Musical Play	5
Mystery Play	4

6. Would a line graph be an appropriate graph in Exercise 5? Why or why not?

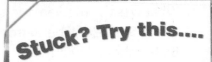

Stuck? Try this....

- What do I know?
- What am I asked to find?
- What diagram can I use to help understand the problem?
- Can I use addition, subtraction, multiplication, or division?
- Is all of my work correct?
- Did I answer the right question?
- Is my answer reasonable?

For another example, see Set D on page 447.

I can make a line graph for bicycle sales.

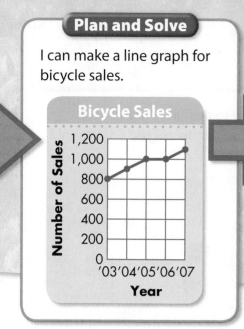

Bicycle Sales

I can make a line graph for skateboard sales.

Skateboard Sales

The sales for bicycles and skateboards have been increasing over the years.

The difference between the number of bicycle sales and the number of skateboard sales is becoming smaller.

For **7** and **8**, a survey of 16 people recorded the number of books people read in one month. Joe made a histogram and Jean made a circle graph to show the results.

Number of people	8	6	2
Number of books	0–2	3–5	6–8

Histogram

Books Read by 16 People in 1 Month

Circle graph

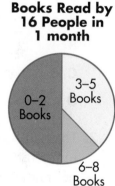

Books Read by 16 People in 1 month

7. Which graph makes it easy to see that $\frac{1}{2}$ of the people read 2 or less books in the month? Which graph makes it easy to tell the number of people in each category?

8. **Writing to Explain** Can you tell from the histogram how many people read 4 books?

9. The data about bicycle sales and skateboard sales at the top of the page could also be shown by a double-bar graph. Part of the graph is shown at the right. Copy and complete the graph.

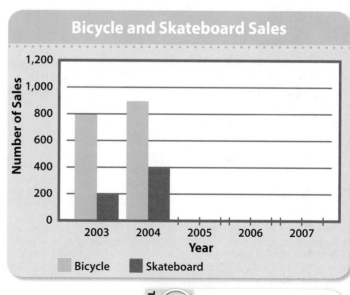

Bicycle and Skateboard Sales

10. A café sells turkey, roast beef, ham, or cheese sandwiches; milk, water, or juice; and yogurt or fruit. How many different meals are possible for a person who wants a sandwich, drink, and dessert?

eTools
www.pearsonsuccessnet.com

1. The line plot shows the results from a survey asking parents how many children they have in the school. How many parents have two children in the school? (18-1)

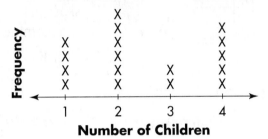

Number of Children in School

A 2

B 4

C 6

D 12

2. The graph shows the Fahrenheit temperature in Old Town taken every hour after 8:00 A.M. What was the temperature at noon? (18-3)

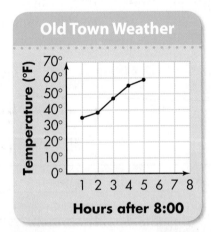

A 58°F

B 54°F

C 47°F

D 45°F

3. According to the circle graph below, about what fraction of the T-shirts sold were X-large? (18-6)

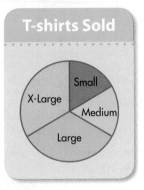

A $\frac{1}{3}$

B $\frac{1}{4}$

C $\frac{1}{5}$

D $\frac{1}{6}$

4. The heights of a group of friends are listed below. What is the mean height of the group in inches? (18-7)

58, 62, 55, 61, 64

A 61

B 60

C 59

D 58

5. The shoe sizes of the starting players on the girls' basketball team are listed below. What is the median of these numbers? (18-8)

7, 6, 5, 6, 8

A 5

B 6

C 7

D 8

6. James is drawing the picture graph below to show the number of license plates from each state he saw on a recent trip. He saw 15 Arizona license plates. Which picture should he draw for Arizona? (18-2)

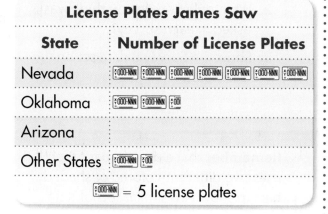

License Plates James Saw

State	Number of License Plates
Nevada	
Oklahoma	
Arizona	
Other States	

= 5 license plates

A

B

C

D

7. How many students scored between 80 and 90 according to the data shown in the stem-and-leaf plot? (18-4)

Student Test Scores

Stem	Leaf
7	2 4 8 8
8	1 1 3 5 6 8 9
9	1 3 3 6 7

KEY: 7 | 2 = 72

A 16

B 12

C 8

D 7

8. The histogram shows the results from a survey asking people how many plays they have seen in the last year. How many people have seen more than 3 plays? (18-5)

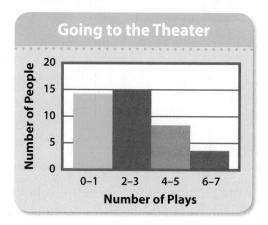

Going to the Theater

A 26

B 15

C 11

D 8

9. If the trend in the graph continues, what will be the company's profits in 2008? (18-9)

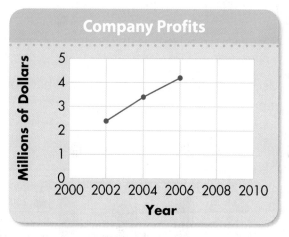

Company Profits

A About 2 million dollars

B About 3 million dollars

C About 5 million dollars

D About 6 million dollars

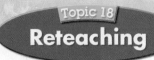
Set A, pages 430–431

These frequency tables use numbers to show how many times a response to a survey occurs.

Survey A

Favorite Video Games	
Snowboarding	6
Save the Whales	5
Pro Hockey	4

Survey B

Number of Video Games Owned	
2 games	4
3 games	6
4 games	2

Remember that survey results can also be shown on a line plot. Each X represents one response.

1. Which survey gathered facts and which gathered opinions?

2. What question do you think was asked in each survey?

3. Show the Survey B data set on a line plot.

Set B, pages 432–435

Use the picture graph to determine how many books were read in March.

Books Read

Month	Books
Jan.	📘 📘 📘
Feb.	📘 📘 📘 📘 📖
Mar.	📘 📘 📖

Key: 📘 = 2 books

Since each symbol represents 2 books, this means that 5 books were read in March.

Use the double-bar graph below. What does the length of the longest bar represent?

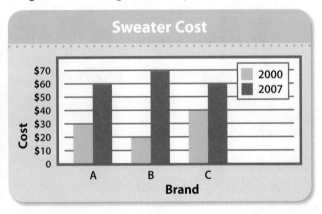

Sweater Cost

(Cost vs. Brand, with 2000 and 2007 legend)

The longest bar shows that Brand B cost $70 in 2007.

Remember that a double-bar graph uses two different-colored or shaded bars to show two similar sets of data.

A picture graph is easy to use when the data involves multiples of the same number.

For **1** and **2**, use the picture graph at the left.

1. How many books were read in February?

2. What was the total number of books read for the three months?

For **3** through **5**, use the double-bar graph at the left.

3. How much more did Brand A cost in 2007 than in 2000?

4. Which brand increased the most in price from 2000 to 2007?

5. What does the length of the shortest bar represent?

Set C, pages 436–439

Make a line graph for the data.

	Day	Newspapers sold
Data	1	6
	2	8
	3	9
	4	10
	5	12

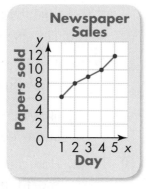

To make a line graph:

1. Use grid paper to draw a coordinate grid.

2. Label the axes.

3. Number each axis with a consistent scale.

4. Plot the ordered pairs and connect the points.

Remember that line graphs show data that change over time.

1. Make a line graph for the data.

	Week	CDs sold
Data	1	10
	2	5
	3	20
	4	15

2. Describe the trend.

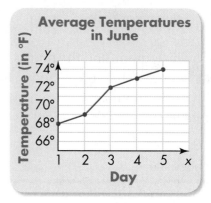

Set D, pages 440–442

The sizes of jeans in stock in one store are listed below in inches.

31, 32, 41, 44, 33, 21, 22, 32, 36, 37, 42, 29

A stem-and-leaf plot can display the data.

1. List the numbers in order from least to greatest: 21, 22, 29, 31, 32, 32, 33, 36, 37, 41, 42, 44

2. List the tens digits in order (20, 30, 40) to the left of the vertical line.

3. For each tens digit, record the ones digits, in order, to the right of the vertical line.

Jean Sizes	
Stem	Leaf
2	1 2 9
3	1 2 2 3 6 7
4	1 2 4
KEY: 2	1 = 21	

Remember to write the data in order from least to greatest before making your stem-and-leaf plot.

For **1**, use the stem-and-leaf plot at the left.

1. How many pairs of jeans in stock had waist sizes greater than 30 inches? How did the stem-and-leaf plot help you find your answer?

For **2** and **3**, make a stem-and-leaf plot.

2. Math scores: 75, 86, 92, 90, 88, 79, 95, 98, and 85.

3. Daily high temperatures: 28, 32, 27, 34, 38, 48, 50, 47, 34, 38, 49

Set E, pages 444–445

David made a histogram to show how many books his class had purchased in the last year.

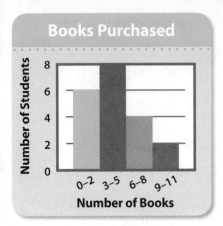

Books Purchased

Number of Students / Number of Books

Using the histogram, find the number of students who purchased 3–5 books. Notice the bar with the 3–5 interval has a height of 8. Therefore, the number of students is 8.

Remember that histograms are a type of bar graph that has no space between the bars and the bars show equal intervals.

Use the histogram at the left to answer the following questions.

1. How many students were surveyed?

2. How many students had bought more than 5 books?

3. What fraction of the students bought 9, 10, or 11 books?

Set F, pages 446–448

A group of 100 students were asked to name their favorite type of television program. Make a circle graph to show the results.

Favorite Type of Television Program	
Comedy	25
Sports	50
Drama	10
Other	15

Data

Comedy = 25 out of 100 = $\frac{1}{4}$

Sports = 50 out of 100 = $\frac{1}{2}$

Drama = 10 out of 100 = $\frac{1}{10}$

Other = $\frac{15}{100}$ = $\frac{3}{20}$

Draw a circle with sectors for $\frac{1}{2}, \frac{1}{4},$ and $\frac{1}{10}$ and label those sectors with the program type. The remaining sector shows $\frac{3}{20}$ or Other.

Remember that a circle graph shows the whole amount (100%) and each sector represents a part of the whole amount.

Jill spent a total of 30 hours exercising last month: Jogging: 15 hours; Cycling: 10 hours; Swimming: 5 hours.

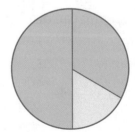

1. Copy the circle graph and label each sector with the activity and fraction.

2. What fraction represents the part of the day Jill spent cycling?

460

Set G, pages 450–453

Find the mean, median, mode, and range for this set of data: 10, 13, 20, 12, 10

To find the mean, find the sum of the data and divide by the number of numbers.

$10 + 13 + 20 + 12 + 10 = 65$

$65 \div 5 = 13$ **The mean is 13.**

To find the median, list the data in order from least to greatest, and find the middle value.

10, 10, 12, 13, 20   **The median is 12.**

To find the mode, find the value that occurs most often.

The mode is 10.

To find the range, subtract the least value from the greatest value.

$20 - 10 = 10$ **The range is 10.**

Remember that if there is an even number of values, you must add the two middle numbers when the data set is ordered from least to greatest, and then divide by 2 to find the median.

1. Find the mean of this data set:
   13, 16, 25, 22, 19

2. Find the mean of this data set:
   3, 5, 9, 2, 4, 6, 6

3. Find the range of this data set:
   1, 19, 2, 8, 6, 10, 4

4. Find the median of this data set:
   27, 21, 24, 32

5. Find the mode of this data set:
   12, 6, 9, 5, 8, 12, 8, 1, 4, 12, 6

6. Find the range of this data set:
   87, 84, 90, 75, 100, 88

Set H, pages 454–455

Students were asked to name their favorite animal. Make a bar graph to show the results.

Favorite Animal	
Penguin	7
Elephant	6
Lion	3
Monkey	4

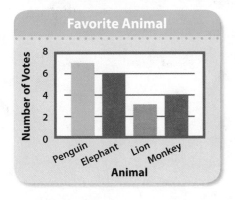

Remember that making a graph makes it easy to visualize data and answer questions about the data.

Monthly Snowfall				
Month	Dec.	Jan.	Feb.	Mar.
Inches	6	12	18	4

1. Make a line graph of the data.

2. Which month has a snowfall 3 times as great as December?

Topic 19

Transformations, Congruence, and Symmetry

1 What would a reflection of this rainbow look like? You will find out in Lesson 19-2.

2 Is this pair of wheels congruent? You will find out in Lesson 19-4.

3

Stalagmites like this can be found in underground caves. What would a rotation of this stalagmite look like? You will find out in Lesson 19-3.

Review What You Know!

Understand It!
The size and shape of a figure do not change when it is translated.

Translations

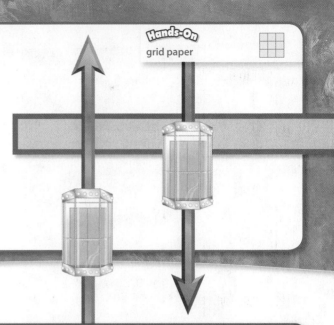

Hands-On
grid paper

How can you describe a translation?

A translation moves a figure up, down, left, or right. An elevator can translate up or down as shown at the right.

Other Examples

How do you sketch translations?

To sketch a translation of this triangle 3 units to the left, move each vertex 3 units to the left.

Point	Original	Image
A	(6, 2)	(3, 2)
B	(6, 5)	(3, 5)
C	(11, 2)	(8, 2)

3 was subtracted from each x-coordinate.

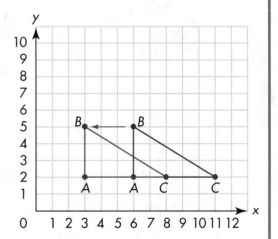

To sketch a translation of this triangle shown by the translation arrow, move each vertex to the right 5 units and up 2 units.

Point	Original	Image
A	(3, 2)	(8, 4)
B	(6, 2)	(11, 4)
C	(6, 5)	(11, 7)

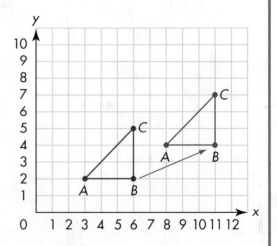

Explain It

1. In the second *Other Example*, how did each of the x– and y–coordinates of the original figure change to the translated image?

You can use a coordinate grid to translate the elevator up 4 units. The size and shape of the figure do not change.

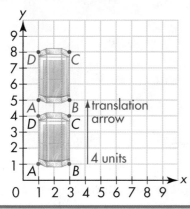

When the figure is translated up 4 units, each of the y-coordinates increases by 4.

Point	Original	Image
A	(1, 1)	(1, 5)
B	(3, 1)	(3, 5)
C	(3, 4)	(3, 8)
D	(1, 4)	(1, 8)

Guided Practice*

Do you know HOW?

1. In which direction did the rectangle move? How many units?

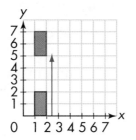

2. In which directions did the triangle move? How many units?

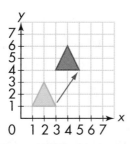

Do you UNDERSTAND?

3. Copy the figure at the right onto grid paper. Translate it 3 units to the left and 2 units up.

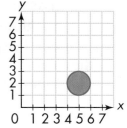

4. **Writing to Explain** How can you translate a book that is on top of your desk?

5. Does translation change a figure's shape or size?

Independent Practice

For **6** through **8**, copy each figure onto grid paper. Sketch the translation shown by the arrow.

6.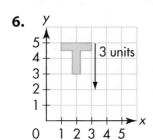

7.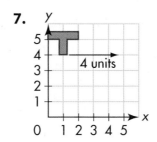

8.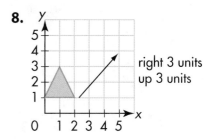

right 3 units
up 3 units

*For another example, see Set A on page 482.

For **9** use the picture to the right.

9. A basketball team has a play where Player A passes to Player B. Player B passes to Player C, who shoots. The letters show the positions of the players. The triangles represent the ball moving in play. Describe the translation of the triangle from A to C.

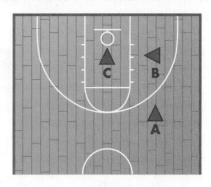

10. A rectangle is located at (7, 6), (9, 6), (9, 10), and (7, 10) on a coordinate grid. Use grid paper. Draw the original rectangle and its translation of 6 units to the left.

11. A square is located at (1, 1), (3, 1), (3, 3), and (1, 3) on a coordinate grid. Use grid paper. Draw the original square and its translation of 4 units to the right and 3 units up.

12. Naomi is translating a square 7 units to the right. If the coordinates of one vertex of the square are (3, 5), what are the coordinates of the same vertex of the image?

   A (3, 12)   **C** (10, 12)

   B (10, 5)   **D** (3, 5)

13. **Think About the Process** Each cartwheel that Veronica completes covers 8 feet. If Veronica completes 2 cartwheels in a row, how many feet does she cover?

   A 8   **C** 8 + 3

   B 8 × 3   **D** 8 × 2

14. A dog walker charges $12 per hour. How much will she charge to walk a dog $\frac{1}{2}$ hour each day for 10 days?

15. **Writing to Explain** How can the movement of a figure either up or right on a coordinate grid both be considered translations?

16. Name the coordinates for the vertices of the translated shape.

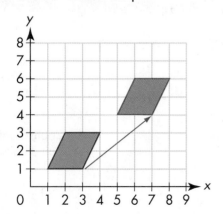

17. **Reasoning** Mrs. Beigler gave away books to students. Jacob got $\frac{1}{2}$ of the books, and then David took $\frac{1}{2}$ of the remaining books. Becky took 4 of the books left after Jacob and David. Jenny and Carey shared the remaining 8 books. What was the total number of books Mrs. Beigler gave to the students?

Translations

Use 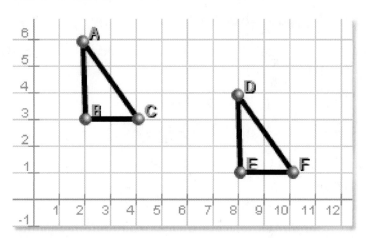 tools
Geometry Drawing

Draw a triangle with vertices at (2, 6), (2, 3), and (4, 3).
Translate it 6 units to the right and 2 units down. Find the
coordinates of the vertices after the translation.

Step 1 Go to the Geometry Drawing eTool. Select
the Cartesian workspace. Then select the Polygon tool
for drawing a polygon. Click on point (2, 6), drag to
(2, 3) and click, drag to (4, 3) and click, and then drag
back to (2, 6) and click to complete the triangle.

Step 2 Click on the copy
tool. Then click on a side
of the triangle to copy
it. Select the arrow tool
and use it to move the
copy of the triangle so it
is 6 units right and 2 units
down from the original
triangle. The vertices of the
translated triangle are at
(8, 4), (8, 1), and (10, 1).

Practice

Use the triangle with vertices at (2, 6), (2, 3), and (4, 3). Find the
coordinates of the vertices of the triangle after each translation.

1. Translate the triangle 1 unit left and 3 units down.

2. Translate the triangle 4 units right and 1 unit up.

3. Translate the triangle 5 units right.

4. Translate the triangle 2 units left.

5. Translate the triangle 2 units right and 1 unit down.

6. Translate the triangle 1 unit right and 1 unit up.

7. Translate the triangle 1 unit right, 1 unit down, 1 unit left,
and 1 unit up.

Reflections

How can figures be reflected?

A reflection of a figure gives its mirror image. A figure can be reflected across any line.

Guided Practice*

Do you know HOW?

In **1** through **4**, tell if the figures are related by a reflection.

1.

2.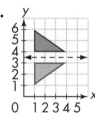

3.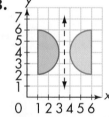

4.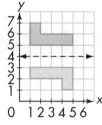

Do you UNDERSTAND?

5. Does a reflection change a figure's size or shape?

6. Sketch the reflection of the figure across the line. Use grid paper.

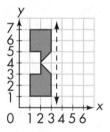

7. **Writing to Explain** How does a reflection differ from a translation?

Independent Practice

In **8** through **11**, sketch the reflection of each figure across the line. Use grid paper.

8.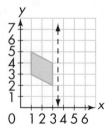

9.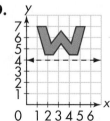

10.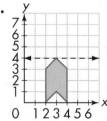

11.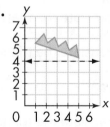

*For another example, see Set B on page 482.

When a figure is reflected, the size and shape of the figure do not change. Reflections can be shown and drawn on coordinate grids.

When drawing a reflection, you can count units from each of the vertices of the original figure to the reflecting line. Plot points the same distance from the line for the image.

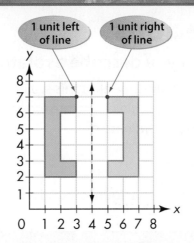

1 unit left of line   1 unit right of line

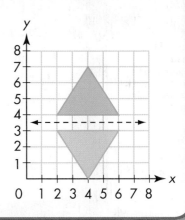

Problem Solving

12. Tell whether the figures in each pair are related by a translation, a reflection, or both.

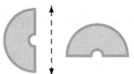

a E Ǝ   b A A   c L L

13. Use grid paper to graph the triangle with vertices (1, 3) (1, 5) and (3, 4). Then, sketch its reflection.

14. Number Sense How can you rewrite the expression below to find the sum mentally?

36 + 29 + 14

15. Which equation does the diagram represent?

51

x	x	x

A $3 + x = 51$ **C** $51 \div 3 = x$

B $51 + 3 = x$ **D** $51 \times x = 3$

16. Antoine was running laps in physical education class. He ran 4 times around the basketball court. The court is 50 ft by 84 ft. Calculate the number of feet Antoine ran.

17. Which shows a reflection of the shape of a rainbow?

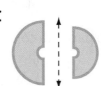

A   B   C   D

Rotations

Understand It!
The size and shape of a figure do not change if it is rotated around a point.

How can you describe a rotation?

Examine the movement of this scalene triangle. The triangle can rotate around a point on a coordinate grid.

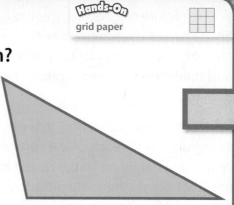

A rotation moves a figure around a point.

Guided Practice*

Do you know HOW?

In **1** and **2**, describe the measure of the rotation.

1.
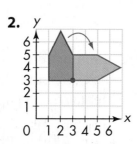

2.
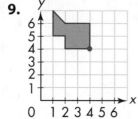

Do you UNDERSTAND?

3. Writing to Explain Why is the image of a 360° rotation of the scalene triangle in the same position as the original triangle?

4. If the scalene triangle moved in a straight direction from its original point, was the movement a translation or a rotation?

Independent Practice

In **5** through **7**, describe whether the figures in each pair are related by a rotation, a translation, or a reflection.

5.
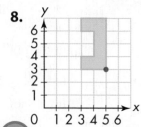

6.
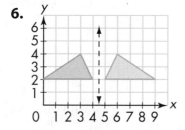

7.
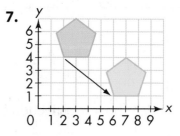

In **8** through **10**, use the grid paper to copy the figure and sketch a 270° rotation.

8.
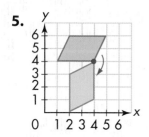

9.
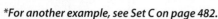

10.
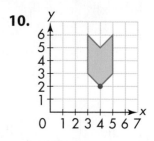

*For another example, see Set C on page 482.

When a figure is rotated, the size and shape of the figure do not change. Rotations can be measured in degrees or fractions of a rotation.

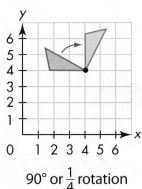

90° or $\frac{1}{4}$ rotation

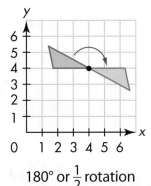

180° or $\frac{1}{2}$ rotation

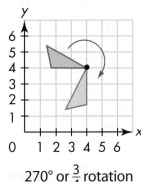

270° or $\frac{3}{4}$ rotation

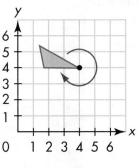

360° or full rotation

Problem Solving

11. Which transformation relates to the guitars?

A Rotation

B Symmetric

C Translation

D Reflection

12. Which transformation relates to the paddle boat?

A Symmetric

B Rotation

C Translation

D Reflection

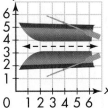

13. Use grid paper to sketch a triangle with these vertices: (3, 3), (3, 7), and (1, 6). Rotate this triangle 90° around the vertex point (3, 3). Sketch the result.

14. **Think About the Process** Keiko wants to rotate a figure a full turn around one of its vertices. How many degrees will Keiko rotate the figure?

A 90°   B 180°   C 270°   D 360°

15. **Writing to Explain** What is the difference between a rotation and a reflection? Explain.

16. **Writing to Explain** You estimate that 2,486 ÷ 65 is about 40. Is your estimate greater than or less than the actual quotient? How do you know?

17. Imagine the shape of this stalagmite rotated 180°. What would it look like?

A

B

C

D

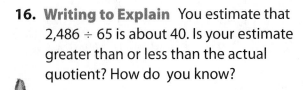

Understand It!
Figures that have the same shape and size are congruent.

Congruence

How can you verify that two figures are congruent?

Translations, reflections, and rotations are three examples of transformations. Figures that are the same size and shape are congruent.

Guided Practice*

Do you know HOW?

1. Tell which type of transformation is represented in each pair of figures below. If it is a rotation, describe it.

a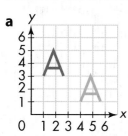

c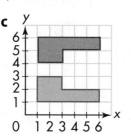

b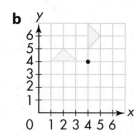

d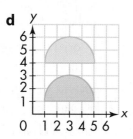

Do you UNDERSTAND?

2. **Writing to Explain** How do you know these two figures are congruent?

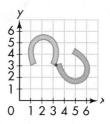

3. **Writing to Explain** Does this diagram represent a translation? Why or why not?

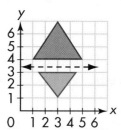

Independent Practice

4. Tell if the figures in each pair are congruent.

a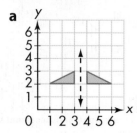

b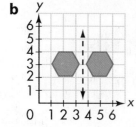

c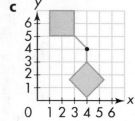

d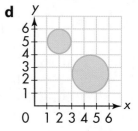

*For another example, see Set D on page 483.

Remember that transformations do not change the size or shape of the figure.

The two figures are congruent because the puzzle piece can be rotated and then translated into the space.

You can test if two figures are congruent by using translations, reflections, or rotations.

Problem Solving

5. **Think About the Process** Draw a triangle with the following vertices: (2, 1), (7, 1), and (7, 3). Move the triangle right 6 units and down 3 units. What transformation took place?

A Reflection   **C** Translation

B Rotation   **D** Congruent

6. **Writing to Explain** Explain how the figure was moved from Position *A* to Position *B*. Are the figures congruent?

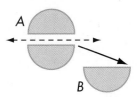

7. Which of these pairs of wheels are congruent?

A   **C**

B   **D**

8. Are the figures shown below an example of a transformation? If not, explain why.

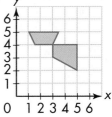

9. The pattern at the right shows a pattern of transformations. Describe each step.

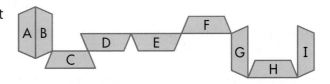

10. **Reasoning** Reflecting a figure to the right and then reflecting it down results in which single transformation?

11. Stefan bought three colors of paint to paint his skateboard. The paint cost $1.29, $2.09, and $0.99. The total tax was $0.42. How much change did Stefan get back from $10?

Symmetry

What is line symmetry?

A figure has line symmetry if it can be folded into two congruent parts that fit on top of each other exactly. The fold line is called a line of symmetry. A figure can have more than one line of symmetry.

Understand It!
Some figures can be folded in half so that one side reflects the other side or rotated so that the figure rotates onto itself in less than a full rotation.

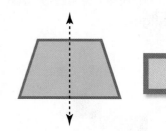

One line of symmetry

Another Example **What is rotational symmetry?**

A figure has rotational symmetry if it rotates onto itself in less than a full rotation.

This octagon has rotational symmetry because a 90° rotation ($\frac{1}{4}$ rotation) rotates it onto itself.

This rhombus has rotational symmetry because a 180° rotation ($\frac{1}{2}$ rotation) rotates it onto itself.

This trapezoid does not have rotational symmetry.

Explain It

1. Explain why the trapezoid above does not have rotational symmetry.

2. Which figure above has both rotational symmetry and line symmetry?

3. Are there any other rotations less than a full rotation that will rotate the octagon onto itself? Explain.

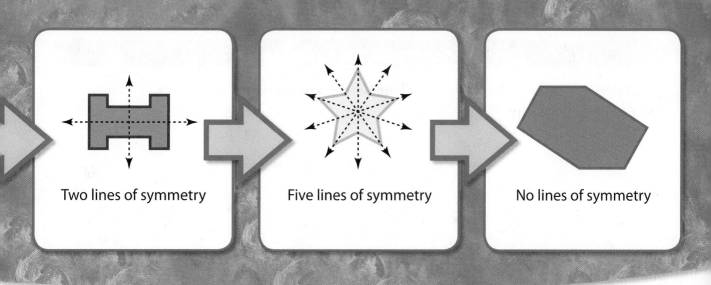

| Two lines of symmetry | Five lines of symmetry | No lines of symmetry |

Guided Practice*

Do you know HOW?

For **1** and **2**, write the number of lines of symmetry each figure has.

1.

2.

For **3** and **4**, give the smallest rotation that will rotate the figure onto itself.

3.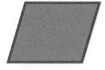

4.

Do you UNDERSTAND?

5. Which hexagon has more lines of symmetry? Explain.

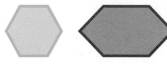

6. Can a triangle have rotational symmetry? Explain.

7. Draw a figure that has both line symmetry and rotational symmetry.

Independent Practice

For **8** through **12**, tell if the figure has line symmetry, rotational symmetry, or both. If it has line symmetry, how many lines of symmetry are there? If it has rotational symmetry, what is the smallest rotation that will rotate the figure onto itself?

8.

9.

10.

11.

12.

*For another example, see Set D on page 483.

For **13** through **16**, copy the figure. Then complete the figure so the dashed line is a line of symmetry.

13. **14.** **15.** **16.**

Many figures in nature, like the starfish at the right, are nearly symmetric, but not exactly symmetric.

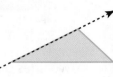

17. Does the starfish seem to have line symmetry? If so, how many lines of symmetry do there seem to be?

18. Does the starfish seem to have rotational symmetry? If so, what is the smallest rotation that would seem to rotate the starfish onto itself?

19. Explain why the starfish is not exactly symmetric.

20. **Writing to Explain** Francine thinks that the lines of symmetry for a rectangle pass through the midpoints of its sides. Do you think she is correct?

21. Michael bought a jacket and a sweater. The jacket cost $28 more than the sweater. The sum of the prices was $146. How much did each item cost?

22. **Draw a Picture** Draw a quadrilateral that has neither line symmetry nor rotational symmetry.

23. Is it possible for a quadrilateral to rotate onto itself in less than a one-half-rotation? Explain.

24. How many lines of symmetry does this figure have?

A 0

B Exactly 1

C Exactly 2

D Exactly 4

25. What is the smallest rotation that will rotate this rectangle onto itself?

A 45° ($\frac{1}{8}$)

B 90° ($\frac{1}{4}$)

C 180° ($\frac{1}{2}$)

D 360° (full)

Animated Glossary, eTools
www.pearsonsuccessnet.com

Tessellations

A **tessellation** is a repeating pattern of shapes without any gaps or overlaps. There are many shapes you can use to make a tessellation. On this page, the tessellations will be made of regular polygons.

Examples:

Squares alone can make a tessellation. There are no gaps or overlaps.

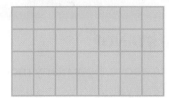

Regular pentagons alone cannot make a tessellation. There are gaps.

Equilateral triangles and regular hexagons can combine to make a tessellation.

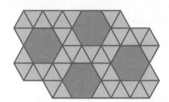

Practice

Tessellations are often used in tile floors. In **1** and **2**, name the regular polygons that were used to make the tessellation.

1.

2.

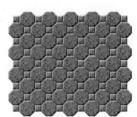

3. Which regular polygons other than squares can be used alone to make a tessellation? Draw each tessellation. You may use Power Polygons to help.

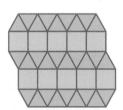

4. **Writing to Explain** Describe how the two tessellations at the right are alike and how they are different.

5. Draw a tessellation by combining equilateral triangles, squares, and regular hexagons.

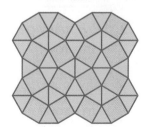

Understand It!
Learning how and when to use objects can help you solve problems.

Use Objects

A pentomino is an arrangement of 5 identical squares in a plane. The squares must be attached to one another edge to edge.

This is a pentomino.

This is not a pentomino.

Using 5 identical square tiles, how can you build 3 more pentominoes that have 3 squares in a row?

Guided Practice*

Do you know HOW?

1. Is the following a pentomino? Explain.

2. Are these two pentominoes the same or different? Explain.

Do you UNDERSTAND?

3. In the example above, how many more pentominoes can you find with 3 in a row?

4. **Write a Problem** Write a real-world problem that can be solved by using objects.

Independent Practice

In **5** and **6**, tell whether the pentominoes in each pair are related by a reflection or a rotation.

5.

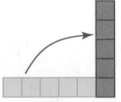

6.

In **7** and **8**, use objects to help you solve the problem.

7. How many pentominoes can you build with 5 in a row?

8. How many pentominoes can you build with 4 in a row?

Stuck? Try this....

- What do I know?
- What am I asked to find?
- What diagram can I use to help understand the problem?
- Can I use addition, subtraction, multiplication, or division?
- Is all of my work correct?
- Did I answer the right question?
- Is my answer reasonable?

Three more unique pentominoes that have 3 squares in a row.

Two pentominoes are the same if they can be matched together by rotating or reflecting.

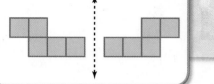

I can use objects to build 3 more pentominoes with 3 in a row.

Here are 3 possible solutions.

• All are attached edge to edge.

• All can be rotated and reflected. None are repeated.

The 3 pentominoes I've made are all unique.

---

9. Suppose each square in a pentomino is a table that seats one person on a side. Draw a table arrangement (a pentomino) that can seat 12 people.

10. The figure below can be folded to form a box. After it is folded, which face will be parallel to face *ABDC*?

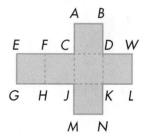

11. Maureen is buying a game that is priced at $15. She has a coupon worth $2.50 off the regular price. After Maureen gives the clerk a $20 bill, how much change does she receive?

12. James and Kurt were paid $176 for landscaping a yard. James worked 9 hours and Kurt worked 13 hours. How much is Kurt's fair share of the earnings? James's share?

13. Use objects to build pentominoes with 2 squares in a row. How many of these kinds of pentominoes can be built?

14. Make an organized list. How many different combinations of coins can make $0.42 if one of the coins is a quarter? One possible combination: 1 quarter, 17 pennies.

15. At the concert, Mischa, Jordan, and Elijah are sitting together in a row. Make a list of the possible orders in which the three could be sitting.

16. Estimation A great white shark can weigh 4,400 lbs. A dolphin can weigh 440 lbs. About how many pounds heavier is the shark than the dolphin?

1. A polygon with a vertex at (5, 8) is translated left 3 units and up 1 unit. What are the coordinates of this vertex after the translation? (19-1)

A (2, 7)

B (8, 7)

C (8, 9)

D (2, 9)

2. Which of the following shows a rotation of the cat pattern? (19-3)

A

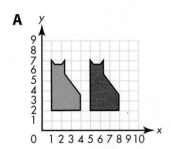

B

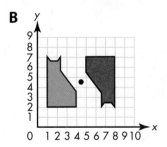

C

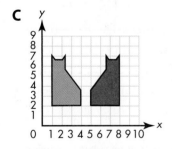

D

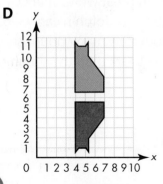

3. Suppose each of the 6 squares in a hexamino represents a table which can seat one person on a side. Which arrangement of 6 tables can seat exactly 12 people? (19-6)

A

B

C

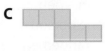

D

4. Which of the following best describes the transformation of the moon? (19-3)

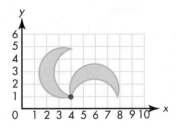

A Rotation about a point

B Reflection across a vertical line

C Reflection across a horizontal line

D Translation to the right

5. Which of the following figures appear to be congruent? (19-4)

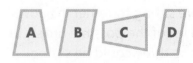

A Figures A and B

B Figures B and C

C Figures B and D

D Figures A and C

6. The symbol shown is a common one found in Native American pottery and means snow cloud. Which of the following describes the translation of the symbol? (19-1)

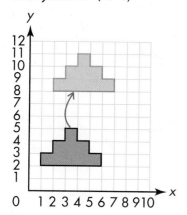

A Right one unit and up eight units

B Right two units and up eight units

C Right one unit and up six units

D Right two units and up six units

7. Which anchor shows a reflection of anchor 1? (19-2)

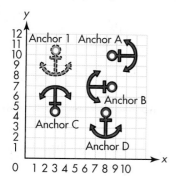

A Anchor A

B Anchor B

C Anchor C

D Anchor D

8. What is the smallest rotation that will rotate the figure onto itself? (19-5)

A 90°

B 180°

C 270°

D 360°

9. Which of the following could NOT be used to describe the relationship between each pair of stars on the flag of Bosnia and Herzegovina? (19-4)

A Translation

B Transformation

C Congruent

D Reflection

10. How many lines of symmetry are there in the figure shown below? (19-5)

A none

B 1

C 2

D 3

Set A, pages 464–466

Sketch a translation of this figure 3 units to the right and 2 units down. Use grid paper.

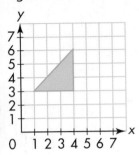

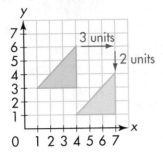

Remember that a translation of a figure moves the figure in a straight line.

Copy each figure onto grid paper. Sketch the translation shown by the arrow.

1.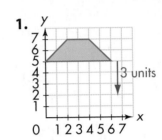

2.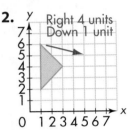
Right 4 units
Down 1 unit

Set B, pages 468–469

Tell if the figures are related by a reflection.

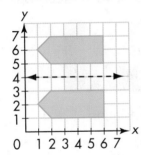

Yes, the figures are mirror images. So they are related by a reflection.

Remember that a reflection of a figure gives its mirror image.

Tell if the figures are related by a reflection.

1.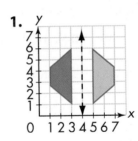

2.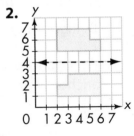

Set C, pages 470–471

A rotation moves a figure around a point. Describe the measure of the rotation.

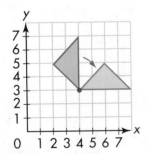

This is a 90° rotation.

Remember that figures can be rotated through angles such as 90°, 180°, 270°, and 360°.

In **1** and **2**, copy the figure and sketch a 180° rotation.

1.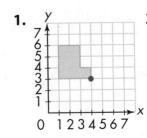

2.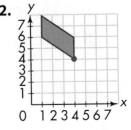

Set D, pages 472–473

Figures having the same shape and size are congruent. Tell if the figures are congruent.

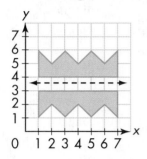

Yes, the figures are congruent.

Remember that figures created by a transformation are congruent.

Tell if each pair of figures is congruent.

1.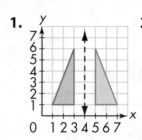

2.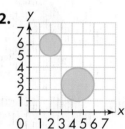

Set E, pages 474–476

Tell if the figure has line symmetry, rotational symmetry, or both. If line symmetry, how many lines of symmetry? If rotational symmetry, what is the smallest rotation that will rotate the figure onto itself?

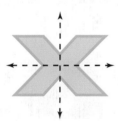

The figure has both line symmetry and rotational symmetry. It has two lines of symmetry. A 180° turn will rotate the figure onto itself.

Remember that a figure has rotational symmetry if it rotates onto itself in less than a full rotation.

Tell if each figure has line symmetry, rotational symmetry, or both. If line symmetry, how many lines of symmetry are there? If rotational symmetry, what is the smallest rotation that will rotate the figure onto itself?

1. B

2.

Set F, pages 478–479

When you use objects to solve problems, follow these steps.

 Choose objects that can best model what is described in the problem.

 Use the objects to make a model of what you know.

 Use the objects to act out the action in the problem. Look for patterns.

Step 4 Find the answer in your model.

Remember to state clearly at the beginning what your objects represent in the problem.

1. How many total bricks are needed if the pattern extends to 4 bricks in the middle row?

Topic 20 Probability

1 Fireworks come in a variety of colors and patterns. How can you predict the number of fireworks shown at a community fireworks display will be red? You will find out in Lesson 20-3.

2 Barrel racing is a popular rodeo event. How many different combinations of saddle and bridle could a barrel rider have? You will find out in Lesson 20-1.

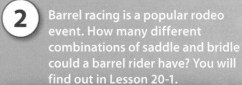

RODEO

Review What You Know!

3

What is the probability of tossing one beanbag through a hole in the top row of a beanbag toss board? You will find out in Lesson 20-2.

Vocabulary

Choose the best term from the box.

- mean
- median
- mode
- opposites

1. Numbers that are the same distance away from zero are called __?__.

2. A(n) __?__ is the middle value in a set of data.

3. The data value that occurs most often in a set of data is the __?__.

4. Another name for the average of a set of data is the __?__.

Simplest Form

Write each fraction in its simplest form.

5. $\frac{6}{8}$ 6. $\frac{15}{24}$ 7. $\frac{7}{21}$

8. $\frac{48}{56}$ 9. $\frac{8}{46}$ 10. $\frac{12}{36}$

Fractions

Writing to Explain Write an answer for the question.

Favorite Type of Movie	Number of Students
Action	3
Comedy	4
Science Fiction	3
Horror	1

11. What fraction of students like action movies best? Explain.

Outcomes

How can tree diagrams help you list possible outcomes?

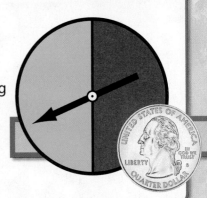

Understand It!
Making tree diagrams and using multiplication is useful when finding the number of possible outcomes.

How many outcomes are possible when spinning a spinner once and then tossing a coin twice?

Use a tree diagram to list all possible outcomes.

A tree diagram is a diagram used to organize outcomes of an experiment.

Guided Practice*

Do you know HOW?

In **1** through **3**, list the possible outcomes.

1. Tossing a number cube

2. Spinning a spinner divided into white, blue, black, and purple

3. Tossing an even number on a number cube

Do you UNDERSTAND?

4. **Writing to Explain** In the example above, how would your tree diagram change if the spinner had 4 colors? How many possible outcomes would there be?

5. Write a multiplication equation to find the possible outcomes of tossing a number cube and spinning a spinner with 4 different colors.

Independent Practice

6. Two spinners are spun. Copy and complete the tree diagram to show the possible outcomes.

Spinner 1

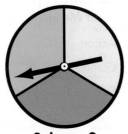
Spinner 2

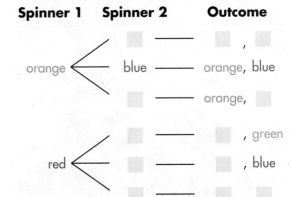

Spinner 1	Spinner 2	Outcome
	▢ ———	, ▢
orange ⟨	blue ———	orange, blue
	▢ ———	orange, ▢
	▢ ———	▢ , green
red ⟨	▢ ———	▢ , blue
	▢ ———	▢ ,

7. Josh and Susan are running for class president. Mark, Maria, Lee, and Eva are running for vice-president. How many possible outcomes are there for electing a president and a vice president?

Animated Glossary
www.pearsonsuccessnet.com

DIGITAL

*For another example, see Set A on page 498.

A tree diagram shows the sample space, which is the set of all possible outcomes.

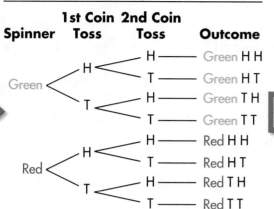

Spinner	1st Coin Toss	2nd Coin Toss	Outcome

Green
H — H — Green H H
H — T — Green H T
T — H — Green T H
T — T — Green T T

Red
H — H — Red H H
H — T — Red H T
T — H — Red T H
T — T — Red T T

You can also find the number of outcomes by multiplying.

Number of spinner outcomes	Number of 1st coin toss outcomes	Number of 2nd coin toss outcomes	Total possible outcomes
↓	↓	↓	↓
2 ×	2 ×	2 =	8

There are 8 possible outcomes.

Problem Solving

8. On four tests, Justin scored 90, 85, 90, and 95. What is the mean score of the four tests?

9. Steve's dog is 10 lb heavier than Marsha's dog. Together, the dogs weigh 42 lb. How much does each dog weigh?

10. John, Andy, and Miguel run in the first race. Sharon, Marie, and Mona run in the second race. How many different outcomes are possible for the winning pairs?

A 3   **B** 6   **C** 9   **D** 12

11. Barrel racers at a rodeo often have a variety of saddles and bridles. If a rider has 3 saddles and 6 bridles, how many combinations of a saddle and bridle can the rider have?

A 6   **B** 9   **C** 18   **D** 36

12. Writing to Explain How does a tree diagram make it easier to tell which outcome occurs most often?

13. Lara's ice skating lesson started at 11:15 A.M. and ended at 12:50 P.M. How long did the lesson last?

14. Think About the Process Jennifer's paycheck was $314.79. She used $205.75 of that money to pay bills. Then she spent $58 on groceries. Which expression shows how to find how much money Jennifer has left?

A $314.79 + $205.75 − $58

B $314.79 − $205.75 − $58

C $314.79 − $205.75 + $58

D $314.79 + $205.75 + $58

15. How many different outfits consisting of one pair of jeans, one T-shirt, and one jacket can you make if you have three pairs of jeans, four T-shirts, and two jackets to choose from?

16. Algebra Find the value of n, if $n \times 400 = 28,000$.

Writing Probability as a Fraction

What is the probability of an event?

Reuben writes each letter of his name on a separate piece of paper and puts them in a bag. He chooses one piece of paper from the bag without looking.

The probability of an event is a number that describes the chance the event will occur.

Understand It!
The likelihood of something happening can be expressed as a fraction.

Another Example What is the probability of two events happening together?

Eva puts the letters of her name into a bag and chooses a letter out of the bag without looking. She puts the letter back into the bag and chooses again without looking. What is the probability that Eva chooses the letter A both times?

Draw a tree diagram.

First Letter	Second Letter	Outcome
E	E	E, E
	V	E, V
	A	E, A
V	E	V, E
	V	V, V
	A	V, A
A	E	A, E
	V	A, V
	A	A, A

Find the probability.

There are a total of 9 possible outcomes when the two letters are chosen and the first is replaced. One of the outcomes is *favorable* because only one of the outcomes has an A both times.

The probabilty of any event ranges from 0 to 1.

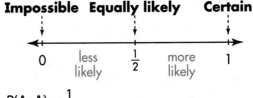

$P(A, A) = \frac{1}{9}$

The probability that Eva chooses an A both times is $\frac{1}{9}$.

Explain It

1. Use the tree diagram above to find the probability of choosing the same letter twice. Hint: Look for pairs of outcomes with the same letter.

2. If an event has a probability of $\frac{3}{4}$, is it less likely, more likely, equally likely, impossible, or certain to occur?

Probability of an event = $\dfrac{\text{number of favorable outcomes}}{\text{total number of possible outcomes}}$

What is the probability that Reuben will choose the letter B?

There is 1 favorable outcome out of 6 possible outcomes, R, E, U, B, E, or N. The outcomes are equally likely (have the same chance of occurring). The probability of choosing the letter B can be written as $P(B)$.

$P(B) = \dfrac{1}{6}$

The probability that Reuben chooses a letter B out of the bag is $\dfrac{1}{6}$.

What is the probability that Reuben will choose the letter E?

There are 2 favorable outcomes out of 6 possible outcomes (since E appears twice).

$P(E) = \dfrac{2}{6} = \dfrac{1}{3}$

The probability that Reuben chooses a letter E out of the bag is $\dfrac{1}{3}$ or $P(E) = \dfrac{1}{3}$.

Guided Practice*

Do you know HOW?

For **1** through **4**, use the spinner shown.

1. Find P(blue).

2. Find P(yellow).

3. Find P(red).

4. Find P(green).

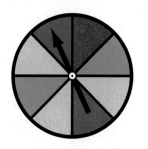

Do you UNDERSTAND?

5. **Writing to Explain** In the example above, is it likely, unlikely, impossible, or certain that Reuben draws a B?

6. What is the probability that Reuben will NOT draw an R?

Independent Practice

7. Write each letter of your first name on a separate small sheet of paper. Put each piece into a box. Do an experiment where you pick one letter and replace it each time. Do this 10 times. Record the number of times you pick each letter, and then write the probability as a fraction.

For **8** through **12**, suppose you toss a quarter and a penny.

8. Make a tree diagram to show the possible outcomes.

9. Find P(one head).

10. Find P(two heads).

11. Find P(quarter heads, penny tails)

12. Find P(no heads)

Animated Glossary
www.pearsonsuccessnet.com

For another example, see Set B on page 498.

13. When a number cube is tossed, there are 6 possible outcomes (1, 2, 3, 4, 5, or 6). If the cube is tossed twice and the outcomes are added, the possible sums are from 2 through 12.

Copy the table and give the probability of each sum.

Sum	2	3	4	5	6	7	8	9	10	11	12
Number of Occurrences	1	2	3	4	5	6	5	4	3	2	1
Probability	■	■	■	■	■	■	■	■	■	■	■

14. Which sum (or sums) has the greatest probability of occurring?

15. Which sum (or sums) has the least probability of occurring?

Problem Solving

16. **Geometry** Kendra tosses a colored cube. Half of the sides of the cube are red, $\frac{1}{3}$ of the sides are blue, and one side is green. What is the probability that the cube will land on a color other than red when tossed?

17. Mrs. Pierre bought 150 pencils to give to her students. She has three classes with 27, 25, and 23 students. She wants every student to get the same number of pencils. How many pencils should she give to each student?

18. **Think About the Process** Jorge put colored cards into a bag. Two of the cards were green, three were red, one was orange, two were blue, and two were purple. Jorge wants to find the probability that he will pull an orange card from the bag. What step does Jorge take to determine the number of possible outcomes?

A Count the number of orange cards

B Count the number of different colored cards

C Count the total number of cards in the bag

D Count the number of cards that are not orange

19. Carlita buys 3 beanbag throws for $1.00. What is the probability she will toss one beanbag through a hole in the top row of this game? Assume Carlita always throws a beanbag into a hole.

20. How many parts of each color should there be to make sure that it is equally likely this spinner will land on each of 3 different colors?

Going Digital

Simulating Probability

Use
Probability

A bag has 5 red marbles, 3 blue marbles, and 2 yellow marbles. Find the probability of getting a blue marble when choosing a marble from the bag. Then simulate choosing a marble 100 times and use the results to find the probability of getting a blue marble.

Step 1 Go to the Probability eTool. Click on the button next to the marbles tool to expand the tool palette. Select the three marbles tool. On the left, type 5 in the box for color 1, which is red, 3 for color 2, and 2 for color 3. At the top of the page, click to toggle on the probability column. The probability of getting blue, or color 2, is $\frac{3}{10}$.

Step 2 Fill in 100 where it says *Draw* ▮▮▮ *Marbles*. Click *Go*. The results may be slightly different each time. Since $\frac{3}{10} = \frac{30}{100}$, the result for blue should be close to 30. If the result is, for example, 26, the probability based on the simulation is $\frac{26}{100}$ because there are 100 possible outcomes and 26 of them were blue.

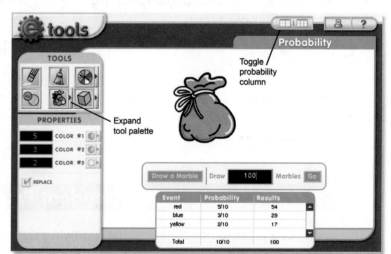

Practice

1. Find the probability of getting a red marble and of getting a yellow marble, based on your results.

2. Find the probability of NOT getting a blue marble, based on your results.

3. Use the broom tool to clear your work. Create another bag with 4 red, 4 blue, and 2 yellow marbles. Find the probability of getting a blue marble based on the information and based on a simulation of 100 draws.

Understand It!
Probability and experimental data can be used to make predictions.

Experiments and Predictions

How can you use probability to make predictions?

A cafeteria sells lunches for 30 minutes each day. Predict how many salads will be sold if 300 lunches are sold.

A <u>prediction</u> is a statement about an event in the future. It can be based on an experiment or on past experience.

Lunch	Number Sold in 30 Minutes
Pasta	20
Salad	15
Sandwich	25
Stir Fry	15
Total Lunches	**75**

Guided Practice*

Do you know HOW?

For **1** through **3**, write each of the following as a fraction in simplest form.

1. 15 out of 25

2. 60 out of 100

3. 28 out of 50

Do you UNDERSTAND?

For **4** and **5**, use the data in the example above.

4. If 150 lunches are sold, would you expect the number of salads sold to be 30. Why or why not?

5. Predict how many sandwiches would be sold if 300 lunches were sold.

Independent Practice

The owner of a pizza parlor collected the following data during one lunch shift. Use the following table to answer **6** through **10**.

6. How many total slices were ordered in all?

7. What is the probability that someone will order a slice of mushroom pizza?

8. What is the probability that someone will order a slice of cheese pizza?

Pizza	Slices Ordered
Cheese	23
Mushroom	10
Green Pepper	5
Combination	12

9. Predict how many slices of combination pizza will be ordered if 200 slices of pizza are ordered.

10. How can the owner of the pizza parlor use these predictions?

Animated Glossary
www.pearsonsuccessnet.com

Find the number of favorable outcomes and the total possible outcomes.

There are 15 favorable outcomes and 75 possible outcomes as there are 15 salads sold out of 75 lunches.

Write the probability as a fraction in simplest form.

Probability $= \frac{15}{75} = \frac{15 \div 15}{75 \div 15} = \frac{1}{5}$

Out of 75 lunches sold in 30 minutes, the probability of selling a salad is $\frac{1}{5}$.

Predict how many salads will be sold when 300 lunches are sold.

Find a fraction equivalent to $\frac{1}{5}$ with a denominator of 300.

$\frac{1}{5} = \frac{\blacksquare}{300}$ **Think** $5 \times 60 = 300$

$\frac{1}{5} = \frac{1 \times 60}{5 \times 60} = \frac{60}{300}$

If 300 lunches are sold, we can predict that 60 salads will be sold.

Problem Solving

11. The table below shows the results of an experiment using a 4-color spinner. What is the probability that the next color the spinner lands on is blue?

Color	Number of Spins
Green	6
Blue	3
Orange	5
Yellow	4

A $\frac{1}{6}$ **C** $\frac{1}{4}$

B $\frac{1}{3}$ **D** $\frac{3}{4}$

12. An automaker compared the time it takes different cars to accelerate from 0 to 60 miles per hour. The times recorded were 8.25, 7.93, 8.47, 8.06, and 8.70 seconds. Order these times from least to greatest.

13. Using the letters in the word MATHEMATICS, find the probability of choosing a letter that is not M?

A $\frac{2}{11}$ **C** $\frac{11}{2}$

B $\frac{9}{11}$ **D** $\frac{1}{11}$

14. The table below shows the colors of the first twelve fireworks shown at a fireworks display. Predict how many fireworks will be red if a total of 60 fireworks are displayed.

Color	Number of Fireworks
Red	5
White	3
Blue	4

15. A researcher studied the color of cars entering a parking lot. Out of 20 cars, five were red. What fraction represents the probability that the next car entering the parking lot will be red?

16. Which word name describes 0.01?

A One tenth

B One hundredth

C One thousandth

D One hundred

Problem Solving

Solve a Simpler Problem

books from reading list

Owen needs to read 2 books from a list of 6 books. How many different combinations of books are possible?

Follow these steps to solve a simpler problem.

1. Break apart or change the problem into one that is simpler.
2. Solve the simpler problem.
3. Use the answers to the simpler problem to solve the original problem.

Guided Practice*

Do you know HOW?

1. Draw a picture to show the number of combinations of pairs for 5 books.

2. Think of extending the table at the top to find the number of pairs for 7 books. What number would you add to 15 to find the number of pairs? How many pairs would there be for 7 books?

Do you UNDERSTAND?

3. **Writing to Explain** Is it easier to use the table or to draw a picture as the number of books increases?

4. **Write a Problem** Write a real-world problem that can be solved by solving a simpler problem.

Independent Practice

Solve each problem.

5. Continue the pattern in the book problem above. How many pairs of books would there be for 8 books? 9 books? 10 books?

6. Find the number of degrees in a hexagon. HINT: Divide the hexagon into triangles.

    a   How many triangles are formed?

    b   How many degrees are in each triangle?

    c   What is the total number of degrees in the hexagon?

7. Using the same strategy as in Problem 6, what is the total number of degrees in a pentagon? An octagon?

Stuck? Try this....

- What do I know?
- What am I asked to find?
- What diagram can I use to help understand the problem?
- Can I use addition, subtraction, multiplication, or division?
- Is all of my work correct?
- Did I answer the right question?
- Is my answer reasonable?

For another example, see Set D on page 499.

Use letters to represent the books.

A —— B   A —— B   A ———— B

2 books:
1 pair

3 books: 3 pairs

C

C —— D

4 books: 6 pairs

Look for a pattern.

Find the pattern. Continue the pattern to 6 books.

Number of Books	2	3	4	5	6
Number of Pairs	1	3	6	10	15

+2   +3   +4   +5

There are 15 different possible pairs.

---

8. Juanita tossed 3 number cubes, and these digits came up.

If each of the numbers 2, 1, and 4 is used only once, which shows all the possible 3-digit numbers?

A 214, 421, 142

B 214, 124, 412, 421

C 214, 241, 142, 412, 124

D 214, 241, 142, 124, 412, 421

9. Jill has 3 colored vases to arrange on a shelf.

Let B stand for blue, O for orange, and G for green. Which list shows all the possible arrangements of the vases?

A BOG, OBG, GOB

B BOG, OBG, GOB, GBO

C BOG, OBG, GOB, GBO, OGB

D BOG, OBG, GOB, GBO, OGB, BGO

10. George was choosing which clothes to wear. In his closet were 2 ties, 5 shirts, 3 pairs of pants, and 2 belts. How many combinations of a tie, a shirt, a pair of pants, and a belt did George have to choose from?

11. The McMillan family wanted to buy a new vehicle. They could choose a van or a car; a black, silver, or white exterior; and a tan or black interior. How many different vehicles can they choose from?

12. After seeing a movie, 2 friends stopped for frozen yogurt. Three flavors were available in small, medium, and large sizes. How many different combinations of flavors and sizes are possible?

13. Algebra Draw a picture and write an equation to solve.

Niko had $17\frac{1}{3}$ ft of fencing. He used $5\frac{2}{3}$ ft to finish a job. How many feet of fencing does Niko have now?

Let f = amount of fencing left in ft.

1. A city baseball league has 7 teams as listed below. During the first part of the season, each pair of teams will play one time. How many combinations of two teams are possible from the list? (20-1)

Mudcats	Rangers
Falcons	Eagles
Stampede	Muckdogs
Green Machine	

   A 21

   B 18

   C 15

   D 7

2. Angel is randomly choosing a pair of socks from a drawer. If there are 3 pairs of white socks, 2 pairs of gray socks, and one pair of blue socks, what is the probability that she will choose a green pair? (20-2)

   A 1

   B $\frac{5}{6}$

   C $\frac{1}{6}$

   D 0

3. A car company has found that 8 out of 25 cars they sell are sports cars. If the company sells 500 cars, how many would the company expect to be sports cars? (20-3)

   A 320

   B 160

   C 32

   D 20

4. Which of the following best describes an event with a probability of $\frac{1}{4}$? (20-2)

   A Less likely

   B More likely

   C Impossible

   D Certain

5. A T-shirt shop recorded the number of T-shirts sold in the table below. Based on the information in the table, what is the probability that the next shirt sold will be blue? (20-3)

Color	Number Sold
White	22
Blue	10
Green	3
Red	5

   A $\frac{3}{4}$

   B $\frac{1}{3}$

   C $\frac{1}{4}$

   D $\frac{1}{5}$

6. The cards shown are placed in a bag and one is drawn without looking. What is the probability Bobby's name is drawn? (20-2)

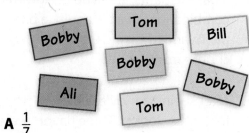

   A $\frac{1}{7}$

   B $\frac{2}{7}$

   C $\frac{3}{7}$

   D $\frac{3}{5}$

7. The menu shows the entrée and side items available at a restaurant. How many different combinations are possible when choosing one entrée and one side item? (20-1)

Entrées	Side Items
Meatloaf	Beans
Chicken	Salad
Roast Beef	Baked Potato
Fish	Steamed Vegetables
	Fries

A 9

B 12

C 20

D 45

8. The table shows the results from one classroom when voting for class president. If there are 240 students in the entire school, which of the following could be used to predict the number that would vote for Asa? (20-3)

Candidate	Votes
Blake	12
Isabel	4
Asa	8

A $\frac{12}{24} = \frac{\square}{240}$

B $\frac{8}{24} = \frac{\square}{240}$

C $\frac{4}{24} = \frac{\square}{240}$

D $\frac{6}{24} = \frac{\square}{240}$

9. A college student plans to take Biology, Algebra, and Literature in the morning. Each letter represents the first letter of each class. Which list below shows all the different orders in which these three classes can be taken? (20-1)

A BAL, BAB, LAB

B BAL, LAB, ABL, LBA

C BAL, BLA, ALB, LAB, ABL

D BAL, BLA, ALB, ABL, LAB, LBA

10. How many 1 × 1 squares are shown in the quilt below? How many 2 × 2 squares? (Squares can overlap.) (20-4)

A 16; 4

B 16; 6

C 16; 9

D 16; 10

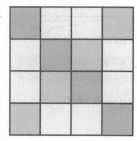

11. Pilar has 4 marbles in a bag. The colors are green, red, blue, and yellow. She chooses a marble without looking, replaces it, and then chooses another marble. If she wants to get a green marble exactly one time out of the two draws, how many favorable outcomes are possible? (20-2)

A 6

B 5

C 4

D 2

Set A, pages 486–487

Judy is choosing what to have for lunch. She can have a hamburger or a chicken sandwich and coleslaw, potato salad, or a fruit salad. How many different lunch combinations can she choose from?

One Way **Draw a tree diagram**

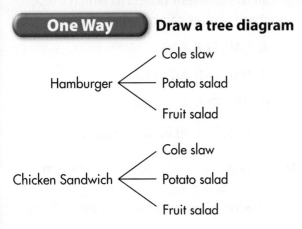

Hamburger — Cole slaw, Potato salad, Fruit salad

Chicken Sandwich — Cole slaw, Potato salad, Fruit salad

There are 6 possible combinations of lunches, so Judy has a choice of six different lunches.

Another Way **Multiply**

2 entrées × 3 sides = 6 different lunches

Remember that when you make a tree diagram, start with 1 item and list all the possible outcomes. Continue with all the items.

1. Make a tree diagram to show the total combinations for tossing a number cube and then tossing a quarter.

2. A car can have an automatic transmission or a manual transmission. The seats can be gray, tan, blue, or black. How many different cars can be made?

3. If you roll two six-sided number cubes, how many possible outcomes are there?

4. If you toss 2 quarters, how many possible outcomes are there?

Set B, pages 488–489

You spin the spinner once. Find P(green).

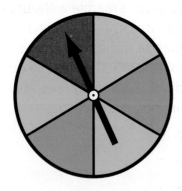

$$\text{Probability} = \frac{\text{number of favorable outcomes}}{\text{number of possible outcomes}}$$

So, $P(\text{green}) = \frac{3}{6} = \frac{1}{2}$.

Remember that when you express a probability as a fraction, always write the fraction in simplest form.

You toss a nickel and a dime.

1. Find P(two heads)

2. Find P(1 head, 1 tail)

3. Find P(nickel tails, dime heads)

4. Find P(two tails)

You toss a number cube and a penny.

5. Find P(3, heads)

6. Find P(even, tails)

7. Find P(a number greater than 3, heads)

Set C, pages 492–493

Data was collected from an experiment about the type of fish caught off the coast of Florida.

Type of Fish	Number Caught
Snapper	12
Grouper	8
Marlin	4

Data

Predict how many times a snapper will be caught if 40 fish are caught.

Step 1 Find the probability of catching a snapper.

Probability $= \frac{12}{24} = \frac{1}{2}$

Step 2 Find an equivalent fraction with 40 in the denominator.

$\frac{1}{2} = \frac{}{40}$ **Think** $2 \times 20 = 40$

$\frac{1}{2} = \frac{1 \times 20}{2 \times 20} = \frac{20}{40}$

So, 20 snapper are predicted to be caught if a total of 40 fish are caught.

Remember to first determine the probability of an event occurring before making a prediction about the number of times that event will occur.

Data was collected on the type of car passing through an intersection.

Type of Automobile	Number Passing Through Intersection
Sedan	16
Truck	6
Minivan	10
Compact car	18

Data

Predict the following:

1. Number of trucks in 100 automobiles

2. Number of sedans in 100 automobiles

3. Number of compact cars in 100 automobiles

Set D, pages 494–495

To solve a simpler problem, follow these steps:

Step 1 Break apart or change the problem into one that is simpler to solve.

Step 2 Solve the simpler problem.

Step 3 Use the answers to the simpler problem to solve the original problem.

Four people shake hands with each other once. How many handshakes are there in all?

Use A, B, C, D to represent the people.

AB, AC, AD,
BC, BD, CD

There are 6 handshakes in all.

Remember you can draw a picture or make a table to look for a pattern in finding the relationship between the simpler problem and the original problem.

1. How many different teams of 2 people can be chosen from 8 people?

2. What is the sum of the angles of an octagon?

acute angle An angle whose measure is between 0° and 90°.

acute triangle A triangle whose angles are all acute angles.

Addition Property of Equality The same number can be added to both sides of an equation and the sides remain equal.

algebraic expression A mathematical phrase involving a variable or variables, numbers, and operations.
Example: $x - 3$

angle Two rays that have the same endpoint.

area The number of square units needed to cover a surface or figure.

Associative Property of Addition Addends can be regrouped and the sum remains the same.
Example: $1 + (3 + 5) = (1 + 3) + 5$

Associative Property of Multiplication Factors can be regrouped and the product remains the same.
Example: $2 \times (4 \times 10) = (2 \times 4) \times 10$

average The number found by adding all the data and dividing by the number of data. Also called the *mean*.

axis (plural: axes) Either of two lines drawn perpendicular to each other in a graph.

bar graph A graph that uses bars to show and compare data.

base (in arithmetic) The number that is multiplied by itself when raised to a power.
Example: In 5^3, the 5 is the base.

base (of a polygon) The side of a polygon to which the height is perpendicular.

base (of a solid) The face of a solid that is used to name the solid.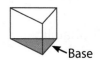

benchmark fraction Common fractions used for estimating, such as $\frac{1}{4}, \frac{1}{3}, \frac{1}{2}, \frac{2}{3}$, and $\frac{3}{4}$.

capacity The volume of a container measured in liquid units.

Celsius (°C) A unit of measure for measuring temperature in the metric system.

center The point from which all points in a circle are equally distant.

centimeter (cm) A metric unit of length. 100 centimeters equal 1 meter.

central angle An angle formed by two radii inside a circle. The vertex of this angle is the center of the circle.

chord Any line segment that connects two points on a circle.

circle A closed plane figure made up of all the points that are the same distance from a given point.

circle graph A graph in the shape of a circle that shows how all (100%) of a set of data has been divided into parts.

circumference The distance around a circle.

common denominator A number that is the denominator of two or more fractions.

common factor A number that is a factor of two or more given numbers.

common multiple A number that is a multiple of two or more numbers.

Commutative Property of Addition The order of addends can be changed and the sum remains the same.
Example: 3 + 7 = 7 + 3

Commutative Property of Multiplication The order of factors can be changed and the product remains the same.
Example: 3 × 5 = 5 × 3

compatible numbers Numbers that are easy to compute with mentally.

compensation Adjusting one number of an operation to make computations easier and balancing the adjustment by changing the other number.

composite number A whole number greater than 1 with more than 2 factors.

cone A solid figure with one circular base; the points on the circle are joined to one point outside the base.

congruent figures Figures that have the same size and shape.

coordinate grid A grid that makes it easy to locate points in a plane using an ordered pair of numbers.

coordinate plane A coordinate grid that extends to include both positive and negative numbers.

coordinates The two numbers in an ordered pair.

cube A solid figure with six flat surfaces called faces. All the faces are squares.

cubed A name for a number to the third power.

cubic unit The volume of a cube that measures 1 unit on each edge.

cup (c) A customary unit of capacity. 1 cup equals 8 fluid ounces.

cylinder A solid figure with two circular bases that are congruent and parallel.

data Collected information.

decimal A number with one or more places to the right of a decimal point.

degree (°) A unit of measure for angles and temperature.

denominator The number below the fraction bar in a fraction.

diameter Any line segment through the center of a circle that connects two points on the circle.

difference The number that results from subtracting one number from another.

digits The symbols used to show numbers: 0, 1, 2, 3, 4, 5, 6, 7, 8, 9.

Distributive Property Multiplying a sum (or difference) by a number is the same as multiplying each number in the sum (or difference) by the number and adding (or subtracting) the products.
Example: $3 \times (10 + 4) = (3 \times 10) + (3 \times 4)$

dividend The number to be divided.

divisible A number is divisible by another number if there is no remainder after dividing.

Division Property of Equality Both sides of an equation can be divided by the same nonzero number and the sides remain equal.

divisor The number used to divide another number.

double-bar graph A bar graph that uses two different-colored or shaded bars to show two similar sets of data.

edge A line segment where two faces meet in a solid figure.

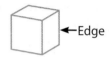

elapsed time The difference between two times.

equally likely (outcomes) Having the same chance of occurring.

equal ratios Ratios that can be represented by equivalent fractions.

equation A number sentence that uses an equal sign to show that two expressions have the same value. *Example:* $9 + 3 = 12$

equilateral triangle A triangle whose sides all have the same length.

equivalent decimals Decimals that name the same amount. *Example:* $0.7 = 0.70$

equivalent fractions Fractions that name the same part of a whole region, length, or set.

estimate To give an approximate value rather than an exact answer.

evaluate To find the value of an expression.

expanded form A way to write a number that shows the place value of each digit. *Example:* 3,000 + 500 + 60 + 2

expanded form (exponents) A way to write a number involving exponents that shows the base as a factor.

exponent A number that tells how many times the base is used as a factor. *Example:* $10^3 = 10 \times 10 \times 10$; the exponent is 3 and the base is 10.

exponential notation A way to write a number using a base and an exponent.

face A flat surface of a polyhedron.

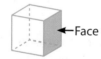

←Face

factor pair A pair of numbers whose product equals a given number.

factors Numbers that are multiplied to get a product.

factor tree A diagram that shows the prime factorization of a composite number.

Fahrenheit (°F) A unit of measure for measuring temperature in the customary system.

fluid ounce (fl oz) A customary unit of capacity equal to 2 tablespoons.

formula A rule that uses symbols.

fraction A symbol, such as $\frac{2}{3}$, $\frac{5}{1}$, or $\frac{8}{5}$, used to describe one or more parts of a whole that is divided into equal parts. A fraction can name a part of a whole, a part of a set, a location on a number line, or a division of whole numbers.

frequency table A table used to show the number of times something occurs.

gallon (gal) A unit for measuring capacity in the customary system. 1 gallon equals 4 quarts.

generalization A general statement. *Example:* A generalization about rectangles applies to all rectangles.

gram (g) A metric unit of mass. One gram is equal to 1,000 milligrams.

greatest common factor (GCF) The greatest number that is a factor of two or more given numbers.

height (of a polygon) The length of a segment from one vertex of a polygon perpendicular to its base.

hexagon A polygon with 6 sides.

histogram A bar graph that groups data into equal intervals shown on a horizontal axis. There is no space between the bars.

hundredth One part of 100 equal parts of a whole.

Identity Properties The properties that state that the sum of any number and 0 is that number, and the product of any number and 1 is that number.

improper fraction A fraction whose numerator is greater than or equal to its denominator.

inequality A mathematical sentence that contains one of the symbols >, <, ≥, or ≤.

integers The whole numbers and their opposites; 0 is its own opposite.

intersecting lines Lines that pass through the same point.

interval (on a graph) The difference between adjoining numbers on an axis of a graph.

inverse operations Operations that undo each other. *Example:* Adding 6 and subtracting 6 are inverse operations.

isosceles triangle A triangle with at least two congruent sides.

kilogram (kg) A metric unit of mass. One kilogram is equal to 1,000 grams.

kilometer (km) A metric unit of length. One kilometer is equal to 1,000 meters.

leaf The ones digit of each data value of a stem-and-leaf plot.

least common denominator (LCD) The least common multiple of the denominators of two or more fractions.

least common multiple (LCM) The least number that is a common multiple of two or more numbers.

line A straight path of points that goes on forever in two directions.

linear equation An equation whose graph is a straight line.

line graph A graph that connects points to show how data changes over time.

line of symmetry The fold line in a symmetric figure.

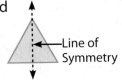
Line of Symmetry

line plot A display of responses along a number line with X's recorded above the responses to indicate the number of times a response occurred.

line segment Part of a line having two endpoints.

line symmetry A figure has line symmetry when it can be folded along one or more lines that create congruent parts, which can fit on top of each other exactly.

liter (L) A metric unit of capacity. One liter is equal to 1,000 milliliters.

mass The measure of the quantity of matter in an object.

mean The number found by adding all the data and dividing by the number of numbers in the set. Often called the average.

median The middle number in an ordered set of data.

meter (m) A metric unit of length. One meter is equal to 1,000 millimeters.

milligram (mg) A metric unit of mass. 1,000 milligrams equal 1 gram.

milliliter (mL) A metric unit of capacity. 1,000 milliliters equal 1 liter.

millimeter (mm) A metric unit of length. 1,000 millimeters equal 1 meter.

mixed number A number that has a whole-number part and a fractional part.

mode The data value that occurs most often in a set of data.

multiple The product of a given whole number and any other whole number.

multiple of 10 A number that has 10 as a factor.

Multiplication Property of Equality Both sides of an equation can be multiplied by the same nonzero number and the sides remain equal.

multiplicative inverse (reciprocal) Two numbers whose product is one.

net A plane figure which, when folded, gives the original shape of a solid.

numerator The number above the fraction bar in a fraction.

obtuse angle An angle whose measure is between 90° and 180°.

135°

obtuse triangle A triangle in which one angle is an obtuse angle.

octagon A polygon with 8 sides.

order of operations The order in which operations are done in calculations. Work inside parentheses is done first. Next, terms with exponents are evaluated. Then multiplication and division are done in order from left to right, and finally addition and subtraction are done in order from left to right.

ordered pair A pair of numbers used to locate a point on a coordinate grid.

origin The point where the two axes of a coordinate plane intersect. The origin is represented by the ordered pair (0, 0).

ounce (oz) A customary unit of weight. 16 ounces equal 1 pound.

outcome A result in an experiment.

overestimate The result of using larger numbers to estimate a sum or product. The estimate is larger than the actual answer.

parallel lines In a plane, lines that never cross and stay the same distance apart.

parallelogram A quadrilateral with both pairs of opposite sides parallel.

partial products Products found by breaking one of two factors into ones, tens, hundreds, and so on, and then multiplying each of these by the other factor.

pentagon A polygon with 5 sides.

pentomino An arrangement of 5 identical squares in a plane. The squares must be attached to one another edge to edge.
Example:

percent A ratio in which the first term is compared to 100.

perimeter The distance around the outside of any polygon.

period A group of 3 digits in a number. Periods are separated by a comma and start from the right of a number.

perpendicular lines Two lines that intersect to form square corners or right angles.

pi (π) The ratio of the circumference of a circle to its diameter. Pi is approximately 3.14 or $\frac{22}{7}$.

picture graph A graph that uses pictures or symbols to compare data that can be counted. Each picture represents a certain amount in the data.

pint (pt) A customary unit of capacity equal to 2 cups.

place value The position of a digit in a number that is used to determine the value of the digit.
Example: In 5,318, the 3 is in the hundreds place. So, the 3 has a value of 300.

plane An endless flat surface.

point An exact location in space.

polygon A closed plane figure made up of line segments.

pound (lb) A customary unit of weight equal to 16 ounces.

prediction A statement about an event in the future.

prime factorization The process of writing a whole number as a product of its prime factors.

prime number A whole number greater than 1 that has exactly two factors, itself and 1.

prism A solid figure with two congruent parallel bases and faces that are parallelograms.

probability A number that describes the chance an event will occur. The probability of an event is the ratio of favorable outcomes to the total number of possible outcomes.

product The number that is the result of multiplying two or more factors.

protractor An instrument used to measure and draw angles.

pyramid A solid figure with a base that is a polygon and whose faces are triangles with a common vertex.

quadrilateral A polygon with 4 sides.

quart (qt) A customary unit of capacity equal to 2 pints.

quotient The answer to a division problem.

radius (plural: radii) Any line segment that connects the center of a circle to a point on the same circle.

range The difference between the largest value and the smallest value in a data list.

ratio A relationship where for every x units of one quantity there are y units of another quantity.

ray Part of a line that has one endpoint and extends forever in one direction.

reciprocal A given number is a reciprocal of another number if the product of the numbers is one.
Example: The numbers $\frac{1}{8}$ and $\frac{8}{1}$ are reciprocals because $\frac{1}{8} \times \frac{8}{1} = 1$.

rectangle A parallelogram with four right angles.

reflection The change in the position of a figure that gives the mirror image of the figure.

regular polygon A polygon that has sides of equal length and angles of equal measure.

remainder In division, the number that is left after the division is complete.

rhombus A parallelogram with all sides the same length.

right angle An angle whose measure is 90°.

right triangle A triangle in which one angle is a right angle.

rotation The change in the position of a figure that moves it around a point.

rotational symmetry A figure has rotational symmetry when it can rotate onto itself in less than a full rotation.

rounding A process that determines which multiple of 10, 100, 1,000, etc., a number is closest to.

S

sample A representative part of a larger group.

sample space The set of all possible outcomes of an event.

scale (in a graph) A series of numbers at equal intervals along an axis on a graph.

scalene triangle A triangle in which no sides have the same length.

sides (of an angle) The two rays that form an angle.

simplest form A fraction in which the greatest common factor of the numerator and denominator is one.

solid figure (also: solid) A figure that has three dimensions and takes up space.

solution The value of a variable that makes an equation true.

solution of an inequality Any number that makes an inequality true.

sphere A solid figure with all points the same distance from the center point.

square A rectangle with all sides the same length.

squared A name for a number to the second power.

standard form A common way of writing a number with commas separating groups of three digits starting from the right.
Example: 3,458

stem The digit to the left of the ones digit(s) in a stem-and-leaf plot.

stem-and-leaf plot A convenient way to organize data using numerical order and place value. The digits to the left of the ones digits are called the stems; the ones digits for each stem are called the leaves.

straight angle An angle measuring 180°.

Subtraction Property of Equality The same number can be subtracted from both sides of an equation and the sides remain equal.

sum The number that is the result of adding two or more addends.

surface area (SA) The sum of the areas of all faces.

survey A question or questions used to gather information.

T

table of *x*- and *y*-values A table used to show how *x* and *y* are related.

tenth One out of ten equal parts of a whole.

tessellation A repeating pattern of shapes without any gaps or overlaps.

thousandth One out of 1,000 equal parts of a whole.

ton (T) A customary unit of weight equal to 2,000 pounds.

transformation A move such as a translation, reflection, or rotation.

translation The change in the position of a figure that moves it up, down, or sideways.

trapezoid A quadrilateral that has exactly one pair of parallel sides.

tree diagram A diagram used to organize outcomes of an experiment.

trend The general direction in a set of data.

triangle A polygon with 3 sides.

underestimate The result of using lesser numbers to estimate a sum or product. The estimate is smaller than the actual answer.

value (of a digit) The number a digit represents, which is determined by the position of the digit. See also *place value*.

variable A letter, such as *n*, that represents a number in an expression or an equation.

vertex (plural: vertices) **a.** The common endpoint of the two rays in an angle. **b.** The point at which three or more edges meet in a solid figure. **c.** The point of a cone.

volume The number of cubic units needed to fill a solid figure.

weight A measure of how light or how heavy something is.

whole numbers The numbers 0, 1, 2, 3, 4, and so on.

word form A way to write a number using words.

x-axis A horizontal line that includes both positive and negative numbers.

x-coordinate The first number in an ordered pair, which names the distance to the right or left from the origin along the *x*-axis.

y-axis A vertical line that includes both positive and negative numbers.

y-coordinate The second number in an ordered pair, which names the distance up or down from the origin along the *y*-axis.

Zero Property of Multiplication The product of any number and 0 is 0.

Illustrations:

4, 6, 38, 152, 229, 300, 304, 323, 324, 348, 404, 471, 473 Neil Stewart; 32, 358, 361, 412 Joe LeMonnier; 45, 68, 147, 296, 298, 299, 302, 307, 314 Dick Gage; 110, 122, 162, 172, 256, 262, 267, 285, 362, 364, 366, 378, 386, 420, 422 Leslie Kell.

Photographs:

Every effort has been made to secure permission and provide appropriate credit for photographic material. The publisher deeply regrets any omission and pledges to correct errors called to its attention in subsequent editions.

Unless otherwise acknowledged, all photographs are the property of Pearson Education, Inc.

Photo locators denoted as follows: Top (T), Center (C), Bottom (B), Left (L), Right (R), Background (Bkgd)

Cover:

Luciana Navarro Powell

Front Matter:

x (BR) Bryan Faust/Fotolia, (BL) Prints and Photographs Division Washington, D.C. /Library of Congress; xi (TL) Dennis Tokarzewski/Fotolia; xii (TL) elswarro/Fotolia, (BR) Getty Images/Jupiterimages/Thinkstock; xiii (BL) 2010 /Photos to Go/Photolibrary, (TR) Kirsten Wahlquist/Fotolia; xiv (TR, BR) 2010 / Photos to Go/Photolibrary; xv (BL) Flipper75/ Fotolia; xvi (BR) Cathy Keifer/Fotolia, (TL) Henrik Larsson/Fotolia;

2 (B) philipus/Fotolia, (TL) Stockbyte/ Thinkstock; 3 (TL) Getty Images, (BR) Michael Legge/Fotolia, (TL) NASA; 5 (BR) Stockbyte/Thinkstock; 8 (BR) NASA; 10 (TR) Vladislav Gajic/Fotolia; 12 (TCR) Getty Images/Hemera Technologies/Thinkstock, (T) Ivelin Radkov /Fotolia, (TR) James Steidl/Fotolia; 22 (TR) Andy/Fotolia, (C, BL) NASA; 23 (TL) Stockbyte/Getty Images, (BL) Jupiterimages/Thinkstock; 44 (TR) ©Robert Marien/Corbis, (CR) ©Royalty-Free/Corbis, Caleb Foster/Fotolia; 56 (TL) 2010 /Photos to Go/Photolibrary, (Bkgrd) Digital Vision/ Thinkstock; 57 (B) Getty Images/Hemera Technologies/Thinkstock, (T) Hristo Shanov/ Fotolia; 63 (B) Digital Vision/Thinkstock; 82 (BR) Comstock Images/Thinkstock, (T) pimmimemom/Fotolia; 83 (TL) 2010 /Photos to Go/Photolibrary; 87 pimmimemom/ Fotolia; 120 (B) Comstock/Thinkstock, (T) Steve Lovegrove/Fotolia; 121 (TL) Jean-Jacques Cordier/Fotolia; 128 (TR) ©Visions of America. LLC/Alamy; 135 (B) Erik Kersten/ Fotolia, (BL) IT Stock Free/Jupiter Images; 144 (TL) 2010 /Photos to Go/Photolibrary, (B) Goodshoot/Thinkstock; 145 (B) Brand X

Pictures/Thinkstock, (TL) Eric Isselée/Fotolia; 168 (TC) Connie Stephens/Fotolia, (CL, B) Getty Images; 169 (BL) ©imagebroker/Alamy; 177 (C) Index Open; 198 (B) 2010 /Photos to Go/Photolibrary, (TL) Getty Images/ Thinkstock; 199 (TL) 2010 /Photos to Go/ Photolibrary, (Bkgrd) Ayupov Evgeniy/Fotolia, (B) David R. Frazier Photolibrary, Inc./Alamy Images; 200 (TR) 2010/Photos to Go/ Photolibrary; 202 (BR) Getty Images; 205 (BL) Michael Flippo/Fotolia; 206 (TR, TC) Jupiter Images; 207 (BR) Ingram Publishing, (BL, BC) Jupiter Images; 209 (BR) 2010 /Photos to Go/Photolibrary; 218 (BR) Paul Cowan/ Fotolia, (TL) Zakharchenko /Fotolia; 219 (T) BananaStock/Thinkstock, (B) Courtesy of the American Sport Art Museum & Archives, Division of United States Sports Academy, Daphne, AL; 240 (CR) Getty Images/ Thinkstock, (BR) Zakharchenko /Fotolia; 254 (B) Shopartgallery/Fotolia, (C) Stephen Meese/Fotolia; 255 (B) Getty Images/Hamera technologies/Thinkstock, (TL) Otmar Smit /Fotolia; 263 Getty Images/Hamera technologies/Thinkstock; 268 (TC) Image Source/Jupiter Images; 273 (CL) ©AbleStock/ Index Open, (C) ©photolibrary/Index Open, (TL, CL) Getty Images; 276 (BR, B) 2010 / Photos to Go/Photolibrary, (CL) Digital Vision/ Thinkstock/Getty Images; 277 (TL) DAJ/Getty Images, (CL) Rubberball/Jupiter Images; 294 (TL) Getty Images, (B) Steve Perlstein/ Courtesy of Mohawk; 295 (T) 2010 /Photos to Go/Photolibrary, (BL) Jupiter Images; 306 (T) Getty Images/Photos/Thinkstock; 307 (TL, TC) Getty Images/Photos/Thinkstock; 309 (BR) Getty Images; 320 (TR) Carbonbrain/ Fotolia, (C) shirophoto/Shutterstock; 324 (Inset) shirophoto/Shutterstock; 346 (BL) Goodshoot/Thinkstock, (CR) Stephen Sweet/Fotolia; 347 (TL) 2010 /Photos to Go/Photolibrary, (BL) picpic/Fotolia; 353 (TL) ©photolibrary/Index Open; 354 (TC) Getty Images; 356 (T) drnickburton/Fotolia; 365 (CL) ©eurekaimages/Alamy, (TL, BL) Getty Images; 374 (B) Anup Shah/Thinkstock, (CL) npologuy/Fotolia; 375 (BL) 2010 /Photos to Go/Photolibrary, (TL) kuosumo/Fotolia; 394 (L) Getty Images/Jupiterimages/Thinkstock; 395 (TL) Getty Images, (BL) vivalapenler/ Fotolia; 410 (TL) NGDC/NOAA, (B) Stockdisc; 411 (TL) Cartographer/Fotolia; 428 (R) Corbis, (TR, BL) Getty Images, (TL) Jose Gil/Fotolia; 429 (TL) Getty Images; 462 (TL) 2011/Photos to Go/Photolibrary, (BR) Eisenmann, N.Y/ Library of Congress; 463 (BL) Getty Images; 468 (TR) Digital Stock; 471 (B) 2010 /Photos to Go/Photolibrary; 476 (TR) Getty Images; 484 (TR) ©Brand X Pictures/Getty Images, (L) MOKreations/Fotolia.

Index